Successful Public Relations
for Colleges and Universities

Successful Public Relations

for Colleges and Universities

by SIDNEY KOBRE, Ph.D.

Professor of Journalism and Public Relations
Director, News Bureau
Community College of Baltimore

COMMUNICATION ARTS BOOKS

HASTINGS HOUSE, PUBLISHERS
New York

Library of Congress Cataloging in Publication Data

Kobre, Sidney,
Successful public relations for colleges and universities.

   (Communication arts books)
   Bibliography: p.
   1. Public relations—Schools.   I. Title.
LB2847.K62   659.2′9′3781   73-12404
ISBN 0-8038-6720-4

Published simultaneously in Canada by
Saunders of Toronto, Ltd., Don Mills, Ontario

Designed by Al Lichtenberg
Printed in the United States of America

CONTENTS

Planning a Cooperative Program—The College Working Staff—Working with Station Personnel—Conference with the Program Director—Preparing News Programs—Interviews and News Events—Special Programs—Writing Style —Mechanics of Scripting—Announcements and News Releases—Scripts for Talks and Interviews—Preparing Visuals —Audio Materials—TV Film Production—Sources of Film —Videotape—Examples of University & College TV Programs

PREFACE

This book seeks to explore in a systematic fashion the special public relations area of senior and community/junior colleges. Throughout, I stress the value of public relations in helping to meet and to solve the problems, especially the communication problems, confronting boards of trustees, administrators, department heads and faculty. I aim to show how public relations representatives interpret through various media the college's important role in the community and present its special advantages, courses and programs to general or specific publics.

The community/junior colleges are multiplying and expanding at a furious rate, because they meet important educational needs of thousands of persons—young people and adults—in every section of the country today. The community colleges, located somewhere between the high school-vocational school level and the four-year university plan, have unique problems in building understanding, good-will and support. I give special attention in this volume, therefore, to these matters and to the techniques of coping with them successfully.

The book should prove useful and informative to several groups. Today, college administrators—presidents, deans, and other officers—need to develop greater understanding of what "public relations" is and what it can do for their institutions. Similarly, admissions directors, department heads and other college officials should become more aware of the significance of public relations for the entire university or college, and particularly for their divisions.

While these administrators may not be experts in all the varied techniques of communication, they should have an appreciation of the importance of the public relations communicator in conveying information on all aspects of the college to its external and internal publics. Likewise, these administrators need to realize the value of the public relations representative in developing a favorable community climate of opinion for their institutions as well as in helping to build financial support.

For those who are entering public relations work at the senior or community college level for the first time, this volume will provide a solid source of ideas and a systematic approach to the information process. Newspapermen, radio or television newscasters and magazine writers often join the public relations staffs or news bureaus of the four-year and two-year institutions, to build these departments from the ground floor or to give a new dimension to their current coverage. I hope that this book will help to orient these professionals rapidly by giving them an over-all viewpoint of public relations, and demonstrating the varied communications methods employed in college information work.

Courses for future administrators and teachers in senior and community colleges have been established already in a number of graduate degree-granting institutions. But additional courses in public relations for administrators, faculty members and public relations personnel would contribute to their understanding of a subject of critical importance to them, once they have entered the day-by-day work of their educational institutions. This volume should serve as a systematic text for such courses.

Most college public relations officers, news bureau heads or information directors are on the alert for new ways to improve their operations. They seek new sources and ideas for news or features, and methods of preparing them for publication or broadcast. The news bureau head wants to learn, too, what the experiences of other colleges have been in conducting special projects or in presenting exhibits. Most frequently, the college information directors want to study examples of striking brochures or photographs that have had successful impact. This book, therefore, supplies selections of such communication tools which can be used for the particular needs of these directors, and can be keyed to local media.

I wish to acknowledge the cooperation given by many public relations directors and news bureau heads of universities, colleges and community colleges throughout the nation, enabling me to give wide scope to this book. They have supplied me with pertinent information about their public relations operations and provided excellent examples of their news, feature articles and photos, as well as brochures and periodicals. A number of representatives sent worthwhile information about their radio and television activities as well as broadcast scripts and motion picture films they produced for various university audiences.

In particular I want to thank representatives of Boston University,

Brown University, University of Chicago, University of California at Los Angeles, and University of California, San Diego Campus, Carnegie-Mellon University, Frostburg State College, Md., Goucher College, Johns Hopkins University, University of Maryland, University of Michigan, Michigan State University, New York University, University of New York in New York City, University of Pennsylvania, University of Pittsburgh, Princeton University, University of Texas, Tulane University and Vassar College. I have also used the public relations materials about Morgan State College and Coppin State College in Baltimore, Md.

Among the community colleges which provided information and public relations materials were: Anne Arundel Community College, Sparks, Md.; Catonsville and Essex Community College in Baltimore County, Md.; Cleveland Community College, Cleveland, Tennessee; Hagerstown Community College in Hagerstown, Md.; Harford Community College, Belair, Md.; Montgomery Community College, Rockville, Md. On occasion I have combined the best features of releases from several colleges and universities, designating the copy as having come from "Central College," "Clearwater College," "Metropolitan College," "City College" or "State University."

Films and film strips were furnished by American University, Cornell University, Duke University, The Citadel, of Charleston, S. C., Ohio State University, and among community colleges, Cleveland Community College and the Community College of Baltimore.

On a sabbatical leave in England, I gathered information and materials relating to the information offices of the University of Aston in Birmingham, University of Leeds, University of Liverpool, University of London, University of Manchester and the University of Oxford.

The staffs of the Enoch Pratt Free Library, Baltimore; of the Baltimore County Library System; and of the Community College of Baltimore have been very helpful at all stages of the manuscript writing.

Without the assistance of my wife, Reva, this book would not have been completed. Her objective analysis of the organization and the copy as well as her editorial criticism were invaluable. Ken Kobre, Boston-based photographer, contributed much to the pictorial quality of the volume.

SIDNEY KOBRE
Baltimore, Md.

Part One

BACKGROUND FOR PUBLIC RELATIONS

Students are the Number One internal public of universities and colleges—
the backbone of these institutions.

1

Public Relations
in Higher Education

A STRONG PUBLIC RELATIONS PROGRAM is needed by colleges and universities
to help meet today's new educational challenges and problems. In a time
when faculty and students are demanding greater voices in the affairs of
the colleges, and in determining significant policies, college officers must
meet these requests in some orderly effective manner. The administrations
have to discover what are the complaints and what adjustments are needed
to keep the segments harmonious and the institutions moving forward. Colleges also have a continuous internal job of building the morale of students, strengthening the prestige of their faculties and their own reputations as solid educational institutions.

They must also communicate their activities to many persons and
groups in the community. Administrators need to find ways to relay information about the colleges' special contributions and to show how these
benefit people. A systematic program of communication, therefore, is essential to inform the public about the colleges—their courses, special advantages, growth and progress and their financial problems.

Of particular interest is the two-year junior or community college, the
fastest-growing institution of higher education in America today—
increasing at the rate of one a month, and spreading into all sections of the
country. Student enrollments are steadily expanding, new instructors are
being added to the faculty, new buildings and special-purpose wings are
being constructed. It is predicted by conservative forecasters that more
than 2½-million students will be enrolled in the junior/community colleges within the next five years. Because of their special nature and special
public relations problems, attention will be devoted to these institutions.

3

While the taxpayers and general public should be informed about these colleges, their budgets are controlled by the officials—city, county and state—who reflect the attitudes, wants and desires of the public. These officials, therefore, have to understand the facts about the institution's value to the community's economic and professional life—essential, too, in connection with any proposed legislation.

THE PUBLIC RELATIONS DIRECTOR

For all of these reasons a strong, effective public relations program is essential today for the senior and the community colleges. The key person in this operation is the public relations director, or representative. In some institutions he may be called information director or news bureau head but, whatever his title, he develops public relations policies for the institution, in consultation with officials, and then he and his staff carry out the program. He is the skilled communicator, who translates educational policies and facts into communication messages, understandable and believable. As a part of his job, the director should serve as a public relations consultant to the board of trustees, to the president of the college and to other administrative heads. What will be the impact of a new policy or program on the publics—students, faculty, community—who would be affected? What media should be used to tell the college's story? What benefit will a new course provide for the student or community? These are some of the questions which are directed at the public relations representative.

On issues with which the college may be confronted shortly, or which have appeared already, officials look to the public relations director for his advice on methods of handling these problems with the best human results and the least ill-will.

To keep abreast of the developments at the college, the public relations director has weekly or semi-weekly conferences with the president and attends the weekly sessions of the administrative council as well as the monthly meetings of the board of trustees. From these contacts, he gets tips on upcoming events and faculty appointments, learning about the general background of policies proposed and obtaining a current knowledge of community college problems and trends. All of this on-the-record and off-the-record information will be valuable later and will be reflected in the perceptive, well-informed communication messages the director prepares.

The public relations program cannot develop successfully without the understanding and cooperation of college administrators and faculty. Presidents of many colleges are becoming aware, therefore, that the public relations director must be on a par with other high-ranking officials, being listed in the directory, catalogue and other publications as a member of the administrative staff.

VARIED UNIVERSITY PUBLICS

To direct the college public relations programs successfully, the director first analyzes the various publics of his institution. He studies the relationship of these groups to the college and the problems which arise as a result of that relationship. His success depends on a probing search for the facts about these groups. As a result of his analysis of their characteristics and their problems, the representative can develop effective solutions to the issues. He can also aim his messages more accurately at a specific target, determining the correct content and style of the communications and the most effective media which should be used.

In public relations work, the term "public" has acquired a special meaning, for it is not the vague "general public" that is used so frequently. Here "the public" means any individual or group related to the educational institution. These people are linked to the college psychologically or economically. They are affected by the college's programs, staff and students; and they, in turn, have an effect on the institution's operations and advancement.

The college has a number of "publics." Through communication, the public relations director seeks to reach them with his messages and to get their "feedback" or response. He desires to build their good-will and to get their understanding as well as cooperation and support. His aim is to help keep the university progressive and to enable it to adjust to the changing times and to meet the changing educational needs of students.

The two general types of the college's publics can be identified as internal and external. Students and faculty fall into the internal class. Parents, taxpayers and future students are in the external public.

The public relations representative recognizes the necessity of identifying the college's publics accurately, and of including as many publics as he can in his program. If he does not make a list of possible publics, and if he does not have a clear idea of their importance, he will be apt to omit some of them from his planning.

His public relations programs may be built around each of the groups, realizing at the same time that many messages he sends out to different publics will contain similar content. As a result of his analysis, he selects more wisely different communication channels to reach different audiences. The selection of the publics with which the director deals, and for whom he develops consistent programs, depends on his time and budget. At one period of the year, or during one week, he will focus on one of these publics; at another period, he may shift his attention to another public and another problem requiring his immediate attention.

In his analysis, the practitioner endeavors to find answers to these questions:

1. Who specifically are the college's publics?
2. What are their essential characteristics—size, sex, age, location, background, desires, interests?
3. What is their relationship to the college?
4. What are the problems growing out of this relationship?
5. What are the best communication channels the director can use to reach these publics?
6. What channels and methods can he employ for obtaining feedback—obtaining the opinions of the various publics on current college issues and discovering what problems have arisen or will arise?

INTERNAL PUBLICS

Students Are Basic

The students constitute the primary internal public, the reasons for the existence of the institution. They are the "consumers" of education for whom the college was established and is maintained and expanded.

Sitting in with the president and the administrative council, the public relations director advises these officials regarding the problems which arise in connection with the student public. He determines also the best means to keep students informed about current developments, and the reasons behind regulations, or changes which have been proposed or are to be put into effect.

At the same time as full and free student expression is desirable, methods of obtaining feedback about courses, educational programs and college services are systematically developed by the public relations department. Repeatedly, lack of information is given as the chief reason for the unrest, conflict or outbreak of violence on campuses: The PR department, therefore, seeks to develop an orderly system of obtaining views and ideas of students, student leaders and student government officers, then of transmitting their reactions and having them considered seriously by administrators.

The public relations director studies the student public on a national scale as well as in his own particular institution, keeping aware of the many grievances students have expressed. To create a desirable university climate, where the various publics will live in harmony and have mutual respect and toleration for each other, and where friction is reduced to the minimum, he discusses with the officials these student grievances and suggests ways they may be met honestly.

He points out to the administrators the students' charges of irrelevancy, concerning those courses that may not have enough bearing on modern living—charges that too few attempts have been made to relate past experience, traditional knowledge and academic methods to the problems and conditions of today—that there must be course offerings which focus directly and concretely upon the contemporary world. Students often claim that they need an education that will provide them with the knowledge necessary to be effective and responsible members of society.

Many students complain also that the quality of teaching they receive is poor. They generally blame excessive outside faculty commitments to research and consulting jobs. The university emphasis upon research and publication causes lack of quality teaching, they say. Faculty indifference to students and their needs, however, rates equally high as a contributing cause to poor instruction.

The public relations director suggests, in conferences with the president and vice presidents, that at all levels of the university, excellence in teaching should be recognized along with excellence in scholarly work, as a criterion for hiring, salary increases and promotion. Many students complain that the graduate teaching assistant system is bad. At many universities, undergraduate education depends heavily on the graduate assistants who do the teaching. Often they are not skilled instructors and, besides, have heavy academic workloads themselves in trying to attain their higher degrees. Perhaps it would be too costly to eliminate the assistants, but steps might be taken to improve their teaching skills and reduce their workloads.

The director may point out that another way of improving the student morale is to increase the variety of teaching styles and learning environments. An extensive investigation by the President's Commission on Campus Unrest found that many students who are capable of taking advantage of the opportunities for higher education are not stimulated; indeed, they are even repelled by the uniform approach to teaching at many American universities. Exclusive reliance upon the traditional lecture method and memorization of facts may deter many students from learning. Colleges and universities are experimenting with and adopting additional styles of teaching and learning. No one educational system will suit the needs of all students. Diversity in teaching approaches and educational programs should be made available within the framework of the university, with the result that more students might find a greater challenge and excitement in their work.

Students also complain of the size of the university. They say a major factor contributing to the loss of their sense of community has been the development of huge universities with as many as 30,000 or 40,000 and even more students on a single campus. As size increases, effective communication becomes difficult, government becomes unwieldy and students have less sense of involvement with the institution as a whole. Additional growth of universities cannot be stopped, but starting new branches under separate systems of governance has been recommended. Large universities are considering seriously decentralization of their current sites or the geographical dispersal of some of their units.

For the university to function adequately, it must create an atmosphere of openness, lively debate and critical discussion. Universities are committed to hear all views and study them for the elements of truth they contain and the contributions they make to the various educational disciplines. This same approach should be maintained in dealing with student views. The public relations director, therefore, assists the president in setting up an official grievance procedure, so that students and their leaders may have access to officials in authority and face-to-face discussions. At meetings these students or their representatives have the opportunity to present their ideas and complaints and to receive serious consideration. In some colleges and universities, students are now serving on the boards of trustees as voting or non-voting members. In other educational institutions, students have places on the college committees, determining curricula, and students serve on administrative-faculty-student committees reviewing new applications for teaching positions (although the students are nonvoting members).

From the public relations standpoint, a university which made such changes would become a university whose students would be there more likely because they genuinely wanted to be. Such a university would offer students a variety of learning styles and educational programs. It would give students also the opportunity to participate in the operation of the institution, particularly on matters which affect them.

Faculty Recognition and Morale

A college succeeds or is ineffective, in large part, because of the instructional staff. No dull subject exists—only dull, uninspired teachers. Effective teachers provide the guidance, inspiration and motivation for students. Instructors furnish the dynamic challenge to make learning exciting at both the senior and community colleges.

At the same time, the faculty member is a human being, a worker and an employe. He must get psychological satisfactions from his work as a teacher, receiving recognition from his superiors and from his students. Although he realizes his salary will not equal the earnings of those who have gone into other professions or into business and industry, his income must be adequate for his needs and those of his family.

The public relations man acts in an advisory capacity to the president and his official administrative family in dealing with these significant faculty relationships. The practitioner's job is to strengthen the faculty feeling of good-will and to show specifically and constructively how this can be achieved.

Recognition of faculty efforts, a problem the president and other key officials face, is largely a public relations problem. The public relations director emphasizes to the officials that the instructors need to understand that their role is considered important, and that the administration, faculty

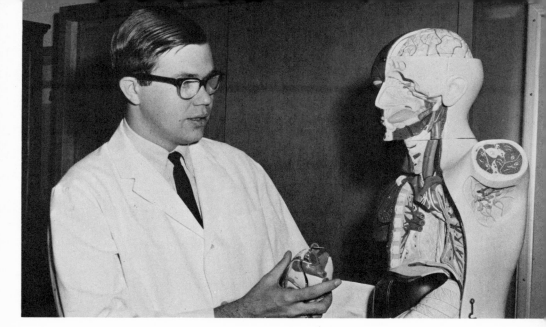

The instructional staff, from instructors to full professors, constitutes an important internal public as the quality of the education students receive rests upon these men and women.

An often-neglected group, the administrators make-up another significant internal public.

colleagues and other personnel in the college are aware of the faculty's effective classroom teaching and research, and of their general contributions to the college. Public relations men develop a systematic program which will give such recognition. They publicize the achievements of professors, their new teaching methods as well as their publications. The PR directors use internal communications as well as local and home-town newspapers. When the faculty news is of general significance to a wider audience, the newspaper wire services are called in for press conferences. The director seeks to feature the faculty on radio and television news or special programs.

We are entering into a new period of the democratic operation of universities and colleges, when faculties seek a more significant role in college affairs. The public relations director works with administrators to advance a plan which would enable the faculty to participate in determining decisions affecting faculty, students and educational programs, for this is important in building morale.

In many higher educational institutions, rivalry between departments for funds and recognition as well as for personnel and even office space, frequently exists and may become critical. The situation may block the smooth-functioning of the institution and prove a hindrance to growth. Students usually suffer, as they are caught between the competing departments or divisions. Searching for methods to reduce or to eliminate interdepartmental trouble which has a bad university-wide effect, the PR director confers with the top administrative officials to develop practical plans to achieve this goal. Involved may be frequent separate or joint meetings with various departments. At these conferences, the problems are defined and clarified, with better guidelines being made for the allocation of funds and office space.

Intercommunication between the president, the administrative staff and the faculty is essential for the rapid transmission of pertinent, correct information. Such information provides not only the facts upon which the various segments of the institution can base reasonable decisions, but also gives an understanding of the aims of a new project, plan or proposed regulation. As one way of achieving this, the public relations director assists the president in developing a weekly or monthly presidential newsletter and in writing bulletin-board information.

Supporting Personnel

Working behind the college scenes are two groups usually overlooked in planning an effective internal public relations program. Constituting the first group, the telephone switchboard operators, office personnel and sec-

Too often overlooked in considering the internal publics, the auxiliary services staffs, from the switchboard operator to the maintenance and custodial workers, play an important role in the efficient operation of the university.

retaries carry important and heavy loads of work. Many of these staff members meet the outside public frequently. The public relations director recognizes, therefore, that they must be considered a significant college public. They can do much to give the institution a favorable reputation, or they can block its growth and mar its educational image with the public. The PR man, hence, gives a prominent place to this group in his planning, seeking to train the staff in good public relations and to keep them informed through various internal media. This helps to build their morale and to develop a spirit of cooperativeness.

Usually silent groups, the plant maintenance and custodial staffs get too little recognition in a college community because of the emphasis on educational matters. An indifferent, impersonal attitude is often demonstrated toward clean-up men, window-washers, electricians, carpenters or food-dispensers. The public relations department, therefore, makes an effort to help the plant superintendent get recognition for the efforts of these employes and to strengthen their pride in their work and the college.

By means of bulletin board posters and notices as well as by printed newsletters, newspapers and magazines, the public relations director keeps these employes informed and focuses attention on them in news features and photos in college publications. The director may suggest to the president or other officials that meetings be held with the maintenance and custodial staffs to listen to their problems and give them recognition for their efforts.

Parents Have a Stake

High on the list of publics of universities and colleges are the parents, who have a direct concern with the institution because the careers of their sons and daughters are at stake. Although many parents, busy with their own families, and social or business affairs, are indifferent to what their children get out of college, most fathers and mothers desire the best education for their children. Parents of college students usually want their offspring to get a better education than they (the parents) may have had, aware of the better-paying jobs open to those with more educational preparation. Many families, too, send their children to colleges at much personal sacrifice, and are therefore particularly interested in the education to be obtained.

The public relations director has the job of informing these parents about news of the college, the general aims of the curriculum, and the contribution a particular program or course makes to the educational well-being of their children. Parents' confidence and even pride in the college are encouraged. It is necessary that progress reports and plans for college growth be given to parents by means of periodicals and newsletters. In addition to various channels of printed and broadcast communication, PR departments conduct Parents' Day or Parents' Night to arouse the interest of mothers and fathers in the college.

Trustees are an important public who take part in the university activities, and have an important role in determining general directions and policies and passing on the budget.

Board of Trustees; Policy-Makers

Comparable to the board of directors of a large corporation, the university board of trustees lays down the general policy for the institution. The board represents the college to government officials, to the public and to legislators. Board members often lead the way in fighting for the educational institution's programs and in meeting verbal attacks on the university. Board members should be well-informed on the value of academic freedom and the need for the university to present various points of view, some not in accord with those of the "establishment." The college or university should be the one place, free from political, economic or psychological pressures, where all sides may be heard.

The public relations representative aids the president in keeping board members informed, giving them an understanding and an appreciation of the education and financial problems the college faces. The public relations man sends to members clippings of important college news and feature articles of significance. He also furnishes board members with newspapers, magazines and brochures the public relations department issues.

Acting as liaison with the press, the public relations man handles publicity for the board meetings. He provides reporters with the agenda of board sessions, obtains advance copies of speeches and background materials for newsmen, so that intelligent, accurate and interesting news about the board's actions may be written. The head of the college news bureau sends news of the board meetings to editors when reporters are unable to cover the sessions.

Alumni Public Influential

College alumni represent a significant public which may help the institution—sometimes possibly hinder it, or move it in the wrong direction. The public relations man has to provide systematic, regular channels of communication with the alumni who send their own children to the college or recommend it to other high schoolers and their parents. The alumni supply funds to the college, and some of the graduates become members of the state legislature, county or city council. All of the alumni may influence the city's, county's or state's budget for college education.

EXTERNAL PUBLICS

Future Students and Their Parents

Outside the college walls are a number of publics which have a bearing on the progress and growth of the institution. Each year hundreds, often thousands, of high schoolers and their parents have to be made aware of the special advantages of the college; moreover, they need to be told about its program, courses and student activities. The public relations man recognizes that this information should go out in a steady stream, so that the high schoolers become acquainted with the college from the time they are high school freshmen to the time they march down the aisle in the auditorium to get their diplomas. The high school students need to learn about the reputation of the college and, if it is a community college, to understand about its college-transfer programs as well as its variety of career-oriented courses.

The public relations man assists the college's counseling department in building a sound, logical and interesting program to reach high school counselors. The PR director recognizes that the high schooler gets his messages also from his student paper, and from radio-listening and television-

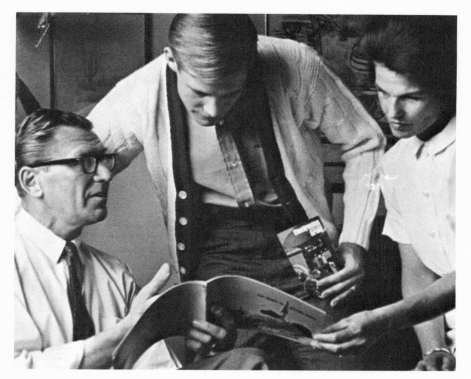

High school students constitute the major outside public, for they make up the chief resource for future college students. Parents also constitute a significant outside public, as they influence their sons and daughters in their choices of an institution.

watching. The director develops brochures and special newspapers written in lively, colorful style, or he produces striking photographs that tell the college story to this high school audience. He works with the college counselors in arranging for them to visit high schools and to present meaningful programs with slides, movies and posters. The director assists in arranging special tours of the college for high school juniors and seniors.

While many independent-minded students say they are not influenced by their parents, particularly in the choice of a college to attend, the majority of such statements may be discounted. In many instances, either parent or both parents make suggestions which are influential. In many families, funds do not permit the wide choice of a college. Frank parents tell their sons and daughters the financial facts, pointing out the availability and the reputation of the local college or state university or community college. Acquainted with the local institution through newspaper articles, radio and television programs, produced by the college's public relations department, parents are more likely to discuss the college's educational programs with their children.

Adults are the second important source for student enrollment, and they provide a growing group at which the college public relations departments aim their communications.

The Adult Market

Community, as well as senior, colleges today are making a strong bid for adults to return to college or to continue with their education. Working during the day, many of these adults realize the need for more education to move ahead in their professions or businesses. They recognize that job promotions come to those with specialized training. The adults return to the college for early morning, late afternoon, evening or Saturday classes. They may enroll in off-campus college centers in various districts. Many adults enroll in the informal non-credit courses and workshops of the community services division of the college.

Among the adults are women who are housewives or mothers. Their children may have grown up or they may be attending school, going to college, or are married and no longer live at home. Seeking to broaden their own backgrounds, to explore the possibilities of entering business or one of the professions, these women enroll at colleges.

The public relations director, aware of this adult public, develops a program to appeal to these adults, then seeks to discover the proper messages and the effective media to reach this audience. He can't use the school counselors to contact this adult public, as he does to reach the high schoolers. He must use newspaper articles, radio, television, shopping center exhibits and other methods to obtain direct contact with these adults.

Cultural Audience: The college also makes an effort to arouse the interest of many men and women in the college's theatrical, musical and art programs as well as its lectures and panel discussions of current events, and of national and community problems. The public relations director is concerned, therefore, with keeping the public informed about such college events and getting interested persons to attend—using all the print and broadcast media to achieve these goals.

General Public—Voters

The public relations director is concerned also with the general public who pay the taxes and vote on bond issues and influence legislation relating to colleges. The director recognizes that they have a stake in the college and their opinion about it is important.

Many in this general public have a low regard for the community college, or they may even be hostile for a variety of reasons to all higher education. These persons may not have gone to college. They may have absorbed a stereotype of the college boy—creating confrontations, holding administrative officials in their own offices, interfering with class instruction and damaging buildings. Millions of people see the college instructor as a radical, taking the part of students in their confrontations. Or the professor is pictured as engaged solely in research or, wearing a white coat, working in his laboratory past midnight.

The job of the public relations director is to refocus for the public these incorrect, blurry images into a truer and more accurate picture of the college. He has to present the positive accomplishments and contributions of the college to the community, telling about the institution's constructive educational value for the students. He develops the image of the local college as a community institution, providing education for those who can benefit from it. He shows the institution's economic contributions to the community, when graduates trained at the university, state college, private college, or community college enter the business and industrial or professional life of the community. The representative seeks to give an accurate picture of the college instructor, showing his educational training and professional outlook, his dedication to the teaching of students. This is particularly applicable to community/junior college teachers, whose primary focus is upon teaching, not research.

All of this program of information will present a full and realistic image of the college to the general public. As voters and taxpayers, they influence directly and indirectly the mayor and city council who pass on the college's budget or vote legislation affecting the institution. Where the senior or community college derives its funds in part from the county or the state, the officials of these governmental units would be influenced like-wise by a favorable or unfavorable climate of general public opinion. The general public often is called upon to approve or disapprove bond issues for the construction of additional buildings or other construction at the col-lege. Hence the importance of the voting public's understanding of the pur-poses and value of the college.

At various times, the public relations director seeks to survey the pub-lic's opinion or knowledge of the senior or community college. In what regard does the public hold the institution? What do people think of its programs? What additional credit programs, formal and informal courses, workshops and lectures would they like to see the college present? What experiences, good and bad, have they had with the college, its faculty? stu-dents? nonprofessional employees? The director uses this information to improve college-community relations.

Government Officials

We have mentioned the government officials on all levels—state, county and municipal—in connection with the general public. But the public relations representative, however, recognizes the particular impor-tance of these officials and realizes the necessity of placing them in a spe-cial category. He is aware that they are a part of that general public and will absorb much of the information which appears in local media, but he aims special communications to these "downtown" or state officials to keep them informed about the college, keeping them on the mailing list for im-portant statements, new policies, programs or plans.

Business, Industry, Professions

Today businessmen, industrialists and professional people are aware of the increasing need for colleges; therefore, this group constitutes a signifi-cant and influential public of colleges. This business and professional seg-ment of the public wants to know, and deserves to know, where and how municipal and state money is being spent educationally. The businessmen are often the large taxpayers in the community. They may encourage their own employes to take evening courses for upgrading, often paying part or all of the tuition fees. The businessmen may recruit their personnel from the colleges' graduates. Businessmen also may serve on advisory commit-tees of colleges. Many qualified persons in local businesses, industry and the professions are willing to become part-time instructors in the evening courses at colleges.

The public relations man, therefore, through various channels brings his institution to the attention of the business concerns and professional people, informing them of the college's activities in teach-ing and service, and he tells management about the graduates who have entered business or the professions and are succeeding.

2

The Multimedia Approach

EFFECTIVE COMMUNICATIONS is not the only key to successful public relations for colleges and universities, but it is certainly basic and important. In planning for an effective college program, the director should use a multimedia approach to his problem of communications. With this method, he employs all printed, electronic and personal communication channels to reach his publics described in the previous chapter.

Often the public relations representative is trained and experienced in one channel of communication, such as the newspaper. Consequently, he gives his major attention to writing news releases about the faculty and students. In other instances, he may be more successful in producing brochures than in obtaining space in newspapers, and naturally this may lead him to concentrate on the printed two- and four-page publications. He may hesitate to try an exhibit because he is not artistically inclined or construction-minded, or has never put together a college display.

Yet, to achieve the best results for his institution, the public relations man needs to become acquainted with a variety of information media and to use them strategically. Some methods of communication he can produce himself; for other media, he may have to hire professionals to do the job. Given time and a few attempts, he may learn to develop and use a variety of communication tools himself.

WHY MULTIMEDIA ARE NEEDED

From a practical point of view, the public relations man realizes that more than one communication channel is needed. The audience he wishes

19

to reach may be exposed to one communication channel, but may miss another totally. Some may read a newspaper, but never listen to radio or listen only occasionally. For others, radio is the prime channel. Men have the radio going full blast while they are getting up in the morning, drinking their coffee, riding to work in their cars; housewives listen to the radio as they wash the dishes, clean the house and prepare supper.

Thousands of persons—especially teen-agers—in the population the director wishes to reach, have never developed the news-reading or news-listening habit. They will attend, however, the college exhibit at the local shopping center, or read a poster about the new law-enforcement course in the window of the local barber shop. The multimedia approach, consequently, *multiplies* the college message, or *increases the chances* for its exposure so that it *may reach more people.* This approach also reinforces the messages' exposure, for the audience may read about the college in one medium, then see or hear the message in a different form in another medium. Two exposures are usually more effective than one.

Using a variety of communication tools, the public relations director knows that each has its special uses. The newspaper article may attract attention but, in the brochure, the representative can go into details and give a more complete explanation of a new college program, for example. Besides, the brochure is more permanent and may be taken home, filed away and read later.

Sometimes the public relations man is blocked by one medium in his efforts to communicate with his publics. The newspaper editor may not be favorable to the institution, or may not have space that day or that week for the college news—but the message is important and must be presented. The news of a career program may be old, but the story about it needs to be retold many times. The director then wisely turns to another medium, say, tabloid supplements in high school newspapers, or speakers to present the college story.

Often a concentrated attack must be made over a short period of time to get a message across to the public. Then, all media will be employed to gain the desired results. "Community College Week" is an example of this, when newspapers, radio, television, exhibits, brochures and speakers are needed and coordinated for the one-week presentation.

Multimedia, thus, enable the public relations practitioner in the college *to reach the maximum number of people with effective college messages, transmitted over the right channels.* The approach compensates for the reading or listening habits of people, besides overcoming the failure of one channel to reach sufficient individuals in the audience. When the importance of a single event calls for concentrated all-out action, all communications media can be coordinated and focused on the one event.

We have presented the basic reasons and advantages of the multimedia communications plan for colleges. With unlimited money, unlimited time, the public relations director can do a complete job for his institution, producing the maximum results, telling the college story frequently and to many people. But, realistically, we know that few directors have unlimited funds or can find more than 40 hours to do the proper job. The director may be working on a small budget in an institution which has not recognized the significance of his department and its work. Therefore, he has to analyze: (1) his financial situation; (2) the amount of time he has; and (3) the number of personnel in his office—and then he needs to use these elements strategically. As the value of his work is demonstrated, administrators will respond, over a period of time, with additional funds for equipment, supplies and personnel.

ADAPTATION TO PARTICULAR ENVIRONMENT

Acquainted with the various tools, the public relations representative applies the multimedia plan to his publics, adapting it to the communication channels available. He analyzes carefully the channels and the media news directors, seeking to learn their characteristics and to determine, by studying their product and by trial and error, what they may want in college news, features, pictures. In some communities, there are daily newspaper editors who desire regular news from the educational institution. The community, however, has no weekly newspaper and its radio stations don't seem to favor the college. Other communities have strong dailies which will publish, according to space requirements at the time, *some* of the college news. Some areas also have suburban and city weeklies which are looking for neighborhood, district or community angles to the community or senior college news.

The college public relations director makes use of all these media. He writes a general story about the college for the dailies, and then redevelops the news from a district or area angle; or he writes a special feature for the weeklies. He next compresses the news into a brief announcement for the radio. For the television station, he persuades its public affairs director to put on a panel discussion sponsored by the college, or a documentary devoted to one or more departments of the institution.

The public relations director discovers that exhibits are held by the local chapter of the American Cancer Society, for example, at the local shopping plaza where thousands of persons come to buy their groceries, clothes, furniture and garden supplies. Why not a college exhibit at this mall, where the college's story can be told to thousands of persons, and brochures can be handed out?

The public relations director learns that industrial or business career-days are held at various local high schools, and he thinks, why not have a College Career Day? Here is a direct channel which would reach the teen-agers and future students of the college. He proposes a College Career Day to be held at the high school or at the civic center, and also produces a special tabloid supplement about the college, the supplement to be inserted in high school newspapers.

The public relations man recognizes that many communities have similar channels he can use to reach his publics, but the towns, counties, cities and metropolitan areas also have different media. The alert practitioner studies carefully whatever is in his environment, to make full use of his communication opportunities. He learns about the successful methods used in other communities by public relations men and he researches his own area for channels. Intensive study will reveal new ones to him—often the public relations man has more communication opportunities than he can handle.

SOME SUCCESSFUL PRINCIPLES OF
PUBLIC RELATIONS COMMUNICATION

1. **Right Message**
2. **Right Style**   **THE**
3. **Right Frequency** } For } **RIGHT**
4. **Right Media**   **AUDIENCE**
5. **Right Timing**

PLANNED SCHEDULE ESSENTIAL

Resultful public relations work in a college means systematic communication planning by the representative. Planning is a habit—a habit which can be acquired, but needs cultivating. The successful practitioner makes planning automatic.

As in any other type of planning, public relations means pre-thinking. Such thinking allows the representative to review all the facts before the event begins—giving him needed foresight, not hindsight. By looking ahead the public relations man can determine with reasoned vision what steps should be taken to accomplish the purpose—whether it be marking the opening of a new art and music wing, or writing a series of newspaper features on the career programs, or developing a brochure on the engineering courses. As a result of the plan, the public relations representative *does not omit important steps*. Such thinking gives him the opportunity to coordinate all parts of the public relations program on paper.

By planning ahead, the practitioner finds he can *time* the events more accurately. He develops a smoother operation and achieves a more balanced performance. Besides, the public relations man is not thrown for a loss by new factors which are unforeseen, but which inevitably arise. As a result of strategic scheduling, he can move his project or communication plan steadily toward the original goal he has set.

In developing a public relations activity, time is an important factor and each step must follow in the proper sequence. A timetable can be set up for the news about an anniversary celebration event, for instance, so that each segment will begin and end at the right time, and the news will be printed according to schedule. No one is ever completely successful in having the news, the feature and photo schedule work out as beautifully as it does on paper. But with no timetable, the program is off the track by hours, by days, even by weeks.

Writing out the program may seem unnecessary since the representative has thought each step through in his mind. The successful public relations man knows, however, that he can look at his program objectively only if he sees it on paper. He has a final opportunity to foresee what reactions might occur, what mis-steps he might take. He can change his plan before it jells into a hard formation.

You may plan thoroughly, but only by carrying out the event will you learn how wise your judgment was, how careful was your analysis of the problem, and the time and money the event required. You make mistakes, plenty of them. Experience on a communications project will enable you to plan better for the next one. Experience is a costly and stern teacher, but a realistic one. We can reduce the experience-cost-factor: (1) by studying the experience of others; (2) by taking time to plan; (3) by restudying the success or failure of our own plans after the event.

PLANNING FOR THE LONG-RANGE

The further ahead the public relations man looks, the more effective his final program and results will be. The representative seeks, thus, to discover at the beginning of the year what events are coming up on the calendar. He knows ahead of time when certain events will occur—homecoming, the Christmas concert, graduation. But he also tries, ahead of time, to get complete information on the students' dances, parents' nights, and the plays and concerts.

He can plan, as a result, more confidently for their coverage. By thinking ahead, he is able to furnish, in advance, news tips for editors, telling them when the events will occur, recommending that they send their own reporters, or making arrangements to cover for the editor. The photographer also may be notified that, on these key dates, pre-coverage of the events and during-the-event coverage will be needed. This advance scheduling is especially essential if commercial photographers are employed.

The public relations man has to dig for the advance information, using all available printed announcements and also interviewing key administrators, department heads and student leaders about their plans for the year.

The public relations man analyzes the contents of the official college catalogue for dates; he studies also the calendars of events which are sometimes mimeographed for the entire year, then revised monthly. The representative has to size up news or feature possibilities of the event, and then make a new public relations schedule for himself to follow.

Here is a sample of an events-schedule for a regular semester, from September through December. From all the sources, the public relations man begins to compile his own type of events which he will cover for the semester. Then he begins to narrow his own public relations schedule down to a one-month period.

SCHEDULE OF COLLEGE PUBLIC RELATIONS EVENTS

September – December

September

Opening of the college	September
Freshman orientation	September 2-3
Faculty meeting--new instructors	September 5-9
Registration	September __
Classes begin	September __
Fall hop for students	September __
Faculty Senate meets Am. Assoc. of Univ.	September __
Profs. Board of Trustees	

October

Administrative Council, Panel Discussion – Crime	October __
Talent Show	October __
Student Gov. Meeting	October __
Board of Trustees	October __
Administrative Council Meets	October __

November

Play – "Caligula"	November __
Concert – Wind Ensemble	November __
Community College Week	November __
Homecoming	November __
Parents' Week-end	November __
Board of Trustees	November __

December

Big Band Plays	December __
TV Discussion	December __
Christmas Concerts	December __
Board of Trustees	December __

This calendar of events was compiled by a Student Activities Director for February through April.

CALENDAR OF EVENTS

These dates are subject to change without notice. Please check in Room 22 for the latest information concerning each event.

Other events will be added to the calendar. Check the bulletin boards, S.I.C., and Crier for any additions.

ACTIVITY	DATE	TIME	PLACE
	February		
Instruction begins	Feb. 3		
Coffee House	Feb. 7	8:00-12:00	Formal Lounge
C.C.B. Symphony Orch.	Feb. 9	8:00p.m.	Campus Theater
Center Stage - "Golden Age"	Feb.13	11:00a.m.	Campus Theater
Student-Faculty Basketball Game	Feb.15	6:00p.m.	Field House
Freshman Dance	Feb.15	9:00-1:00a.m.	Cafeteria
C.C.B. Players	Feb.20	11:00a.m.	Campus Theater
Coffee House	Feb.21	8:00-12:00	Formal Lounge
Peabody Chamber Orch.	Feb.23	3:30p.m.	Campus Theater
Class Meetings	Feb.27	11:00a.m.	
Freshman			Field House
Sophomore			Campus Theater
	March		
Career Day	Mar. 1	9:00-3:00p.m.	Cafeteria
Peabody Orchestra	Mar. 2	3:30p.m.	Campus Theater
Spanish Night	Mar. 7	6:00-11:00p.m.	Cafeteria
Scholarship Assembly	Mar.13	11:00a.m.	Field House
Red Cross Blood Program	Mar.18	9:15-3:30p.m.	Formal Lounge
Spring Hop	Mar.22	9:00-1:00p.m.	Cafeteria
Faculty Concert	Mar.23	8:00p.m.	Campus Theater
Informal Grades	Mar.25		Advisors
C.C.B. Players	Mar.27	11:00p.m.	Campus Theater
Spring Vacation Begins	Mar.29		
	April		
Classes Resume	Apr. 7		
C.C.B. Players	Apr.15	11:00a.m.	Campus Theater
Afro-American Jazz Group	Apr.17	11:00a.m.	Field House
Afro-American Dance Group	Apr.22	11:00a.m.	Field House
S.G.A.&Soph Elections	Apr.24	9:00-3:30 p.m.	Informal Lounge
Concert	Apr.27	8:00p.m.	Campus Theater

Here's a two-week schedule of public relations events, enabling the representative to focus his attention on the immediate upcoming events he should cover in words and pictures.

COLLEGE PUBLIC RELATIONS EVENTS

Overall 2 Week Schedule

April 1-15

EVENT	DATE	PERSONNEL Writer	Photographer
Allied Health and Pix (Future Use)	April 2		
Doorbell Campaign and Pix	April 3		
Allied Health Event Pix	April 10		
Library Week	April 12		
Art Dept.	April 15		
Board of Trustees Meeting	April 16		

April 16-30

EVENT	DATE		
Summer Promotion	April 16		
Administrative Council	April 16		
Play - "The Tempest"	April 20		
Concert - Community Symphony	April 22		
Evening Division Promotion	April 24		
Board of Trustees Meeting	April 25		

The Single News Event's Coverage

The public relations representative also needs to plan a schedule for each news release, feature article or radio newscast. Such a schedule enables him to visualize the entire communications message. He determines when the news should be distributed, what media should get the releases. The schedule also enables him to recognize what angles should be developed. He is able also to coordinate his picture coverage more adequately, as the photo assignments have to be made in advance; the commercial photographer, if used, requires a week's or month's notification.

The public relations director also needs to check up and to determine the coverage he has received. This check-up system enables him to see clearly the media which have not published articles. If he is on a friendly basis with the editor, the representative may call him by phone or pay a visit to the newspaper office to check up on the news that didn't appear. Perhaps the secretary or switch-board operator responsible for mailings at the college failed to send the copy out in the first place, or for some reason delayed the news. The article never arrived at the newspaper! In another instance, perhaps, the editor has sent the articles to the composing room where they were linotyped, but he has not had the space to publish them. Sometimes the news may be buried in a pile of other releases and letters. If the news warrants it, the public relations director can call the importance of the article to the attention of the news editor (or feature or departmental editor) who may then scoop it out from his pile of copy and publish it.

The public relations news release schedule sometimes reveals to the representative that, during the last month, he has sent a number of articles to the morning paper. But only some were published, some were not. Perhaps he has been overloading the city editor of that paper with the college news. It is now time to shift the distribution of releases to a departmental editor, or to a Sunday supplement editor, or to the city editor of the afternoon paper. Maybe the public relations man will then get better results.

At the end of the year, the representative will make a report on his annual activities and programs. At that time, he will find it easy to complete the report of the public relations department from these individual daily or weekly schedule sheets.

SCHEDULE OF COLLEGE NEWS, FEATURE RELEASES, PHOTOS TO NEWSPAPERS

Event _____   Date of Event _____

Publication	Angle	Pictures	Release Date
Daily Newspapers			
Sunpapers			
Morning Edition			
City Editor			
Department Editor			
Evening Edition			
City Editor			
Department Editor			
Sunday Edition			
City Editor			
Department Editor			
News-American			
Afternoon Edition			
City Editor			
Department Editor			
Sunday Edition			
City Editor			
Department Editor			
Community Newspapers			
Afro-American			
City Editor			
Department Editor			
Northwest Star			
The Guide			
Enterprise			
Jeffersonian			
Special Publications			
Catholic Review			
Jewish Times			
Labor Herald			
College Publications			
Crier			
Courtier (Yearbook)			

RADIO-TELEVISION SCHEDULE OF A RELEASE

EVENT _____ DATE _____

Radio Stations	ANGLE	DATE
WFBR		
News Editor		
Public Affairs Editor		
WBAL		
WCBM		
WSID		
Television Stations		
WJZ–Channel 13		
News		
Public Affairs		
Calendar		
WBAL–Channel 11		
WMAR–Channel 2 (CBS)		

SAMPLE OF SCHEDULE SHEET FOR NEWS-FEATURES RELEASES

CCB News Bureau Activities   Dr. Sidney Kobre

Afro-American Cultural Exhibit

Publication	Sent	Published	Length	Head Size	Page	Pictures

CCB NEWS BUREAU ACTIVITIES
DR. SIDNEY KOBRE   NOVEMBER 19—

Model Case Study

Publication	Sent	Published	Length (Story &Head)	Head Size	Page Appeared	Picture Size
Daily Newspapers						
SUN						
Evening	11/17	11/19	6"	#1 24 pt.		
Morning						
Sunday						1-3x5
NEWS-AMERICAN						
Daily	11/15	11/18	10"	#2 24 pt.	City-Co.	
Sunday						
Community Press						
East Baltimore						
Guide	11/23	11/25	10"	#3 24 pt.		1-3x5
N-W Star	11/30	12/3	10"	#2 24 pt.		
Enterprise	11/30	12/3				
Jeffersonian						
(Towson)	11/23	11/30	9"	#2 24 pt.		
Parkville						
Reporter						
Harford Rd.						
Booster						
Catonsville						
Times						
Special						
Afro-Am.	11/23	11/25	10"	#3 36 pt.		1-4x5
Jewish Times						
Catholic						
Review						
AFL-CIO News						

TOTALS   7 articles   55 inches   3 pictures
                                                                  50 inches

Analysis – No. of Articles _____   Total|No. of Inch. | _____ Heads
          Daily Newspaper _____   % | % |
          Community News _____   % | % |
          Specialize   _____   % | % |

                                            _____ Photos Size
                    Daily   _____
                    Community _____
                    Specialize _____

**TALLY SHEET SHOWING FACTS ABOUT NEWS RELEASE CAN BE USED FOR DAILY;
WEEKLY; MONTHLY; AND YEARLY CHECK-UP**

SUMMARY NEWS BUREAU ACTIVITIES   NOVEMBER 19—

Subject: Tuition Fight

*Own reporter
**Delayed

Publication	Sent	Published	Length	Head Size	Page	Pictures
DAILY						
Evening Sun	11/8	11/11	3"	1 col.	8 (top)	
Morning Sun						
Sunday Sun	11/15	11/17*	7"	1 col 24 pt.		
News-American "Young World"	11/25					
News-American Sunday	11/15	11/17	10"	2 col 24 pt.		
COMMUNITY						
Guide	11/8	11/21**	12"	4 col 30 pt.	5	
N-W Star	11/8	11/28**	12"	2 col 24 pt.	3	
Enterprise	11/23	(none)				
Jeffersonian	11/23	(none)				
Catonsville Times						
Belair Rd. Booster						
Harford Rd. Reporter						
SPECIAL						
Afro-American	11/8	11/11	12"	2 col 24 pt.	8	
Jewish Times						
Catholic Review						

Part Two

PRINT MEDIA−I

NEWS OFFICE / VASSAR COLLEGE / POUGHKEEPSIE, NEW YORK 12601

news from vassar

Robert H. Hevenor, director / Telephone (914) 452-7000

FROM: Anne Newcombe
       621-3500
       Ext. 7271

FOR IMMEDIATE RELEASE

 PITT

University of Pittsburgh
Department of News and Publications

 UNIVERSITY of PENNSYLVANIA
NEWS BUREAU, Franklin Building
3451 Walnut Street, Philadelphia 19104

Carnegie-Mellon
University
Schenley Park
Pittsburgh, Pennsylvania
15213

NEWS SERVICE

[412] 621-2600 x318

uw
news

From The University of Wisconsin News and Publications Service, Bascom Hall, Madison 53706 • Telephone: (608) 262-3571

UCLA

UNIVERSITY OF CALIFORNIA, LOS ANGELES
Office of Public Information
405 Hilgard Avenue · Los Angeles, California 90024
Dial: "UCLA-585"

Release

Immediate

UT NEWS

THE UNIVERSITY OF TEXAS AT AUSTIN
News & Information Service · Director: Amy Jo Long
Box Z, University Station, Austin, Texas 78712   Area Code 512 · 471-3151

Samples of news release "letterheads" used by public relations departments and news bureaus. Note that they tell who can be reached for further
details, although these names are often typed in.

3

Newspapers

COLLEGE PUBLIC RELATIONS MEN recognize the importance of the basic "print media"—the daily newspapers and the weeklies—in relaying the colleges' messages quickly to a large public. While electronic journalism has moved into the communications orbit, the print channels still have certain undeniable advantages.

Almost every family in the community subscribes to a daily newspaper, or subscribes to (or gets free) a weekly community publication. Thousands of readers buy both morning and afternoon newspapers, or they buy the morning newspaper and one of two competing afternoon dailies. In analyzing the possible channels for transmitting the college news, one should not overlook the wide readership of the Sunday editions of the daily newspapers. From first page to last, neighborhood residents read their local community weeklies, which are usually favorable to senior and especially to community colleges and, therefore, print a steady stream of such educational news.

The exposure thus given the college message through print media is large—with the *chances high* that, during the course of the week, nearly every resident has seen the news or feature article *in one or the other of the local publications.*

If the editors are interested in the college news, they will provide sufficient space to tell the news bureau's story. These articles may vary from 3 inches to 10 inches, from a half-page to a full page with pictures. Space is available somewhere during the week in the 7- or 8-column standard-size newspaper, or in the 5- or 6-column tabloid. Sufficient details to make the story meaningful can be included. Unlike news on the radio, the printed news will not be confined to a brief one- or two-sentence announcement.

The public relations representative recognizes, too, that the printed communication has permanency. If the article is an informative one about the new courses being offered at the community college in the fall, readers often clip the story and save the news to be read more thoroughly afterwards, and acted upon at a later date. Parents mark or clip out of the newspaper articles about the programs and tuition costs at the community college, so that their sons and daughters, who are considering college, may read the stories later.

Special articles about the faculty or students—features which would not be carried by the electronic media in public service news announcements—constitute the stock-in-trade of many dailies. Experienced public relations representatives also know that articles in the dailies can be reprinted later as promotional pieces about the colleges. In some instances, editors print 5,000 extra copies of supplements containing articles concerning the programs at the college. These supplements are used by the news bureaus of colleges for six months after the original articles were published.

Public relations men, therefore, make the printed media the *foundation of the college's communication messages*. The news directors recognize the importance of radio, however, and of the increasing number of hours devoted to television. As a starting point, the news bureau chief often writes the news for the printed media, then he re-adapts the information for the electronic channels.

THE DAILY NEWSPAPERS

The public relations director, as indicated, needs to make an in-depth study of the characteristics of the newspapers in his community. He analyzes what the editors publish in daily, weekly and Sunday editions. He learns the differences between the morning and afternoon editions in news policies, in styles of writing and in length of college articles they print.

Whenever he can, the representative discusses with the editors what they want in news and features about the college. The representative, as indicated, carefully studies the style of writing in the dailies. Re-examining his own published releases, he determines what parts of his article were used, what paragraphs were trimmed out. He asks: Did this trimming occur because of space requirements, or because of the writing and news policy of the daily? A consistent, systematic study of his results will yield some useful answers. For better results, the college news bureau director compares the news policy and writing styles of the dailies with the policies and styles of the community paper editors.

Attractively-printed headings for their news releases are used by Boston University and Brown University. Some information offices print the headings in color.

City Editors

Relying on their previous experience, or on a current study of the press, public relations directors for colleges recognize that daily newspaper city editors desire news of *general interest*. They want news about the college, news which has *impact or significance* to many of their readers. Such news may concern a new admissions policy which would affect high school students. Other significant news may deal with a change of top deans. The college representative recognizes and remembers that the news with the greatest amount of impact gets the strongest "play" in size of headlines, in space and in position in the paper. If the editor is community-minded, news of the progress being made at the college will be welcome news to him, because it will reflect favorably on the town or city in which the paper is published.

The daily editor is looking also for news with *human-interest appeal* —not necessarily all-important but unusual or humorous. The city editor desires off-beat news which doesn't fall into the usual, routine category of college news. Consequently, the college news director is on the lookout for this type of news at his institution. Instead of a story about the usual Christmas concert with the traditional hymns, the public relations director provides an article about the Latin-American beat or the 'round-the-world flavor being given in the holiday concert this year. The music director may combine Christmas carols with Channukah songs in the programs, producing news which is a little-bit-different, hence more acceptable to the city editor, and even worth his featuring it with large headlines, considerable space and possibly a photo.

The city editor of the daily is also *time-conscious*. He wants to publish important news quickly. He doesn't desire to print news of the board of trustees three days after the board meets, nor does he care for news of the appointment of a top dean, or the letting of a contract for a new physical education building, a week after these events have occurred. The college public relations man, thus, doesn't hold back the important news for the city desk; he writes the news, or telephones it to the editor *quickly*. The news bureau head is conscious, too, of the editor's deadlines, and seeks, in professional fashion, to conform to them.

The college public relations man, as indicated, studies the writing style of the reporters on the dailies. Perhaps the city desk wants the college news written in straight 5-w fashion, giving the bare facts, using no direct quotes. The city editor's own reporters can write the same news in feature style, leading off with specific situations or direct quotes. But the college news bureau head is not a paid staffman of the daily. In other instances, the editor of the daily may want more color in the college articles, but no representative has ever produced such pieces for the paper. Personal discussions with the editors, after deadline-time, may provide the key to the future news-style of the college stories. This writer advocates a more informal feature style for news releases.

College Features

In addition to straight news, the city desk of the dailies may occasionally want general news-features about the college. Maybe these features would deal with the importance of the new recruitment programs, the new admissions policy, the type of instructors who teach in the evening division.

City editors and news editors differ in what constitutes readable, interesting news. Consequently, the public relations director, as indicated, makes a thorough-going study of the product of each city editor on the morning or the afternoon editions, and he studies also the Sunday newspapers. The college article which may be rejected, or trimmed to the bone, by one city editor may receive, however, a strong display in the competitive publication. The public relations director soon learns to aim his news at the editor *most favorable* to the college news, or most favorable to *certain kinds* of college news.

The public relations representative is also aware of the various departments within the daily, where the editors specialize in certain kinds of news and will accept the college information if it fits into their page or section. The public relations man, hence, studies the women's section to determine the kinds of articles being published and the style of writing being used.

Women's Page

The representative may be able to develop some news or news features of particular interest to women. Certain health-related occupations, such as physical therapy and occupational therapy, are opening to women who can receive such training at the community college. Two new heads of departments have been appointed: they are women. On the city desk side of the daily, these stories may be considered routine, run-of-the-mill college releases. For the women's page, the articles have a special flavor and appeal. The editor of the women's page may give the occupational therapy story a column of space; she may allow a half-page with pictures for the women heading up, for the first time, the business administration department or the music department. One of these features, the women's page editor says, might fit into the column, "Focus on Women," of which she is especially proud. Fortunately, for the college, "Focus on Women" has a wide, consistent readership.

Music Editor

The music editor or columnist for the daily is more favorable to the news of music activities of the students and the faculty at the college than is the city desk. For the city editor, the news about the college's producing a light opera may be fifth-rate in importance—he considers it cultural news, of interest to a limited few. Seeking to report fully the music events in the community, or desiring to give encouragement to

---

New Pharmacy Program

New Externship Program Helps Train Budding Young Druggists

By David Lightman

For pharmacy students working may no longer be synonymous with employment.

The University of Maryland's pharmaceutical school this year became the first school in the country to institute an externship program or course credit, thus eliminating the traditional post-graduate on-the-job training program for budding druggists.

Dr. Ralph F. Shangraw, University program director, called the step " the most radical in pharmacy education since the 1880's," when Universities began organizing curriculums for pharmaceutical studies.

The step from graduation to a

pharmacy of one's own is always difficult, Dr. Shangraw said, because schools provided no means by which a graduate could receive on-the-job training without actually being an employe.

"He often had to do what was needed just to keep the pharmacy running," Dr. Shangraw said. "This way, he spends his time doing what he needs to learn something."

Schools Encouraged

The university program, first of its kind in the nation, involves six months of clinical experience, beginning in June of the fifth year. Included in the training is one month with a

community pharmacist and one month in a hospital pharmacy.

The National Association of Boards of Pharmacies has encouraged schools to undertake similar programs, but other Universities have only gone halfway, by giving students credit for the "apprenticeships" they find.

The traditional externship last a year. Mr. Shangraw was not worried, however, that his program's graduates would suffer from only serving half that time.

"There'll be no trouble. We've documented this to other areas," he said, "although you just can't

tell in individual cases. I can't speak for all 50 states."

Half The Year

The externship occupies half the student's fifth year. In September and October, they take courses in advanced therapeutics, professional practice, clinical toxicology and administration.

In November, students begin patient-care experience, working in hospital wards and ambulatory care areas, noting use, management and effects of drugs.

The final months are spent alternating classroom and on-the-job experience.

New college programs often get feature headline display in newspapers.

young people with musical talent, however, the music editor will print the college music news readily on his page or in his columns. He may also accept a longer story, with names of students taking the various roles in the opera, and will use a 4 x 5 glossy photograph of the leading character in the production. The same departmental editor may be responsible for the writing and production of the Sunday cultural page or section. Having more space, then, he is looking for interesting articles about local musical activities. The student musical may get a half-page of space in the weekend edition.

Business Industrial Editor

The business and industrial editor of the daily may accept a general article about the college's business administration department, or a specific one about the training of data-processing personnel—all of interest to businessmen who read the editor's page. When the college, for example, conducts a "Profits Clinic for Small Businessmen," the representative may find space on the business pages for this news.

Sports Editor

The college's sports news provides good copy for the sports editor, who will take news of games which are coming up and reports of games which have been played. As in other news areas, the community college sports news rates somewhere between the high school sports and the senior college or professional sports news.

An intensive study of local departmental editors and the types of news and features they publish will reveal new outlets for special community college articles. The public relations representative re-analyzes his own college sources for ideas for such articles.

Sunday Editor

Most city editors and feature editors of the Sunday editions of daily newspapers are on the lookout for readable, well-written, straight news stories and features to appeal to their thousands of readers. Much of this news has to be created, growing out of a news-peg or feature-peg supplied by the daily news menu during the week.

Sometimes the important news about the college will be held a day or two for Sunday release. The public relations director believes that the city desk of the Sunday edition will appreciate the significance of the news and, because of the sparcity of other big news happening on Saturday, will give the college news a strong play on Sunday morning. The public relations director, too, believes that the college news will get a wide readership in the Sunday paper. Many people devote more time to reading the Sunday paper than the daily publication.

The Sunday edition is also the place for special features about the senior or community college. While one section of the Sunday issue is devoted to live, immediate current events, most of the pages are filled with features. They may be in-depth, background articles interpreting the trend of current news or explaining the meaning behind specific events on an international, national, state and local level. But the Sunday edition also covers human-interest features, personality sketches related to the news, and articles with a strong appeal but no time-element.

The Sunday edition has more space than the dailies for such features, publishing them in regular, standard-size sections or in special supplements, some of which are produced locally, dealing with local personalities, places, and events.

The college public relations director, therefore, aims part of his communication program at the Sunday edition. He may have the opportunity in this edition, for example, to tell about the new student recruitment program the college is launching for students in the suburbs or inner city. The Sunday supplement editor may provide space for a special feature on the new techniques being used in the Art Department of the college to teach drawing or oil painting. The public relations representative can place in the Sunday edition an article about the college's Danish professor of history who assisted in the resistance movement in his native Denmark during World War II. The student with an average of 99 for two years may make a readable personality feature. Having more space than the daily, the Sunday editor may be willing to use photos to illustrate these college articles, thus increasing manyfold the readership for them.

Frequently, publishers carry in their Sunday editions special teen-age or high school pages, and even entire sections devoted to the young readers. In Baltimore, the *News-American* issues *Young World,* produced by a staff of young writers and high school and college correspondents. Well-written community college articles, with photos, are welcomed by the alert editor. Community college articles may deal with student activities, such as "Homecoming" or concerts or plays, but the articles often feature also new educational programs of interest to high-schoolers. Such teen-age Sunday supplements are read intensely by hundreds of thousands of young people—potential students of the local community college.

Making Friends, Getting Respect

The public relations college representative seeks to make friends with various city editors and departmental editors of the daily publications and to get on an easy-going, possibly, a first-name basis with them. A number of city editors, news editors and reporters still look on all public relations representatives as being necessary space-grabbers. A number of newsmen consider that many (even most) of the college representatives are incompetent non-professionals, who exaggerate the facts or are unreliable in getting names, dates and other facts correctly. The newsmen claim that copy is written poorly or in unjournalistic style, more like a catalogue or an advertisement than a news or feature story. The editors say the physical appearance of the college release is smudgy, and full of typing errors. The copy doesn't look like a news story—and according to professional standards, it isn't.

Somehow, *by word and deed,* the senior and community college public relations representative or news bureau head must overcome this hostility or indifference, this low opinion of his work. He has to get the point across that the college is an educational institution and the public should be informed about its activities. In his conversations with the editor, the representative must emphasize the fact that the college is making a contribution to the lives of thousands of young people and adults, and to business and the professions in the local area, the state and even the nation.

By gathering the facts carefully and thoroughly, and by writing them into readable, interesting news and feature articles which tell the college story truthfully and accurately, the public relations man seeks to *build the confidence* of all the editors in his product. The college information man wants to reach the point where the editor knows *he can rely on and depend upon the college representative for accurate, reliable news, written in acceptable, journalistic form and delivered on time.*

In dealing with reporters and editors, the college public relations representative must seek to keep the institution's channels open to the print and broadcast media. The director needs to provide easy access to top officials when reporters call. The newsmen and newswomen don't want to spend time trying to reach the *right* college administrator for specific information. The representative makes the proper contact quickly for the reporters. Nor do the newsmen want to be blocked in their efforts to interview the president, for example, when the editors want the newsmen to follow up stories relating to the college. The public relations director encourages the president to talk to reporters and to understand how to treat them and to answer their questions honestly and fully. The director emphasizes the need for courteous, not curt, treatment of the press.

The public relations man also prepares for the verbal attacks which are made on students, members of the faculty, administrators or on the whole college. In developing a plan to handle such situations, he encourages the officials to provide accurate information and to try to show the larger picture of a particular event which has become newsworthy, and yet may be an isolated or infrequent occurrence.

Likewise, in news stories which reflect unfavorably on the institution, the public relations director seeks to persuade officials to provide complete and accurate information. Many news stories have a police angle, and if the college doesn't give out its own version of the event—with the facts placed in context—the situation may worsen, because the reporters will get all of their information from police headquarters. As a result, the story which is published may be distorted or incorrect. In some instances, reporters may have picked up rumors which will hurt the reputation of the institution, and call the college for confirmation. The director can then give the correct facts, and call attention to unfavorable results which will occur if the rumors are published as actual news. He makes no attempt to ask that such stories be suppressed, but he can refer to the sense of fair play the newspaper has exhibited in the past.

Most newspaper editors are busy people, preoccupied with deadlines. It is difficult to find a time when they are at leisure and can talk about college news. But the public relations man tries to find a time when the newsman can talk about college news and features. These sessions will give the college news representative the opportunity to indicate his own interest in the college, his professionalism and his desire to produce readable copy.

He will have the chance also to discuss future news events coming up at the college and to outline briefly some possible features which might be written. The editor is not an educator, nor does he know all the ramifications of internal operations and activities of a college—what news exists, what features lie behind its walls. The editor can recognize readily, however, the reader-interest in the news or feature which the public relations man outlines and may give the "go" signal to some suggestions. When the editor shows interest in special articles, the news bureau head can write these with a fair chance that they will subsequently find acceptance.

The college representative is also aware that if the editor is interested enough, and has the manpower available, he will send his own reporters and photographers to cover a big news event at the college. Under these circumstances, the event has a stronger chance of getting coverage and a better position or display than if the college representative covered it and wrote the article himself. Unless the event is of such importance and a reporter has been assigned the "college beat," the city editor often will rely on the college's representative for coverage.

If reporters are sent from the daily to cover regularly the college beat, or to write about a specific event, the news bureau man seeks to help them without interfering. To save the newsman's time, the representative arranges interviews with busy deans, or gets students to come to an office where they can be interviewed by the reporter. The college news director supplies agendas of meetings the reporters have been sent to cover, providing lists of names and titles of persons who will speak or participate in discussions. The representative arranges for a special table or seats up front for the newsmen and the photographers of the dailies. He may give necessary background to the reporters so that they can understand the discussion of, for instance, a new proposal made at the board of trustees meetings.

Visits to Editors

Although he has a busy schedule, the public relations representative tries to visit the daily editors regularly. If the newspaper is located in the same city, the college representative may visit the newsroom once a week or every two weeks. If the newspaper office is situated some distance away, monthly visits may be scheduled. Most of the time the visit is kept short; the representative may hand a piece of copy to the assistant city editor, let him read it to see if he has any questions to ask, and then leave. Telephone calls may be used to tip the editor off on any important event coming up, or to ask: How much coverage does the city desk want? Are any pictures desired? What kind?

Although officials, department heads, faculty and students at the college become deeply concerned when news in which they are interested and think important is omitted or trimmed down mercilessly, the public relations man has to "keep his cool." He has to explain that he has no control over the disposition of the news or feature article, once it has been delivered to the editor. The news bureau chief explains that the editor has a physical limitation on the amount of news which can be published. Space for news is also determined by the number and size of the advertisements that day, the information man explains. He points out that the editor is the final judge of what news is to be published and the amount of attention it gets—explaining, too, that the news article which didn't appear a day after it was delivered may appear at the end of the week or during the next week.

The public relations representative cannot afford to argue with the news editor of the daily. In most instances, the PR man must accept the editor's judgment on the value of the news and must recognize the space limitations on news. Instead of arguing, he returns to his typewriter the next day and writes a piece on another activity at the college. This article, perhaps, will better meet the requirements of newsworthiness and he may be lucky enough to hit on a day when the editor has plenty of space to fill.

If the college news is important enough but has not appeared, the representative can casually make polite inquiries about the omitted news. As explained before, perhaps the news never reached the city desk for one reason or another. Or maybe, when the article was received at the newspaper office, the editor decided to use it some days later when he would have a larger edition. On the other hand, the editor might think your college has had its fair share of space, even though the news is important to you, and he now wants to give other institutions some space this time. Your college then has to wait its turn.

THE COMMUNITY NEWSPAPERS

More than 10,000 weekly newspapers are published in the United States, but they are often overlooked by senior and community college news bureaus. Many of these newspapers are published in small towns and reach a limited rural audience. Others are issued in larger communities and subscribed to by the town-dwellers as well as those living on farms.

With the expansion of the cities in the last few decades, enterprising newsmen and advertisers have established neighborhood or community weeklies in metropolitan areas to cover the news of their areas which large-circulation newspapers have not had room for. The public relations man notices that the community press reporters write about local school events, Parent-Teacher Associations' meetings and playground activities. The community editors also carry on vigorous campaigns for health centers and recreational facilities.

A new principle, free distribution, has been instituted and has become popular in many cities. Circulations of 5,000, 10,000 or 50,000 can be guaranteed the advertiser.

Community college men know that similar weekly publications have also been launched in suburban communities. Often six to ten weeklies will ring a metropolitan city; even dailies have been established to meet local needs. Reporters for the suburban weeklies and dailies cover local news intensely, develop special features appealing to women and use local pictures to attract attention. Many of the weeklies have paid circulations. Recognizing that they had interests in common, the publishers organized the Suburban Press Foundation, obtaining Dr. Curtis D. MacDougall of Medill School of Journalism, Northwestern University, as consultant.

The college public relations director recognizes the special advantage of the community press for his news, but he also studies their special requirements. The weeklies do not have as large circulations as the dailies, but they have an intense readership, which is generally partial to college articles. Because of the college's importance to the community and to the families among the subscribers, the editor may give the news or feature more attention and a more prominent place than will the city editor of the daily newspaper. The community editor may "play" the news with large headlines, extended space and top position on a page—and he may use pictures to illustrate the article, which the daily cannot do because of space limitations. Avoiding crime and other heavy news, the weekly editor gives considerable space to education and to other local, constructive community activities. In addition, college news may be well-written with plenty of color, and therefore have considerable appeal for the readers.

The four-year or community college may be located in the area in which the publication is issued, and the editor takes pride in having such a worthwhile institution in his district. He does not have a large reportorial or photographic staff to cover all the news in the area, so the community editor welcomes well-written, readable college releases and well-posed and professionally-developed photographs. The college news is read, too, because the weekly is usually smaller than the daily. Often the weekly is printed in tabloid form, with the result that readers are more apt to see the college news.

The college bureau head recognizes that these district weeklies have a certain market to which they appeal, and that their readers have certain definite interests. The editor cannot give them the identical news they get in the daily newspapers, although news about the college may often be of such general importance that it would be of interest even if readers also saw it in the dailies. Besides, in some sections, there are a great many people who may not even subscribe to the dailies. Hence, the weekly editor is willing to publish on a Thursday the same important college news which appeared in the dailies on a Tuesday or Wednesday—and the college news bureau often seeks to give weeklies a break by aiming the news release at a Thursday edition.

But the editor of the weekly, being a professional newsman, prefers that the news articles for his paper be given a new angle or written in a different style from the daily's news. His viewpoint is not dissimilar to that of the editors of the weekly newsmagazines, such as *Time* and *Newsweek*. College news bureau directors recognize and are grateful that some weekly editors will grant considerable style leeway in writing the college news, allowing a more colorful or a personal style than the dailies will permit.

Above all, the weekly editor is looking for *fresh articles about the senior or community colleges, news or features which have not been published elsewhere in the dailies.* The alert public relations director, therefore, seeks to meet this definite need by developing ideas for articles about local or area students, programs and professors. Personality sketches about the deans and faculty members may be written for the weeklies. Special features about the career-courses offered by the college also might be acceptable as part of a series of such articles (the dailies may not be willing to allow space for a series of this kind).

But *localization* of general news stories and other features about the college is what the weekly editors most desire. The articles may cover groups of students, or particular students from the area in which the publication is distributed. For example, a special feature on the area students who are studying in the data-processing program, telling about the training given at the college, will be welcomed eagerly by the editor. The same principle of localization also applies to photographs. Hence, every time the news bureau head gathers the facts about a college story, he thinks of the local-area angle, particularly of where the students live, and what newspapers are distributed there. Out of the same event, such as homecoming or graduation, the college newsman can develop a general story for a downtown daily or Sunday newspaper, and then four or five separate articles for local community weeklies.

The public relations man is aware of the special deadline problems of weekly editors. He knows that the great push is on the weekends, and on Monday and Tuesday for Thursday or Friday publication. He plans ahead for both covering the event and writing the news, as well as shooting and processing photos, in time to meet the Monday or Tuesday deadlines of these papers.

As with the daily editors, the college information head seeks to develop a first-name relationship with the weekly editors. He visits these editors—but not on days when they are facing deadlines—to tell about the college's activities which may make news, and he may submit a list of possible features which may be written for the publication. His objective is to generate enthusiasm for some articles, with indications from the weekly editor that the pieces will get "good plays," if written well and if proper local pictures are provided. But, of course, some of the representative's suggestions may merely get editorial shrugs.

Many of the weekly community editors are particularly time-conscious, and want news of the big events immediately after they happen. Mrs. Elizabeth Murphy Moss, the Supervising Editor of the *Afro-American* newspaper, in Baltimore, a publication which is issued twice weekly, demands the news of "Homecoming," graduation and meetings of the board of trustees within 24 hours after these events occur. When the college representative complies with her requirements, the institutional news is not only published, but featured with strong headlines and large photos in the *Afro-American*.

To the weekly editors, the director of the college news bureau demonstrates by his performance that he is a professional newsman. He acts as though he were a paid member of the staff of the weekly publication, sizing up the college news for its importance and interest to the weekly's readers, gathering the facts, writing them in straight news or feature style. He develops strong leads, striving for accuracy and completeness in the entire news article. Then he makes a strenuous effort to get the copy to the editor as quickly as possible, sometimes telephoning the late-breaking news, and on other occasions delivering the article personally.

SPECIAL PUBLICATIONS

Special publications, such as those issued by the Association of Commerce, will accept general articles on the contributions made by the educational institution to the state, county or city. Editors of these publications may be interested in news of special programs for adults, or will accept an article on the evening classes. The university news bureau head develops a list of such publications and their editors by checking the Yellow Pages of the telephone book, the local library and other sources. Then he calls on these editors and discusses possible news and features about the university, articles that the editors would find newsworthy.

Labor Newspapers

Labor paper editors are interested in news or feature articles built around the courses in labor-management relations, labor history or economics. The editors will accept articles dealing with courses specifically related to the interests of union members. Such news may deal with construction and mechanical technology, but also with accounting, business law and other subjects of value to union members who are seeking to advance themselves. News and features dealing especially with evening courses—offered to workers at the main campus or in off-campus centers, such as manufacturing plants where workers are employed—are sought after by many labor paper editors.

Union members have cultural interests, too, and news relating to speeches, plays and concerts to which the public is invited find space in the labor press. Some of these editors are particularly responsive to special events which universities and colleges conduct, such as anniversaries, or the opening of new buildings. On the Silver Anniversary of the Community College of Baltimore, *The Affiliate,* an independent labor newspaper, devoted almost its entire issue to the college.

A state-wide or city-wide labor publication may be issued, but individual unions may publish their own tabloids. The union press may have an extensive circulation among those persons or families which the college desires to reach. Hence, the college representative visits the labor editors to discuss college news, features and photos the publications would be glad to run.

Business Publications

Outlets for college news and features may also be found in state and local business publications. Interviews with professors of economics or of business administration may yield general features on the major trends in national or state business developments, or on other subjects timed to the current news. Research being conducted, or the results of investigations, may furnish the basis for acceptable articles.

Specialized business periodicals, such as contractors' magazines, may find it worthwhile to print features on the college's construction engineering program, giving space also to awards won by the department, the chairmen or the instructors, or to the new departmental appointments to the faculty.

4

News of the Administration and Faculty

In this and following chapters we will pinpoint the various types of college news stories and feature articles which have been found to be publishable. We will give examples of typical news articles, analyzing the facts upon which they were built, to show what many editors and their readers want. In some instances, we will indicate how the news might be angled toward community weeklies. Using these articles as guidelines, the public relations director or news bureau head may adapt them to his own institution and to the local media requirements. Other facts which might be included in these articles, other angles of the same news which might be featured, or additional news which might be covered will undoubtedly occur to the reader.

We will deal first with the general news about the university or college, such as the opening of the semester, then we will focus on news and features dealing with the various divisions or groups within the institution: board of trustees, president and administrators and faculty in one chapter. Then we will single out student news in another chapter.

Some of the articles may be placed in other categories than those indicated here, or they may originate from more than one source, but this is not too important. The main purpose is a practical one: Get the story out to as wide an audience as possible.

OPENING OF COLLEGE SEASON

The news of the opening of the college would be of interest to the general public, for such articles keep citizens informed about the activities at the institution. For some high school students and their parents, the story-seed implanted now may bear results a year or so away when the family determination of what college to attend becomes an immediate and real issue. Some newspapers publish "Back to School" and "Back to College" sections or special editions; consequently, this general type of article about the opening of the college may be suitable also in these specials.

The opening article might contain some or all of these facts, depending upon the local situation and the media outlets:

Enrollment
>   Expected enrollment
>   Comparison of enrollment this fall (or spring) with that of last year
>>   (These figures could be expressed in numbers and percentage of increase.)

>   Reasons for the increase
>>   Expansion of community
>>   Greater acceptance of college
>>   Introduction of new programs and courses
>>   Construction of new building
>>   Special recruitment drives
>>   Additional funds for scholarships

New Faculty
>   General statement about numbers added
>   New positions created
>   Old positions filled
>   Background of faculty
>>   (a separate article on the faculty may be desirable)

New Courses and Programs
>   Titles of courses
>   Reasons for introduction of courses
>>   Cultural
>>   Occupational
>   Instructors

New Buildings or Wings Constructed
>   Cost of building
>   Purposes of building
>   Special features of construction

New Cultural Programs Planned
>   Theatrical
>   Musical

Community Services
  Workshops
  Informal courses

Student Activities Planned

Application, Registration Dates
  Last day for filing application
  Registration dates
  Dates of beginning of all classes
  Tuition fees charged

Here is a sample of such an article, with some of the facts or angles suggested above woven into the copy. Certain facts about the opening—the dates—are standard. Other parts of the article are included or omitted, according to the space requirements of the publications.

City College
News Bureau
Telephone

City College this year more than ever before is gearing itself to the educational needs of more than 7,800 persons who will attend the various divisions. This will represent an increase of almost 1,500 over last year's enrollment for day, evening and summer sessions. **Lead**

Enrollment

At the same time, because it is an urban institution, the college will meet the needs of business, industry and the professions in the metropolitan area of trained personnel, who have acquired general background knowledge as well as specific skills to fill thousands of jobs that go begging. **Meets Needs of Community**

The college is adding 30 new members to the faculty to meet the steadily increasing number of students. These instructors will help keep down the size of classes, so that students will receive more personalized instruction. President Thomas Jones said that 19 of these appointments will fill positions created by the rise in enrollment; 11 instructors will replace those who have retired or resigned. **Faculty Added**

The faculty backgrounds and educational experiences are varied, with instructors getting their degrees from local colleges, as well as educational institutions in many states of the nation. The students will benefit from the wide perspective and background which instructors will bring to the classroom, the president said. **Value of Wide Background**

Adding strength to the staff, three new top adminis-   **Top**
trators have been approved by the Board of Trustees. New   **Administrators**
dean of the faculty is Dr. Richard Rovere, who will bring   **Appointed**
to the college his extensive experience in college work at
the Midwestern Community College. Mrs. Francine Liver-
more has been appointed director of Developmental Studies Program, which will help students bridge the gap between high school and college successfully. Mr. James
Fielding, who has been in charge of curriculum, will become assistant dean of the faculty. . . .

This spring registration story from the University of Maryland started
with a catchy opening:

COLLEGE PARK, Maryland, February 4—Beards, leggings, sideburns
and short skirts under maxi-coats were the order of the day at the University of Maryland, College Park, as thousands of students signed up
this week for spring semester, to begin February 8.

During the first two days of spring enrollment, which usually totals about 90% of the fall enrollment figure, 6512 students had registered. The early applicants, coming in from 20-degree temperatures
with reddened cheeks and noses, created a busy—but not frantic—
scene in the Reckord Armory. Gone were the long, long lines and
frenzied atmosphere that formerly characterized registration weeks.

"I think we have all learned how to improve our procedures," com-
mented William C. Spann, coordinator of records and registrations. Tables were more fully staffed and juniors with 87 or more credit hours
and all seniors have been pre-registered. During last fall's registration,
when 34,500 students enrolled, incoming freshmen had also pre-registered during the required summer orientation session. . . .

(Other paragraphs covered new courses and registration procedures)

FACULTY APPOINTMENTS

Another significant news article at the beginning of the semester deals
with the appointment of deans and department heads and the addition of
faculty members to the staff. Some of the points to be covered include:

Numbers
  Total number of additions to faculty
  Newly-created positions
  Additions because of retirements

Reasons for the increase

General discussion of sources of educational background of instructors, meaning for students

New Deans and Department Heads

Names and titles

Educational background, degrees

Teaching experience

Other work experience—of value to teaching at college

Publications

Organizations

Previous travel

(Personal facts if desired: marriage, children, special interests)

New Faculty Members

Names and titles

Colleges, universities attended; degrees

Teaching experience

Other work experience

Travel

Publications

(Personal facts, if desired: marriage, children, special interests)

The public relations officer may believe that the newspaper-reading public can absorb only a few names at a time, therefore he writes a separate article devoted to the new deans and department heads. The following is an informative piece on the appointment of three top administrators to a college:

Metropolitan College
News Bureau
Telephone—Extension

MC'S 3 ADMINISTRATORS

Three key administrators of the Metropolitan College were appointed by the Board of Trustees at their last meeting and will join the staff for the fall semester according to President Sam Jones.

Dr. Samuel S. Rich will become Dean of Faculty, Mrs. Mary J. Moses will be Director of Developmental Studies, and Mr. R. Raymond Feld will serve as Assistant Dean of the Faculty.

Dr. Rich replaces Dr. Louis M. Bales, who has become professor of education at Eastern College. Dr. Rich is currently assistant dean of special academic services at Nassau Community College in Nassau County, Long Island, New York where for two years he was administrative assistant to the president. . . .

Special Publication Releases

Sometimes for special publications with Jewish, Catholic or other ethnic readership, special articles might be written. These articles would be developed in accord with the policy of the president and administrative council. The religion or other ethnic background does not have to be mentioned in the news. Many Negro publications consider themselves to be community-newspapers and should be treated as such. The editors are justly proud when black persons have been appointed to top positions or to the teaching faculty of a college. These editors prefer a special story on the appointments. The college news director may lead off his article with these appointments, or he may write the usual release, giving additional details about the particular appointments in which the editors are interested.

FOCUS ON NEW COURSES

When a new course is introduced the reader wants to know the name of the course, its content, its value to him, the credits the course carries. He would like to know the instructor and his background and, finally, the time the course is given.

You will note the lead in the following news story mentions generally the new courses, with the second and third paragraphs directing attention to the types of adults who enroll in these and other courses.

A number of new courses will be given in the Evening Division of Midwest College when the fall semester begins. These will be among the 150 courses offered in the division.

"Each semester we seek to key our courses to the educational and occupational needs of those who work during the day," said Herman Jones, associate dean in charge of the Evening Division. Some of these adults take single courses, others work toward the Associate in Arts (AA) degree. **Courses Keyed to Job Needs**

"Many of the students enroll in courses which will help them move ahead in their occupations in business, industry or the professions. Others desire to widen their educational background and improve their skills and abilities." **Value to Students**

For the first time, MC Evening Division is giving a labor-management relations course, which will appeal to both persons in business or industry as well as union members and representatives. The course will also be of interest to those who would like to enter this expanding personnel field or who have an interest in labor problems. . . . **New Labor Management Course**

Registration will be held September 8 through 12,   **Dates of**
with classes beginning September 15. Counselors are avail-   **Registration**
able for consultation and prospective students may call
(telephone number) or write for a free brochure and catalogue of all courses listed. Address: Associate Dean, Evening Division, Midwest College, (address) . . .

If the previous article was sent to the morning and afternoon papers,
owned by one publishing company, the news bureau head may rewrite or
reangle the story for the Sunday issue, or for the opposition dailies. In this
article the director selects one new course, labor-management, which
would have wide appeal, and concentrates his lead on that course. Some
history of the introduction of the labor-management course and the reasons
behind its being offered as well as some details on the instructor are
woven, as background, into the article. Because of its content, this particular article would be of interest to the labor newspapers in the area.

A woman's institution, Goucher College, led off its extensive article on
spring courses and enrollment information with a description of this unusual offering:

A "how-to-fix-it" course in the applied chemistry and physics of
maintaining a home is among the 55 courses and seminars available to
students during the first January term at Goucher College.

Students enrolled in the course, entitled "Chemistry and Physics
Applied: Nuts and Bolts in Contemporary Society," will learn principles
of house maintenance such as methods of wood preservation, simple
electrical and plumbing repairs, the application of soil chemistry to care
of the yard, small appliance repair, automobile tune-up and numerous
other operations. Students may also elect to build, from a kit, a stereo
FM receiver or an AM table radio.

The class, believed to be the only one of its kind offered by a
four-year, liberal arts college for women, will be taught by Dr. Barton
L. Houseman and Dr. James L. A. Webb, of Goucher's chemistry department. It will meet three hours a day, Monday through Friday,
through January 29. Members of the Goucher faculty and staff have
been invited to submit appliances in need of repair to the class. . . .

BOARD OF TRUSTEES

The boards of trustees of the universities and colleges produce "hard
news" because they are the governing bodies of the institutions. News of
their activities is usually of considerable interest, and often it has widespread significance. The boards approve the appointments to top administrative positions at the institutions, and the trustees make policy affecting

present students and faculty as well as future students. As taxpayers or voluntary contributors, the people have a stake in the action of the trustee boards.

NEW BOARD APPOINTMENTS

The appointment of members of the board by the governor, the mayor, the county executive or by the governing body of the university is always news. As board members' terms expire, or as members resign for one reason or another, new appointments always produce top news.

In many instances, this news originates in the office of the government official making the appointments; as a result, the dailies' capital correspondents, or the city hall or courthouse reporters, may get such news first. On their own, the dailies would publish the news; however, the college's news bureau chief might give additional details, obtained from the president, or from the chairman or secretary of the board. For the community weeklies and the specialized press, the college news bureau head writes articles about the appointments, furnishing attractive photos. Readers would like to know about the board members, their educational and geographical backgrounds and their occupations. Any previous interest or connection the new board member may have had with education would be informative, in addition.

The election of Harold C. Fleming, noted for his fight for civil rights, to the Board of Trustees of Vassar College was covered in this fashion by the college's representative:

POUGHKEEPSIE, N.Y., Dec. 22—Harold C. Fleming, president of the Potomac Institute, Washington, D.C., has been elected to an eight-year term on the Vassar College Board of Trustees, according to Vassar President Alan Simpson.

Long associated with various civil rights organizations, he has attempted to advance the cause of equal opportunity by influencing public opinion and public policy through programs shaped by research, information and education.

Born in Atlanta in July, 1922, Mr. Fleming attended public schools in Georgia before entering Harvard University in 1940. Three years later, he was drafted into World War II duty with the Army, where he entered as a private and left as a captain. He returned to Harvard in 1946, and a year later was graduated cum laude and member of Phi Beta Kappa. . . .

(The writer covered other details of Mr. Fleming's professional experience, his marriage and children in the remaining paragraphs.)

Here is one article on the board of trustees of a community college. The college board had been the same as the city school board for 20 years, and this was the first time the college obtained a board devoting itself exclusively to the college's problems.

News Bureau
Metropolitan College
Telephone

NEW COLLEGE BOARD REPRESENTS CROSS-SECTION

The new members of the Board of Trustees of Metropolitan College represent a cross-section of professions and businesses as well as ethnic groups in the city.

A professor at Clearwater University, as well as a filling station operator; an executive in a soap manufacturing company, as well as a vice president of a union; a newspaper executive, as well as a civic worker . . . all sat around the board table at the first meeting of the Board of Trustees (recently) (Wednesday) (last night). Both men and women, whites and blacks, joined together to guide the policies of the college and to assist President Lee Jones in advancing the welfare of the two-year institution. . . .

This was an historic meeting. . . .

Searching for additional news or feature coverage, the information representative of the college suggested to the women's section editor of the local daily a special feature on the two women appointees to the board. The editor accepted the idea, publishing a half-page spread on the new women board members, with large photos.

BOARD MEETINGS

Several days in advance of the meeting of the board of trustees, the news bureau head gets in touch with the city and local wire-service editors to inform them about some of the important appointments or other actions to be taken. If the agenda of the meeting can be obtained (from the president or secretary of the board), the representative writes an advance article about the meeting and delivers it to the various media. If, on the other hand, a reporter from the local newspaper or wire service is assigned to the meeting, the college information officer will assist him in every possible way, furnishing meeting agenda, names and titles of the speakers, and so on. The reporter may wish to get additional background on policy or the program to be discussed, and he may need information for a more detailed story than the brief discussion at the meeting provides—for instance, special interviews with deans, department heads or students involved. The PR man should try to assist the reporter in getting the necessary information.

Following the board of trustees meeting, the college representative takes several actions as quickly as he can. First, he sizes up the strength of each item and action at the meeting. He may review his own detailed notes and other printed or mimeographed material handed out at the meeting. Often such meetings are complicated and provide a variety of different kinds of news. The news bureau head, going about his work systematically, outlines briefly for himself the main points of the meeting. He then calls the morning newspaper or the afternoon daily which did not send a reporter to cover the meeting. Using his own notes, the representative outlines for the city desk the best news items which the meeting yielded. The city editor may assign the telephoned story to a rewrite man. However, the city editor, remembering that he has a short staff that evening or morning, may say, "The story will keep. Write it up and get it in. We may be able to run it tomorrow."

The news bureau head may ask: What feature of the meeting did the editor want "played up"? or what length article did the editor want? The college newsmen may get definite instructions, or a noncommittal, "Use your own judgment." He then proceeds to follow-through and write the story quickly, before it gets cold.

For the weekly newspaper editors, the news bureau writer then reexamines his notes and develops new angles. He has several journalistic alternatives:

1. He may write an article giving the same news of the meeting, but using a different style, adding more color.

2. He may write a new lead, including some additional details.

3. He may rewrite the entire article, featuring a different lead for the readers of the weekly newspaper. Other details of particular interest may be included for specialized publications.

4. He may write a special by-lined column, interpreting the news of the meeting and giving its deeper meaning for the general public, the probable impact on readers of the weekly or specialized publication.

The various types of news items worthy of reporting might include: (1) approval of various new educational programs; (2) appointment of a committee to study a new policy; (3) approval of the promotion of a college official; (4) report of progress being made on a new campus addition.

Metropolitan College
Public Relations Dept.
News Bureau
Telephone

COLLEGE TRUSTEES MEET, APPROVE NEW COURSES, MAKE NEW APPOINTMENTS

In various official actions, the Metropolitan College Board of Trustees yesterday approved the development of two new courses and appointed a committee to study a new policy, proposed by a trustee.

Fire Protection Technology, designed to provide in-service opportunities for fire protection personnel and make it possible for persons to prepare for careers in the fire service, was approved.

The board also approved the promotion of Mrs. Natalie Wiles, from Acting Training Director to Training Director of the New Careers Program. She replaces Mr. Joseph Mason, who recently resigned to accept another position.

Dr. William C. Lock, dean of the proposed Harbor Campus, reported on the progress being made on that branch of the college, which will be located downtown. He said that studies of similar campuses in other cities were to be made, and architects would be able to submit their drawings within the next month. . . .

An article, with backgrounds, about members of the board who are identified with particular occupational groups may be sent to specialized publications. If John McQueen, an official or active member in the Association of Commerce, is appointed to the board, this would call for a special release on Mr. McQueen to be sent to the editor of *Progress*, a publication of the association. If John McGuire, an AFL-CIO representative, is appointed to the college board, an article about him might be welcomed by the editor of the *AFL-CIO News* in the town or state.

The public relations director is alert to the various types of resolutions and actions which the board might take at its regular meetings, as any one of them or all of them might produce news of general interest. We list here some of the board actions which the representative watches for:

Appointments of deans, department heads and faculty
> Considerable investigation and discussion of these appointments usually precede the action.
>
> While the inkling of the new appointments proposed may have leaked out before, the board action is the first official action taken. Hence the rumor has been denied or confirmed—which makes news.

General Policies developed

Resolutions passed

Special action taken

Discussion by the college president—
> Background of events at the college
>
> Trends in college education today as they affect the local institution
>
> Progress report on the past month at the college
>
> Future growth or plans outlined
>
> Problems of the college requiring consideration

Recommendations of the president for the board to consider
The budget which is being prepared or has been prepared

Reports of board committees
   Financial committee
   Parking committee
   Building committee
   Faculty-administration-trustee relations committee
   Student welfare committee

Discussion by divisional deans or department heads

Discussion of proposals by Student Government Association or by other student groups or individuals

Outside speakers who present facts, views of importance to college and board of trustees
   Representatives of college council speak
   Representatives of state college board speak
   Representatives of other colleges speak

Reports of official visits made by board members on college business

BUDGET NEWS

Budget news, which usually comes out of the board of trustees meeting, is the top news of the financial side of the university or college. The general public, the faculty and the students desire to know what the operating budget of the institution will be for next year. They would like to learn also what the increase in the requests will amount to. The budget projected by the president will also reveal how many students are expected, and the number of instructors to be added to the faculty. Perhaps the president will also reveal new building plans for the college.

The head of the news bureau studies carefully the budget figures, interviewing the president of the college and the business manager for an interpretation of the significance of the figures. Discussion of the budget may have occurred at one of the meetings of the college's administrators. By attending these meetings, the news representative has the opportunity to familiarize himself in advance with complicated budget details. *Somehow he has to simplify the figures and make them understandable to the newspaper readers, the listeners of radio news and the viewers of television.* He discovers that his best approach is to focus on the over-all figures and give reasons behind the increases asked for.

He follows the budget story later through the state legislature, the county board of commissioners or the city board of estimates and the city council. The daily newspapers, radio and TV stations may have reporters at these key news points, but the college representative covers for the weeklies and the specialized press.

Clearwater College
News Bureau
Telephone

CLEARWATER COLLEGE TO ASK FOR $6,900,000 BUDGET

To meet the expected increase of 450 students and the increased costs of operation, Clearwater College will ask for a budget of $6,960,-767 for next year.

This budget was adopted (last night) (Wednesday) (this week) by the Board of Trustees, following a presentation of the college's budget by President Samson Folks. The budget represents an increase of 33 per cent over the current budget of $5,199,477.

Reasons for the increase were outlined by President Folks, who told the trustees that the population explosion is finally catching up with the college, that families in the area are recognizing the business and cultural value of a college education.

Twenty-five instructors will be added to the faculty to take care of the increased teaching load and to keep down the class-size, according to the college president . . . Top administrators will be hired to co-or-dinate new programs at the college.

Included in the budget is the item for instruction, which will increase from $3,409,455 to $4,244,303. This will provide for the salaries of the new instructors, while raising the salaries of the present staff, so that the college will move up from a "C" rating to a "B" rating on the scale urged by the American Association of University Professors.

General administration will jump from $785,004 to $943,257. To operate the college's plant, President Folks is asking for $533,706. Students' services will amount to $844,771, providing for counseling and other student aids. . . .

COLLEGE PRESIDENT MAKES NEWS

The appointment, speeches, statements, actions, campaigns and projects of many university or college presidents furnish excellent material for news articles, produced by the news bureau. As the official representative of the college, the president's name and his statement and actions carry news-weight. Often, because of his identification with high-level educational activities, and because of his active participation in state and local community affairs, the president becomes a news-personality. Realizing this, the news bureau director fully reports all newsworthy views and activities of the president. The PR director sets up weekly or semi-weekly conferences with the president, discussing the college's public relations problems. The schedule of the university head for the week is reviewed, outlines of possible news articles are drawn up, advanced statements are written. If, for example, the president is to deliver a speech before the college at convocation, before a national educational organization, or before the local Exchange Club, the PR representative gets the official to write out the talk as far ahead as possible—sometimes a little "arm-twisting" is necessary to accomplish this objective. The representative then has mimeographed copies made for the press, if the speech has wide-spread interest. And he studies the speech for ideas that may develop into a news story.

When public-supported colleges were faced with the demand by the federal government to integrate, one college president presented what his institution was developing to accelerate the integration process.

Metropolitan College
News Bureau
Telephone

DR. BOWERS SEES COLLEGE SETTING
RACIAL EXAMPLE

State colleges faced with a federal integration order might look to Metropolitan College for programs which work, the college's president, Dr. Martin Bowers, said today.

By going to the inner-city to recruit black students and by offering them opportunities for help once they reach campus, Dr. Bowers said, the college has increased its Negro enrollment from 7 to 8 per cent five years ago to 27 per cent this year.

The college president said that figures may climb a few percentage points this fall. . . .

Among the points Dr. Bowers cited as reasons for his college's success with integration was recognition of the need to take a hard look at attrition—students dropping out. The college offers tutorial services and counseling to students so that they don't lose hope if their grades drop, the president said. . . .

The problem of student protests and student desires to gain a greater voice in university and college policy-making was faced by almost every institution of higher education in the country. It is likely that this will be an on-going struggle and so continue to make news. One college bureau released this story:

Clearwater College
News Bureau
Telephone

HEED STUDENTS, EDUCATOR SAYS

Educators should recognize that student protesters "have something to say, though we may not approve of their manners," the president of Clearwater College said today.

"As I see it," added Dr. Franklyn Pierce, "the answer to student revolt is not hysteria or suppression."

Dr. Pierce's remarks were made when he spoke at the twentieth convocation of St. Francis College.

"The strange part of the students' revolt on the campus is that research by educators is bearing out some of the claims of the student manifesto," he said.

"The Muscatine Report on student disorders at the University of California campus at Berkeley shows that what matters is the personal interest and firmness when necessary of teachers during student confrontations," he continued.

Dr. Pierce echoed a Stanford University professor whose research on student problems indicated that young people who study abroad get "closer" to teachers, and, as a result, profit more than they do from studies at home. . . .

FACULTY NEWS

While the board of trustees and the president furnish the top "hard news" of the university or college, readable, current news and features about the faculty, heads of departments and other administrators are welcomed by the public and sought by editors.

Such news rounds out the college picture, personalizes it, and shows the activity going on throughout the institution—not just in the president's office. With such news of the faculty, the public relations director keeps the public informed about the teaching personnel, the new methods of instruction being explored, the scientific research being conducted. Such news reveals the human side of the professors, helping to alter the stereotype of the college instructor, lost in a world of his own. Some articles about the faculty give background on current issues, useful information supplied by an authority or expert on the faculty and desired by the public.

MR. ESTY

News about faculty members who are engaged in research or who have won particular honors, or speak on current issues before outside groups is welcomed by city editors.

More than any other single source, the faculty and administrators provide the newspeg opportunities to tell the public about what is happening *inside* the institution.

We offer here a general list of the types of news and features which find acceptance both by the public and by the city desks of dailies, weeklies and special publications.

New instructors who join the faculty. These may be grouped by departments, with brief or extended background sketches, personality profiles in-depth of some of these new instructors.

Personality sketches of present members of the staff. These may be offered as single profiles or a series.

Background articles on current issues, with information supplied by faculty members—historians, economists, sociologists, scientists, teachers of literature and the drama.

New grants being made by state or federal governments for certain departments.

Research being conducted by departments.

New teaching and laboratory techniques being used to enliven college instruction.

Faculty attendance at conventions, papers read, work done on committees.

Faculty books being written or published; articles being published in professional, trade or general interest magazines.

Advanced degrees being awarded at various universities to faculty members.

Field trips being taken by instructors and their classes.

Faculty who will take, or have taken, unusual vacations in various parts of the world.

Faculty senate meetings, the actions proposed and taken.

Faculty honors won.

Faculty musical recitals being given.

Faculty exhibits of books at college library or city library.

Faculty retirements.

The news bureau head also uses the appointment of a new department head or instructor as a newspeg on which he can "hang" the story of the significant work of a department. The following news-feature about the appointment of Mr. Herman E. West as dean of the Evening Division of a college, gave the director of the college news bureau the chance to tell about adult education and to promote the interest of adults in returning to college. It will be noted that this is in accord with the new journalistic trends in writing such personality sketches: The focus is on views and experiences or the personality of the person, with the writer then shifting at the end to biographical details.

Central College
News Bureau
Telephone

NEW EVENING DIVISION DIRECTOR
PROMOTES ADULT EDUCATION

(This is the first of a series of personality portraits of new administrators who have been appointed at Central College. The articles, filled with human interest material, will tell about the goals and ambitions of these new administrators, and how they view their positions, which will have a bearing on residents of the city.)

The new director of the Evening Division of Central College, Herman West, has one great all-consuming goal in life: the promotion of adult education.

In a special interview for the . . . , he explained that his most important problem was to reach thousands of adults and urge them to continue their education.

"You know that most people believe that their education is finished when they get their high school diplomas," the educator pointed out.

"But the truth of the matter is that we should never finish studying and learning.

"And I believe that regular study under a competent instructor is the best way to acquire knowledge and to increase abilities and skills."

"There are actually thousands of men and women living in the East, Northeast and Southwest sections of the city who could benefit by their attendance at the Evening Division of Central College," the new director asserted. "Our challenge is to find them and give them the message."

Mr. West grouped these adults into several categories. The Evening Division, he said, can benefit those who want better jobs, who desire to advance themselves. The 113 courses offered by the division provide general background for positions in industry, commerce, banking and governmental work. Other adults desire to train for different occupations than the ones they now fill, and they get the opportunities at the college.

Today a high school education is not enough. . . .

(The college writer continued then with a biographical sketch of the new appointee.)

Personality sketches of members of ethnic or religious groups who are college instructors or researchers are desired especially by editors of specialized publications. The news bureau is on the alert for such feature possibilities. The News Bureau of the Community College of Baltimore produced this feature for the *Baltimore* (Md.) *Afro-American:*

MRS. WYLLIS, DIRECTOR OF NEW CAREERS

Mrs. Natalie H. Wyllis is the first woman director of the New Careers Program at the Community College.

The program is designed to offer rewarding jobs for unemployed persons in the city as well as for those who are locked into low-paying jobs, but are ambitious to rise.

Mrs. Wyllis finds that the new position to which the Board of Trustees appointed her is both challenging and stimulating. "It affords me the opportunity to contribute towards bettering people's lives," she said. (The college reporter then outlined Mrs. Wyllis's background.)

Interesting and significant research being conducted by university physical, biological and behavioral scientists provides many opportunities for the university newsmen to write news and features desired by editors and their readers, as the following articles demonstrate. Only the first few paragraphs of these fascinating stories are given here:

JHU Sociologist Plans Research In American Hiring Patterns

Recruiting and hiring practices of American business and how they affect employment patterns in the American labor force will be the subject of a scientific study by a Johns Hopkins University sociologist.

Dr. Peter H. Rossi, professor of social relations, will undertake the investigation with the support of a grant of $109,000 from the National Institute of Mental Health. He will collaborate in this study with Professor Richard Berk, of Northwestern University, and Professor

Bettye Eidson, of the University of Michigan.

The study will concentrate on 100 firms in the Detroit metropolitan area which employ more than 100 persons each.

Dr. Rossi and a survey team will interview managers, personnel officers and several thousand employes, using specially designed questionnaires.

Policy Examination

Dr. Rossi say" the researchers hope to gain a new understanding of the effects of business policies on the employment of different groups, for example,

young people, blacks, old people and women.

"The question of personnel selection and wage-setting policies is up in the air at this time because of the recession, the wage freeze, activities of the Equal Employment Opportunity Commission and other factors," Dr. Rossi says.

Methods Study

Managers don't know what the problem really is, or what they will be facing over the next 5 to 10 years.

"We will be looking into the ways in which different types of

firms tie themselves into their labor markets. We think the gist says studies have shown that a great deal depends on individual definitions of what is appropriate work for women.

"To cite two extremes," he says, "you find very few if any women on the production line of a steel mill, but plenty of them at the telephone company."

"An interesting thing we have seen is that a surprisingly large number of firms in the blue collar area depend on their existing work force to spread the word and bring in new employes when they are needed. This is fatal to the recruitment of blacks where the existing work force is predominantly white."

study will have important implications as far as employment opportunities are concerned for the country as a whole."

Both of Dr. Rossi's collaborators on this project are former students who recently earned doctoral degrees in the department of social relations at the in regard to the employment Hopkins.

Services For Illicit Users

UM To Test Potency Of Drugs

By Jon Franklin

Illicit drug users who suspect they are not getting what they are paying for will soon be able to take samples to a laboratory on the University of Maryland Medical school campus for analysis.

The laboratory is financed by a $30,000 grant from the state's Drug Abuse Administration and is run by Dr. S. Edward Krikorian, Jr., a School of Pharmacy chemist.

He said the lab is already in

suspect operation, but the touchy question of how a drug user can get samples to him without exposing himself to possible arrest is still unanswered.

Without Risk

Dr. Krikorian said it was his understanding that the drug user would be able to get the questionable drug to the lab without risk of exposure. He said the Drug Abuse Administration would probably act as a confi-

dential messenger between the user and the lab.

But Philip Greene, head of the Drug Abuse Administration, said today that such drug transactions would be confidential "as far as the School of Pharmacy is concerned."

He said that in some instances parents may be told.

Mr. Greene said the part of the drug abuse authority law that insures confidentiality for

[Continued, Page C 6, Col. 4]

Barker Book Is Winner Of Emerson Award

Charles A. Barker, professor of American history at Johns Hopkins University, has won the Phi Beta Kappa Ralph Waldo Emerson Award for his book "American Convictions: Cycles of Public Thought, 1600-1850."

He received the $2,500 award Friday night at a dinner meeting of the Phi Beta Kappa Senate in Washington.

Published in 1970 by the J.B. Lippincott Company, "American Convictions" focuses on American thought that concerns public affairs, institutions and policies.

give recognition to interpretations that carry forward the great tradition of humane learning—comprehensive, over-arching studies that make for a deeper understanding of man.

Previous winners include John Herman Randall, Roberts Coles, Winthrop D. Jordan, Peter Gay and Rollo May.

Working on New Volume

Dr. Barker is on leave to work on a companion volume to his prize-winning book, to be entitled "American Convictions.

Activities of the faculty capture the interest of the editor and the make-up man who places 2-, 3-, 4- and even 5-column headlines on such news.

SIMPLE RESTRAINTS MAY SAVE YOUNGSTERS'
LIVES IN AUTO ACCIDENTS

Many of the yearly one million automotive injuries to children might be prevented with the adaptation of standard adult lap belts to restrain youngsters in cars.

So reports Dr. Alan Nahum of the UCLA Medical School. Dr. Nahum, Arnold Siegel and Michael R. Appleby made a study of 46 automobile collisions involving injuries to 82 children.

An unrestrained child is catapulted through the car in an auto collision. Since most children tend to be in a back seat they usually strike the roof (or header) of the car or back of the front seat. Sometimes they are propelled over the back of the front seat and strike the instrument panel or rear view mirror.

The result is usually severe facial injuries, skull or other fractures, and occasional brain damage. . . .

✿ ✿ ✿ ✿ ✿ ✿ ✿

COVINGTON, La.—Captive wild-born chimpanzees at Tulane University's Delta Regional Primate Research Center here are showing a remarkable ability to learn skills and outwit experimenters.

The chimps have been found to spontaneously manipulate sticks and poles for use as ladders to reach otherwise inaccessible treetops and wall ledges.

This was noted in a group of wild-born chimpanzees under study at the center's field observation compound. Dr. Emil W. Menzel, Jr., research associate at the center, is preparing a scientific report on this first-known occurrence among captive chimps. A preliminary report appears in the current issue of "Delta Primate Report" published by Tuland and circulated among research scientists and institutions. . . .

THE FACULTY HEADGEAR EXHIBIT ADVENTURE

One day the director of the news bureau of the Baltimore Community College was visited by Professor Beverly Chico, of the History Department, who told the director about the Headgear Exhibit she planned for the college. She had collected a wide variety of military, religious and artistic hats. The director spotted this story as having strong human interest elements. It had some social significance, too, because Prof. Chico linked the hats to the development of civilization and to the changing cultures of peoples throughout the world. She conveyed a lively enthusiasm which was very infectious.

Prof. Chico gave the bureau full cooperation on this faculty feature—with good results. She was asked to write a complete résumé of the hats—what they represented, where she obtained them, and any other facts of interest and significance. She wrote a preliminary, extensive article on the exhibit. Then the news bureau head reworked the material in journalistic feature style, with an acceptable lead.

Next, he called the editor of the *News-American* Sunday features department and the editor of the morning *Sun's Woman's Section* as he believed, based on his experience, that these particular editors would be the most interested in the hat article. He told the editors about the article, emphasizing its general human-interest features. The college newsman recommended that the editors have their own reporters or feature-writers interview Prof. Chico, and said that the college news bureau would supply a number of the basic facts in typewritten form for a start. He also promised to provide striking photos. The editors agreed hesitantly, as they didn't want to "buy" the article without seeing it.

Armed with the written copy, the photos and some of her best hats, Mrs. Chico, following the bureau head's suggestion, paid visits to the newspaper offices. Because of her teaching responsibilities and some home duties as a wife and mother, she had difficulty making the appointments, but managed to meet the editors somehow. The editors, or their writers, caught Mrs. Chico's enthusiasm, and responded more favorably than the college news head had hoped for or had been led to believe by the editors. They read the basic copy prepared by the news bureau and then asked Prof. Chico a number of questions. Each of the dailies gave the Headgear Exhibit a half-page, with text and photos.

Here is an excerpt from a fact sheet sent by the news bureau:

Community College
News Bureau
Telephone

HEADGEAR AND HISTORY EXHIBIT
AT THE COMMUNITY COLLEGE

"Off the Top of My Head," an unusual exhibit of headgear, will be held September 25 through October 25 at the Community College.

The exhibition is developed around the nucleus of a hat and headgear collection owned by Mrs. Beverly Chico, instructor in history in the Social Science Department of the college. She gathered the hats from all over the world during her travels.

Types of headgear ranged from two eighteenth century Japanese Sumari helmets to a nineteenth century Prussian Infantry Officer's helmet; from the Sorcerer's Four Pointed hat of Lapland to a bullfighter's hat of Spain—and even to a 1968 local political campaign hat.

The extensive exhibit, sponsored by the Social Science Department and the Art Department, will be open to the public Monday through Friday between 9 A.M. to 4 P.M., and Saturdays from 10 A.M. to 2 P.M. On Sundays visitors may see and enjoy the exhibit from 1 P.M. to 5 P.M. in the Art Gallery of the college, 2901 Liberty Heights Avenue.

"The history of man's headcoverings seems to be almost as old as man himself and is tied in somehow with his primitive home," Mrs. Chico explained. "The word 'hat' probably came from haet or hutt, the name early northern Europeans gave to their primitive shacks or huts."

Over the years, man has devised humorous uses for his headgear; originally hats were used as a protection against climate and physical violence. Some tribes used headgear as ceremonial badges of rank and service. The aesthetic development of hats came fairly late in man's history. . . .

LECTURES, CONFERENCES, EXHIBITS

The public relations department has the responsibility of publicizing lectures, symposiums, workshops and conferences held on the campus by various organizations with which the faculty is connected. The news bureau also sends out releases on art exhibits, concerts, films and plays held for the benefit of students, faculty, and often for community residents.

Lively lecture topics, such as those relating to drugs, sex or social change, make news which many editors want. When these subjects are combined in one speech, the college news bureau has an article which will find acceptance. This one was sent to wire services, local papers, radio/TV stations and education editors.

AUSTIN, Texas (Sept. 1)—"Freedom and Responsibility—Drugs, Sex and Social Change" will be the topic of the opening lecture Thursday (Feb. 4) at Challenge '71 on the University of Texas campus.

Dr. Joel Fort, considered an authority on the contemporary scene, will speak at 4 P.M. in the Texas Union Main Ballroom.

"There is something compelling about Fort's humanity and honesty, his deep understanding of dissident forces of society and his sharp eye for the liars and totalitarians in the power structure," according to the *Saturday Review.*

Dr. Fort, the author of the analysis of today's drug culture entitled "The Pleasure Seekers," is a physician specializing in public health, social psychiatry and drug abuse. He created the San Francisco Center for Solving Special Social and Health Problems. . . . (The background of Dr. Fort followed, together with other facts about the symposium.)

Crime is front-page news, and college institutes devoted to almost any aspect of this subject, particularly the prevention or rehabilitation of offenders, will produce news, as the following shows:

Rehabilitation of the Social Offender will be explored in a one-day institute to be held Wednesday, Feb. 17 at Boston University's Sherman Union Conference Auditorium, 775 Commonwealth Ave. Focus will be on the alternatives to incarceration and how to prevent recurrent aggression.

Professional organizations and social agencies working with offenders have been invited to the institute, which is cosponsored by the Massachusetts chapter of the National Rehabilitation Association and Boston University's Sargent College of Allied Health Professions. . . . (Other details on the conference and the speakers followed.)

In writing about art exhibits, the public relations representative usually is not an artist, but he has to be a good reporter to develop a newsworthy art story. He asks sufficient questions of the sponsoring art department or group, questions about the general scope and significance of the exhibit, seeking to get a new angle on the event. He seeks to show its interest and relevance to the general public as well as to the art-minded persons who might attend. The college writer gets information about the background of the artists who are exhibiting and he describes some of the principal works on display, concluding with facts about the time of the gallery showing, perhaps the opening reception for the artists.

Similarly, in preparing to send a news article on a concert, the college newsman gathers facts about the scope of the concert, searching for some interesting news angle which will capture its flavor, its general and special interests to potential audiences. He gets the correct names of compositions, often not easy to do because of the foreign names involved; the composers; and the musicians performing. Additional information on each of the concert pieces and on the background of the musicians helps to build interest; otherwise, the story consists mostly of a listing of the program items.

Morgan State University in Baltimore, Md. held a four-day conference on the development and present status of the Negroes' experience in religion, literature, education, medicine and human rights, with the news writer sending out a release which was accorded extensive display in the local *Afro-American* newspaper, as the following headline over the article shows:

Morgan conference opens April 18 for new look at Black Experience

Interviews with college instructors whose subjects relate to the news are welcomed by some editors, especially editors of Sunday editions and Sunday supplements. These interview articles can provide background and can give depth to spot news. Professors may be encouraged to write such articles, which are placed by the university news bureau. Interviews with magazine writers may be set up by the bureau.

The following interesting article was based on an interview or collaboration between Dr. Povl W. Toussieng and Arthur Henley. Dr. Toussieng is a Professor of Child Psychiatry, University of Oklahoma.

DEFIANT KIDS WILL MAKE THE BEST ADULTS

It has become increasingly apparent that more and more children do not want to be like their parents; they dress differently, think differently, and aspire to different goals. Youth seems to be going its own way, not the way its elders want it to go. But is this necessarily so bad?

My answer as a child psychiatrist is a resounding, "No!"

Working with teen-agers has always been one of the things I enjoyed most and thought I did best. We always seemed to "dig" each other. About a year ago, I became aware that I wasn't getting through to them any longer, and I began to worry about it. Finally, after a lengthy and intense personal crisis, I began to understand why these young people and I had ceased to communicate. It wasn't the kids who had become estranged from me; it was I who had not kept pace with them. . . .

The "ideal children" who are the envy of the neighborhood because they are "such good kids and no trouble to anyone" aren't really growing up, or even trying to solve the crucial problems of adolescence. Yet many children whose behavior worries their elders most *are* actively struggling with the tasks of growing up and are likely to do better as adults than their "ideal" contemporaries. . . .

Information on the background of faculty members is often difficult to obtain in a hurry. The public relations department should get the facts about faculty members as soon as they arrive on campus.

This letter and form are used by one college public relations man to get information from faculty members.

MONTGOMERY COLLEGE
Rockville—Takoma Park

MEMORANDUM

TO: All full-time Faculty and Staff

FROM: Helmuth O. Froeschle, Administrative Assistant,
           Public Information

SUBJECT: Background Information for News Release

The world will little note nor long remember what you did in this life unless you let me tell about it.

One of my tasks is the maintenance of a current biographical file for faculty and staff. This file will be used for background information for news releases when I hear of something newsworthy. It will also provide me with the data needed to determine where the release should be sent.

Most of us have very little news value to the major Washington dailies. But, we are news to our original home town and the home town of our parents and spouse. Also, publications of college fraternal associations, professional organizations, and similar memberships are interested in us.

A story about YOU is a story about MONTGOMERY COLLEGE. I want the world to note you and learn more about Montgomery College.

Please complete the attached form—Background Information for News Release—and return it to Public Information Office, Room 229 of the central staff building, Rockville.

FACULTY RECORD

For Public Relations Office

Date _____

Name _____

Department _____ Room No. _____ Telephone Sys. ___
  (Building _____)

Rank or Title _____

When Appointed _____

Date of Birth _____ Place of Birth _____

Secondary Schools Attended:
  (Location of School)   (Date of Graduation)

_____   _____

_____   _____

Institutions of Higher Learning Attended:
Name of Institution)   (Date of Graduation)   (Degree)

_____   _____   _____

_____   _____   _____

Title of theses written for Master's Degree _____

Title of dissertation _____

College honors: (honorary societies, fellowships, assistantships)

_____

FACULTY RECORD - For Public Relations Office (continued)

Professional societies, including offices held: _____

_____

Principal Civic Activities: _____

Military Experience, including branch of service, length of service,
ranks and honors: _____

Teaching experience: Secondary Schools
     (Location)   (Date)   (Subj. Taught)

_____   _____   _____

_____   _____   _____

Teaching experience in colleges or universities:
(Name)   (Location)   (Date)   (Subj. Taught)

_____   _____   _____   _____

_____   _____   _____   _____

Publications, dates, titles: _____

Research activities and interests: _____

Promotions in rank at this institution:
     (Date)   (Title)

_____   _____

_____   _____

Wife's Name: _____

Children: (Name)   (Age)

          _____   _____

          _____   _____

          _____   _____

Home Address: _____

Telephone: _____

5

Student News

STUDENTS MAKE UP THE HEART of a college. They are the reason why the colleges have been established in the first place, and are operating today. The university student activities furnish news of considerable interest to the general public as well as to the parents and relatives of the students. News about the undergraduates deals with their scholastic attainments, their departmental work, but also is concerned with their extra-curricular activities—the plays and musicals as well as the clubs and the student government association, in which they participate.

Such news and features give recognition to students, making them aware that the college takes notice of their academic achievements, and the strenuous work and time extra-curricular activities often require. Students are pleased when outsiders, their relatives and friends, have read about their college work; consequently, students are spurred to continue with these activities when such news appears.

Publicity about the college dramatic productions, musicals, art exhibits, and the yearbook and newspaper also stimulate high school students to enroll in college later. High schoolers may have strong interests in theatrical work or in music or journalism; thus, when they read about such activities of students in the college, they realize that they can continue with their interests and move closer toward their professional careers.

Many of the serious plays or musical productions of students in college drama and music departments are of interest to the general public, to current high schoolers and to special interest groups in the community. News and feature articles in daily and community newspapers and specialized publications inform these potential audiences about such events at the college, the publicity helping to draw larger audiences.

A variety of student activities can be turned into news stories and feature articles; hence, the news bureau is alert to student news for the daily newspapers and the hometown newspapers, as well as for the city and suburban weeklies and special publications. Here is a partial list of student events college public relations writers watch for:

Theatrical Productions:
>   Serious Dramas
>   Light Comedies
>   Revivals of Shakespeare
>   Revivals of Greek Plays

Musical Productions
>   Musical Comedies
>   Operettas
>   Symphony Orchestra Concerts
>   Wind Ensemble Concerts
>   Student Talent Shows
>   Christmas Concerts
>   Musical Festivals

Special Productions
>   Afro-American Nite
>   Spanish Night
>   Other Ethnic Group Nights

Student-Sponsored Concerts of Outside Musical Organizations
>   City Symphony Concerts
>   Jazz Combos
>   Rock Productions

Special Events Honoring National Leaders

Cultural Shows
>   Student Art Exhibits
>   Student-Faculty Photo Exhibits

Panel Discussions of Current Issues

Student Government Association Meetings, Projects

Polls of Student Opinion on Current Issues

Unusual Students at the College:
>   High scholarship students; blind, handicapped, oldest, youngest students; women, police, firemen, cab drivers who are enrolled; students from particular city districts

Student Award Night

Homecoming Activities

May Queen Vote and Ball

Graduation Events

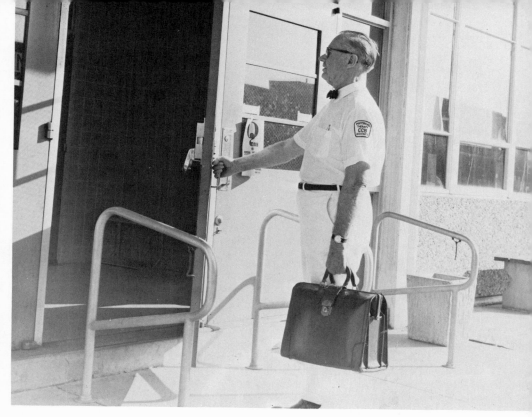

This was one of a series of photos accompanying an article on the oldest student at the Community College of Baltimore. The sequence was published in the Women's and Feature section of the *Evening Sun* in Baltimore. This photo pictures the student, with briefcase in hand, on his way to the college library.

An instructor helps the student in the laboratory.

STUDENT PLAYS

Watching the college calendar of events, the news director learns about the play to be produced by the Speech and Drama Department, or he finds out about the event through his contact with the head of that department. The newsman seeks to get the information about the play as far ahead as he can, so that he can prepare the copy and obtain pictures of the players in time for the various deadlines he must meet. He realizes that the city editor of the daily may accept an attractive, striking photo two days, or even a day, before the curtain goes up. But the Sunday editor and the editor of the Youth Supplement, the tabloid which appears on Wednesday or Sunday in the daily newspaper, require all copy and pictures to be ready a week or more ahead. And the college reporter has a greater chance of getting those departments or editors to publish the feature about the musical event than he has of obtaining space from the day city editor.

The college news writer interviews the director of the play for facts about the plot, searching to find some unusual or significant "angle." He seeks to discover a feature which he can play up, such as the fact that the plot deals with a modern problem of society; or if the play is concerned with the ancient peoples, he looks for modern parallels which can be drawn. He outlines the plot briefly. Then he writes in the character parts which will be played by the students. The cooperation of the production director is helpful in learning the students' hometowns or the districts in the city where they reside. Later the college newswriter may use this information for special articles for home-town newspapers or for community weeklies in the city or the suburbs.

Here is a news story about the play "Caligula," an article which the news bureau head wrote for general distribution. Note the attempt to show modern parallels in this contemporary play which deals with an ancient Roman.

Public Relations Dept.
News Bureau
Telephone:

COLLEGE STUDENTS GIVE "CALIGULA"
ROMAN DICTATOR

A realistic play about a Roman emperor, Caligula, who has modern counterparts in current dictators throughout the world, will be presented by drama students at Metropolitan College on Friday, Saturday, and Sunday (March 14–16). Curtain time in the Campus Theatre is 8:30 P.M.

**Comparison
with
Modern
Counter-Parts
Drawn**

More than 30 students will play parts in Albert Camus' classic play, *Caligula*, which takes its title from the famous or infamous Roman emperor who held sway during the time Rome was at the height of its glory and power. Professor Jerry Gold directs.

Number of Students Involved

The play has a number of controversial scenes. The young emperor had a great love for his sister, and therefore when she died, he became insane and increased his tyrannical hold on his people. Caligula killed his subjects without ceremony and trial. His will was supreme, and he executed without reasoning or any concern about his acts.

The Romans, however, refused to take it any longer. They formed a conspiracy and developed a plot to kill Caligula. They succeeded, and thus ended an early tyrant. This represented symbolically man's efforts to overcome all oppressors.

Brief Outline of Plot

Playing the lead role of Caligula is Jerry Holste. Other players include Gene Timberlake, Anthony Davis, Chet Kadlunowski, Ed Litrenta, Emil Zant, Bruce Foster, Greg Cohen, Tom Douglas, Robert Wilson, Rod Morgan, Estelle Goldenson, Bruce Haas and Bob Cook.

Also in the cast are Diane Wilson, Donna Levin, Sue Spellman, Deborah Fortson, Marsha Mintry, P'nina Cohen, Ernie Horton, Betty Skrutch and Donarda Tutman.

Names of Students Given

Special feature articles focusing on county and on neighborhood students taking part in the production were written and sent to weekly publications.

The college students and many members of the outside community welcome the opportunity to see something different. One college news director recognized that the Afro-American cultural show given at his institution had general interest as well as timeliness; therefore, he wrote a detailed story for dailies, weeklies and ethnic publications. The significance of the production was stressed in the lead.

An Afro-American Culture Show, featuring a dance group, a jazz combo, fashions and art objects, will be presented at the Clearwater University. A lecture giving the history and significance of the African culture, which has infiltrated and influenced American developments, will be part of the show.

Lead: Combines All Events

A faculty-student group is now planning the event which will be held at the university on November 15. "We wish to make this show interesting and meaningful for col-

Direct Quote

lege students and for the general public, including adults, high school, junior high school and elementary school students," said S. Joseph Saudo, director of student activities.

(Then followed the names of participants and the plan for the program. Also given were the time and place when the events would be held.)

The editor of the local Negro newspaper asked for full coverage of the event, plus pictures of the artists and speakers. Complying with the request, the college news director wrote an extensive news article and offered 10 photos, two of which were printed, each three columns wide.

Each year the art departments of many colleges hold elaborate exhibits of the students' work. Desiring to call attention to the activity in the art department, the public relations director of one college wrote an article relating to the three top winners, who happened to be freshmen. Some biographical detail was mentioned.

Metropolitan College
New Bureau
Telephone

FRESHMEN WIN ART SHOW

For the first time in the eight-year history of the student art shows at the Metropolitan College, freshmen have captured a majority of the top prizes.

Ruth Rofsky, Lyne Julius and Tom Cordner were awarded the first, second, third prizes in the 8th annual Student Art Exhibition at the college.

Miss Rofsky, a freshman art major at the college, is a graduate of Milford Mill High School. Miss Julius, also a freshman majoring in art, came to the college from Northwestern High School. Mr. Cordner is a sophomore art major who was graduated from Sparrows Point High School. He is a candidate to receive the Associate in Art degree from the college next month and has already been offered a position as a commercial artist with a local advertising agency.

Honorable mentions were awarded to Leslie Engle, Sharon Lugouri, Gerard Pilchowski and Emily Turk.

Judges for the art show were six members of the Metro College Art Department. A total of 84 of the college's art and art education majors participated in the one-day campus exhibition.

SPECIAL EVENTS: SPANISH NIGHT

The college news director is aware that the city editors of daily newspapers, as well as the feature editors and departmental editors, all are on the look-out for off-beat articles about college students. When the news bureau head finds out that "Spanish Night" is being planned by the modern language department, he makes some further inquiries about the event. He discovers the event has considerable human-interest potential. He develops a plan for writing the news and releasing it to produce the maximum results from the event:

1. Regular news article for daily No. 1.
2. New lead on story for daily No. 2.
3. Special articles for music and women's departmental editors of dailies, regular edition and Sunday editions.
4. Fresh angle and new lead for community and hometown newspapers, stressing local students and giving additional newsy details.
5. New angle on story for youth department supplement in Sunday edition of daily, favorable to this type of feature.

The college representative developed the following general article for the daily No. 1, giving the program and pointing out the purpose of the event. He mentioned, too, those sponsoring "Spanish Night."

Central College
News Bureau
Telephone

COLLEGE TO HOLD SPANISH NIGHT— PUBLIC INVITED

An outstanding guitarist and a number of dancers will be featured in "Una Gala Espagnola," at the Central College on Friday evening, March 7.

The Spanish Night will not only present entertainment native to Spain, but a Spanish dinner will be held also. The purpose of the event is to acquaint students of Central and other colleges and high school students and adults with Spanish cultural life as well as the foods of that country.

The program is being sponsored by the Student Government Association, of which Steven Becker is head, by students in the Foreign Language Department and by instructors of Spanish. Dr. Rena C. Tansky, head of the

LEAD:
Summary
of Events,
Especially
Guitarist,
Dancers

Purpose
of Event

Sponsors
of Event

department, and Janet Reymann, student, are making the arrangements.

The delicious Spanish dinner will feature paella, arroz con pollo and other Iberian dishes. For those who wish to come to the dinner, the charge is $2.50, with the entertainment thrown in free. For those who wish to enjoy the entertainment, admission is free. Tickets may be obtained from Mrs. Tansky. The event will be given in the formal lounge of the Central College, 2224 Raven Heights Avenue. . . .

Foods Featured

Place of Event

(The remainder of the article dealt with the background of the guitarist and the Spanish dancer, and told about the illustrated talk on bullfighting.)

CHRISTMAS CONCERTS

Most universities, four-year colleges and community/junior colleges produce Christmas concerts. The music department works hard for a month or six weeks before the holiday event to produce a creditable performance. The concert is designed for students and their parents as well as for the community. The college news director, however, realizes that the Christmas concerts are traditional and have been presented in similar fashion for years. He is aware that the editors will be deluged with news of such concerts being given by high schools, elementary schools, other colleges, churches. All their productions are newsworthy, but they have a certain sameness. The college news director tries to discover some unusual feature which will set his college's Christmas concert off from those of other institutions. Perhaps the songs which will be sung will be unusual; perhaps the theme, out-of-the-ordinary. Maybe the instruments used will furnish some off-beat angle. In the following article the various instruments gave the news a fresh twist:

Guitars, bells and Caribbean percussion instruments will be used to accompany the Christmas Spanish and French folk carols presented at the various programs of the Central College this pre-holiday season.

"These instruments will give the event a realistic atmosphere," said Mrs. Blanche Bowlsbey, director of the choir. "A calypso Christmas carol will be sung and native instruments will supply the background. These songs in the original language will be given in addition to our traditional carols and special numbers."

Robed in their white and crimson gowns, the choir, assisted by the college band, will present a candlelight processional and recessional. The stage will be decorated in the holiday spirit.

The major work to be performed at the annual Christmas Concert, which the public is invited to attend on Sunday at 8 p.m. in the Campus Theatre, will be "Die Kindheit Jesu," a cantata by Johann Christoph Bach, son of Johann Sebastian Bach.

(Also given were the names of student participants and the musical numbers they performed.)

The following year, the news bureau head learned of the variety of songs, including Christmas carols and Hannukah selections which were on the program. This gave him the feature angle he was looking for.

Featuring Christmas spirituals and carols and Hannukah selections, Indian and Caribbean carols, the Central College will present "Winter Celebrations" at 8:30 P.M. next Sunday in the Campus Theater. . . .

For the *Young World,* the tabloid supplement of the Sunday edition of the local daily, the news bureau stressed the modern beat. After shooting pictures of students in the chorus and the instrumentalists, the bureau head submitted the live photos to the editor, who was happy to get the story and photos. He gave the event a half page of space.

When the students observe the birthday of Washington, Lincoln, Robert E. Lee or Martin Luther King, this event may produce a newsworthy article if some strong statements are made with general appeal or some unusual event occurs. The commemorative event honoring Dr. King was covered thoroughly at this college by the Community College news bureau reporters.

OVER 300 HEAR PROGRAM HONORING KING AT CCB

By

DR. SIDNEY KOBRE

and

CARL SMITH

Community College of

Baltimore

The need to carry on Dr. Martin Luther King's commitment to non-violence and to improve social and economic conditions for everyone was the recurrent theme stressed by speakers at the King memorial at the Community College of Baltimore this week.

Central Emphasis of Speakers Given

More than 300 students, administrators and faculty members attended the exercises remembering Dr. King's birthday. The services were held in the Campus Theatre on Tuesday morning. . . . (Details of each speech followed.)   **Number Attending, Place**

Baltimore (Md.)
Afro-American

STUDENT ELECTIONS

News about students who are elected to the offices of the Student Government Association becomes newsworthy for many publications. Some background material on the newly elected president may be included in the news article. This is the type of news in which home-town newspapers of the students would be particularly interested.

Steve Fedder, a freshman majoring in Arts and Sciences, has been elected president of the Student Government Association at State College.

During the freshman year, Steve was elected councilman, or a representative to the Student Government Association (SGA). He was busy also with the social committees which are part of the organization.

(Steve's other activities were listed then. His hobbies were mentioned. Additional officers also elected were named.)

The election of the first Black student as president of a Student Government Association was of particular interest.

Robert Wilson, Jr. became the first Black student in State College history to be elected President of the powerful Student Government Association. His VP is Bennie Frazier. Lydia Gallant and Kate Leonard were elected Secretary and Treasurer, respectively.

Commenting on his victory, President-Elect Wilson said, "Although there were some heated emotions on the part of a few students over the results, this is to be expected. However, despite this, I will be President of all of the students, representing all students and showing partiality to no special interest group." . . .

Polls taken of student opinion on current national issues or candidates for election are of interest, reflecting how the college students are reacting and thinking.

COLLEGE CLUBS

The activities and projects of student clubs can be developed into readable features. Here is one about the International Club.

One of the recurrent topics of conversation at the International Club of the State University is national humor. Students from all over the world who attend the university find out that what seems humorous in one country is "blah" in another land. Good jokes fall flat on foreign ears—and the students wonder why.

At the International Club 25 members munch Asian arare and European blintzes. Members listen to the beat of an Indian tabla and hear the dreamy strum of an Italian mandolin. They also dance the hora from Israel, and are amazed when a student from the Ukraine, dressed in billowy silk pants, does his intricate steps.

State University has indeed gone international. Its melting pot of foreign students represents such diverse countries as Japan, Turkey and Czechoslovakia. Students come from as far as Tunisia and the Ukraine. Some have lived in Sweden and Greece at one end of the world and Hawaii at the other. . . .

Most of the foreign student's social life is centered around the club. It was organized last fall as a means of developing new friendships among students, the idea for such a group being conceived by Sharon Hess, who became the club's president.

Discussing the club, Sharon, a former resident of Hawaii, said, "I saw the need to form some type of organization which would introduce foreign students to each other as well as to the local students from Baltimore.

"Although the club was originally formed to promote new friendships, we have expanded our purpose to include human understanding and empathy of the world's peoples through education."

The foreign students get many of their impressions of America through their association with the students. The American students, in turn, learn about the culture of other lands. . . .

(Interesting information was given about several of the foreign students and a list of all the students and their native countries was included.)

FOCUS ON INDIVIDUAL STUDENTS

Students who are unusual in scholastic attainments or who are attending college despite unusual handicaps provide good human interest copy. These students may have obtained "straight A" averages, or they may be blind or come to classes in wheel chairs. They may also be newsworthy because they are twins. Other students become news copy when they are given scholarships. These are excellent stories to send back to the hometown papers.

The following news story deals with the winning of television station awards and covers what the students will do and some of the background.

2 STUDENTS ARE AWARDED WMAR-TV SCHOLARSHIPS

Two City College students have been chosen as the first recipients of scholarships in electronic technology awarded by WMAR-TV, the local television station.

Thomas E. Fitchette and Dennis Hatton have been provided with $200 each for tuition and books from the WMAR-TV Scholarship Fund.

In the program established by WMAR-TV, the two students will be employed part time to learn the electronic techniques of the station while they are completing their college studies.

Work With Engineers

Mr. Fitchette and Mr. Hatton will work with professional engineers at WMAR-TV to learn the technical operations which they have studied in school.

On completion of their courses at the college they will begin full-time work with WMAR-TV.

HOMECOMING EVENTS

Here is an announcement which the news bureau receives, telling about Homecoming activities. This is one of the big annual events which produce news in most of the media outlets of the news bureau.

Date: October 28, 197_

TO: All the faculty
FROM: S. Joseph Salvaggio, Student Activities Director
SUBJECT: Homecoming

Homecoming Game and Dance will be this Saturday, November 2.
There will be a reception for Alumni at 1:00 p.m. in the Formal

Lounge. Many faculty members may wish to be present to meet former students. We are expecting about 100 Alumni to attend.

The football game will be Central vs Nassau, and it will begin at 2:00 p.m. During half-time the Homecoming Queen will be crowned.

The dance will be from 9:00 p.m. to 1:00 a.m. and will feature Tommy Vann and the Professionals. At about 10:30 there will be a special program honoring the Queen and football team.

You are all cordially invited to attend as guests of the Student Government Association.

This sets the bureau writer(s) off on news stories which may last for several weeks.

Newspaper editors like mysterious angles in the news, and therefore the news bureau featured the mystery angle of the May Queen selection for the local youth section of the Sunday newspaper:

News Bureau
Telephone

The Number One question at the Central College for the past two weeks has been—who will be the May Queen for 1972?

The rumors floated around the college, but the name of the queen was not known—not even to student leaders or President Harry Barnes.

(Names of the various entrants as well as the place and time of the dance, the band and other information were given. The committee which worked to make the affair a success was included.)

Here is the story which cleared up the mystery:

Lynn Dodd, brown hair and brown eyes, with top grades, is the new May Queen of Central College. A sophomore, she expects to graduate in June and continue with her education at Towson State College, studying to be an elementary school teacher.

Miss Dodd was elected in a college-wide vote. More than 25 coeds were nominated for the honor several weeks ago. After students voted, the Queen's official court was cut to ten girls. The top winner, Lynn, became May Queen.

The coronation took place at the Civic Center in elaborate ceremonies before an audience of more than 1,000.

(Similar information given before in the news was repeated here— the names of the attendants, escorts, band which played.)

COVERING THE GRADUATION

Graduation ceremonies provide good news copy for most colleges because the commencement speakers often are prominent and say something which furnish strong quotes. In addition, every graduating class has students with high averages, or who get their diplomas in spite of many handicaps—physical or financial. Twins, mother-and-daughter graduates, students who are beyond the usual age for graduating seniors may provide human interest copy. These the representative must search out before the ceremonies begin. Some newspaper editors like the graduation stories because they furnish the newsmen with the opportunity to publish many names. They want, too, the names of the scholarship and other award and high honor winners. The college newswriter may compare the number of graduates with those last year, or ten years ago. As in other traditional, it-happens-every-year, college stories, he must find the unusual angle. On graduation news, he is in competition with other colleges and local high schools for space and attention.

The public relations values of the graduation news or feature are many. Attention is again focused on the institution, giving it exposure. Preparation is the keynote for successful coverage by the college public relations department. It is almost too late to begin the coverage of the news on the afternoon or evening of the ceremony itself. The event moves too fast, the happenings occur too quickly—and the graduation is over. Obtaining a list of the graduates as soon as they can be released by the director of admissions or the dean of the faculty is essential. Getting the names of top students with the highest averages and obtaining the scholarship and other award winners enable the public relations representative to build background sketches of these students before the event begins and to have the information ready as soon as the last graduation note is played by the college band. If the representatives desire to aim some of the news articles at the hometown papers of the students, the writers get breakdowns of towns and city districts from the directors of admissions.

The representatives make a determined effort to get copies of the speeches of the principal speakers and the college president long before the graduation event begins. The college newsmen size up the news value and begin to select the best statements for the final stories. Securing an outstanding speaker with something of value to say demonstrates that the college is providing a forum to bring the views of individuals to the public.

Centering interest on scholarship and award winners, especially those with great brilliance, shows that brains, too, are rewarded at colleges, spurring others to achieve. Demonstrating that students can graduate in spite of handicaps provides an example for high schoolers with similar difficulties to emulate. By listing the graduates, the news bureau has given

Mom, 37, Gets Degree

Mrs. Clarice Pitts of the 2700 block E. Federal St. recently graduated from Morgan State College.

What's so unusual about that? Only that Mrs. Pitts is 37 years old and during the four years she was studying at Morgan she was also keeping house, raising her children, taking care of her husband and — for all but six months — working fulltime for the Community Action Agency.

But Mrs. Pitts' graduation from Morgan is only the happy ending of a long story of patience, perseverance, ambition and hard work.

She was born in Apex, N.C., one of 9 children. At the age of 16, while a tenth grader, she dropped out of school, got married and had a child. That's when she moved to Baltimore.

THE MARRIAGE didn't work out, however, and ended in divorce. That's when she met — and married — William A. Pitts and, with his support and encouragement, she started on the long road that climaxed with a bachelor's degree in sociology from Morgan.

First she studied dressmaking at Carver High School, followed by employment in several garment factories.

Then it was Douglass Evening School — and graduation in 1959.

With time out for another child it was back to school again, at Baltimore Junior College (now the Community College of Baltimore). Then another period of working fulltime.

AND FINALLY, evening classes at Morgan for more than three years — while still working fulltime — and a six-month leave of absence last year from the CAA to finish her studies.

It's a happy story that has a moral, according to her husband.

"You hear a lot about kids dropping out of school," he said.

"They don't seem to realize how important an education is and they don't seem to know that it's a lot easier to get an education while you're young.

"Maybe the example of my wife will help convince some kids that they ought to stick with school and that they really don't have it as tough as they think."

Collector sells comics for tuition

David Faggioli leafs through one of his Captain Marvels.

Salt Lake City (AP)—Superman, Captain Marvel and Flash Gordon are helping to put David Faggioli through college.

The University of Utah junior earns his tuition by collecting and selling old comic books. He has made more than $2,000 so far.

"Like most little kids, I started a comic book collection," Mr. Faggioli said. "Later I got turned on to comic strip art, to its combination of graphic design with motion. I decided to make a profit out of that interest."

In neat piles

Hundreds of comic books, some dating back to the late Thirties, are stacked in neat piles in the Faggioli home. Many of the older editions are sealed in plastic bags.

Mr. Faggioli, 20, sells most of his comics by advertising in a national comic collectors' magazine. He puts his more valuable acquisitions up for bid.

He was recently offered $200 for his most precious comic, a 1939 Marvel Mystery. It will be his biggest sale.

The value of a comic is largely determined by its rarity, Mr. Faggioli said.

"Comics published in the Forties are the most valuable because most got thrown out during wartime paper drives," he said. It's not unusual to sell a wartime comic for $50 or more.

"The Fifties were not good years for comics," he added. "They're more common and their quality isn't as good. Some of them wouldn't even bring 5 cents."

The current nostalgia craze has been a boon for comic book sellers, he said.

"People like old, funky things now, and they like to look at the world the simple way it was 20 or 30 years ago. Comics do a good job of showing the world.

"During World War II, comics were intensely patriotic—totally behind this country with slogans like 'Be Too Wise for Those Axis Lies' and 'A War Stamp a Day Keeps Hitler Away.' "

"Idealism was the key word. Crooks were total bad guys, and the heroes were clean-cut and decent."

"Blew my mind"

Most of those who collect comics of the Forties, Mr. Faggioli said, are in their 20's and older "because they're the only ones who can afford to pay $50 and up for a comic."

He added, however, he recently received a letter from a 7-year-old, who bid $100 for a comic. "That blew my mind."

Mr. Faggioli, a music major, says he hopes to end his comic-selling career next year and open a shop dealing in graphics and rare jazz and classical records.

The 37-year-old mother (top) and the student who collects and sells comic books (bottom) to help put him through college make appealing human interest features and, at the same time, show the public the determination of some students to learn and get their degrees. Such news may spur other persons to continue their education.

recognition to all the seniors. Their friends in high school may be stimulated to attend this college or another institution.

Here's a graduation story which began with the strong statements made by a former congressman. The college newswriter then gave the other details regarding the graduating class, finally returning to the other main points of the address. The writer then included the high honor graduates, the special award winners and concluded with the names of the graduates.

"In every area our nation is troubled and deeply divided. The voices of extremism are growing loud and the voices of reason are all too often silent."	**LEAD:** **Direct** **Quote of** **Speaker**
This is what former Congressman Carlton R. Sickles told the largest graduating class in the history of the Central College.	
The 28th commencement exercises were held in the field house of the college, where 353 students received the associate in arts degree and 32 were awarded certificates. President Harry Jones introduced the speaker and conferred degrees.	**5 W's** **Large** **Graduating** **Class**
The speaker said that, "without being unduly optimistic, we can see progress and improvement all about us . . ."	**Return** **to Speaker**
(More quotes followed and then the writer told about the students who graduated with high honors and the others who were presented special awards.)	

A feature about Lawrence Lehmann, son of a carpenter who was graduated from college with highest over-all average, but made it in three years, provided interesting reading for many readers of the *Towson* (Md.) *Jeffersonian*. The feature would inspire other students to make full use of their potential.

LEHMANN ENDS 4-YEAR COURSE IN 3 WITH HIGHEST OVERALL AVERAGE

Lawrence Lehmann, son of a Baltimore carpenter, graduated from the University of Maryland June 7 not only with the highest overall average in the College of Engineering (3.6), but with a record of having made it through the program in just three years.

His older brother John, now an electrical engineer with Westinghouse Electric Corp. here, also graduated from the university's College of Engineering in three years in 1967.

In addition to his high scholastic achievement, Lawrence participated in many other extra-curricular activities: he was vice president of his residence hall, head of the judiciary board of the dorm, on Hill area council, member of the student faculty committee on administration.

The second son of five children (four boys, one girl) of Charles F. and Mary T. Lehmann, 5935 Leith Walk, Larry financed his college education all the way by earning scholarships and working part-time during the school year and full-time summers as a carpenter in the construction industry. . . .

(The article then included the honors Lawrence had received and his plans for the future.)

News bureau directors are on the lookout for unusual students who, in spite of handicaps, get their diplomas. Here is a human interest feature about housewives who received their diplomas late in life. Such stories set examples for other adults, suggesting indirectly that they, too, might continue with their education at a college or university.

They ignore dusty houses

By LUANNE W. PRYOR

Long Beach, Calif.

"Going back to school when you're over 30 means you are serious and you really want that education," says Alison Averill, 33, mother of three and one of 3,000 "mature women students" at California State University at Long Beach.

She and her husband, Ted, moved to California nine years ago, and three years ago Mrs. Averill decided to go back to school.

"When I started back I had to learn how to study all over again," she says. "The kids and Ted had to put up with crazy hours, my running off to the library, and my miserable disposition when I had a final coming up.

"My house was a mess," she adds, "but I decided that a dusty house wasn't going a lot at night and often early to matter that much.

"Of course I had to study in the morning. I have found, though, that the more I do, the more I can do.

"Our home life is different. Somehow it is more valuable. We've all learned not to dissipate out time so that our activities aren't as frivolous as they used to be."

She works, too

Another student at the Long Beach campus, Irene Marsi, mother of four, says: "My husband and my children make it possible for me to continue at the university and hold down a job, too."

Mrs. Marsi works daily at a part-time job from 7 A.M. to 11 A.M. She already has one degree and is now enrolled in a education course.

When asked how she manages all her activites, she answers, "Well, there is the sock that dangles from the chandelier—the result of an ill-aimed hook shot; there are mornings when no one, but no one, has clean underwear; there is the wrecking of the budget when university fees are due at the beginning of the semester; and there is the planning and organizaton required so that I can sit down for a relaxed chat with my husband."

She explained that her children leave for school when their father does. She is always home in the afternoon. The children do a large part of the housekeeping and yard work and, for the most part, do it willingly and cheerfully. "If they did not," she says, "I simply could not manage it by my-

continued on next page

self. I have to have time to study."

Commutes daily

Jacquelyn Kimmich commutes daily to the Long Beach campus, where she's working toward a master's degree and a junior high teaching credential.

"Last year I did my student teaching while taking classes at the university, too. It was rather difficult at times, especially those nights I was up until 3 in the morning studying and grading papers," she says.

Recently divorced and the mother of two girls, Mrs. Kimmich chose school over the business world, where she once was an executive secretary.

"Sometimes the pressure is terrific," she admits, "and then, on top of it, I have the added responsibility of being a single parent."

She is always home when her girls return from school. They swap stories about the day and then go about their business.

"The girls have activities of their own now," Mrs. Kimmich says, "and that leaves me time to study. Sometimes, though, I'm washing the kitchen floors pretty late at night. But I don't care. You learn when you return to school that the chores aren't anywhere nearly as important as you once made them out to be."

Husband helped

With graduation just a few months away, Harriet Danufsky says she often feels sad that her college career is almost over. "I've had the opportunity to do all the things I always wanted to and never could," she says. "I've sung in the college chorus, taken folk dancing, piano swimming and sailing. Imagine all that in addition to a full academic schedule!"

Mrs. Danufsky will receive a B.A. in English from California State. She has a 3.25 grade average—around a B-plus.

Her husband has helped her the most by not applying pressure. "He doesn't insist upon fancy meals or a perfect house."

However, she is quick to say that her college career hasn't all been easy. "One night I took out the typewriter—to write a letter, mind you—and the girls, Shoshana, 9, and Tomar, 7, said, 'Oh, Mom, you aren't going to write another term paper!' "

"What it amounts to," she continues, "is that the kids get upset when they think my schooling interferes with them. But on the other hand, they see me as an individual instead of as a servant."

(c) Christian Science Monitor

Part Three

PRINT MEDIA—II

A Student Prospectus for Vassar College / 1970-71

Vassar College is not unique.

Every Vassar student is.

Designer of the Vassar College brochure made use of white space to attract attention. Notice the narrow band of a campus scene at top and the unique catch-lines at bottom right.

6

Brochures

Leaflets, brochures and pamphlets have certain outstanding advantages which newspaper and magazine publicity cannot equal. The entire story of the college can be told in one convenient, printed package. One phase of the institution's activities or the courses of one department may be presented in another publication. These printed publications have a permanency which news and feature articles in newspapers do not possess.

Although the categories frequently overlap, leaflets may be considered as four-page publications, while brochures usually involve six or more pages. Brochures are printed on both sides of a large sheet and then folded so as to produce the various pages. Pamphlets are more elaborate booklets with eight or more pages, requiring a saddlestitch or metal fastener to hold or staple the pages together. Attractive publications may be designed for students, faculty and the general public. In this chapter we will use the word brochures to represent all these types of publications, as the same principles apply to them.

The college public relations representative must be aware of the tough job his brochures must do. They have to stand alone, depend solely on their merit. If a publicity news article appears in a daily or weekly newspaper, or trade magazine, the message has a ready-made audience which may glance at the headlines and read on, perhaps to the college article. The reader has formed the habit of reading the news in his hometown newspaper, where he has found pleasure-giving and informative reading matter before, written and presented in the way he likes it.

The public relations man for the college, thus, has a better-than-average chance of getting thousands to read his feature article, when it appears in the general news section of the daily newspaper, in its special college section, or in the tabloid feature supplement given away with the big Sunday edition. The college news which gets a strong display in the weekly also captures the readers' attention. But the brochure must stand on its own merit.

The college brochure must do a varied job: It must get attention; arouse interest and hold it; and convince—all within a short time.

The college writer can't bore the reader. He can't include material which could cause his audience to lose interest quickly. If he does, the brochure goes flying into the wastebasket, or it is politely filed away.

VARIETY OF UNIVERSITY PUBLICATIONS PRODUCED BY PUBLIC RELATIONS DEPARTMENTS

FOR STUDENTS
General information about the university
History of institution
Combined (History and General Information)
Combined (History, General Information and Programs)
University programs
Departmental programs
Individual courses
Catalogues
Preparation for careers
Intern preparation
Student handbook
Life at the college
Library services
Counseling services
Financial aid for students
Housing information
Art Museum Guide
Chapel information
Guide to buildings
Guide for minority students
Maps of campus, buildings

FOR FACULTY
Faculty handbook
Governance of university
Introduction to campus

ADULT STUDENTS
Informal programs, courses
Off-campus centers

GENERAL PUBLIC
History of college
Special events
Dedication (buildings, etc.)
Anniversary
Cultural programs for year
Speakers' Bureau
Annual report
Financial report
President's report
Reprint of presidential speech(es)
Reprint of newspaper article, special columns
Reprints of conference speeches
Publications of university press
Cultural events
   Art gallery exhibitions
   Concerts
   Theatrical productions
Meetings, conferences, institutes

EDITORS, REPORTERS, BROADCASTERS
Facts about university (information and statistics)
Campus calendars
   Main events
   Cultural events
Campus maps

How, then, can you produce effective brochures with which you will get the desired results? No pat prescription is available at the corner drug-store. But we can point to some steps which will prove helpful in finding your own special formula, meeting your own needs.

PRELIMINARY STEPS

Before any writing is done, the representative makes a careful study of the facts about the department on which he is focusing. He saturates himself with information. He collects all the previously-printed matter—not to copy it slavishly, but to study the material as a guideline. He next moves through the department for clues—reads notices and other information on bulletin boards. He examines the aims of the department, the courses it offers, and he asks about the graduates. He talks to the chairman of the department, instructors and students. Slowly, the significant points begin to emerge, the ideas for the brochure to jell.

Determine the Purpose

As in all effective college communications, the practitioner has to determine—in consultation with the chairman or division head—what the aim or aims of the brochure will be. He may be producing a brochure for the arts or science department, or he may be developing a brochure giving perspective on the entire institution. On other occasions, he may work out a brochure about the arts festival or college week. Each brochure has a different and a distinctive purpose.

Make an Audience Analysis

The public relations man sizes up the audience for whom he is writing the brochure. When he writes a news or feature article, he can say, "I'm aiming at the 'general public.' " He can aim his brochure at the general public also; however, he also can select a specific group as his target and then direct his communication to this audience.

The closer, the more accurate his analysis of the specialized public he desires to reach with his brochure, the most result-getting will be his final product. If he desires to interest the reader in the social work program at the college, for example, he analyzes first the desires of these prospective students. What are their ambitions? What kinds of training do they want and need? What are the opportunities in social work for the young high school graduate who desires to get professional training? What rewards will social work offer the adult seeking a new career?

A specific checklist for background of the audience might include: (1) age; (2) educational status; (3) economic level; (4) general interests; (5) special interests.

The writer then determines what are the advantages to the reader of this university or college. What background and specialized courses are offered by the sociology or urban affairs department, and what is the specific value of the courses to the future social worker? Is there any outside field work undertaken by the class? What teaching and professional experience do the instructors have? The writer then checks on the graduates of the college's social work program so that he may include a few paragraphs on the type of jobs they obtain upon graduation, and later, as they gain experience on the job.

Writing a Prospectus

The publications writer now develops a brochure prospectus to define clearly in writing his objectives, the general theme of the publication and to whom it will be addressed. He determines in preliminary fashion some of the details of its production, such as size, number of pages, illustrations and copies to be printed. He may revise the prospectus later and get cost estimates from the printer. Throughout the production steps, the prospectus serves as a guideline for the writer. In the event the public relations director has to consult with department heads and college officials regarding the publication, or if he has to secure additional or special funds for it, he can use the prospectus.

PROSPECTUS FOR BROCHURE

Brochure's Value
    Will it help entire college, or what specific department or divisions?
Purpose(s)
    What are the purposes of the brochure? What are the goals or aims of the message—give information, attract students?
Audience(s)
    Whom do you want to read the brochure? It may be general public, or specialized groups, or a combination of audiences.
General and Specific Themes or Topics
    List the general as well as the specific points you will cover in the brochure. An outline would serve the purpose.
Size of the Brochure
    What is the over-all page-size of the brochure? Length and width?
Number of Pages (preliminary estimate)
    How many pages will the brochure be—4? 6? 8? 12?
Number of Illustrations
    How many pictures, drawings, charts do you think will be needed? Approximate size of each? List and identify each on a page labeled "Photos Needed," giving reduction in size needed for each.

Color or Black & White Printing

What do you choose? Consider value and cost; see below under "Printing Estimates."

Number of Copies

How many do you think you need? 1,000, 5,000, 10,000, 50,000? Consider the audience and the length of time you believe the brochure can be distributed effectively—1 month, 6 months, 1 year, 2 years?

Methods of Distribution

Where will the brochure be distributed? On what occasions? What methods will be used to distribute it?

Get Printing Estimates

Estimates from two (2) printers for offset and letterpress for 1,000 copies, for 2,000 copies and for 5,000 copies, etc. Get size of type needed.

Your table should read:

PRINTING ESTIMATES FOR
BROCHURE FOR —————————

Printer "A" (name and address)

	Offset		Letterpress	
	Bl. & W.	Color	Bl. & W.	Color
1,000	$	$	$	$
2,000	$	$	$	$
5,000	$	$	$	$
10,000	$	$	$	$

Printer "B" (name and address)

	Offset		Letterpress	
	Bl. & W.	Color	Bl. & W.	Color
1,000	$	$	$	$
2,000	$	$	$	$
5,000	$	$	$	$
10,000	$	$	$	$

When can deliveries be expected? ———

PRODUCTION STEPS

Out of the welter of material he has gathered from observation, reading and talking, and after considering his purpose and audience, the practitioner selects his information. He picks the facts and ideas, the incidents and illustrative stories for his brochure. Ordinarily, he cannot use all the information he has acquired. Thus he must choose material which is interesting, pertinent and convincing. Often the writer has to compress important facts because he is not writing a book but a lively, readable brochure.

Outline the Material

The knowledgeable college writer now groups his material, placing similar points and related incidents together, and arranging the facts according to some logical but interesting pattern. His outline enables him to look at the material objectively and to check it out before he begins to write the first draft. The writer is able to determine also how much copy he has and how much space he needs to say what he wants. He may alter his copy later, for the writer goes through a trial-and-error process before he completes his brochure.

Many college brochures are quite dull, for they appear to have been lifted from the institution's catalogue, which is primarily concerned with fees and a listing of the courses and programs. Brochures do not have to be academic in their approach. They can be as interesting and as exciting and original as the public relations writer can make them. Many brochures are attractively written and the copy is developed in a lively, appealing manner.

In some ways, the brochure and the news or feature article are similar. The first few paragraphs must get the attention and arouse the interest of the reader. The 4-, 8-, or 12-page publication can rely also on the pull of the cover headline, picture and text for its appeal. Nevertheless, once the reader has been attracted to the inside of the brochure, the writer must take over and lure him further into the material. The techniques outlined in the section on news and feature articles may be applied to brochure-writing. As in the news or feature article, various devices have proved successful:

The Descriptive Lead

The descriptive lead depicts a situation or scene, the writer seeking to produce a visual image for the reader. For a brochure relating to the college's teacher-education program, this lead describes a classroom situation in which the young graduate might find himself a few years away:

Picture yourself as a teacher of a group of small children. The class is in the ghetto of a large city. The little boys and girls, age 6, sit in their seats quietly. They are dressed in plain clothes, but their minds are active. Potentially, they have many different abilities. Some may become scientists, doctors or lawyers. This is their formative time of life, and you can shape them forever. . . . Elemenatary teaching is a rewarding profession that contributes much to the community.

For another brochure showing the intellectual excitement and friendly social atmosphere at the college:

The freshman at ——— College enjoys an exciting life and has rewarding experiences. At 9 A.M. he listens to a lecture on Ancient Civilization by a man who has actually dug in the tombs of the Egyptian pharaohs. The instructor has brought some magnificent color slides back from his trips and he shows these photos . . . At 10 o'clock, the freshman takes part in a stimulating discussion of the problems of urban life today. He learns what is wrong with our cities and contributes his views. . . .

The Summary Statement Lead
Often, in developing the copy for a brochure relating to courses that lead to specific careers, the college writer develops the broad occupational needs of industry or the professions for trained persons. Or he may tell about the future in which the reader would find himself.

One of the important facts you should consider in planning your future is the role of women in today's business world. Between 1950 and 1965, the number of women in the United States who were employed outside their homes increased from 19 million to 27 million. Most were married. Increasing participation of women in the business world in the years ahead is virtually a certainty.

If you get your education and training now, you will be rewarded now as well as later on. . . .

The Opening Statement
Many knowledgeable college brochure writers open with a strong statement about the need for the graduates of the institution. Here is one which tells in an interesting fashion about the needs in mechanical technology:

Ninety per cent of all scientists who have ever lived are alive today. Their discoveries require a constantly increasing amount of implementation by technicians rather than engineers. By 1975 more than half of our country's labor force will have to be involved in the middle-level technologies, at less than engineering, but more than trade skills (skill levels which require two-years of college education, but not necessarily four).

To tell about the careers open to graduates of community colleges in the Baltimore metropolitan area, the public relations representatives developed this opening for a brochure:

Skilled, well-trained young people in the technical and semi-professional level are urgently needed in the Baltimore metropolitan area, by industry, commerce and public agencies.

More than 30 programs providing the specialized training are presently being offered—and more are being developed each year at local community colleges.

The Question Lead

The question lead is always useful, for it arouses interest and gets the reader to wake up. The U. S. Army Intelligence Service produced this lead for one of its brochures:

Do you want a job that is intriguing—exciting, yet exacting? Would you like to travel to strange places in foreign countries? Or maybe even work in your own home town? Could you lead a life of adventure—sometimes under hazardous conditions—and at unusual hours? Want to work with a top-flight organization—playing an important and distinctive role in our country's defense?

The writer thus sought to arouse feelings and emotions of the prospective candidate by picturing the life of an intelligence service representative, and raising provocative questions which would appeal to the adventuresome-minded reader.

The Direct Address Lead

The writer of this brochure speaks directly to the reader who has already signed up for the college.

Congratulations

You have taken the first step toward an exciting and rewarding career as a secretary.

This booklet has been prepared to give you guidance in selecting superior professional training and education. . . .

The General Appeal

Michigan State University writer Eugenia Smith said:

Bewilderment and frustration usually greet the new student during his first term at Michigan State University. Trying to find one's way around the megaversity is often a traumatic experience for even the veteran student. The information in this booklet is designed to help the student to find solutions to some of the problems which are likely to confront him. Included are descriptions of university units offering financial, legal and counseling assistance to students. Also listed are minority group faculty and staff at Michigan State. . . .

Boston University opened its pamphlet, *This is Boston University,* with:

As Boston University enters its second century of service in the advancement of learning, it is characterized by broadness and intensity of instruction and a humanistic air of lively inquiry.

One of the nation's largest independent universities, Boston University offers strong professional education, emphasizing a liberal arts core of study . . .

Each of its 16 separate Schools and Colleges has the closeness and informal atmosphere of a small institution, yet together they provide the resources and facilities of a major institution.

When William F. Stokes, of the *Wisconsin State Journal,* wrote some pieces about the University of Wisconsin at Madison, these were reprinted in a booklet, *A Little Look at Our Intellectual Bean Patch,* which had a catchy opening:

HAIR!

The University of Wisconsin students are a joy to behold, worrisome to contemplate, and wondrous to hope upon.

They are picket-face farm boys, wild-haired New York youths, lonely-homely daughters of factory foremen, and pretty coeds showing enough thigh to make grandma groan like a ghost.

They wear beautiful masks of confidence and arrogance, and they writhe within to find out who they are. They do their identity dance with long scarves and hair . . .

An appropriate opening for the *Bulletin of the Rhode Island School of Design* gave the educational philosophy of this college in Providence:

Man is a maker, his long history measured by the tools he has devised, the materials mastered, and the enduring marks left upon his sur-

roundings . . . from Stonehenge to spacecraft, from adobe hut to vertical cities in steel, man has sought both symbolic and physical mastery
of his world by design. . . .

To prepare the student for such a world, Rhode Island School of
Design is dedicated to a deep-reaching educational experience that goes
far beyond the student's specific training as a professional. It must en-
rich his growth as a feeling and reflective human being. . . .

DEVELOPING THE BODY

After the lead has been written, the remainder of the brochure material unfolds naturally, with the points presented in logical order. The outline made before proves helpful to the college writer. In the body of the
article, he presents now his best evidence and facts, adding the most interesting incidents and illustrations. Finally, at the end, the writer seeks to
arouse some action. It may be enrollment in the college, or in a special department. The action may be contributing funds to the college, or participating in Community College Week. The contents of the publication will
vary, depending upon the general and specific aims of the brochure and
the audience.

Typical of other general introductory publications for students, the
booklet shown on page 94, *Vassar College is Not Unique. Every Vassar student is,* contains the following contents:

Learning at Vassar	Who Comes to Vassar?
New Options for Study	After Vassar
Three Approaches to a Degree	Degree Programs
Beyond the Campus	Student Services
The College Community	Courses of Instruction
Life on Campus	Admission and Financial Aid
The Faculty	Faculty names, degrees and background

A reference for editors, *This is Michigan State* has a map of the university, administrative officers, organizational chart of the administration
and faculty, description of each building and each department. The fact-
book also contains statistics giving the number of graduates from 1861
through the present year, the services of the university, something of the
history of the institution. The writer also gives the names of the presidents
since the beginning, student expenses and a calendar of events.

Guide for Minority Students, also issued by the same university, tells
about the Center for Urban Affairs, the Equal Opportunity Programs, and
Support Services for Minority Students. The booklet also gives a description of the student organizations of particular interest to Black students,

the State University's financial assistance and counseling services. Several pages are devoted to academic information such as registration, pre-enrollment, late-drops and adds. The booklet concludes with sections on community activities in Lansing, businesses and special interests in the area, and Minority Group Faculty and staff.

Contents of Career Programs

Brochures relating to career programs in community colleges usually contain most of these general points:

Challenge of the career
Opportunities of the career
Rewards of the career
Overall academic requirements
Reasons for general background courses
Specific requirements for the career program
Schedule of courses to be taken each year, together with credits
for each course
Brief description of each career course
Details of cost
Registration information
Faculty background and qualifications

EYE-CATCHING HEADINGS

In most newspaper or magazine publicity, the writer is not concerned with the top headings or sub-heads. The editor determines what these should be. In the production of brochures, however, the college practitioner is his own editor. He must consider:

a. Into what logical divisions does his material fall?
b. What headings should be included?
c. Where should they be placed?

Brochure writers find that headlines on the front page stop the reader and lure him inside. They help also to break up the solid text on inside pages. The headlines, too, provide additional opportunity to summarize key points, focusing the readers' attention on these points. Such headings make the page appealing, for the heads can be set in different size type. from the body of the text. Inside the brochure, the headings stop the reader as he thumbs through the publication and lead him to read the copy underneath the headlines.

The writer may choose one or several of these constructions for his heading: (1) full sentences; (2) phrases; (3) single words. Where he has a full sentence or phrase, a strong verb will develop impact for his copy and message. Newspaper copy-editors and advertising writers for commercial products and services, searching for the catchy headline, have evolved valuable principles which apply to the writing of college brochures. Excellent books have been written on newspaper copyediting, and other volumes are available on the preparation of advertising copy. Some of these works are listed in the references at the end of this book for those college publications writers who wish to go deeply into this subject.

Whether headlines can be classified is highly debatable; moreover, the classifications overlap. A few clues and examples, however, will enable the college writer to think systematically, even creatively, about headline construction. Headlines should grow out of the situation, the audience and the educational services he is publicizing. The writer also considers the purposes behind the brochure.

News

When the brochure has some new feature, new development or other important points, a newsy front-page headline can be used. The writer, trying to pack as much as he can into his concise statement, chooses each word carefully for its full impact—perhaps to focus on one outstanding point. The headline also may be a summary "5-w" type—giving the who, what, where, when and why. For example:

14 PROGRAMS TO PREPARE YOU FOR A REWARDING CAREER

This gives quickly the number of educational programs available in the college and what they can do for the student.

Emotional Appeal

Some brochure writers, however, use an emotional appeal to gain attention and arouse interest:

STUDY—LEARN—BUILD—for Your Future

This is the headline over a dramatic photo of a student on the front page of a brochure issued by the U. S. Army Recruiting Service to spur young men to think ahead.

Another brochure emphasizes the getting-ahead aspect of college:

WHAT YOU NEED TO GET AHEAD—
PLAN A CAREER IN LAW

The symbols of the key and the open door have been used thousands of times, but still are found useful in picturing graphically the value of a college education:

THE KEY TO PROSPERITY
YOUR KEY TO THE FUTURE
YOUR KEYS TO YOUR FUTURE
OPEN THE DOOR TO THE FUTURE

Study...
Learn...
Build...
for your future

ASSOCIATE
DEGREE
CURRICULUM

LEGAL
SECRETARY

A CAREER PROGRAM

ESSEX COMMUNITY COLLEGE
BALTIMORE COUNTY, MARYLAND
21237

COLLEGE BOUND?

??

The close-up photograph of a student studying with background of books on the library shelf is attractive, and given meaning by the headline. Essex Community College announces its legal secretarial curriculum, while Baltimore Community College asks the question "College Bound?" the whole length of the brochure.

Everyone is interested in pleasure, so this drive may be applied to education, too:

MAKING STUDY A PLEASURE

or this:

_____(Name)_____ College MAKES LEARNING A PLEASURE

A strong appeal to self-interest may be stressed in this front-page headline:

COLLEGE GRADS EARN MORE OVER A LIFE-TIME

Inside the brochure the copy would tell about the income earned by college graduates compared with the earnings of high school graduates. Tables could illustrate the point graphically.

Other headlines which stress the economic future:

TAKE A GIANT STEP FORWARD

THE SECRET OF GETTING AHEAD

EXCITING OPPORTUNITIES AWAIT YOU

_____(Name)_____ COLLEGE HELPS YOU BROADEN YOUR HORIZONS

Or this one:

Opportunity Is Spelled

J · U · N · I · O · R

C · O · L · L · E · G · E

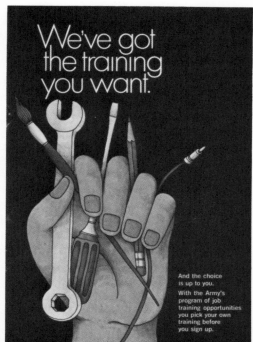

The picture on this brochure gives an instantaneous message to the reader. The headline, "We've got the training you want," is illustrated effectively with the hand which is holding the wrench, screwdriver, pencil and paint brush, used in the courses which the Army offers.

Choose the training you want.

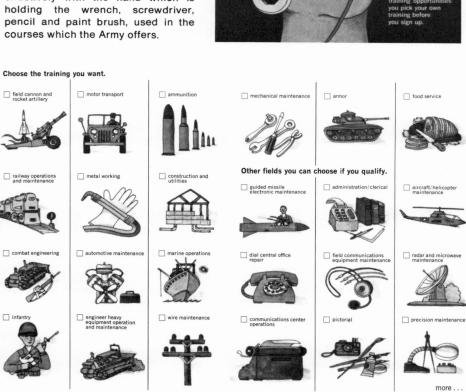

☐ field cannon and rocket artillery

☐ motor transport

☐ ammunition

☐ mechanical maintenance

☐ armor

☐ food service

☐ railway operations and maintenance

☐ metal working

☐ construction and utilities

Other fields you can choose if you qualify.

☐ guided missile electronic maintenance

☐ administration/clerical

☐ aircraft/helicopter maintenance

☐ combat engineering

☐ automotive maintenance

☐ marine operations

☐ dial central office repair

☐ field communications equipment maintenance

☐ radar and microwave maintenance

☐ infantry

☐ engineer heavy equipment operation and maintenance

☐ wire maintenance

☐ communications center operations

☐ pictorial

☐ precision maintenance

more . . .

The University of Wisconsin at Madison addressed new students with this provocative headline and an interesting design-drawing on page one:

The Critical Years
Focus on Freshman and Sophomore Instruction
at the University of Wisconsin——Madison

Brochure writers can be imaginative, not following the usual routine style. Carnegie-Mellon wanted to show that the old stereotype about Pittsburgh, where the university is located, had been altered, hence printed a brochure with a skyline and this headline on its front page:

Carnegie-Mellon
University
is in Pittsburgh!

The second and third pages carried out the theme, with a skyline drawing and a large photo of four students. The caption headline in large type underneath the picture said:

Pittsburgh! Bleughk!

The reader turned the page to see what this was all about and found in large type:

But
Pittsburgh is not
the "smoke city."
It hasn't been
since 1945!
(That's twenty-five years ago)

The page opposite showed a photo of the new city with the large caption line: "Now that that's settled." The following pages told about the institution in lively prose and a multitude of pictures. If your institution is located in a town or city with a negative image, a similar approach might be used to overcome the unfavorable impression. A brochure can also picture the advantages of the location in a big city, or away-from-it-all rural area.

Conversational Style

Headlines may be written in a conversational style for college brochures. Such headlines should be written so that they seem to be lifted out of a conversation the writer is having with the reader, or they may be drawn from a chat one student seems to be having with another one. This headline is aimed at a high school senior:

C'MON NOW: WHAT DO YOU
THINK <u>(name)</u> COLLEGE IS ALL ABOUT?

These have the same appeal:

C'MON NOW! WHAT OTHER COLLEGE
HAS THESE ADVANTAGES?
C'MON NOW! WHERE ELSE COULD
YOU GET THESE OPPORTUNITIES?

Question Type

It will be noted that the above headlines are cast in the form of questions, the purpose of which is to arouse interest or curiosity. But the main purpose is to get some kind of reaction from the teen-agers. For example:

WANT A REWARDING CAREER IN SOCIAL WORK?

Or this one, focusing on psychology as a career:

LOOKING FOR A CHALLENGING CAREER
WORKING WITH PEOPLE?

Consider this:

ARE YOU SEARCHING FOR A COLLEGE
WITH A BROAD LIBERAL ARTS PROGRAM,
DEDICATED TEACHERS, SMALL CLASSES?

Sophisticated Appeal

Often the college brochure writer thinks about the changing times and that what will appeal is a sophisticated approach to headlines. He may use for his front page this line of thought:

HERE COMES
TOMORROW

On the inside he tells about the rewards to come for those students who have foresight to plan ahead.

Inside Headlines

Headlines inside of the brochure call attention to the main points of the contents, and also help to break up the solid type and produce

an attractive page. The writing of inside headlines follows the same principles as those employed for the front-page heads. They may be phrases:

> GENERAL VIEW OF PROGRAM
>
> COURSES OFFERED
>
> CREDITS NEEDED FOR GRADUATION
>
> OPPORTUNITIES FOR GRADUATES
>
> COLLEGE ACCREDITED
>
> TRANSFER OF CREDITS

Some writers cast the headlines into brief statements with nouns and
verbs.

> PROGRAM GIVES PERSPECTIVE
>
> VARIETY OF COURSES OFFERED
>
> OPPORTUNITIES AWAIT GRADUATES
>
> COLLEGE HAS BEEN ACCREDITED
>
> CREDITS EASILY TRANSFERRED

University
of London

Extra-Mural
Studies

1971-72

UNIVERSITY CLASSES FOR ADULTS

The University of London publishes a brochure, *University Classes For Adults*, which is sold on newsstands throughout the city and other locations in England. Front-page photos show the types of adult students attending the courses and enable the readers to identify with these other students.

ecological psychology

michigan state university

The new psychodelic trend in posters is used in the production of brochures to attract students who are accustomed to and like this form of art and design.

Public relations staff is often called upon to produce brochures for the cultural activities of universities and colleges. An impressionistic drawing of Beethoven plus the composer's name in distinctive script gave interest to the Michigan State University Bicentennial Festival.

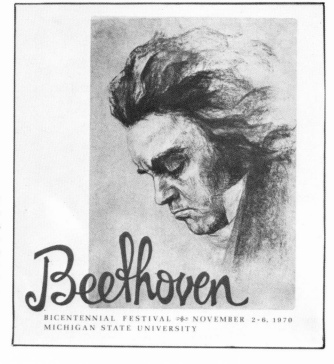

Beethoven

BICENTENNIAL FESTIVAL ᪈ NOVEMBER 2-6, 1970
MICHIGAN STATE UNIVERSITY

PLACING THE HEADLINES

Brochure writers place their headlines in various positions on the page to achieve different effects. Headlines may be used on the front page, a topic which will be dealt with later when front pages are discussed. If the writer has only one headline on an inside page, he may place it at the top:

headline }   **XXXXXXXXXXXX**

in the middle

headline }   **XXXXXXXXXXXXX**

or even at the bottom:

headline }   **XXXXXXXXXXX**

The single heading consolidates the information on the page and, as indicated, breaks up the copy and makes the page more attractive.

When the public relations man has a number of heads on a page to top off each paragraph, he can use the large heading in addition to small ones:

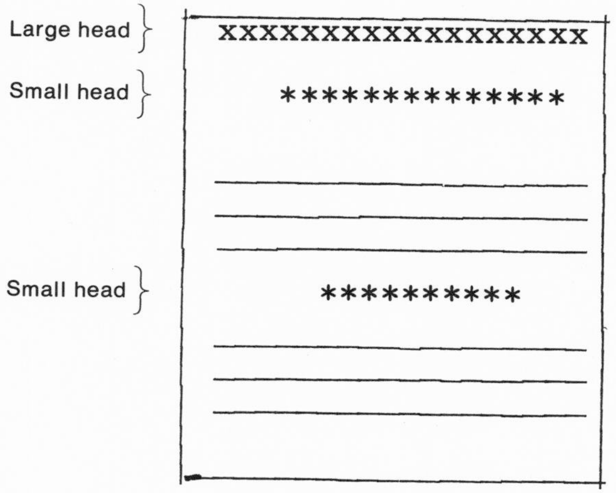

Large head ⎬ | XXXXXXXXXXXXXXXXXX

Small head ⎬ | **************

Small head ⎬ | *********

If the writer believes that this design overdoes the headline bit, and that it produces clutter, he can eliminate the larger headline.

It should be noted that the smaller headlines may be centered or set flush-left, that is, toward the left-hand margin. The previous example shows the centered head. The following example indicates the flush-left type:

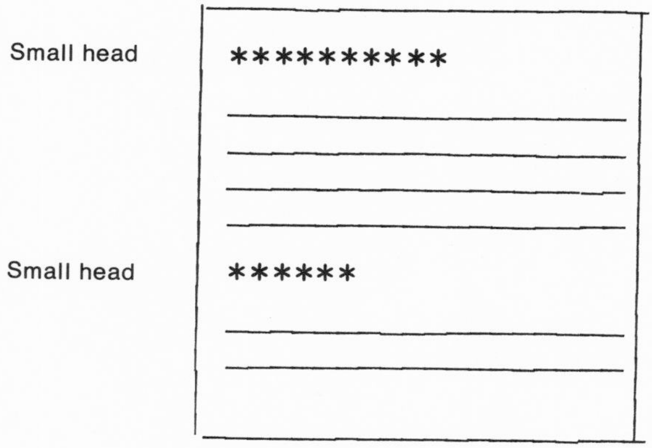

Small head | *********

Small head | ******

Sometimes, in their search for new page designs, brochure writers will place the bold, striking and large headlines on the side of the page:

```
          ┌─────────────────────────────────┐
          │  XX  _____ │
   H      │  XX  _____ │
   E      │  XX  _____ │
   A      │  XX  _____ │
   D      │      _____ │
   L      │                                  │
   I      │                                  │
   N      │                                  │
   E      └─────────────────────────────────┘
```

USING ILLUSTRATIONS EFFECTIVELY

While he is writing the copy for his brochure, the practitioner thinks about the types of pictures and drawings he can use. He gathers systematically his photos throughout the year. He now realizes the value of building his "photo file" (described in the chapter on publicity photos). He digs down into this file for pictures which will suit the purposes of the brochure, or he has new photos taken.

He reasons that photos and drawings strengthen and reinforce the text, illustrating graphically and realistically the writer's points. Such illustrations may transmit part of the brochure's message without elaborate prose. As do headlines, photos help break up the solid pages of the brochure, making the pages more attractive.

When the photos, or other illustrations, appear on the front page, they arouse the attention of the reader—the first step. The photos lure the reader inside. When they are printed on the inside pages, the photos help hold his interest. Newspaper or magazine editors may not accept his pictures; but when the representative produces his own brochure, he can include the illustrations if he thinks they help.

Selection

The question usually is not whether you will use photos—but which ones? Will the cost be prohibitive for the many photographs you desire to use? Do you have the space you need for the excellent shots you have taken?

The brochure writer should seek to obtain photos which represent every phase of the subject he is presenting so that he may have a wide variety from which to choose. Let him, then, select: a) the most graphic; b) the most pertinent; c) the most appealing.

Fortunate are you if you have many shots from which to choose. Select the ones which are striking and unusual. Action pictures are more attention-arousing than dull, lifeless ones (see the chapter on photos). Pick pictures which show students, faculty, administrators doing things, in illustration of the points made in the text. The "mug shots," showing students staring into the camera lens, should be avoided. The best photos are those which appear to be casual, taken when the student was in a class, or in the lab with a chemistry bottle. This does not mean "candid" shots, taken of people off-guard to point up some weakness or peculiarity of face or dress. Photos taken from a high or low angle, instead of on the usual eye-level, prove more interesting to view. The chapter on photos deals more fully with this problem.

Size and Position

The size of the photos is important and, as we have noted, the choice of size depends on the size of the brochure page and the emphasis you wish to give the picture.

A photo for a large brochure might call for an 8 x 10 inch picture. Smaller ones to be placed in a brochure 4 x 9 inches might call for a photo 4 x 4 inches to cover a half page. And still smaller ones, 2 x 2 inches, may be placed at the top of the page or on the side.

Large pictures, 8 x 10 inches, may be reduced to the size needed by the printer or engraver. Some sample brochure pages with pictures may be seen in the later section on dummy make-up or page design.

Photo Engravings

The public relations man should know about the two kinds of photo-engravings, halftone and linecuts, used in printing.

Halftones. Halftones are used by printers to reproduce photographs, paintings and other illustrations. The halftone is created by photographing the original copy through a fine screen placed between the camera lens and the film or plate which is to become the negative. The image transmitted through the screen appears on the negative as a pattern of broken or dotted lines. Dark areas in the copy are reproduced as heavy dots. Lighter areas are recorded as rows of smaller dots.

The most commonly used halftone screens are 55-, 65-, 100-, 110-, 133- and 150-lines. The designations indicate the number of dotted lines in a linear inch. The practical application is that, for low-grade paper stock such as newsprint, the coarser screens are used—the 55-, or the 65- or the 85-line screens. For glossy paper stock the 100-, 110- and 120-line screens are employed. For enamel or smooth-coated stock, the 133- and 150-line screen may be used. The finer the screen, the greater the amount of details retained in the engraving process.

Line-cuts. The public relations man often uses line engravings, which are straight reproductions of solid tones, such as in drawings or cartoons. Line engravings are made without the screen. They reproduce well on any type of paper stock. Most line engravings are etched on zinc and are referred to as zinc etchings.

Captions

Most photos or other illustrations require some headlines over the top or caption-lines underneath. Rare is the illustration which tells completely and adequately its own story. Captions or cut-lines explain the action in the picture, identify the activity, or the person or the place shown. Brochure-writers may use several sentences to point out what the photo shows, or they may think a sentence or phrase is sufficient. The practitioner depends on the text to do most of the story-telling, and so he makes the caption-lines brief and concise. He avoids "the picture shows. . . ." He identifies the persons, the action and place.

Cartoons and Drawings

Because of the widespread appeal of cartoons, some public relations men believe that such drawings can be used with positive results in brochures.

They may consider that some of their messages can be put across best with a cartoon—serious or humorous. Sometimes humor can josh people into doing the right thing, or make them see themselves more clearly than serious messages can do. We have seen some excellent cartoons used in mental health brochures and they had a light, rather than serious touch in spite of the illness with which they dealt. Cartoons also may be a relief from the sameness produced by photos. Don't overlook the fact that cartoons and photos may be used jointly in one brochure. Cartoons may be used on the front page of the brochure and/or on the inside pages.

Charts and Graphs

In the newspaper news or feature article, the public relations man has an opportunity to present charts and graphs, summarizing statistical material. The chances are against the newspaper editor using them, although this should not stop the representative from submitting the illustrations if he thinks they are pertinent and newsworthy.

Because he becomes his own editor when he produces the brochure, the practitioner can include whatever charts he thinks necessary—a choice of pie-charts, line-graphs, bar-charts and diagrams. Many public relations men are employing increasingly the pictogram—a pictorial representation of figures and statistical material which can be understood easily by the reader. A chart can be made more interesting and graphic by combining it with a photograph, as will be shown.

Just to throw in a chart does not solve the writer's communication problem. The chart's meaning must be made clear to the reader. This can be done with labeling and caption lines. The text may refer to the chart and explain it more fully.

MAKING A "DUMMY"

The next step in the production of a brochure is the designing of a "dummy." This involves the assembling of the headlines, text materials, photos and their captions. The dummy is a blueprint for the brochure, and it gives the public relations writer an opportunity to see what his publication will be like when the reader picks it up. The dummy will serve also as a guide for the printer. He is not a mind-reader. He can guess what he thinks you need, but it is better for you, assisted by your staff artist, to determine what you think the format of the brochure should be and *then* show it to the printer. With some pattern to follow, the printer can improve on the format, suggest various possibilities. He can tell you, moreover, what he, as a printer, can do or can't do. He can estimate how much the brochure will cost. If the printer has an art department, so much the better. The artist can improve on your basic design, or develop an original creative design, acceptable to you.

Pages and Size

Now, decide on the number of pages and the size of the brochure. These two elements depend on the amount of copy, the audience and the purpose.

Sizes of brochures vary. One popular size is 4 x 9 inches, because it can fit easily into a Standard Number 10 business envelope. Other sizes are: $3\frac{3}{4}''$ x $8''$, $3\frac{3}{4}''$ x $8\frac{1}{2}''$, $4''$ x $8''$. Or a brochure might have a nearly square size, $3\frac{1}{2}''$ x $5\frac{3}{4}''$.

A brochure telling about a new building, about your university or a school or department within the university—each may require a multi-paged, expensive publication.

Get together with your printer and explain to him your brochure-printing problem, for he may have previous brochures he has produced and can show you them, or he can cut you some sample paper in sizes suitable for your publication.

"Front-Window" Copy

Now you may begin to visualize how the text material, photos and headlines will appear on each page.

What catchy headline can you use on page one? This, as already indicated, is the "front-window" display used to lure the reader inside. Some universities and colleges just use a catchy headline printed on colored paper stock to lure the reader.

Inside Pages Layout

What will you place on page two? Do you need a strong headline to start off? What about the picture or pictures to accompany the text? The photos can be placed at the top, on the sides and even at the bottom. The illustrations may be large-size or several small ones may be selected, each to occupy a small space.

Here are a few sample layouts:

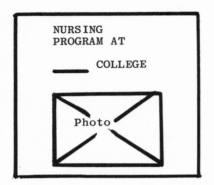 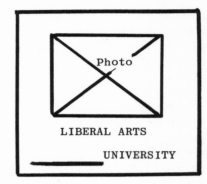

This attractive front page depended upon its choice design, small type and vertical photo to lure readers.

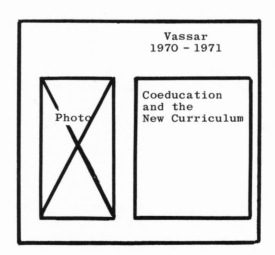

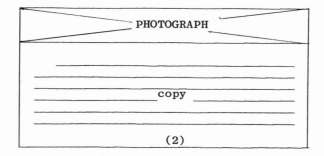

Photo at top of page, copy underneath.

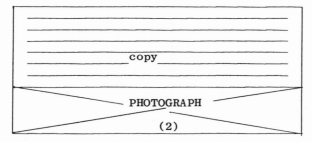

Copy at top, photo at bottom.

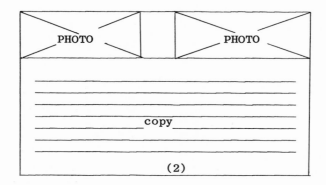

Two small photos at top, copy underneath.

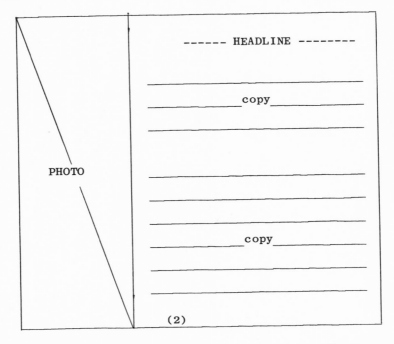

------ HEADLINE --------

copy

copy

PHOTO

(2)

Photo (long) on left. Copy takes up remainder of page. Headline centered. White space between paragraphs.

Some designers of university brochures have adopted the three-column width for the wider publications.

Proceed in the same way to determine what goes on each page of your dummy. Block in the headlines, then the text, then show where you want the photos to be placed.

Many brochure writers use an "esquisse." This is a miniature layout model of the brochure, usually drawn to about the same scale. The esquisse enables the writer to visualize more easily each page of the brochure. He draws in or positions the headlines and pictures on the small-scale page. Brochure writers say that this method enables them to change and modify layouts more quickly, resulting in a more experimental approach than if they worked with the full-size-page dummy sheet.

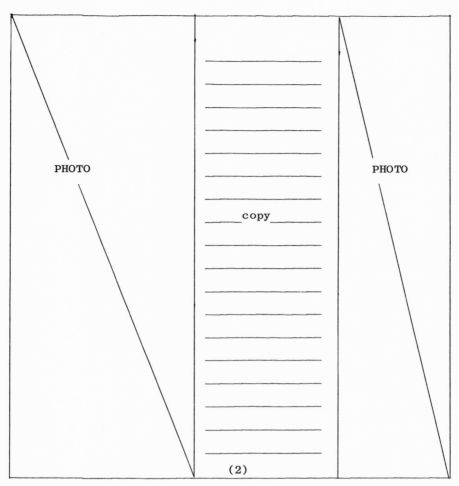

PHOTO

copy

PHOTO

(2)

Photo (large) left; smaller, narrow photo (long) on right. Copy in center.

copy

PHOTO

PHOTOGRAPH

(2)

PHOTO

Copy in middle; two small photos on right side; large photo at bottom left.

TWO-PAGE SPREADS—7¾″ x 10″ TRIM SIZE

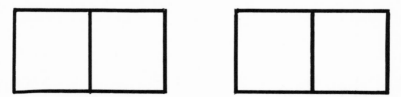

Examples of esquisse, a small-scale dummy for a brochure.

Typing Copy

Copy may be typed on the dummy, but it is preferable to draw headlines in, and then to mark the copy as, for example: "Page one, Block A." Type the copy on a separate page, labeling the typewritten copy for identification, as "Copy A." Other paragraphs should be labeled, "Block B," "Block C," etc. with corresponding block letters or copy letters on your typewritten copy. The printer will then be able to follow your dummy and your directions more easily. Label each Photo No. 1, No. 2 with proper identifications, such as "Person getting check-up." Then list photos on separate page with correct number and label. See the following examples:

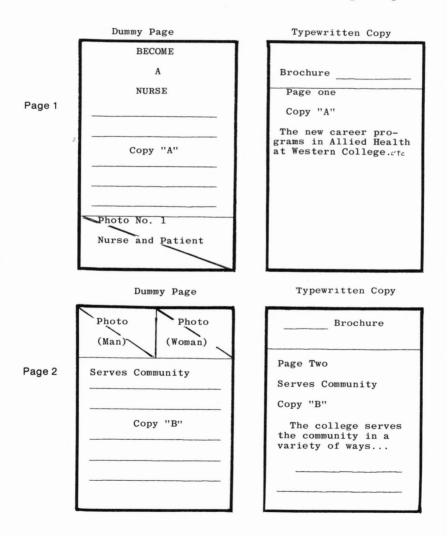

The new trend in publication work is the treating as one the two inside pages, facing each other. Thus pages 2 and 3 would be considered a unit; 3 and 4 would be treated similarly.

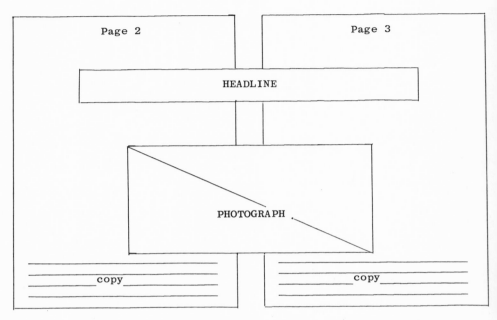

Headline runs across page 2 and page 3, so does the large picture.
Both combine for powerful impact.

COPY FITTING

You can estimate roughly the number of words you will need on a page, or part of a page, in a simple way. If you expect to use type about the size found in a newspaper, the type will be about 8 point; 10 point is a little larger.

1. Count the number of words in a line in the newspaper column (about 2 inches).
2. Now measure the probable length of a line in your booklet. How many words will be in the line?
3. Calculate how many lines to the inch in your booklet.
4. How many inches on a page (omitting the border top and bottom)?
5. Now determine the number of lines on your booklet page. (Divide number of lines per inch into the number of inches on page.)

6. Multiply the number of words on a line by the number of lines and you will have the number of words you need for each page.
7. Determine this for each copy block ("A," "B," "C").

Don't overlook the space for the picture, which must be subtracted from the total available space.

PRINTING THE BROCHURE

The public relations man should have at first a speaking acquaintance, then later a deeper knowledge of the several types of printing. He should understand the advantages and disadvantages of each. After gaining experience in producing several brochures, he will be in an even better position to judge their value and to estimate printing costs.

Letterpress Printing

Letterpress printing involves all the various methods of printing from raised letters or plates. It is called relief printing. In letterpress printing, the type is either set by hand or on a linecasting machine, such as the Linotype or Intertype. The compositor assembles the type and places it in a form, held together by an iron frame. The form is then placed on a printing press, where the type is inked by a roller. The paper is pressed against the raised letters and the impression comes off on the paper.

The advantages of letterpress are pointed out by printers. The brochure may be printed on inexpensive newsprint or uncoated paper. Copy changes may be made easily during the "run" or at each printing—in the event of error, or the writer's change-of-mind. When brochures are printed by letterpress, a high-grade coated stock may be used, and illustrations appear sharp and clear.

Letterpress, however, has a number of disadvantages. If you desire to rerun your brochure after a period of time, the printer has to reset the type, which is usually thrown into the "hell-box" soon after the first printing, unless he is instructed to do otherwise. Even then, the printer will not keep the type standing for long because he does not want his money tied up in type. In many shops, letterpress may cost more than offset, especially if many pictures are used. For letterpress printing, pictures have to be made separately by an engraving process.

Offset Printing

Businessmen and public relations men are turning to offset increasingly to produce their brochures. What is the essential difference between letterpress and offset printing? In letterpress, as indicated, the copy is printed directly from raised type. In offset, however, the copy is first set on the linecasting machine. Sharp reproduction proofs are pulled and then pasted down on a layout sheet together with artwork, such as photos. You can also by-pass the expensive linecasting operation by using a typewriter, or a Varityper—a special typewriter which evens up or squares off the right-hand margins. This copy is finally photographed by a special camera. The resulting negative is made now into a printing plate. The plate, unlike letterpress, is inked but does not print directly on paper. The plate touches a rubber cylinder, or blanket. The press (or offset) is transferred from the cylinder to the paper, with thousands of copies being printed from the offset plate.

The offset printing method is used widely because of its various advantages. If you have many pictures or some artwork, which would require expensive engravings or electrotype, it is less costly to use offset than letterpress. For, as indicated, in offset, the artwork and photos can be pasted on the same sheet with the copy text and photographed. Or they can be photographed separately and joined together by the offset layout man. Offset also permits the use of special paper stocks that are not practical in letterpress printing. Many printers claim that offset permits soft gradations in tones not possible in letterpress.

An important advantage of offset is the economy of storage space, because the offset plates take up little space and they can be used for another printing. The type does not have to be reset years later. Finally, offset plates do not wear out so quickly as do letterpress forms, for offset plates can be used again and again.

What Kinds of Type?

A familiarity with the principal kinds of type will prove useful to the public relations man producing brochures. In discussing your publication with your printer, you may ask him for his specimen or type style book, which he has prepared for customers' use. From this specimen booklet you can select the kinds of type you wish to use in the text, picking the type for large headlines, division heads and picture caption-lines.

Color

Surveys have shown that: (1) color catches the attention better than black-and-white; (2) color causes the reader to retain the image and message longer. The definite trend in brochure printing is toward color. Printing in color is often more expensive than black-and-white, but many practitioners believe that the additional costs are offset by the increased interest given the publication. The black-and-white enthusiasts, however, think that, on a limited budget, the public relations director would do better to concentrate on interesting pictures, attention-compelling headlines, selection of type and lively copy.

Color for a brochure may be produced by a variety of paperstock or by ink. Color would show up in the text, or copy, but it would be particularly attractive in the reproduction of pictures to give them graphic power and realism. To make an intelligent decision on the question of black-and-white or color, have a full discussion of color possibilities and the costs of the brochure with your printer.

Paper Stock

The public relations man who expects to produce effective brochures needs to know a few of the different kinds of paper which he can use. The attractiveness and readability of his brochure can be increased by a wise choice of paper. Letterpress and offset require different kinds of paper, and various kinds of engravings for pictures call for specific paper stock.

News stock is the least expensive of the book papers and has a thin, porous body and a rough surface. It comes mostly in white, but the qualities vary. News stock will print zinc plates well and 65-screen halftones. This kind of paper would not be used usually in brochures, except on special occasions. Large tabloid-size circulars are printed on news stock for public relations departments because rotary presses can be used to produce such publications inexpensively. Machine-finish paper is especially appropriate for brochures because this is the least expensive of the book papers which print halftones effectively. Coming in a moderate range of colors, machine-finish paper is used widely. You can produce drawings and photographs with 120-screen, and the paper creases well.

The public relations man may desire a heavier cover on his pamphlet than he would on a four-page brochure. He can choose antique paper, which has a rough surface and comes in a broad range of finishes, or he may select an enamel-coated stock, which is the acme of cover stocks in its good looks and is able to reproduce halftones with a 133-, 150-, and 175-screen.

Most large printing companies have specimen booklets of papers which are available. The public relations director obtains a copy and consults with his printer about the choice of papers for a specific brochure.

7

Periodicals

THE NEED FOR INTERNAL COMMUNICATIONS in universities and colleges exists, and this need has been recognized by many persons. Dr. A. Westley Rowland, vice president for University Relations at the State University of New York at Buffalo, has pointed out that deficiencies in communications cause misunderstanding, anxiety and dissent on the campus.

James Cass, writing in the January 16, 1965 issue of *Saturday Review* concerning the problems at the University of California's Berkeley campus, pointed out that as a result of size and circumstance, communication within the university broke down—communication between student and teacher, between student and administration, and even between faculty and administration.

Recently, 22 members of the U. S. House of Representatives, under the leadership of Representative W. E. Brock, of Tennessee, visited more than 50 universities of all types and sizes, and met with more than 1,000 students as well as many faculty, administrators and other concerned adults. In analyzing the factors contributing to unrest on the campus, this group of congressmen found that one of the most important internal causes was communication failure. Specifically, the report said:

> On campus after campus we found wide-spread criticism from students who feel unable to communicate with administration and faculty. They believe that no adequate channel is open to them to make their views known. Channels which do exist provide only limited access to individuals who will take responsibility for major decision.
>
> In some cases, the university structure itself seems at fault. In these

130

instances, the modern university is so large, and decision-making so fragmented, the student often finds it difficult to identify the individual or organization that has the final responsibility for a particular policy.

The *Chronicle of Higher Education* for February 2, 1970, in discussing the development of university newspapers, said:

The internal communications mechanisms of American colleges and universities have traditionally functioned by word of mouth, supplemented by the student newspaper and an occasional letter from the president to the whole community.

Today in an era of physical bigness that has brought repeated alarms of student and faculty alienation, many university administrations feel they need regular and reliable ways of communicating with their most immediate publics—students, faculty members and staffs.

To meet the void of communication on the campus, and to give a balanced account of what was going on, the State University of New York at Buffalo, as well as Cornell, Harvard, Pittsburgh, Columbia, Penn State, Boston University, Stanford, and University of California at Los Angeles and others, have established their own university newspapers. Letters and bulletin boards are used by university officials to communicate with faculty, secretarial and maintenance staffs. The university student newspaper is usually read by faculty, students and staff, and may serve as a channel to reach the internal publics.

All of the foregoing communication methods prove useful to the public relations department and to the institution's officials at one time or another.

REACHING PUBLICS SYSTEMATICALLY

Periodicals issued by the public relations department on a systematic basis do special communication jobs in special ways no other media can duplicate or equal. When the college issues a periodical, the institution gets information to its various publics on a *regular schedule, giving the message in an interesting, appealing style and format.*

The public relations department presents this information in different ways in a number of issues of the publication. Besides the PR departments tailor each publication to its special audience.

Such periodicals provide *regular* communication channels for both internal and external publics. For internal communication, a single university-wide faculty newsletter or tabloid newspaper is issued on a regular basis. One of the important trends now is the publication of a newsletter by each school or department within the university to keep the institution informed about departmental activities. If the university is large enough, an employees' publication for staff personnel can be mimeographed or multilithed at regular intervals.

The external publics of an institution of higher learning are many, hence a single publication or a number of different periodicals logically may be issued. Most universities and colleges distribute an alumni magazine. And often newsletters are sent to parents. To reach high school officials, counselors and students, special periodicals are printed regularly. Still another general college publication may be distributed to state, county or city officials as well as to the general public, among whom are potential students, parents of students, as well as voters.

Special university publications may be issued on a set schedule for adults employed in commercial concerns, industries and government agencies, while other periodicals may be addressed to homemakers.

University publications issued on a regular basis have demonstrated their value as public relations communication channels. Such periodicals keep specific outside publics informed about the activities and developments at the institution, telling of its problems and plans, providing an understanding of its aims and long-range educational goals. The effects of the publication may keep the name of the institution before the publics, and may be a genuine prestige-builder. A university publication also may be a channel to build financial support for the institution, urging contributions from alumni, companies and foundations as well as informing the general public about the need for construction loans to be voted upon, and in getting public support for such improvements.

Internal publications issued on a regular basis keep faculty and staff informed *systematically* about news and significant developments at the university. These periodicals may provide stimulating forums for the consideration and discussion of proposed academic plans and programs, and for current issues affecting faculty and students as well as staff. The publication of articles about administrators, faculty and departments stimulates pride and encourages better performance at all levels. Instructors, lab assistants, librarians, secretaries, maintenance men get recognition for quality performance, or that beyond the call of duty. Publications can encourage loyalty among employees, and even strengthen safety, health and other necessary regulations in the institution.

THE **Johns** SUMMER 1967 60¢
hopkins
MAGAZINE

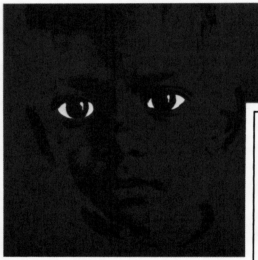

THE WAR AGAINST SUFFERING

NOTES FROM THE FRONT LINES

THE WAR AGAINST SUFFERING

The weapons of science are deployed against
disease and malnutrition in developing countries

THE BATTLE against human suffering invites few comparisons
with a military campaign. For one
thing, the enemies are bewildering
in their number and variety; for

investigators on a variety of medical research projects. Some of these
projects are classifiable as "ecolog-
ical"; essentially they are informa-
tion-gathering activities.

Johns Hopkins Magazine featured
on page one a picture illustrating an
important article to be found on the
inside of the publication. "The War
Against Suffering," a battle in which
Johns Hopkins scientists participated, was played up with strong,
bold headlines in the magazine.

campus report

The University of Wisconsin-Madison

January 21, 1971

University News and Publications
Service, 10 Bascom Hall, Madison

Volume 7, Number 2

The editor of the *Campus Report*, issued by the University of Wisconsin-Madison, featured a striking photo of bicycles parked in the snow outside of a campus building. Specialized periodicals for individual schools within the universities are also published.

SCHOOL OF LAW NEWS   UNIVERSITY OF PITTSBURGH

Vol. 2, No. 1   October, 1970

DEAN'S COLUMN

PREVIEW OF THE 1970-71 ACADEMIC YEAR

The Faculty

With the start of the academic year 1970-71, our faculty profile has changed slightly. Professor R. Stanton Wettick will continue on a partial leave of

ALUMNI PRESIDENT'S COLUMN

At our Annual Meeting of the Law Alumni Association held at the Annual Dinner on May 2, 1970, the following officers and members of the Board of Governors were elected and invested with the duties of their respective offices:

President: Honorable David Olbum

The University of Pittsburgh has its own *Law*, for the School of Law news, with the masthead carrying a drawing of the balance of justice and the symbol of the university, a candle.

134

THE SEARCH

In the nature of things, greatness and unity go together; excellence implies a center. John Henry Newman

Volume 1, Number 7 UNIVERSITY HEALTH CENTER OF PITTSBURGH *October-November, 1970*

REGIONAL MEDICAL PROGRAM:
The Part that Encompasses the Whole

by Graham W. Ward * *Maureen Ryan* **

Most people picture the Health Center as that crowded canyon of medical expertise down in .... physicians are plentiful and

Medical Programs are the first federal health program for which Washington did not supply the plan. Instead, the government has called on

Pittsburgh also publishes *The Search* for the university health center, with the masthead showing a strongly contrasted black-and-white picture of the buildings.

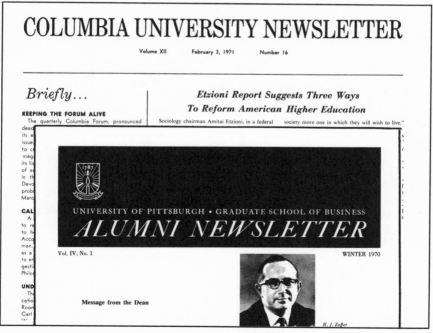

In addition to regular magazines, universities distribute newsletters to the alumni and friends of the institutions as well as the faculties.

135

PRODUCTION STEPS

Whether the public relations director launches a general university periodical or one designed for a special public, he determines first the definite purposes to be served by the publication. The director, or the publications editor he employs, writes down his ideas to clarify them and to make them more specific. Even those university editors who have well-established periodicals need to audit their goals each year and to clarify their own thinking about their objectives.

Planning

Planning is the backbone of successful publication. The publications director designs a masterplan for the periodical and its operation. Questions he raises are: "How will the public relations staff go about producing the publication?" "What specific steps should we take?" "What do we need for a staff?" "What editorial and pictorial matter would we require to carry out the objectives?" "How can I go about getting this copy and these pictures?" If the first issues are planned carefully, the reader gets a feeling of freshness as well as imagination. The reader will appreciate the fact that the editor has put some thinking into each article, has avoided unnecessary duplication of news articles and has produced an attractive, informative publication.

Advisory Council

While the public relations department is responsible for the design and production of the periodical, the director will gain from the formation of an advisory council, who may be drawn from the administrative staff as well as from the departments of the institution. Meeting at regular times, the council may be a source of ideas and information for the editor. If an internal newsletter is to be issued, a member of the library as well as maintenance staff and other service departments may be selected to serve on the council.

In polite, but in unmistakable terms the editor must state the position of the council members. The representatives are welcomed as advisors, but they are not censors, nor should they seek to dominate. The publications editor makes it clear that he has the sole responsibility for the contents of the publication.

MAKE AN AUDIENCE ANALYSIS

Who will read the periodical? Alumni? General public? High school students and counselors? The periodical editor makes an audience analysis

UNIVERSITY TIMES

A PUBLICATION FOR THE CAMPUS COMMUNITY AND FRIENDS OF THE UNIVERSITY OF PITTSBURGH

ENCOUNTER iN EdUCATION

ALTERNATIVES ANd iNNOVATIONS

Vol. 3, No. 11   PITTSBURGH, PENNSYLVANIA   · Thursday, January 28, 1971

A provocative discussion of campus issues appears in each issue of the *University Times,* issued by the University of Pittsburgh. The tabloid folds in half easily, with the logotype being printed vertically and a strong picture topping the front page.

to determine at what group he is aiming and what their characteristics and interests may be. The editor, with his advisory council, appraises the audience to determine their backgrounds. To keep on the line, many college publications editors aim their publications at specific external persons they know, like Francis Wills, the senior at Western High School, or Mr. Samuel Kling, 1960 alumnus. If it is an internal publication, the editor has a mental image of Frank Fortunato in maintenance and Miss Clara Sims in the secretarial pool, specific readers. The editor asks: What kinds of editorial content, pictorial display, methods of writing, would keep the interest of these readers?

With funds, public relations departments frequently have to find some common denominator among many publics. Outside publics have potentially one common bond: they would like to be informed about the current news at the institution and its old and new programs and courses of interest—perhaps of direct value to them. All readers will enjoy human interest articles about the administrators, faculty or students. The editor realizes, too, that although the format may vary, the same copy material and photos may be featured in different publications for different audiences.

137

FREQUENCY OF PUBLICATION

One of the early decisions to be made is the determination of the frequency of publication. This depends on a number of factors: the public relations department's purposes, the amount of money the director has to spend, and the time and personnel necessary to do the job satisfactorily. The decision as to frequency also rests on the size of the periodical and the number of copies to be issued.

A *daily* publication has one big distinct advantage: it enables the public relations department to reach its audience rapidly. Such a publication might suit a large university where the administration needs to give news about the institution quickly and frequently to faculty and staff members. Occasionally, daily publication might be necessary, in an emergency situation, to dispel misinformation and keep the staff posted on a rapidly-changing scene. In a campaign for a building construction loan, daily bulletins might be issued. But institutions will find that, ordinarily, daily publication on a regular basis requires a considerable amount of money and a large staff.

The *weekly edition* has similar advantages, with the latest developments being told quickly. Published on a once-a-week basis, a newsletter can generate considerable interest for an internal publication. The *biweekly,* issued every two weeks, allows more time for gathering and writing the news and features, for snapping photos and for producing the periodical. News of recent events do not get stale, while announcements of up-coming events can be told immediately.

A *monthly* college periodical fits the needs of many institutions. Whether in newspaper or magazine format, the monthly publication allows more time for planning and production. Internal publications issued less frequently than the monthly run into the danger of loss of interest—the news is often old by the time it appears.

For certain external audiences, such as high school counselors and students, or alumni, the public relations director may choose quarterly, semiannual or annual frequency for his publication.

FORMAT

The editor has a choice of several types of publication format to present his editorial and picture material. Some editors favor the newspaper format, claiming this is the only one which can generate enough interest. Others assert that a magazine or news-magazine does the job perfectly. There is no magic formula. The success of the publication depends on its content more than anything else. The format may give the institution prestige and aid the editor in presenting the news, features and photos more attractively. Readers get used to one format and they like it; but they don't object too much to a changeover, when the editor finds the new style more practical or economical. Certain advantages and drawbacks have been experienced by editors for each type of format.

Newspaper Style

Editors have found that readers of college publications are accustomed to newspaper style, and the newspaper format, therefore, gets ready acceptance. With an elastic deadline schedule, the editor can insert the latest news quickly; or when he is right on the deadline, he can place on page one a few paragraphs about important late-breaking news at the college.

Production costs for the newspaper are low, and once the editor gets used to the format, the newspaper can be prepared easily; making up the pages is not difficult. The newspaper, however, is skimmed hastily by the reader. It may not be kept for later and more thoughtful reading. Some publications directors believe that serious educational material is not very successful when published in a newspaper format.

Of the two newspaper sizes, the standard format with 7 to 8 columns, 22 inches long, is the least used. This size is physically awkward to handle. The tabloid size is more common, because the copy is boiled down and each article gets a strong display. The tabloid format is flexible, the pages usually having five columns to the page, with columns 15 to 17 inches long. The 5- or 6-column tabloid is usually 18 inches deep overall and can be folded easily for mailing.

Magazine Format

Editors of university periodicals have found distinct advantages in issuing magazines. Printed on slick coated paper, magazines lend prestige to the institution. Solid feature articles may be printed, and readers keep these publications around the house perhaps longer than the newspapers. General surveys show that magazine-reading habits differ from newspaper-reading habits. Leisurely reading is customary for magazines. They are read and reread long after being received. Color can be used readily and the magazine can be printed on a better-quality paper. Both color and paper add to the feeling of quality, lending prestige to the publication.

The disadvantages of the magazine are many. Magazines may prove more costly in production, and some editors find that more careful planning and scheduling are needed. Because of magazine costs, these periodicals are apt to appear less frequently, hence current news gets stale by the time it is published. University editors also have developed picture-magazines, news-magazines and even pocketsize periodicals.

Newsletter

The least expensive type of periodical is the newsletter. It is effective and efficient for quick transmission of information to a limited number of readers. The newsletter is an economical format. Generally 8½ x 11 inches in size, the college newsletter has a printed masthead. This type of periodical may be reproduced by mimeograph, by multilith or by some other duplicating method in the office, or it can be sent out to a commercial company for printing. The newsletter can be prepared quickly with the cutting of stencils; it is, thus, a low-item production. Some editors believe that the newsletter gives a personal feeling. The bulletin, a one-page publication with two sides, usually is 11 x 17 inches, which folds into an 8½ x 11 inch size.

The newsletters and bulletins produced by offset or multilith processes may use headlines, artwork and other devices to attract attention and interest. The number of pages may be increased at low cost. And, most important, photographs are easily used in offset and multilith newsletters.

PERIODICAL CHECKLIST FOR FREQUENCY, FORMAT

The following points are considered by editors in determining the frequency of publication and the format:

1. What are the major objectives of the publication?
2. Is timeliness an over-riding factor in the publication or of secondary importance?
3. How important is prestige value?
4. Is leisurely-reading significant?
5. How much money is the institution setting aside for the publication?
6. How important is fine reproduction of pictures?
7. What printing facilities does the college have, or what facilities do nearby commercial printers have? What type of publication can each shop handle best?
8. How will the publication be staffed?

BUSINESS NEWS - JOURNAL

Published By Public Relations Students, School Of Business, Dept.
Advertising, Communications And Public Relations, Florida State
University, Tallahassee, Florida, Spring, 1962

Bobbi Mooney, pretty School of Business co-ed, is on her way to classes.

Students strolling to Morrison's for relaxing coffee-break.
See story, Page 4.

Dean Charles A. Rovetta discusses student organizations' problems with Jim Sanborn, student representative, and Prof. William Heck, co-ordinator of the dozen student groups at the School of Business.   See story, Page 1.

PHOTOGRAPHS BY BELCHER AND SHOVER.

The *Business News-Journal*, produced by students of public relations classes in the School of Business, Department of Advertising, Communications and Public Relations, at Florida State University, was printed by a combination of offset and mimeograph methods on a low budget. Only pages one and two were printed in offset because of the need for pictures; the remaining ten pages were produced inexpensively on the department's mimeograph machine, and 1,000 copies were issued.

CONTENT OF PERIODICALS

The contents of the weekly faculty newsletter, or the annual tabloid issued for high school students, or the slick alumni magazine have similarities but also differ in many respects. The content of such university periodicals depends on a number of specific factors: the aims of the periodical, the readers' interests and backgrounds, the amount of space available in the publication, and the funds appropriated for producing it.

News

News of the institution gets top priority in most periodicals, with coverage being given the president's office and the activities of the deans and other administrative officers. The editor also tells about new programs and important courses in various departments, and he may decide to feature the research activities of faculty or their participation in meetings or community cultural events. Outstanding student activities and projects are of interest to many readers of the college periodicals. When new members of the board of trustees are appointed and when the board makes major decisions affecting the institution, such news finds a place in the publication. The editor includes in his editorial pattern news of the non-teaching staff when their activities are newsworthy, especially if a faculty-and-staff newsletter is being produced regularly. New university equipment in science or data-processing departments, as well as the construction of additional wing or buildings, furnish the basis for other news articles.

Feature Articles

Depending on the type of the university publication and its potential readers, a variety of longer feature articles may be developed by the editor. Human interest articles and special interviews with administrators, faculty and students will be read by both general and specific audiences.

Serious educational articles and explanatory background features dealing with new educational programs may find a place in the columns of the periodical. Information about educational innovations being tried at other colleges and material on proposed government bills which will affect all institutions of higher education can be developed into informative features.

The publication also may be used as a forum for the discussion of plans being considered by the university—such as the elimination of examinations, the introduction of the quarter-term system, or the class-attendance (or unlimited cut) proposal. Controversial issues—the policy of "publish or perish," changes in the tenure system for faculty members—may be presented by means of interviews with faculty members and students. Instructors can develop their views in feature articles also.

To stimulate interest in better college teaching, deans, instructors and students may be asked to contribute articles on this subject, perhaps one of the most critical of all academic problems. Editors may publish extended résumés of university conferences on innovative teaching and of meetings dealing with wider participation by faculty and students in institutional affairs, and with problems of increasing governance by the instructional staff. The special problems faced by minority students—Blacks, Puerto Ricans and Chicanos—may be explored in feature articles.

Special By-lined Columns

Newsletters, as well as tabloids and magazines, print special columns with by-lines for the authors. A president's column, in which he has the opportunity to state policies, to explain and even to defend actions and plans, improves the content of a publication. Guest columns, with unlimited freedom, are requested from faculty deans and department chairmen. The chairman of the board of trustees may be given the space to discuss problems of the board and his own outlook, and perhaps that of other board members. Serving as an inquiring reporter, the periodical editor may also get thoughtful reactions of faculty and staff as well as readers to the institution's programs and future plans which have been announced. Or the editor might ask, what educational directions should the college pursue?

Sources of News

The editor of the university periodical, aided by his staff, covers the institution as a city editor of a daily newspaper covers the city. The campus editor has to keep posted on what is going on and what will happen. He checks with the president's office as well as with the other administrative officers. He learns the news and picks up ideas for features in his rounds of departments, interviewing both chairman and faculty members. He uses the publicity releases as a start, either printing them "as is," or he develops new angles and expands the background for his purposes. Requesting news-tips and feature-ideas from the faculty, he follows up these when they indicate some news-worthiness. With his staff, he has editorial sessions which seek to develop new and creative ideas for the publication.

PICTURE APPEAL

University publications have taken their cues for pictures from the successful commercial magazines and newspapers. Many publication editors seek to use one or more photos on the cover or front page, with each inside page carrying photos of the institution's activities.

University editors are aware that photos strengthen the appeal of their news and features, giving impact to the copy. Illustrations also help to

High School Grads Opt For Relevancy,
Pick CCB Transfer, Career Programs

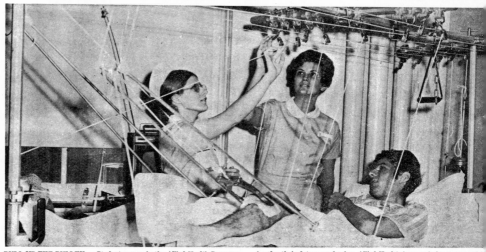

PULL UP THE PULLEY — Student nurses in the Allied Health Program at the Community College of Baltimore adjust the pulleys for a patient at the Johns Hopkins Hospital, where they are getting the practical training for their future profession. Allied Health is one of the many exciti and rewarding career programs at CCB.

ENVIRONMENTAL PROBLEMS — Records which recreate the sounds and problems of our environments today are used in the Urban Affairs classes to give reality to the discussions of critical, vital issues affecting students and adults.

Grads Make Grade At Colleges

You'll find graduates of Community College of Baltimore if you walk across the campus of the University of Maryland, in College Park, or in Baltimore County, or visit the university's professional schools on Greene street in downtown Baltimore.

Stroll through the corridors of Morgan State College Towson State, the University of Baltimore or Loyola College. You'll discover CCB grads enrolled in a variety of programs. You'll bump into them also over at Homewood, where

Johns Hopkins University is located.

And if you happen to be visiting colleges in Washington, D. C., you will meet CCB grads taking courses at American University or George Washington University. On a number of campuses in New England, New York, Pennsylvania and Virginia, you'll also find Baltimore Community College grads taking A.B. and B.S. programs and doing well.

About a third of those who attend CCB are enrolled in the college-transfer programs.

Climb Ladder In Business, Professions

In the accounting office of a large manufacturer in downtown Baltimore . . . in the public relations department of a local utility . . . in the data-processing division of a whole-sale concern . . . on the sales and marketing staff of a local concern . . . you'll find graduates of the business career programs at the Community College of Baltimore. Working for lawyers as secretaries are pretty CCB coeds who learned their stenography and typing and good English on the Liberty campus.

You'll find graduates, too, on the engineering staff of a local construction company, or working in the production department of a local electronics organization.

CCB students, with their Associate in Arts degrees, received after two years' study, or others with certificates, awarded after a year's course, are working in hospitals and dental offices and chemical laboratories. Other grads are employed by the city, county or state governments as urban planners or in law-enforcement and fire-protection.

Having taken the recreation leadership program at the college, some of the grads may be found at recreational centers in all sections of the city and county.

Flexible CCB Courses Designed For You

DR. SIDNEY KOBRE
Director, News Bureau
Community College
of Baltimore

Your high school is taking an active part in Community College Opportunity Month.

The purpose of this event is to focus on the educational opportunities and special advantages which community colleges in the Baltimore metropolitan area have for you.

Such colleges are the fastest-growing educational institutions in America today, because they are flexible enough to meet nearly every educational need. You should find out what the Community College of Baltimore, in particular, has to offer you, as you wisely plan your future lowing your graduation high school.

A number of activitie planned for Community lege Opportunity Month lege representatives will be able to answer questions seniors have. Other colle ministrators and faculty bers will talk to local clubs and organizations.

Exhibits of every d ment at the Community lege of Baltimore will b played at shopping c which will feature live onstrations of students tion and will show num classroom activities. papers and radio and sion broadcasts will news about significant e

Through the co-operat the principal of your school, the publication ad and the editor of your paper, this special Com ity College tabloid is bein tributed with your news to bring to you directly a a printed package the aspects of the college st

In this tabloid, you wi factual information abou two-year programs of un sity-parallel courses and many career programs.

WHAT MAKES PEOPLE TICK — Students in the Psychology Department at the Community College of Baltimore study the behavior of animals. Then they seek to apply some of the principles to discover what makes people tick and do the things they do. A variety of interesting, informative courses in psychology are offered, giving you a new dimension for thinking about people.

Universities and colleges also publish periodicals aimed at high school students. Community colleges in the Baltimore metropolitan area join together to issue a four-page tabloid newspaper, with lively pictures and easy-to-read prose, covering educational programs and extra curricular activities at the colleges.

break up the solid gray of the periodical's printed pages. Some editors devote an entire page to pictures in a four-page publication, with the pictures and cutlines and a small block of type telling the story. Forida State University's *Florida State Reports,* a four-page printed publication distributed to the families of students and graduates, featured on the front page of one issue an article headlined, "Students Tackle Unique Jobs To Pay Their Way Thru College," illustrated with a color photo of Jack Neeley who got paid for skinning, sewing and stuffing specimens for collection purposes and for use in ornithology courses. His subjects included cranes, egrets, redbirds and sparrows as well as bats, squirrels, rats and mice. On page two the editor printed a brief article, "The Administration in Action," describing the daily work of President Stanley Marshall and the vice presidents. The page was filled with five photos of these administrators conferring. Page three carried a feature, "Florida State Snap-sules," topped by a large photo of instructors who won excellence awards. The last page showed a photo of Marcel Marceau, the French pantomimist, who was to appear in the University's Artist Series.

When the occasion calls for it, editors can use the pictures-in-series technique to tell the institution's story. These photos relate to one subject, showing the different angles of the news event or the various personalities involved. Attractive headlines help draw attention, with concisely written captions under the pictures.

HEADLINES

In writing news releases and feature articles for submission to commercial editors, the public relations man does not top them off with a headline. If he does write one, it serves only as a suggestion, or is offered to tell briefly what the news is all about. However, when he produces college brochures and when he issues a periodical, the representative writes his own headlines and uses them. Like those in the brochure, the periodical's headlines attract the reader to the news and, when a headline is coupled with a photo, together they make a strong team of attention-getters. The headline helps to arouse interest in the feature article and gives the nub of its contents to the reader.

When publishing a university periodical, the editor seeks to write headlines in the style commercial newsmen and magazine copyeditors have found successful. Headlines are simply written to convey ideas and information quickly, without the reader being forced to puzzle over them. They are concise, omitting unnecessary words, or they may leave out articles, such as "the," "a" and "and." The fewer the words, the greater the impact. The editor seeks short words because they carry a punch; besides, he can then get more words into the space allotted. He tries to get a verb into the headline to give it some action, omitting the weak verb "is" and all of its forms, such as "will be." For instance, "Plan Is to Be Submitted Tomorrow" becomes "Plan Submitted Tomorrow" or using an active verb, "Officials Submit Plan Tomorrow."

The editor knows that only so many letters and spaces between the words can be included in the headline to fit the width of the column. The number of letters, therefore, has to be counted out. Headlines may be one, two or three lines deep, and may extend over one, two, three or more columns on the page. The editor works out a headline schedule with the printer and then makes up a printed schedule with all sizes of headlines for 1-, 2-, 3-column-wide heads.

Some editors use "decks," or secondary heads below the main one, but the trend is away from this, except for the top-of-the-page heads. Most headlines are informative, merely giving the highlight of the news which is underneath. But editors also use question headlines such as, "What Do You Think of the Trimester System?" Or folksy ones, "Hello, Newcomer!" Some headlines use alliteration, "Ping Pong Players Play for Prizes."

Magazine headlines may be informative, but many editors seek to arouse interest and use any device which they can create. Magazine editors are now writing short top headlines, but including longer, explanatory decks across the page to arouse interest.

PRODUCING EFFECTIVE LAYOUTS

You can write readable news and features and have top-quality pictures on hand, but these are only the raw materials. As editor, you have to organize and display the news and features effectively. The editor has to develop a "dummy" for the guidance of the printer. The editor follows a similar procedure to the one he uses when he writes brochures. Each page of his newspaper or magazine must be studied, with special attention being given the front page. This page usually contains the most important and interesting of his editorial and picture copy.

Various styles have been evolved for newspaper front pages and these can be used by publication editors. To produce the balanced format, the make-up man draws an imaginary line down the center of the page. Then he places headlines of equal size on each side of the line. The off-balanced make-up gives variety and is not so somber. Various sizes of headlines are used on one side of the page, usually the right, to cause the unbalance.

Because of the way most readers read, the editor places his most important story on the upper-right-hand side of the page. He has these possibilities open to him: a) a "banner" or "streamer" across the entire top of the page; b) a 3-column large headline on the right side; c) a 2-column head on the right side; d) a single-column headline on the right side. Each of these would require a "deck," or subsidiary headline in smaller type, giving more details.

After the strongest story has been selected and placed in this spot, the remainder of the make-up is easy, because the other news falls into place—1-, 2- and 3-column heads are placed at the top of the page, with the others filling in the bottom.

The editor next considers the various pictures he has at his disposal and places them strategically alongside the news and features they illustrate. A 1- or 2-line headline across the two columns may top a picture with a news story following underneath. A single column picture may fit into a single news column.

Inside pages receive similar consideration. Banners may top the pages, but usually 2- and 3-column heads with several lines each will be sufficient. For variety, however, banners can be employed effectively across the top of the pages. Pictures are placed on each page. Headlines in magazines are placed alongside the articles.

```
+---------------------------------------------------------+
|                      MASTHEAD                           |
+---------------------------------------------------------+
|////////////////////////////// /////////////////////////|  5-column banner
|/////////////////////// HEAD /////////////////////////// |
|XXXXXXXXX|           |           |XXXXXX Deck XXXXXX      |
|XXXXXXXXX|           |           |                       |
|XXXXXXXXX|  Photo 1  |           |                       |
|XXXXXXXXX|           |           |                       |
|XXXXXXXXX|           |           |                       |
|XXXXXXXXX|           |           |                       |
|XXXXXXXXX|           |           |XXXXXXXXX| XXXXXXXXX    |
|XXXXXXXXX|XXXXXXXXX  |XXXXXXXXX  |XXXXXXXXX| XXXXXXXXX    |
|XXXXXXXXX|XXXXXXXXX  |XXXXXXXXX  |XXXXXXXXX| XXXXXXXXX    |
|XXXXXXXXX|XXXXXXXXX  |XXXXXXXXX  |XXXXXXXXX| XXXXXXXXX    |
|XXXXXXXXX|XXXXXXXXX  |XXXXXXXXX  |XXXXXXXXX| XXXXXXXXX    |
|XXXXXXXXX|XXXXXXXXX  |XXXXXXXXX  |XXXXXXXXX| XXXXXXXXX    |
|XXXXXXXXX|XXXXXXXXX  |XXXXXXXXX  |XXXXXXXXX| XXXXXXXXX    |
|XXXXXXXXX|XXXXXXXXX  |XXXXXXXXX  |XXXXXXXXX| XXXXXXXXX    |
|XXXXXXXXX|XXXXXXXXX  |XXXXXXXXX  |XXXXXXXXX| XXXXXXXXX    |
|XXXXXXXXX|XXXXXXXXX  |XXXXXXXXX  |XXXXXXXXX| XXXXXXXXX    |
|XXXXXXXXX|XXXXXXXXX  |XXXXXXXXX  |XXXXXXXXX| XXXXXXXXX    |
|XXXXXXXXX|XXXXXXXXX  |                                    |
|XXXXXXXXX|XXXXXXXXX  |XXXXXXXXXXX Head XXXXXXXXXXXX        |  3-column head
|XXXXXXXXX|XXXXXXXXX  |           |                       |
|XXXXXXXXX|XXXXXXXXX  |XXXXXXXXX  |XXXXXXXXX| XXXXXXXXX    |
|XXXXXXXXX|XXXXXXXXX  |XXXXXXXXX  |XXXXXXXXX| XXXXXXXXX    |
|XXXXXXXXX|XXXXXXXXX  |XXXXXXXXX  |XXXXXXXXX| XXXXXXXXX    |
|XXXXXXXXX|XXXXXXXXX  |XXXXXXXXX  |XXXXXXXXX| XXXXXXXXX    |
|         |           |XXXXXXXXX  |XXXXXXXXX| XXXXXXXXX    |
|         |           |XXXXXXXXX  |XXXXXXXXX| XXXXXXXXX    |
|  Photo 2|           |XXXXXXXXX  |XXXXXXXXX| XXXXXXXXX    |
|         |           |XXXXXXXXX  |XXXXXXXXX| XXXXXXXXX    |
|         |           |XXXXXXXXX  |XXXXXXXXX| XXXXXXXXX    |
|         |           |XXXXXXXXX  |XXXXXXXXX| XXXXXXXXX    |
|         |           |XXXXXXXXX  |XXXXXXXXX| XXXXXXXXX    |
|         |           |XXXXXXXXX  |XXXXXXXXX| XXXXXXXXX    |
+---------------------------------------------------------+
```

Front Page Make-up: 5-column banner headline; 3-column head; 2-column pictures

MASTHEAD

/////////////////////// HEAD ///////////////////////   5-column banner

xxxxxxxxx | xxxxxxxxx | xxxxxxxxx | xxxxxxxxx | xxxxxxxxx

xxxxxxxxx | xxxxxxxxx | xxxxxxxxx | xxxxxxxxx | xxxxxxxxx

xxxxxxxxx | xxxxxxxxx | xxxxxxxxx | xxxxxxxxx | xxxxxxxxx   News at top of page

xxxxxxxxx | xxxxxxxxx | xxxxxxxxx | xxxxxxxxx | xxxxxxxxx

XXXXXXXXXXXXXXXXXXX | XXXXXXXXX | XXXXXXXXXXXXXXXXXXX   Two 2-column heads
                                                              One 1-column head
xxxxxxxxx | xxxxxxxxx | xxxxxxxxx | xxxxxxxxx | xxxxxxxxx

xxxxxxxxx | xxxxxxxxx | xxxxxxxxx | xxxxxxxxx | xxxxxxxxx

xxxxxxxxx | xxxxxxxxx | xxxxxxxxx | xxxxxxxxx | xxxxxxxxx

xxxxxxxxx | xxxxxxxxx | xxxxxxxxx | xxxxxxxxx | xxxxxxxxx

XXXXXXXXXXXXXXXXXXX | XXXXXXXXX | XXXXXXXXX | XXXXXXXXX   One 2-column head
                                                              Three 1-column heads
xxxxxxxxx | xxxxxxxxx | xxxxxxxxx | xxxxxxxxx | xxxxxxxxx   (This could also
                                                              be made up with
xxxxxxxxx | xxxxxxxxx | xxxxxxxxx | xxxxxxxxx | xxxxxxxxx   one column head
                                                              on left and a 3-
xxxxxxxxx | xxxxxxxxx | xxxxxxxxx | xxxxxxxxx | xxxxxxxxx   column head on
                                                              right)
xxxxxxxxx | xxxxxxxxx | xxxxxxxxx | xxxxxxxxx | xxxxxxxxx

Front page horizontal make-up with 5-column banner and story at top.
Two 2-column and one 1-column heads in the middle. At the bottom are one
2-column head and three 1-column heads.

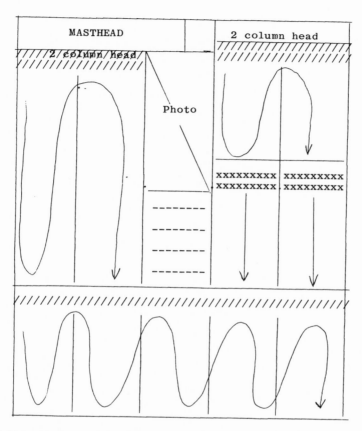

Tabloid with shifting masthead on front page.

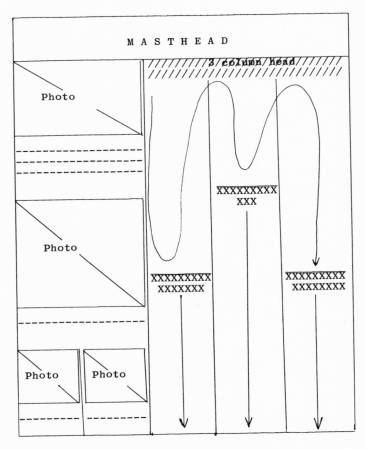

Format with pictorial emphasis; four illustrations on left side.

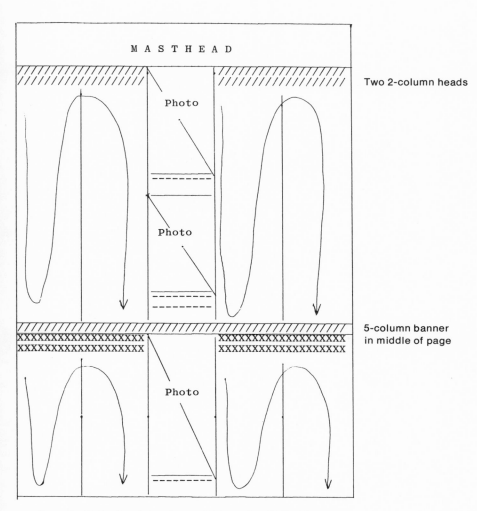

Two 2-column heads

5-column banner
in middle of page

Format with horizontal make-up. Pictures in middle of page.

PRINTING METHODS

The editor has several printing alternatives open to him: letter-press, offset and mimeograph. The points made regarding letter-press and offset in the chapter on brochures may be applied to publication production. Similar advantages and disadvantages may be found. They should be reviewed before any steps are taken, with both quality as well as cost being considered. The cheapest printing is not always the best.

Mimeographing is the least expensive of the various printing methods. While it does not have the attractiveness of the other methods and does not convey "prestige," acceptable publications can be produced. Where funds are low and where the circulation of the periodical is small, mimeograph may very well be resorted to. The job can be done by secretaries in an office, or the entire publication can be produced by commercial mimeograph companies. If the work is done in your own office, the chief expenses are paper, stencils and ink—plus employees' time.

The chief drawback is producing pictures by mimeograph; however, stencils for photo-printing are available. Some editors have combined mimeograph with offset. A page or two of pictures are produced by offset, then combined with the mimeographed sheets—a method especially valuable for front-page display.

METHODS OF DISTRIBUTION

The editor of any type of publication has to be concerned with the final step: distribution. In the university or college, the internal newsletter or bulletin is distributed to the general faculty and staff by means of post-office mail boxes. If the members of the secretarial or maintenance staffs do not have individual boxes, the publications are distributed in a bundle to responsible heads of these divisions. Many editors of company publications distributed to employees believe this is a wasteful method, however. They say that if the publications are distributed while the employee is at work, work stops. If the issue is given to him, or he picks it up on his way home, the chances for him to read the publication are dim—it may be thrown into the nearest wastecan. The periodical, costing so much to produce, will not be read nor will it reach home, where the employee's family can look it over.

When the editor mails the newsletter directly to the college employee's home, the staff knows that the publication will be delivered for a certainty. The editor has a reasonable assurance that the news will get a better reading than otherwise. Some editors think that the employee has more time to read the news, is more relaxed and receptive. Wives and even children have the opportunity to read the periodical, too, and will pick it up if it contains special articles of interest. The cost of mail distribution, however, is higher. Many editors believe, nevertheless, that the additional cost is not significant and that it is offset by the benefits of home-distribution.

University editors make up careful lists for distribution of periodicals intended for the external public. These lists may include alumni and, if the coverage is extended, parents. Editors also compile lists of high school principals and counselors.

Other college presidents may be interested in the news of the institution. Newspaper editors, radio and television news and public affairs editors constitute another list, as these newsmen may pick up an article or an idea for a news-feature which might have been overlooked as a possibility by the college news bureau. Public officials on state, county and city levels may be kept informed by the outside publication.

The public relations officer for the Montgomery College in Rockville, Maryland, distributes *Montgomery County In Review,* a 12-page tabloid, to thousands of residents each year. These constitute half the voters in the area; then in the following year, the officer distributes his tabloid to the other half of the residents in the county.

Distribution of the *Community College Bulletin,* a 4- to 8-page tabloid issued annually by the Community College of Baltimore and other metropolitan community colleges, such as Catonsville, Essex, Anne Arundel and Harford Community Colleges, is distributed through high school publication advisors and editors. The number of copies needed is ascertained ahead of the printing date; then the copies are delivered in bundles of 500 to the high school advisors. They have the *Bulletin* copies inserted in the schools' newspapers.

DETERMINING COSTS

The editor should determine, before publication, the costs of his printing. He shows business wisdom if he obtains estimates from at least three (nearby) printers. Such printing estimates vary.

The editor studies these estimates carefully, because what may seem to be a bargain could turn out to be a high-cost headache. The reputation of the printer is the first consideration. You have to size this up by talking and asking pertinent questions about the printer's facilities and personnel. Does he have the equipment to produce your periodical on time? How will he make the engravings? What kinds of type does he have for setting headlines? What kind of paper will the magazine be printed upon? Does he make a specialty of publication work, or is he just fitting your job into other commercial printing? Are there any further fringe or additional charges involved? Once the answers to these questions are received, the editor makes a detailed comparison of printing estimates.

PRINTING COST ESTIMATE FOR PERIODICAL

Printer A _____

Address _____

Number of Copies	PERIODICAL		No. of Pages	Size	No. of Photos	Cost
	Tabloid Newspaper	Magazine				
500						
1,000						
2,000						
5,000						
10,000						

Staff members will co-operate and save your funds if they know how much you have to spend. Less friction will result. A total budget for the year should be settled on, with specific portions allocated to each issue. If the editor intends to have special issues, such as the Christmas or anniversary issue which would be larger than the other editions, he should set aside sufficient money to cover these special occasions.

The editor often has to persuade officials of his university to earmark enough money to produce a quality publication which will capture attention, be influential and be a credit to the organization.

EVALUATING READER INTEREST

All public relations programs should be re-assessed at regular intervals; the college publication, as a part of that activity, should be audited similarly. While the finances should be re-examined, equally important is the re-evaluation of reader-interest. This assessment will enable the editor to see where he and his publication stand. The results of the survey can be shown to administrators to arouse further interest in the publication. Additional funds for strengthening the staff and providing funds for supplies and printing purposes are more apt to be appropriated.

In a small college, the editorial staff can conduct a poll to determine the acceptance and influence of the college newspaper. In a large organization it is desirable to conduct the survey on a more extensive and formal basis. Either the entire university can be polled or a sample of each department may be obtained. If funds are available, an outside research organization may be brought in to construct the questionnaire and do the survey. Various readership techniques have been developed, and one or several of the methods can be used. In other chapters we have outlined the methods which can be used for readership surveys.

154

8

Advertising

THE PUBLIC RELATIONS DIRECTOR realizes that he must use the most modern and effective methods to promote the college or university. While the university does not have products—such as tractors, shoes or groceries—to sell, the director merchandizes the institution's educational services, just as commercial concerns do their products or services. He uses, therefore, advertising space in the print media, and paid-for time on radio and television.

The director applies to education the findings of business and industry regarding the economic advantage of advertising and its psychological value. He makes use of the principles of consistent promotion and the methods of producing effective informational copy. He is aware that the college needs a strong supplement to the publicity news and features which editors and broadcasters accept. Similarly, the college requires advertising backup for its other communication tools: brochures, catalogues, speakers' bureaus.

The director thus needs to place in the annual college budget a sufficiently-large appropriation earmarked for advertising. While the university is an educational institution, performing a community service, the institution has a business side too—an employee payroll, funds for current expenses and maintenance, and a capital outlay item for construction and the buildings. If the printing of brochures and catalogues is included in the university budget, as printing usually is, then it is entirely legitimate, logical and business-like to incorporate an advertising section in the annual expenses.

Executives of commercial concerns know that to keep their businesses operating and to continue their progress, they must set aside a certain per-

155

centage of their sales for advertising; this percentage varies from business to business, ranging from ½ of 1% to 6% or more.

Businessmen consider that advertising is a fixed expense, just as lights, heat and similar "overhead" items are. Over the years, advertising has proved its value for all types of businesses. It has been demonstrated that the cost of advertising is outweighed by the results it produces—specifically, profits from the increased sales.

A university or college should incorporate in its budget ½ to 1 per cent or more of its total budget for paid advertising space in publications, or for time on the air.

On the other hand, some public relations men find strong opposition against paid advertising to promote the educational institution systematically. They hear from the college officials that advertising is not traditional at the institution, and that money has never been provided for such expenditure before. Some college officers say that advertising for the college is a waste of money; besides, they believe that the press and the broadcast media should provide college news as "a public service." Some college deans say that advertising is "undignified for an educational institution such as ours." In a number of places, the municipal, county and state higher educational institutions run into opposition for paid advertising from governmental officials and budget-directors who control ultimately the finances of the colleges. The philosophy of these officers is that advertising is an unnecessary waste of the taxpayers' money and has no place in the educational budget; in addition, the funds could be, and should be, used for other expenses. It should be noted that these officials are usually lawyers or accountants, with limited experience in promotional work or marketing. In some universities, the claim is made that no additional students are needed, so why advertise?

ADVANTAGES OF EDUCATIONAL ADVERTISING

An increasing number of public relations directors realize that advertising must be used as a supplement or significant auxiliary to their publicity messages. From the directors' experience, they know that they can't always rely on the editors, no matter how cooperative, to provide the necessary newspaper space or airtime for the college message. Through paid-for advertising, the PR representative can get the *amount* of space and *time* the college needs. The editor may think the news about the opening of the evening sessions worth about five inches; the make-up man may be pressed for space himself that day, having an abundance of important news stories to squeeze in. He does manage to place four inches of the college news on page 26. The college, however, needs a lengthy story to tell about the new courses and new instructors and the time students may register.

Through paid advertising, the PR director gets his message across *when* it is needed. The news article on the evening division may find space on the day of registration; but to be most effective, the news should have reached the public a week ahead.

The director needs to give the message in a *certain way*, emphasizing specific points. This he can do in a paid advertisement. The editor may treat the evening division story strictly from a news viewpoint, as he is not interested in motivating potential students to enroll. Unfortunately, he may place a dull lead and a static headline on the article. The university PR director, however, can emphasize in the headline and copy of his advertisement a selling point to motivate the reader. "If you work for a living . . . You can find courses to advance you on your job at _____ University."

By paying for space for the advertising message, the college PR director can get a *continuity* his message needs. Once the story of the evening classes, for instance, has been published, the editor thinks the same news after that is dead. But to get impact and results, the college needs *to repeat* the message a number of times, perhaps in different ways. The director relies on advertising to do this job. To reach adults who are out of school, he can't use the high school counselors; he must use the publication or broadcast media.

Many editors realize that the college or university is not a profit-making institution, but an educational or cultural organization and that it doesn't have the large advertising budget of, say, the local grocery chain or department store. If the college does advertise whenever and wherever it can, such as before the opening of the semester or in the educational supplement, the publisher will appreciate this expression of good-will.

OCCASIONS FOR ADVERTISING

Institutions of higher education need year-round advertising just as any business or industrial organization does. It is undesirable for the college to use advertising only when there is an immediate need for it. Advertising men representing publications and broadcast stations say they can't spend too much time on higher educational accounts, because the universities are sporadic in their placement of advertising, or only "come in once or twice a year." Hence, the indifferent, step-child treatment universities get in the advertising departments of many publications which fail to spur college officials and promote educational advertising.

A systematic 12-month plan for the university's advertising, developed by the campus public relations department, in conjunction with advertising representatives of the print and broadcast media, will produce the best results. Inserted on a regular basis, university advertising builds a favorable impression and gets public acceptance for the institution throughout the year. Such advertising also lays the psychological groundwork for later advertising and publicity at the time of student recruitment, or when support of alumni and voters for campus construction projects is needed.

Advertising can be used wisely on a number of occasions. The public relations man can place advertising before the opening of the semester. He may schedule college advertisements in May and June, and in August and September for the fall semester; in December and January for the spring semester; and in May and June for the summer sessions. A number of progressive newspapers issue educational supplements, called back-to-college or back-to-school editions, which contain educational news, features and photographs, and which depend on advertising for support. If these supplements are carefully planned and contain informative articles of genuine interest and value to potential students, rather than being filled with fluff and filler, they will hit the targets for the university public relations department. The supplements will prove effective media for university and college advertising. This author has suggested to some advertising men the publication of educational supplements. When they were issued, the publishers benefited as did the colleges in the area.

When the college introduces a new curriculum or a single course, and strong promotion is needed to tell about this educational innovation repeatedly to a large number of potential students, the director can develop an advertisement or advertising campaign for this purpose. Advertisements are particularly needed if informal courses for adults or homemakers are offered for the first time or, when enrollments are low in certain courses and need building up. In the advertisement, the director thus can make sure the message reaches the *right people, in the right way, far enough ahead of time.*

The director may wish to promote the entire evening division, with its programs and courses appealing to working adults who want to advance themselves on their jobs and to widen their educational horizons. He uses large advertisements to present his message, repeating the information in different ways with each insertion. Special promotions may be needed also for the summer sessions, because the college must reach working adults, homemakers and other college students returning home from out-of-state institutions. These students desire to pick up college credits while on vacation.

When the university theatre presents a play, or the college orchestra performs in a concert, or when the film club screens old-time classics, effective paid-advertisements can supplement the news and feature articles. The college officials want to make sure that the messages about the cultural events reach the community, attracting a good-size audience to the modern Pinter play or the all-Beethoven symphony. Paid advertisements are appropriate especially if the play or concert requires paid admissions. The cost

Special educational supplements of daily and weekly newspapers, issued several times during the year, concentrate the attention of thousands of readers on courses and programs at the institutions of higher learning. The periodicals carry news, features and photos of the colleges along with the educational institutions' advertising messages.

of the advertising will be paid for in the sale of only a few extra seats. By implication, the advertisement may show, in addition, that the college is active culturally and is making a contribution to the community. Using only the publicity of legitimate stage or professional concerts, some editors place college productions in the amateur class, hence ignore their public relations releases. The use of paid advertising *guarantees* that the readers in these publications will learn about the campus performances.

The public relations director develops the ideas and writes the advertisements himself, or he may assign this job to a member of his staff, the finished copy to be checked out by the director. The director may get the assistance of the college's publication or broadcast advertising representative in designing the copy, determining the appeals and layouts. In some areas, universities turn over their advertising to advertising agencies whose marketing men, copywriters and artists carry out the assignments. The advertising agencies get commissions from the publications in which the universities' advertisements appear.

NEW COMMUNITY COLLEGE REPORT

The Parkville Reporter is featuring a report
this month on the Community College of Baltimore,
(pages 13-16), formerly known as the Baltimore
Junior College. The two-year,fully-accredited
institution meets a particular need for students
looking for education beyond high school.Graduates
may attend to continue vocational training, to
gain time in making a final decision on a career
choice, or to receive two years additional education. Read about the purposes and functions of the
Community College of Baltimore in this special
report.

Special news story in a community newspaper promoting a community college section in the paper's pages. The box appeared on page one.

MEDIA FOR COLLEGE ADVERTISING

Large advertising departments in commercial concerns and advertising agencies have media-buyers who determine the best media to be used
for particular products and services. The media buyers take into consideration the circulation, special audience, editorial matter, and rates of the
publications or broadcast stations. In the college public relations office, the
director, the publication editor, or both jointly, serve this function because
the department has to analyze the types of publications and radio and television stations where the institution's advertisements will be scheduled.
The department has to budget the limited funds to get the maximum results for the college. The director may choose one, two or a combination of
media (1) to get the widest possible audience (2) to repeat the message
during the same week or on following weeks.

Daily Newspapers
In placing the advertisements, the director knows the extensive circulation the daily newspaper can provide. He schedules the college advertisements for the regular run of the paper which is wherever the layout
man happens to place the advertisement, or he may pick certain pages for
the advertising message. The back page in some newspapers is divided
evenly between news and advertisements. Through the years, this page
has proved to be an effective marketplace for products and services, as
readers have become accustomed to checking the advertisements which are
readily seen. In promoting a play or concert, the director may choose the
amusement, entertainment or cultural pages. These special pages may
have higher rates, but they appeal to and reach specific markets.

Sunday Newspapers

Some directors believe that the best time to reach the college-minded audience is on Sundays when there is more free-time to read. The large number of advertisements in the Sunday editions backs this view. A number of publishers on Sundays issue special sections or pages relating to educational news, and build followings for this information.

The "youth supplements" in the Sunday papers attract not only high school students, but adults as well. Such supplements provide channels for paid advertising for the colleges. Back-to-school, college and other educational supplements, mentioned before, usually are published in the Sunday editions.

Weekly Newspapers

Many college public relations men have discovered that the weekly newspapers, published in rural areas, in metropolitan city suburbs, or in inner-city neighborhoods, are result-getting media for advertising. Individually, these publications do not have circulations which compare to the dailies; but the total circulation of the community press in an area may

The *Afro-American* newspapers, with headquarters in Baltimore, Md., publish an attractive educational supplement yearly. The tabloid is filled with lively, informative news and feature articles about colleges and universities in all parts of the nation, and carries a significant amount of advertising.

reach thousands of readers, in some instances equalling the daily in the city. If the public relations man of a college wishes to build up interest and enrollment in a particular section, he turns to the community publication in that area.

Many of these weekly publications issue editions with fewer pages than the daily press; hence the college advertisement may have a greater chance of exposure than in the daily, the public relations men say. Likewise, many of the weeklies are printed in tabloid form, hence the chances for the reader to notice the college advertisements are high.

Community newspapers have an intense readership because readers are looking for local news which they don't get elsewhere. Fred Serrot, advertising director of the *Fullerton* (Cal.) *News Tribune* pointed out in an *Editor & Publisher* article (March 1, 1969), that circulation is not the final answer in judging the advertising value of a newspaper. He concluded that "it still takes readership, i.e. in-depth perusal, or page-traffic to get optimum potential exposures to an advertisement." A media buyer, he said, chooses a newspaper with the highest penetration factor because it proves that it has a much better reader-acceptance. He cited the "Continuing Study of Newspaper Readership" of 142 newspapers which showed that the smaller newspapers achieved higher page-readership while the large newspapers obtained lower page-readership. The advertising rate of the weekly press generally is lower than that of the daily newspaper.

The media advertising buyer for the college is faced, therefore, with the problem that the rate for the daily may be higher than for the individual weekly, but he gets a larger circulation in the daily. To cover the same city market as the daily, he would require a number of weeklies, whose total rate might exceed that of the daily. Many public relations men attempt to use a combination of media, therefore, placing a percentage of advertising in the dailies and a percentage in the weeklies.

Directors often find that the original appropriation for the dailies will not be cut, but the college officials just add more to the advertising budget to include the weeklies.

Radio-Television

Sometimes, to reach a general audience and, at other times, to appeal to specific audiences, campus directors use radio and television spot announcements. The directors say that they have achieved excellent results from radio. The short, to-the-point, repeated messages come to the housewives as they cook in their kitchens in the morning or evening. The radio broadcast also reaches the husbands as they drive to work in the morning in their cars, or when they return to their homes in the afternoon. The radio stations which teen-agers listen to for certain music provide excellent channels to reach high school students, telling them about the new college programs. To reach cultured audiences to tell them about the new (or old) courses in music, arts, literature or current events, the director picks a station which concentrates on high level, or non-rock-and-roll, music and on serious discussions and news.

The cost for the radio spots seems high, the college directors say, but actually the cost is cut down considerably because of the two-paid-for-one-free spots the station arranges. Television is the most costly of the media, but because of its universal appeal, it will become a more important advertising medium for universities in the future. Some colleges, such as Adelphi Suffolk College, in New York, which have used TV for paid air-time, have reported excellent results.

MARKETING SURVEYS

The college public relations director, performing the function of advertising manager for his institution, searches for an understanding of the programs and services of the college and of the present and future enrollees.

He makes marketing surveys, one dealing with present students in the college, the second covering high school seniors.

Present Students

Current students can be given questionnaires, or in-depth interviews during their first week at college as well as after the first semester. Some questionnaires may be filled out in classes. The director can obtain applications and other records in the admissions office; if the office has any other facts about students, this information would be helpful.

The survey attempts to develop a profile of freshmen (and other classes), the researchers seeking to discover who are the students: where do they live, in what state and city. The area of the city or county in which they reside would be particularly important to the public relations director of a community college. He wants to find out in what kinds of homes the students live—upper-economic, middle-class, white-collar, or blue collar. What are the occupations of the students' fathers? Did these parents attend high school? college? The advertising of the college might be designed to overcome the lack in many families of a tradition of attending institutions of higher learning. What are the students' goals? What high schools did they attend?

College and High School Graduates

Colleges make surveys of their graduates to determine which occupations they enter, and whether students continue on to graduate work. This information may become a part of the advertisements of the institution in the future.

The large majority of college and university students come from public and parochial high schools and private preparatory schools; hence, such students constitute the principal target for obtaining undergraduate students at the colleges. The marketing survey would follow similar lines and develop parallel questions as did the survey of present college students.

Employed Persons

Many universities and colleges make little or no attempt to appeal systematically to employed adults. But an increasing number of other rural, urban and metropolitan universities and colleges are searching actively to arouse the interest of working adults in furthering their education.

The public relations student market survey of adults are of two kinds. One focuses on the present adult students. Mass questionnaires are handled by instructors in classrooms; or in-depth interviews among fewer students are conducted by public relations personnel. The techniques for obtaining survey information are explained in some detail in a later chapter on this subject. Similar questions are asked of the adult students as were asked of the young students.

Future Adult Students

The problem of obtaining information about future adult students is more difficult because the students are located out there in the offices, stores, manufacturing companies. A point of concentration for the survey might be a company, such as a utility, or a government agency, which encourages its employees to get additional education, sometimes paying for all or part of the tuition and book expenses.

Homemakers

The advertising man wants to get profiles of the women who are homemakers and are potential students. Who are they? What are their educational backgrounds—high school? college? He wants to learn what are their educational goals? Such information can be obtained at meetings of women's clubs and at shopping centers. He interviews those homemakers *now* enrolled so that he may get information which he can use later in his advertising. He asks are the women enrolled in college to get general background, to develop some ability, such as writing, painting or playing a musical instrument? Do they want to take business or professional refresher courses prior to entering jobs? Are they working for a degree?

How do they get their information? Do they read the daily newspaper? the Sunday edition? women's page? Do they subscribe to the community weekly? the ethnic newspaper?

The informational survey would like to find out about their homes. How many children do they have? grandchildren? What are the occupations of their husbands? How do the women manage to do their housework, prepare dinner, take care of children, and still come to class and to study? This type of information can be the basis for effective advertising copy addressed to other homemakers.

FEDERAL HILL COMMUNITY COLLEGE EXHIBIT
SURVEY FOR COMMUNITY COLLEGE OF BALTIMORE

Date _____

Name _____ Address _____ Age range _____

Occupation _____ Place of Employment _____

If a student, what high school? _____ Year _____ Major _____

EXHIBIT INFORMATION

How did you like the exhibit of C.C.B.?
Excellent___ Fair___ Poor___ Informative___ Not too informative___

What did you like best about the exhibit? _____

After seeing the exhibit, what was your impression of the College?
Very favorable ___ Not too favorable ___

What else would you like to know about the College? _____
_____

KNOWLEDGE OF CCB

Did you ever hear of the Community College of Baltimore before?
Yes ___ No ___

Is C. C. B. a four-year College or a two-year College? Four___ Two ___

Generally, what types of programs does it offer? _____
_____

Does the College give a degree? Yes ___ No ___
Which degree ? _____
Do you know the cost of tuition?_____ How much? _____

COLLEGE RATING

How would you rate C.C.B. as a community college? Tops___ Fair___ Poor___

ENROLLMENT

Have you ever enrolled at C.C.B.? Yes _____ No _____
Have any of your children or other relatives enrolled at C.C.B.?_____
None _____

READING

Where did you get your information about this exhibit? _____

CATALOGUE DESIRED

Day _____ Evening _____ Summer _____ Informal Courses _____

If you are a high school student, what more information would you like
about the Community College?

Older Citizens

Older people more than ever before are keeping alive and alert. The lives of retirees are being extended, and Senior Citizens Clubs are being developed everywhere to provide recreational activities. Men are retiring earlier than they did in previous years; they are not working right up to the grave, nor even to the time when they are incapacitated. Colleges are discovering now these older persons as potential student markets. Surveys, therefore, are made of present older students attending college to discover who they are, what characteristics they possess and what educational aims they have. The survey of these senior citizens may reveal how the college can serve their needs better, with advertising based on sound appeals.

PSYCHOLOGY OF ADVERTISING

In the development of his advertising program, the college PR man uses the successful principles discovered already about the psychology of selling and of advertising. The college representative knows that advertising must crystallize the desires of the public into action, keeping in mind that the person will buy only those things which satisfy his needs or wants. The public relations director is aware that advertising which gets results must have certain characteristics: advertising must *attract*, it should *interest* and *create a desire*. He knows that effective advertising *overcomes obstacles* and *induces favorable action*. To express these principles in a brief statement: Successful advertising is seen, read, heard, believed, remembered and, finally, acted upon.

Viewpoint of the Public

The university advertising representative recognizes the importance of keeping in mind the viewpoint of the public. The human being is primarily interested in himself and his family. He wants to know what advantages *he* will derive from an educational program—what want or need certain courses will satisfy. Serving as the advertising representative, the public relations man takes the "you-viewpoint" rather than the "we-viewpoint." The commercial advertising agency sells "homes" rather than houses, "comfort" rather than oilburners, "protection" rather than insurance, "musical enjoyment" rather than musical instruments—all in the effort to show how the product will benefit the individual. Similarly, the college representative promotes education and what it can do for the youngster or the adult, rather than always focusing on the names of specific courses, or on the prestige of the institution.

Advertising Appeals

Advertising points out specifically what contributions the product can make to the purchasers. Advertising also appeals frequently to the negative, such as when manufacturers of auto tires feature the accidents which may happen if tires are worn. Although not used much heretofore in college advertisements, results of failure to get a college education or of being an educational dropout may become part of advertising campaigns in the future. Such advertising may focus, for example, on the dead-end jobs that high school graduates fall into, or their being anchored to poor-paying positions, because of the lack of specialized higher education and the necessary training required in today's professions or in business and technical occupations.

Timeliness of Advertising

The college advertising representative is concerned about the time *when* students make up their minds to apply for admission to the institution. Do high school seniors decide in the autumn to enroll in one college or another for the following fall semester? Do they wait until Christmas or spring to make the decision? Do some students delay registering until right before the semester opens.

These behavioral patterns are important for the university advertising man to know, as they will determine when his campaign should be launched and when it should be repeated. Some students will be early-birds and apply a year ahead, knowing the competition for places; besides, many colleges and universities require applications to be filed almost a year ahead. Other students will delay their applications until spring; and still others will wait until the last minute, getting in just on the final deadline. How do students go about deciding on an institution of higher learning—do they give deliberate thought to this question, gathering all the facts, regarding programs and costs and location, then making a decision? Or do they "buy impulsively," selecting a college on the moment, right before the semester begins?

The advertising representative needs to learn these facts about high school seniors, as well as working adults and homemakers, so that he can time his advertising wisely.

Some community college PR directors believe that many high school students begin to make up their minds about college attendance when they are in the second or third year of high school. Promotional campaigns, therefore, have to be designed with this fact in mind. On the basis of some good evidence, many community college officials think that it is necessary to begin their promotional campaigns down in the junior high schools—particularly in urban areas and inner-city neighborhoods—for the attitudes toward college are beginning to be shaped then, and the idea of attending college should be implanted at that time.

BASIC APPEALS

In developing his college advertising, the representative searches for basic human appeals which will motivate the reader, listener or viewer of the institution's messages. He ties in the university advertising with old wants and develops new desires, all related to education. He selects the points of the campus programs and courses, and so presents the advantages that may impel the consumer to enroll.

Some psychologists say there are only three basic human interests— fear, love and hunger. Other authorities disagree and cite as many as 24 wants. A practical, but limited, working list of human motives is needed to serve as a guideline for the college advertiser. His advertisements may contain one appeal or a combination of several to fulfill these motives.

Acquisitiveness. Most people have this basic motive, which involves a desire for money, power and material possessions.

Love and Sex. This motive rates second and is concerned with the desire for romantic love and normal sex life.

Esteem. This universal desire indicates that the individual wants to be attractive, popular, praised. He needs recognition for his effort, work, looks, abilities.

Health. The desire for good health, longevity, youthful vigor rates high on any list.

Fear. This is a negative motive, but necessary for survival, as it involves the fear of pain, death, poverty, loss of possessions and dear ones.

Hero-worship. We all desire to be like the people we admire—football heroes, professional and business successes.

Comfort. This motive implies a yearning for physical comfort, rest, leisure, peace of mind.

Curiosity. The desire to seek and engage in new experience is universal.

Mental stimulation. People want to have mental excitement, rather than follow a dreary, dull routine.

A number of familiar products consistently reflect one or more of these basic human wants in their advertising, which is built around appeals to these desires—using different words, slogans and copy approaches to express them. Essentially, advertising is built on a central theme that appeals to the prospect through one or more of his basic human interests or needs.

The advertising representative for the university is aware of these appeals and studies methods of applying them appropriately to the institution's print and broadcast advertising. He asks, what do people want which can be fulfilled through higher education? He breaks down the "people" category into a group of sub-publics to discover more precisely their needs, then, in his advertising, he directs his appeals to these groups.

The High School Student

The high schooler has economic needs which a university can help gratify. He eventually wants to make a living, earn a top income, be a manager or executive in a large company, or own a small concern. In college he often prepares for a specific career in business, the professions and government service. Each career may be analyzed from the standpoint of wants which it gratifies. A career in business administration provides a good income for the businessman or industrialist. From a larger social view, the executive or owner is engaged also in a satisfying occupation of supplying products or services to the community, and he makes a contribution to the general economy of the city, state and nation. The physician's income is high, he heals the sick and relieves pain, and aids the health of the community. Similar analysis can be made of each of the careers which the college prepares for. This information may be used in advertisements in making appeals to students to obtain a university or college education to prepare to enter these vocations.

The high school student has need also for additional *background information.* He wants to be informed better about the world and get an understanding of it. He follows up old interests and explores new ones. In social sciences courses, the instructors deal with human beings, their history, economic behavior, psychology, and their social and governmental problems. The physical sciences enable the student to understand the worlds of chemistry and physics, while the biological sciences give him knowledge and an appreciation of the bases of human and animal life. His desire to learn about the arts is satisfied in the courses in art and music; and his effort to find out about man's experiences, and reactions to experiences, is gratified in the literature courses.

In college, the high school student may *improve on his already-developed skills,* or *develop new ones.* He may learn to play the piano, to paint, to sculpture, or to write. These courses may prepare the student for future careers, but they also widen the high schoolers' knowledge, deepen his appreciation and enlarge his personality.

College education and degrees help the high schooler to achieve greater status in the community—to "be somebody," he says—as the college graduate and the more educated person generally are more highly regarded. A college degree gives a feeling of accomplishment and confidence. Education provides a sense of security, which most persons want.

The high schooler wants personal attention, and if the college is able to provide individualized instruction in small sessions and laboratories, the institution will satisfy this desire. He wants instructors to take a personal interest in him and "be treated like a person," which means recognition of him as a human being.

The college advertising man continues to study the needs of high school graduates and weaves this information into his advertising appeals.

Employed Adults

The advertising man knows that the employed adults who take college courses have economic needs. These adults want to advance in their jobs, earn more money for their families, and possibly explore new job opportunities. For many, the degree means a step-up on the economic ladder. Without the degree, these adults are handicapped in many professional and business organizations. College gratifies this need by providing a variety of general business and professional programs as well as specialized courses. The employed adult also "wishes to be somebody," to achieve status. He wants to be successful in economic and social life.

Other adults desire more *general background*. They want to fill in the educational gaps. Their high school diplomas did not provide enough general education for them; they want to learn more about history and sociology, about current governmental and social problems, explore new findings in psychology. Their knowledge of the physical and biological sciences is weak, and they want to increase their information about these aspects of life.

Personal improvement is the goal of some working adults, as they want to learn to play the piano, write a poem or story, take a photo, make a movie. They want to develop their leisure-time pursuits. They are interested in intellectual stimulation, too, and enjoy discussing new ideas and current problems—a desire which is filled in many college classes. Their need to associate with other adults, exchange experiences and get new ideas is gratified in college programs.

Homemakers, Housewives

Homemakers or housewives may have economic needs, filled by attending college classes. They want to improve their present skills, or develop new knowledges and skills to prepare for future jobs. These adults may wish to explore new careers which are opening up to women. They, too, want "to be somebody," desiring a degree which they could not obtain before, for one reason or another. Other adults may wish to stretch their general background of knowledge in the sciences and the arts, and to develop themselves personally. They yearn for the stimulation of educated people and the excitement of a classroom where they exchange ideas and experiences with other adults.

Out of these desires, the college advertising representative selects and blends his appeals to meet the needs of large groups of people. His success depends on (1) attractiveness of the layout; (2) effectiveness of his headlines and copy; and (3) striking illustrations.

BASIC BUILDING BLOCKS

The copywriter for the university has a number of materials with which to work. Each element is important, but how he blends them will determine the effectiveness and success of his appeals. The building blocks of his advertisements provide an opportunity for creativeness, as each ingredient has an almost infinite variety of approaches from which he can choose.

His building blocks consist of the following: (1) major headline; (2) body copy and subhead; (3) illustration; (4) border; (5) signature or identifying logotype; (6) layout.

HEADLINES

The purpose of the headline in the educational advertisement is to attract the attention of a large and variable group of people.

Are headlines or illustrations the best means of flagging the attention of readers? This is an old argument which has been going on between copywriters, photographers, designers and art directors. There is no precise answer. Actually, the copywriter has only three ways of shouting "Stop and Read" to prospects: (1) headline alone; (2) illustration alone; (3) combination of both. The last method has proved most successful and logical. In most effective advertisements, the words and illustrations are so closely allied to one another, that probably neither copywriter nor artist could tell you which was the original thought.

By means of the headline, the copywriter stops his readers by offering something they want, thus inviting their interest in further exposition of the appeals the copywriter will make. Educational headline writing varies: (1) with the types of markets the university wishes to appeal to; and (2) with the media in which the advertisement is placed.

All books on commercial advertising include lists of headline types. As in the listing of the basic human appeals, some writers name four or five types of headlines, while others discover as many as 50. While this issue is controversial, it is desirable to present some of the standard types so that the educational copywriter can think in some orderly fashion about organizing his ideas and writing his advertisements. Some of the commercial copywriter's techniques may be applied, others may not. There is *no one right way* to present an educational institution to the public.

Direct and Indirect Approach

You can use either a direct or indirect selling approach in educational advertising. A direct-selling headline uses one or more of the primary sales features of the institution as both attention-getters and sales-influencers. For instance, the following headline selects the important features of Western University to capture audience attention and get persons to read further.

Western University Offers You
Varied Courses, Taught
By Dedicated Teachers

The indirect selling headline makes no attempt to do anything but stop the reader and get him to read past the heading. For example, consider the headline:

Graduates With College Degrees
Earn More In the Long Run

This message focuses on the general economic benefits of a college education and a degree. The question therefore arises, *when* do you use a *direct* selling approach in your advertisements, and *when* an *indirect* one? This depends on what you want emphasized. If you are promoting your institution, you select its best features and weave these into the direct-selling headline. If you desire to focus on the general benefits of a college program, you use the indirect-approach.

News Approach

In educational advertisements the most common method of headline treatment is the news approach. This technique calls for the same devices used by the newspaper copyeditor who writes the heads for international, national, state and local news. The advertising copywriter selects the outstanding features of his institution and presents them quickly, clearly and attractively. In writing news headlines more than in developing other types, a high value is placed on sentence structure. You have much to say and must say it in a minimum of words. Brevity is a powerful virtue in all advertising headlines, but you can't afford to be so brief that you omit sales features or fail to state your case with clarity. The educational copywriter uses attractive nouns, colorful adjectives and lively verbs. He may be as creative as he can in the selection of words, and perhaps he may invent new combinations of words, such as "educational power." He avoids the screaming exclamation point, because he believes the news packs enough punch.

When the copywriter uses a news approach, he determines quickly whether he has a news story: Does his institution have special characteristics and qualities which can be focused upon? Are there new programs, courses and divisions to be offered? New buildings, art wings or theatres to be opened? A new series of lectures to be presented?

The news headline has to be backed up with some evidence in the following copy. If you have gained the attention of the reader, you must also gain conviction as you develop your copy later on. You can't sensationalize the educational headline and retain credibility for your advertising and the institution.

Typography plays an important part in the success of a news headline, chiefly because of the extra length ordinarily involved in headlines. The copywriter becomes familiar with type faces and learns how many letters and punctuation marks he can get in each type of advertisement of a certain size.

Headlines on most educational advertisements follow a routine news announcement style. In the headline, the copywriter stresses one, two, three or all of the following:

> name of the institution
> time when the semester begins
> new programs or courses offered

Thus we find:

Mid-Western College Begins
New Semester September 15

Or this one:

REGISTRATION WILL CLOSE
January 6 For Spring Term
Franklin State College

Apparently, the officials of the institution and the copywriter in the public relations department believe that the name of the college and the announcement of the beginning, or closing dates for registering and applying are sufficent news. It will be observed that no attempt is made to provide "sales copy," encouraging, stimulating students to enroll.

The remainder of the copy most frequently presents a list of the degrees awarded, or the courses offered, and where the applicant may write for further information or apply in person.

Sales Approach

This one adds a kicker at the top which turns the straight advertisement to one which has some sales appeal:

Notable careers have their beginnings at

POLYTECHNIC INSTITUTE OF BROOKLYN

Individual and degree programs leading to
Baccalaureates, Masters, Doctorates in
ENGINEERING, HUMANITIES, MANAGEMENT,
SCIENCES, SOCIAL SCIENCES

Note that a subhead gives further information about programs. The body-copy which follows gives sales appeal, telling about Polytechnic, a "Center of Excellence," as one of the nation's most highly-respected educational research centers.

Adelphi Suffolk College in Oakdale, N.Y., used this sales appeal aimed at students who may be weak in certain subjects:

how to
succeed
as a college
freshman

The body amplified the headline, pointing out that freshman year is crucial and Adelphi helps to strengthen basic skills of reading, writing and clear thinking.

An appeal aimed directly at the potential student who is conscientious and wants to take time and make the effort to succeed, was used by Brooklyn Center of Long Island University in a 2-column 6-inch advertisement:

6 weeks . . . 12 weeks . . . 2 years . . . 4 years . . .

If you have
the time for you,
We have the time for you

In the copy which followed, the copywriter amplifed the point that whether your college progress would be best served in a 6-week summer session, or whether you are a community college graduate and require two more years for your degree, Brooklyn Center would benefit you.

Another post-high school institution wanted to appeal to recent high school graduates who might be interested in careers in fashion merchandising and other occupations, hence the copywriter used as a heading:

Good-Bye
High School ...
Hello World!

and addressed the high school seniors directly, saying that "the chances are you will marry. Chances are, too, that you will work at a job for 25 years of your life. Why not train for something you will enjoy—in a field with glamor and prestige?"

The Arundel Institute of Technology in Glen Burnie, Maryland, focused on opportunities in careers in its headline, and used a directive approach in this one. The subhead spelled out the careers: electronic technology, drafting and design technology.

CAREER OPPORTUNITIES
Register Now for Fall Classes

An appeal to the desire of employed adults to advance themselves was made in this advertisement of Loyola College in Baltimore, Maryland, reproduced on the next page.

The New York Institute of Technology used just two words for the main heading, provoking the curiosity of the reader to get further into the copy. The copywriter wrote "Night Light" in white letters superimposed on a student working in the evening in a darkened laboratory, with a bright light from electrical equipment shining.

NIGHT LIGHT

The subhead answered the query about "Night Light's" meaning with: Add the light of learning to your nights with degree or individual evening course at the New York Institute of Technology.

Thinking about
SELF IMPROVEMENT?

Think Loyola

EVENING COLLEGE

Here's Why

- ☐ Most classes are limited to fewer than 30 students to provide careful personalized instruction
- ☐ You can work during day — study and earn credits in the evening
- ☐ Loyola is fully accredited and coeducational
- ☐ Loyola offers an MBA program
- ☐ Loyola offers 5½ year evening degree program
- ☐ Loyola provides each new student with personal counseling

Choose from over 100 courses in the areas of:

Accounting	Business Law	Business Administration
History	Education	& Economics
Mathematics	English	Fine Arts
Physics	Political Science	Language
Sociology	Psychology	Philosophy
Science	Theology	Communications Arts

Classes Start February 2

Send Coupon or Call ID. 5-2500

LOYOLA OF BALTIMORE

REGISTRATION CLOSES JAN. 31   CR 1/23

Please send me complete information.

NAME . . . .

ADDRESS . . . .

CITY . . . . STATE . . . . ZIP . . . .

LOYOLA COLLEGE — UNDERGRADUATE DIVISION
4501 N. Charles St., Baltimore, Md. 21210

Loyola College, Evening College, appeals to economic self-interest in 3 column 8½ inch advertisement.

Headline: Appeal to economic desire with "Thinking about SELF IMPROVEMENT?" a question-type of heading.

Bodycopy: Reasons for attending Loyola College presented, with small box before each reason.

Subhead: "Choose from over 100 courses in the areas of:"

More copy: Listing of each course in parallel style. Other registration details.

Free offer: Coupon for complete information at bottom of advertisement.

Layout: Interesting layout with desk lamp as background for type. Provides natural heavy border at top.

Signature: Design of college with name at the bottom.

A different approach was taken by Wagner College, of Staten Island, N.Y. when the copyrwriter wrote:

A college
where
students
level
with the
president.

The copy pointed out where Wagner was located and stressed the fact that "the college's education environment included programs like meetings between President Arthur O. Davidson, to provide a well-rounded kind of learning that goes beyond static knowledge."

In seeking to attract students to its summer session, the University of Baltimore used a catch line with a subhead:

got a
Summer?

**Use it to further your education . . .
It puts you out front in the Fall**

Another series of advertisements of this university used an indirect approach, focusing on the themes, "careers" and "education," in the heading, "Don't Just Get a Job . . . Study for a Career," as shown in another illustration in this section.

Also aimed at the working adult in the offices and factories and stores in Baltimore was this curiosity-provoking advertisement, stressing an indirect approach to the economic motivation, "If You Work For a Living," as illustrated in this chapter.

A follow-up advertisement published at a different time of the year, used the question approach and focused on "you."

Do You Work During The Day?

with the subhead:

Why Don't You Continue With Your Education in the Evening?

Size:	7 inches wide by 6½ inches deep.
Headline:	Catches interest of reader with play on words: "Don't Just Get a Job . . . Study for a Career." Has economic appeal.
Copy:	Expands on headline and tells difference between job and career. Tells about courses at the University of Baltimore.
Photo:	None.
Border:	Heavy border, top and bottom.
Logo:	Special design of university plus name.
Layout:	Attractive off-balanced advertisement, with plenty of white space on left and right and bottom.

178

Evening Division, Community College of Baltimore advertisement, 2 columns x 5 inch.

Headline: Aimed at the worker, "If you work for a living?" (and who doesn't?)

Subhead: Economic appeal, "Get ahead and move up . . ." Copywriter re-enforces idea in the next sentence: "You can increase your earning power," and "Don't spend your evenings—invest them."

Bodycopy: Emphasizes full accreditation of college, and gives the fact: 120 courses to choose from.

Detailed information: Registration facts.

Signature: Name of college set up in attractive type.

A single-column 15-inch ad running down the page stressed the financial rewards of education to the adult working man and woman:

INCREASE
YOUR
EARNING
POWER

The copywriter used the same theme in his subhead:

Make this a
Profitable summer
Enroll at the
COMMUNITY
COLLEGE
of Baltimore

Special Audience Approach

Advertisements can and should be keyed to suit the audience, and in this advertisement the University of Baltimore copywriter aimed his headline at potential law students . . . He wrote:

the party of the first part... THAT'S YOU

He followed up this curiosity-provoking headline with the argument that "when you enroll at the U of B Law school, you become the party of the first part. Personal attention keeps you the party of the first part the entire time you are a law student . . ."

The Community College of Baltimore copywriter sought to produce a newsy head and emphasize the excitement and rewards in its programs:

Openings Available Now
In These 7 New
Exciting and Rewarding Careers

The copy followed this with a strong subhead and a listing of the various courses and the opportunities they provided.

The educational copywriter may direct his target to special people who may become students. In these advertisements women, housewives, mothers of all ages were appealed to:

WOMEN. All Ages
An Exciting & Rewarding Career Awaits You!

This was followed by the types of careers for which the Maryland Academy of Medical and Dental Assistants prepared the women.

don't Spend your evenings. Invest them

Whether for a course for fun, to fill a special need or earn a degree, CC of B can meet your needs. Registration for spring term: January 26, 27, 28, 29 and 30, 1970 — 6:30-9:00 p.m. Instruction begins February 2, 1970.

Your fully accredited low-cost Community College, 2901 Liberty Heights Avenue, Baltimore, Maryland 21215. Note: A multi-class center at the Patterson High School will offer a selection of college courses for the convenience of residents in that area. Call 523-2151, Ext. 285, 286 or 287 for further information.

in the Division of Continuing Education* of the Community College of Baltimore
* FORMERLY EVENING DIVISION

Headline: Catchy phrase used, "Don't spend your evenings. Invest them." Appeal is made to economic interest.
Photo: The dollar sign against background of stock quotation newspaper page reinforces point of headline.
Copy: Tells why reader would want to enroll—for fun, for special need or for a degree. Tells what courses will be offered.
Logo: Reverse cut (white letters on black background) used with aerial view of campus. Produces strong black border for advertisement.

In another advertisement, the same institution made a different appeal to those who were working already:

UNHAPPY IN YOUR PRESENT JOB?

an exciting and rewarding career can be yours

A humorous, sophisticated approach was used in an advertisement, when the copywriter, having some understanding of the problems of women, wrote:

"HOUSEWIVES . . . MOTHERS! Do you have the Stay-At-Home Blues?" The advertisement with the follow-through subhead, "Are you bored with taking care of Children, Cooking?" is shown in this section.

Headline:	Advertisement aimed at housewives, mothers.
Subhead:	Creates interest with question, "Do you have stay-at-home *blues?*" Specifics are added: "Bored with taking care of children, cooking?"
Bodycopy:	Expands on what housewife can do. Take courses. Begin college education. Pick up where you left off.
Subhead:	Repeat of previous ads. "Don't spend your evenings. Invest them."
Copy:	Registration details.
Logo:	Name of college in attractive type.

of course
it's good
...it's
Leftovers
from
Morrison's

Humor is employed in advertising addressed to high school and college students, as they respond to this appeal. The above advertisement was developed by a Florida State University student to advertise the Morrison Food Service for students at the institution. The ad appeared in the *Flambeau,* then a weekly newspaper.

BODYCOPY

While the headline flags the reader's attention and arouses his curiosity, the bodycopy of the university advertisement sells the benefits the institution has. Here the copywriter persuades the reader to follow through and enroll or support the college or come to the campus theatrical production.

Unlike headlines, which can be broken down into an almost never-ending list of types, body text falls into a few well-defined categories. Each category is used in accordance with the general format and theme of the college advertisement. The tone or key of the copy will be set by the headline and illustration. Here are some bodycopy types:

Straight-line copy, in which the body text immediately begins to develop the headline and/or illustration idea in direct selling of the product or, in this instance, college educational service.

Narrative copy, or the establishment of a story or specific situation which, by its nature, will logically lead to a discussion of a university's selling points.

Dialogue and monologue copy, in which the students illustrated in the advertisement do the selling in their own words by means of testimonials, symbolic testimonials, continuity panels.

Picture and caption copy, in which story is told by a series of illustrations and captions rather than copy alone.

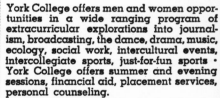
Small one- and two-column advertisements can be catchy and pack consider-
able information in them. "Build a Future," "Good Grief Why Not?" "The Standards are high. The rewards are great" are strongly motivational. "Flexibility!
Innovation! Experimentation!" summarize Cedar Crest College's appeals
briefly, but also in a stimulating fashion.

The layout and catchy headlines create interest for these small ads. University of Denver set its name vertically on the left side, while the adjacent ad made an appeal on its headline, "Courses Now Offered for Para Medical Careers . . . Some Require no H. S. Diploma."

The dental technician ad had an alluring headline, "A Dental Technician has a College Man's Future without a College Degree." Mt. Aloysius emphasized its name along with catchy head and brief summary of the college's advantages and the courses offered.

185

Straight-line Copy

Straight-line or factual copy is the most used type in educational advertisements because, in a majority of instances, newspaper or magazine space is bought for one purpose—to tell people what you have to offer. Straight-line copy is most readily applicable to all situations. As a white shirt, it is correct for any institution. This does not mean that straight-line copy is ideal for all advertisements, simply that it can be used for any approach, whereas the other types have more specialized functions.

Straight-line copy proceeds in a straight and orderly manner from beginning to end. It does not waste words, but starts immediately and directly after the headline, to promote the institution on its own merits.

Straight-line copy demands good, sound preliminary organization before an advertisement is written. By organization is meant the careful review of all the selling points you may wish to get across to the reader, and a close study of the importance of each.

The copywriter is aware that he can oversell. He realizes that if he is too enthusiastic in making claims which cannot stand up, he will ruin the value of his message. He can overclaim the value for all people to get a college education at his institution. A more modest claim is far superior and gives the reader a feeling of believability.

The bodycopy in a straight-line educational advertisement includes two or more of the following blocks of information: (1) types of courses and programs and degrees offered; (2) a follow-up on the selling point made in the headline; (3) facts about the time and dates of registration, or times and dates when the courses will be offered; (4) coupon for further information; (5) signature or logotype, designed by the Art Department as a means of identification of the institution.

The effective presentation of the information about the courses depends on the attractiveness of the typography and the layout. The advertisement of the evening college of Johns Hopkins used subheads to give the degree programs and a listing to tell about the credit courses:

```
    The Evening College of the Johns Hopkins University
offers over 300 graduate and undergraduate courses leading
to the following degrees and certificates:

    Master's Degrees--With majors in applied physics.

    Bachelor's Degrees--With majors in accounting, business.

    Certificates--With majors in accounting, arts and sciences.

    Credit Courses are offered in the following areas:

Applied Physics  Business Accounting  English  Numerical Science
Archaelogy                           French
Art
```

> Registration for credit courses in Shriver Hall
>
> Wednesday, Sept. 3, 6 to 9 P.M. (for those whose last names
> Thursday, Sept. 4   begin with G-O)
> Friday, Sept. 5
> Saturday, Sept. 6

A coupon and the logotype of the college were found at the bottom of the advertisement.

In his body text, the copywriter for the Polytechnic Institute of Brooklyn expanded the selling points of his headline about Notable Careers having their beginnings at the institute. He wrote:

> "A Center of Excellence," Polytechnic is one of the nation's most highly respected education and research centers. It is the first institution of higher learning in the greater New York Metropolitan area to receive a national foundation Center of Excellence grant.
>
> Its graduates are eagerly sought by America's leading industrial and research organizations. Last year, the Placement Services office assisted almost 400 firms recruiting on campus. Polytechnic graduates have the distinction of being fourth highest winners of coveted Woodrow Wilson Fellowships in the Connecticut-Metropolitan New York region--surpassed only by Wesleyan, Yale and Columbia Universities.
>
> Undergraduate engineering programs stress individual project work that stimulates independent study, creativity and significant engineering experience.
>
> Graduate courses are also available at the Long Island Graduate Center, on Route 110, Farmingdale, N. Y.
>
> Apply now for Summer and Fall Admissions.

A coupon containing the logotype and lines to be filled out by the interested reader followed. Blocks were provided for checking whether the individual wanted undergraduate, day and evening, or graduate, day or evening, or September, February, or June sessions.

The Adelphi Suffolk College advertisement followed up the headline about how to succeed as a college freshman with:

Freshman year is crucial in a college career. Adelphi Suffolk College Preparatory Program helps strengthen basic skills of reading, writing and clear thinking. Eases the transition between twelfth grade and freshman year college. Quickens ability to express ideas in speaking and writing.

Then the copywriter told about the programs and their costs.

Art, Music, Literature Courses Deepen Cultural Backgrounds, Improve Skills For Many Adults

By DR. SIDNEY KOBRE
Community College Of Baltimore

Seeking to increase their appreciation of art, music, writing and to develop their talents in these subjects, adult and recent high school graduates are enrolling in the evening classes at the Community College of Baltimore.

Opportunities range from painting with water colors and oil to listening to some of the great musical masterpieces.

Students who have never picked up a paint brush and others who desire to brush up on old skills attend the evening classes. The highly creative teachers and the modern studios provide unequalled opportunity for the beginner as well as the advanced student.

Recent evidence from psychological laboratories have shown that man's potential capacities and abilities are never fully tapped. He has creative talents below the surface that are never brought to light. Man's natural imagination, as can be seen in any five-year-old child, is paralyzed by his static environment.

It is possible to regain these capacities through training, according to Associate Dean Herman E. Westerberg, of the Division of Continuing Education, which sponsors the evening classes. "Man's perception of the world around can be intensified through courses in art and music appreciation, and his creative skills in drawing, painting and writing can be expanded."

For those interested in the written word, CCB provides courses in writing and composition and in the surveys of English and American literature. Stress on the spoken word is found in courses in public speaking, fundamentals of acting and stagecraft.

To understand sounds of the past and the future, a music appreciation course is available. Both the cultural and commercial aspects of the visual arts are studied by the students in the art department.

The opening musical bars will be played and the first brush strokes will be applied as classes begin on Monday, February 2. Registration for the courses will be held January 26 to January 30 from 6:30 to 9 p.m.

ART INSTRUCTION—Adults and teen-agers enroll in the art classes at the Community College of Baltimore to increase their appreciation of all forms of art. A course in "Art in the Culture" traces the development of art throughout the ages. Other students desire to develop their artistic ability, while some study commercial art, expecting to enter this occupation.

MUSIC APPRECIATION—A number of Baltimoreans want to explore the pleasures of music in the appreciation course at CCB. The great composers are studied and their works are played and analyzed. CCB has a Brass Ensemble, a Wind Ensemble and a Community Symphony Orchestra.

Explore The World With The Scientists

Science today is remaking our world. The scientist has probed the nature of the universe, exploring the world of the atoms here on earth as well as the plants in the sky. The United States has sent two successful missions to the moon, with the next stop, Mars.

CCB is aware of the importance of science in our everyday life, and is offering a variety of courses in the day and evening for those who want to explore this fascinating world, to widen their knowledge or to advance themselves in their professions, where science is used.

For the beginner, "Science Concepts" and "Natural Science" are offered. For those who wish to sit in an armchair and go on a tour of the planets in space, a course in "Introductory Science" is given. Courses are also presented for those interested in biology—including general botany, zoology, anatomy and physiology—and in general inorganic chemistry.

Courses Given in Various Places

The Division of Continuing Education is given courses in various sections of the city beginning in February. In addition to the programs offered on the Liberty Heights campus, courses for full-credit are being given at the Patterson Center at Patterson High School.

Students may enroll also at Enoch Pratt Library Centers, including Branch 8, Walbrook, North Ave. near Hilton St., No. 10 Northwood, Loch Raven Blvd. and Cold Spring Lane, No. 23, Patapsco Ave. at Third in Brooklyn; or at No. 31 Reisterstown Rd. and Kenshaw Ave., and at Ft. Holabird in Dundalk.

WRITING ABILITY—CCB day and evening classes give students opportunity to learn how to express themselves in words in the English Composition Courses. Many students also study American and English literature.

Well-Paying Business Career Open Up For Those Trained In CCB Evening Classes

FAST, ACCURATE TYPISTS—Community College students in the day and evening classes become competent typists, as the instructors are dedicated to getting the best out of students. The students aim for accuracy and speed, and they use modern machines in their practice work.

By DR. SIDNEY KOBRE
Community College of Baltimore

Today wide-awake, ambitious persons who work for a living in business, industry or one of the professions know that you can't move up in your career without that extra training.

That is why more than 2,500 recent high school graduates and mature adults enroll in the business courses given in the evening at the Community College of Baltimore.

"These courses are designed to help ambitious Baltimoreans move up the business and professional ladder," said Associate Dean Herman E. Westerberg, head of the Division of Continuing Education, offers the courses.

CCB offers courses in business organization and as well as one concerned business law and another business mathematics, so damental in all business operations. For those ested in the sales side of ness, they enroll in the and the marketing co Related closely is the relations course, which employes as well as exec need if they are to be cessful.

CCB offers courses in management as well as labor arbitration.

A number of courses i counting, including acco ing principles, cost accou are studied by those who to learn more about this ject.

Data processing is a growing profession as the puter has been introduce to nearly every type of ness and commercial o tion. The fundamentals taught along with punch data processing, fortran puting.

Registration will be held 26 to 30, from 6:30 to 9 Classes begin Monday, Fe ary 2.

BUSINESS MACHINES—Besides getting a strong general background in business organization and practices, students in the evening and day classes at CCB learn the technique of operating business machines. Modern office equipment is in good supply at CCB.

COMPUTER AGE—Nearly every business and professional organization today sees the enormous value of the computer in speeding up operations and providing information needed. CCB has a number of evening and day classes where beginners as well as advanced workers can learn more about computers and programming. Well-qualified instructors teach with advanced machines.

Courses Given in Various Places

The Division of Continu Education is giving course various sections of the city ginning February 2. In a tion to the programs offe on the Liberty Heights pus, courses for full-credit being given at the Patte Center at Patterson School.

Students may enroll als Enoch Pratt Library Cen including Branch 8, Walbr North Ave. near Hilton St., 10 Northwood, Loch Ra Blvd. and Cold Spring L No. 23, Patapsco Ave. at T in Brooklyn; or at No. Reisterstown Rd. and I shaw Ave., and at Ft. Hola in Dundalk.

The writer of the Brooklyn Center of Long Island University expanded the theme about "having time to study" (referred to before) by developing the time point more fully:

Whether your college progress would best be served in our 6-week summer sessions or if you're a 2-year college graduate seeking to complete four years . . . or if you're a high school graduate with your college career ahead of you . . . you'll find the Brooklyn Center of Long Island University dedicated to your future, offering an exciting and rewarding educational experience . . .

Visiting students are welcome to our two 6-week full course summer sessions.

Apply now for

Summer and Fall Admissions

The line "for further information, contact the Director of Admissions," was followed by the signature of the center and the logotype.

Dialogue and Monologue Copy

Testimonials have proved their ability to produce outstanding results in selling commercial products. The reader identifies himself with the person talking in the advertisement. The message, if natural and realistic, is more believable than the straight prose copy of the copywriter, making the same points. Copywriters for commercial products have found that good plain talk is absolutely necessary in the testimonial type of advertising. The phony note has to be avoided. The copywriter tests the finished advertisement on somebody who is not in the advertising business. He lets the person read the statement and say whether or not he or she would make such a remark.

Institutions of higher learning have not used the dialogue type of advertising, for two reasons. Educational advertising has been several decades behind commercial advertising, lacking imagination and boldness in approach, and many college officials would usually frown on this type on the ground that it is not dignified. However, dignified college advertisements, based on the personal approach, may be written.

High school students can be quoted on their reasons for choosing Western College. With permission being received from them, the students can be featured in headlines and in bodycopy, with pictures to reinforce the message. The reasons for their selecting the particular institution may stress: (1) its variety of educational programs; (2) the sound preparation for careers; (3) the smallness of the institution; (4) the distinguished and interested faculty; and (5) the research being conducted; or (6) other. Freshmen, sophomores, juniors and seniors may be quoted in their own words for their favorable experiences and the knowledge gained at the institution. The copywriter can also search for graduates to learn about the educational foundation they received at the university, preparing them for life.

If the copywriter prefers, for one or another reason, not to use specific names of persons, a generalized quote from a class or type may be employed. Thus, the copy may read: "Freshmen Say They Enjoy the Stimulating Classes at_____." Or: "Graduates Tell About Sound Education They Got Along with Their Degrees." "Employed Adults at Local Utility Say Evening Classes Help Them on Jobs." Or: "Local Utility Workers Give Credit to Evening Classes for Advancement. Why Don't You Benefit Too?"

ATTENTION-GETTING ILLUSTRATIONS

Educational advertisements can depend on strong headlines plus effective, persuasive solid body copy, set up in attractive typographical style. Many such advertising messages are produced. But the educational copywriter is aware also of the value of effective illustrations in his advertising. Such photographs or hand-drawn pictures can contribute much to the appeal of the advertisement. Striking illustrations, as indicated, can be used in combination with headlines to attract attention and to reinforce prose-points used in the headlines. Illustrations, with caption lines can be used, however, with little or no body text. Educational copywriters use photographs frequently and hand-drawn pictures sometimes.

The copywriter has many types of pictures to draw upon to flag readers' attention and to arouse interest. Copywriters use illustrations of campus buildings. These may be aerial shots of the entire campus, ground shots of key buildings, or photos of single buildings relating to the headline of the bodycopy. The university advertisement may show attractive photos of the inside of the buildings, including classrooms and laboratories, lecture-halls and field houses. Copywriters can select also action photographs of administrators and faculty in classroom and laboratories. In his advertisements, the writer can portray students busy in classrooms, in the laboratories or in the library. He may also picture successful graduates of the institution and photos of the Board of Trustees, drawn from many occupational levels and geographical areas.

The copywriter searches the photo file for those pictures which have strong appeal and which bear out the point of the advertisement. He may have to request new photos to be taken to get just what he wants, for he needs photos with a different angle to arrest attention. He searches for the apparently candid shot, for example, taken when the professor was intent on teaching and was unaware of the presence of the camera. To illustrate the science courses, the copywriter picks those close-up photos showing the student and the laboratory equipment. The writer selects the building shot to show the activity on the campus or/and to give the reader an impression of what the campus looks like.

COMMUNITY COLLEGE BULLETIN

Community College of Baltimore, 2901 Liberty Heights Avenue, Baltimore, Maryland, 21215

Students Choose From:

44 TRANSFER, CAREER PROGRAMS

Industry Needs Many CCB Grads

Baltimore's metropolitan area has many chemical plants, paint companies, plastic factories, electronics and pharmaceutical corporations—all searching for students who get their training at the Community College of Baltimore.

Many banks and insurance companies, and a number of wholesale and retail establishments, too, are looking for Community College graduates in business administration.

Hospitals and clinical laboratories also eagerly hire CCB graduates of the .science programs. Construction companies and manufacturing concerns want those trained in the excellent construction and mechanical engineering technologies of the college, which have experienced teachers using the most modern equipment.

The college also provides transfer programs for those interested in entering science-oriented professions. CCB graduates may continue in four-year colleges to become engineers, pharmacists, physicians or dentists.

The instructors are stimulating and interested in their subjects as well as in guiding students into suitable vocations. As a result, students for the first time develop their interest and desire to be a chemist, a botanist, a microbiologist or engineer.

Freshmen To Receive Help

It is natural that high school seniors are anxious about starting a new academic and social life in college.

They are curious about how to get started, what college is and how to be successful. They have a right to be concerned, for it is important for them "to make it."

A course "College and How to Start It" will be offered this summer at the Community College of Baltimore. The course is designed to answer critical questions asked by students who will become college freshmen. Areas essential to success — attitude, study skills, English writing, and social adjustment will be discussed.

In the Fall semester, the usual orientation program for students will be given, designed to assist them in their first year at the Community College.

Summer Session

Two interesting and informative summer sessions are offered at the Community College of Baltimore. The first session extends from June 1 to July 17; the second is from July 22 to August 23.

College Is Work, But There's Fun-Time Too

The largest portion of the successful student's time at CCB will be devoted to learning in classrooms and laboratories, in the library and at home.

But the college's total program also includes a wide range of extra-curricular activities enjoyed thoroughly by the 3,500 students who attend the day and evening classes.

The college provides an opportunity for participation in social activities, politics, sports, publications, and a nearly unlimited number of clubs.

Dances Featured

Dances featuring the favorite music of the "college crowd" are held regularly in the spacious Student Center wing, and there will be another series of formal dances and "gigits" or informal affairs again next year.

Some students are interested greatly in politics, and they get plenty of practice in students organizations. The student Government Association, the Sophomore Class and Freshman Class Associations are strong and active. They organize and conduct various social affairs and carry out student-oriented projects of benefit to the students and the college.

Operating within the framework of the Student Government Association, a wide variety of clubs catering to many interests have been established and are going groups. They range from teacher-education to psychology, modern language to science, business to secretarial, skiing to creative writing, to chess and checkers.

Art students display their works in an outdoor show or in the art gallery each spring. Student talent often pays off, as painting and sculpture are purchased by fellow-students, faculty and the public. Students interested in music join the choral group, the instrumental band, or the Community College Symphony Orchestra.

CCB's radio station WBJC-FM, provides additional opportunities for announcers and technicians to gain experience during afternoon and evening broadcasting sessions. Closed circuit TV programs are televised within the college.

The college produces plays which are performed before audiences. Plays range from works of Shakespeare to Tennessee Williams.

A series of films and lectures related to all areas of the current scene is presented. The Psychology Department this year presented "Critical Problems of our Times," with outstanding speakers discussing the communication gap between parents and teachers. At one event panelists talked about the causes and means of prevention of crime.

Two publications attract those interested in writing and photography and layout. The *College*

Janet Gingrich
Co-Ed of the Month
Co-Editor, Courtier,
CCB Yearbook

Crier, a weekly produced by off-set printing, is written and edited by a student staff. The four-page tabloid tells the week-by-week happenings at the college and has a strong editorial page. The *Courtier*, the college yearbook, is a splendid publication, containing hundreds of pictures and many articles about the college activities for the year.

Northwest
Star
Special

The Community College of Baltimore, formerly known as the Baltimore Junior College, is celebrating its twentieth anniversary this year. Yet today there are many persons who are unaware of the status, purpose, programs and advantages of CCB as an institution of higher learning within the Baltimore metropolitan area.

The aim of this special supplement is to inform high school students and others about the college. The publication's purpose also is to encourage high schoolers to continue with their college education and prepare for the complex world which demands good education and special training for successful living and for the better positions in the profession; business and industry.

This edition is issued by the college's Community Services Division, of which Andrew M. Bohle is director. The publication was produced by Dr. Sidney Kobre, head of the News Bureau. The information was supplied by President Harry Bard, Miss Leona S. Morris, Dean of Student personnel, and many members of the CCB faculty. Their help is gratefully acknowledged.

Fully Accredited College Offers 1 And 2-Yr. Programs

The Community College of Baltimore offers a wide-variety of courses and programs of study, taught in small classes by qualified, experienced teachers interested in the progress of each student. The college is a fully-accredited, low-cost institution of higher learning.

Located at 2901 Liberty Heights Avenue, it is convenient to all sections of the city. Saving expenses for their families, students may live at home and commute to the college, attending classes either in the morning, afternoon or evening.

Community College of Baltimore is housed in a beautiful complex of buildings valued at more than $7.5 million. Attractive classrooms, up-to-date science laboratories, a new planetarium and modern gymnasium are enjoyed by the students. They appreciate and make use of the splendid library with 50,000 volumes and the Campus Theatre, music rooms and art gallery.

Baltimore's only city and state-supported college has 170 courses and 44 different programs designed for freshman and sophomore levels of education. The first and second year subjects at CCB are recognized as equal to those offered at four-year institutions. Credits earned at CCB may be transferred to other colleges in Maryland and throughout the United States.

CCB's recognition of status was obtained from the Middle States Association of Secondary Schools and Colleges which accredited it in 1965 when it was known as the Baltimore Junior College. Both one-year and two-year programs are offered.

Graduates of CCB have several choices. One, they may transfer their credits at CCB and enter the third year of a four-year college or university. Two, they may begin a career. In either event, after completing the two-year program, graduates receive the Associate in Arts, or AA degree.

The Community College of Baltimore recently introduced a number of aide or assistant programs for positions in social welfare agencies, health, recreation and other departments. These aide programs are one-year in length.

President Harry Bard
"High schoolers welcome!"

CCB offers an unusual educational opportunity for a majority of students who have completed the twelfth grade, or have passed the Maryland High School Equivalency Test. CCB enables excellent high school students as well as those with good or average records to obtain the first two years of a college education. For many students with ability who did not work up to their potential in high school, CCB offers an opportunity to further their education.

Admission requirements include successful scores on some standard tests, an evaluation of high school records and personal interviews. CCB has a liberal admissions policy to give a second chance to students who did not do their best in high school. These students are enabled thus to recognize their mistakes and make up for them by getting essential education and training so needed in today's cultural, business and industrial world.

Community College of Baltimore offers distinct advantages. Tuition is low because more than two-thirds of the college's budget is financed by the City of Baltimore and the State of Maryland. A full-time CCB student pays only $250 a year for tuition and fees ($125 a semester of four months). The cost at other schools for a year's tuition is nearly $2,000. Part-time students at CCB pay $10 per credit hour, about one-third the amount charged at many other accredited colleges.

Grads Succeed in Colleges

"Graduates of the Community College of Baltimore are meeting success in advanced study or in the job market," Dean of Student Personnel Leona S. Morris reports. "Financial aid opportunities are increasing for junior college graduates who seek transfer. Johns Hopkins, Loyola, and Goucher, in our city and many colleges in the United States, are eager to have and to help good students complete their bachelor's degree."

The career graduate at CCB has always found a rewarding position, but now he finds special salary categories in many corporations and he finds additional education available.

For instance, Janine Smith, 1966 graduate in laboratory technology, after working a year, entered Mt. St. Agnes College this September in medical technology. She received enough transfer credits so that with one summer she will graduate in two years.

Undecided? The Community College Might Be Your Answer!

A four-page supplement issued for high school students by the Community College was inserted, with a few adaptations, as a paid-for promotion in community weeklies in the Baltimore metropolitan area.

Photo-and-Caption Type

The possibilities of using single large photographs with a small amount of caption matter underneath, to tell the college story in advertisements, has not been explored by educational institutions. The photo-and-caption approach has distinct advantages. This method gives the information quickly to the busy reader. Such an advertisement lures him to write to the college for a catalogue or a brochure about specific programs. After all, an advertisement never replaces a catalogue, listing all courses and programs and giving all the information needed. Instead, the picture-and-caption approach gives the reader the atmosphere of the institution and whets his appetite to learn more about its programs. In addition to the single photograph with caption lines, the college advertisement may picture a series of photos together with captions, each illustration telling about a dif-

STUDENTS AT WESTERN KNOW THEY WILL PROFIT
BY RELEVANT COURSES, TAUGHT BY
DEEPLY-COMMITTED TEACHERS

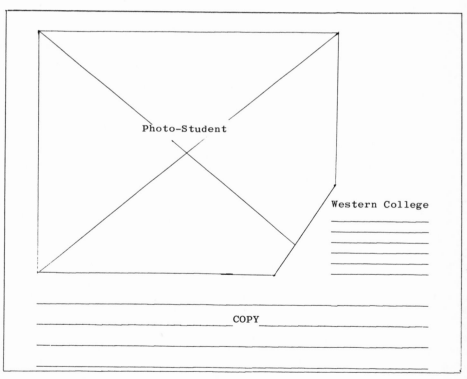

Example of advertising layout for single student testimonial type of advertising. One photo, blown up, dominates the advertisement.

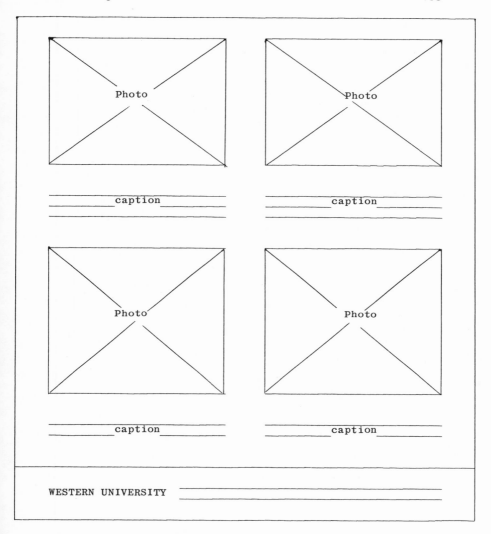

Example of layout for advertisement with four students' photos and their identifications and statements about the college used as captions.

ferent student attending the institution. In other advertisements with the same pictorial emphasis, a combination of pictures of buildings, faculty and students may be used effectively.

This type of illustration approach requires more space, perhaps, than a regular advertisement as a variety of photos, large enough to be recognizable, is required. Experimentation and consultation with the advertising representative of the publication may suggest ways to have small illustrations which are effective.

EFFECTIVE LAYOUTS

All of these elements—headline, bodycopy and photographs—must be brought together in an effective well-organized pattern or display. Layout is the physical grouping of all the elements in an advertisement as planned by the copywriter and/or the art director. Layout serves as a blueprint so that the copyeditor and college official who has to approve the final advertisement can visualize what its appearance will be when published. The layout also enables the printer to follow the college's copy ideas in setting up the advertisement. The building blocks of the advertisement have to be arranged in some orderly, balanced manner.

The copywriter has to determine how much space will be needed for the advertisement. The amount of space is controlled by the money to be spent and the rates of the publication in which the message is to appear.

The copywriter seeks to fit his copy and illustrations into the amount of space allotted. If too much copy is written, it will have to be trimmed or the amount of space enlarged. Advertising is figured on an agate 14-line-to-the-inch basis. Most newspapers are printed in columns which are about two inches wide, hence the advertisements are thought of in terms of 1 column by 14 lines, written 1 x 14.

The copywriter goes through several steps in a methodical, systematic fashion. First he develops a rough sketch of the advertisement, placing the various elements where they belong. This is called a *rough* or *visual*. Headlines are sketched in, position and size of photos are determined. The next step is taken when the copywriter does a *finished layout* or *comprehensive*.

To make it easier for the printer to follow the layout and because all copy cannot be crowded into the layout and still be legible, the copywriter goes through certain mechanical procedures. He positions the elements—headline, illustrations, copy and signature—on the layout page. The top copy is marked "Copy A" on the layout. Then the copywriter types the copy on a separate page, labeling the typewritten copy "Copy A" for identification. Other paragraphs receive labels, such as "Copy B" and "Copy C." The copywriter, the art director, or the advertising man representing the publication, mark the size and kinds of type for each of the headlines and copyblocks.

Design Principles

The copywriter is aware of the basic principles of layout design. The consumer may know nothing of these rules, may not know how to distinguish good art and layout from bad. But he will know which advertising arrangement pleases him and attracts his attention. Layout is an art in itself, and many layout men are finished artists. Quite often, however, the copywriter who makes the layout does not execute the finished drawing.

The copywriter arranges the elements into effective composition. Objects are arranged so that the eye will recognize important detail at the first glance and take in the remainder as mere accessory background. Composition accentuates and focuses attention upon the significant part of the picture, yet at the same time subtly connects and coordinates the detail. To accomplish a pleasing effect, balance, rhythm and harmony are skillfully combined.

The educational copywriter uses formal or perfect balance. The see-saw is a good illustration. Perfect balance occurs when two persons of equal weight, each the same distance from the center, balance the see-saw. Perfect balance occurs also when a heavy person sits nearer the balance point and a lighter person farther away from the balance point. Either way, the result to the viewer is one of satisfaction. So in a picture or layout we can use the first kind of balance or "bi-symmetric."

The copywriter can use also informal balance, satisfactory to the eye, by placing the larger objects nearer to the center line, while locating the smaller elements farther away. He can place a large mass on one side of the vertical center line, balanced by several masses on one side of headline or name. A picture, thus, may be balanced against the heavy type display.

Layout takes liberties with these principles just mentioned. Often to secure attention is more important than to follow the conventional rules of composition. In such cases, to gain attention may compensate for the disregard of artistic forms.

LAYOUT TECHNIQUES

The first step in making the layout is to determine the shape of the advertisement. The shape may be limited in advance by the selection of the media. If a magazine has been chosen, the size of the page or the part thereof is standard. A full page may be 7 inches by 10 inches or 9 inches by 12 inches, and a half-page, a proportionate part of these sizes. If a newspaper is to be the medium for the advertisement, more latitude is possible. While the width will be in multiples of column width, the height may vary from an inch up to the full vertical length of the newspaper page. The copywriter uses, as a general guideline, the "golden rectangle" principle, which is believed to have the most pleasing proportions for an advertisement. This is a rectangle of 1 to 1.62, approximately five inches wide by eight deep or multiples of these figures; such as 10 by 16, 20 x 32.

Depending upon the material to be displayed, often a long narrow column is effective, such as a single column. Occasionally a wide short advertisement may be desired. Also the size and shape of the illustration(s) are considered in determining the space.

The copywriter determines whether the headline or the illustration should be placed at the top of the advertisement. An illustration always increases the attention value of the advertisement. But whether the headline or the picture will come first depends on the logical sequence of thought. If the attention value of the picture is greater, then the picture should come first. The ability of the headline to transfer the reader's interest into the copy should be considered.

There has been a tendency in recent years to strive for individuality —to be different. Some commercial advertisers have put the illustration at the bottom of the advertisement. Unfortunately, the reader's attention thus

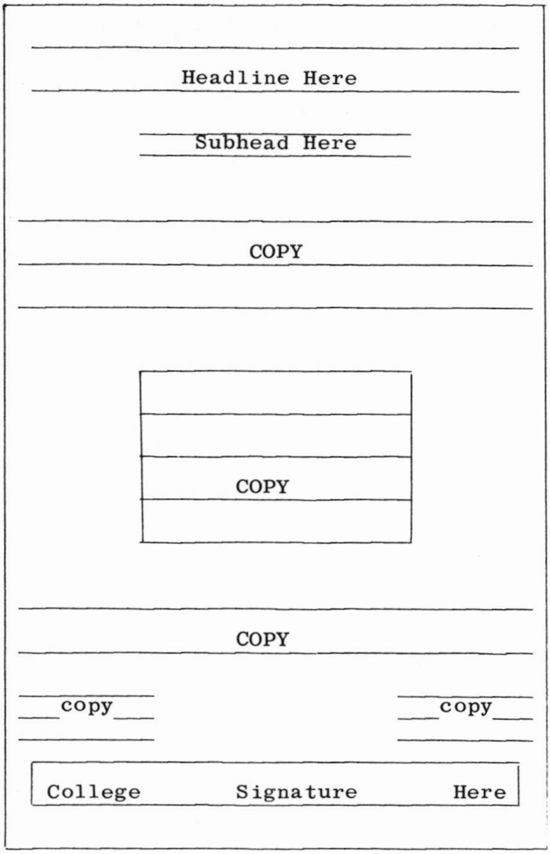

Headline Here

Subhead Here

COPY

COPY

COPY

copy   copy

College   Signature   Here

Perfect Balance Without Photo

may be attracted first to the bottom of the advertisement, with the risk that the top of the announcement will be permanently overlooked.

White Space

White space often greatly increases the attractiveness of the college advertisement. The amount of white space to be used in a layout has often been discussed. Certainly an advertisement should not be crowded. It should look easy to read, with open spaces to let in "daylight," as advertising men say.

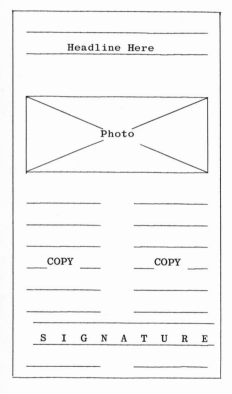

Perfect Balance With Photo

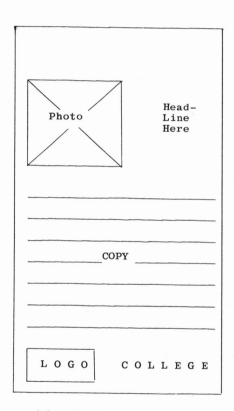

Informal Balance

Narrow Photo At Top of Advertisement.

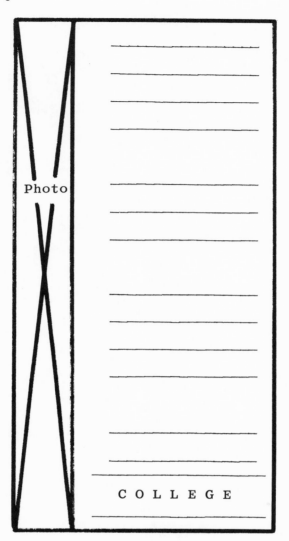

Photo

C O L L E G E

Vertical Photo on Side

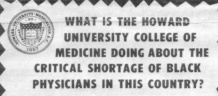

WHAT IS THE HOWARD UNIVERSITY COLLEGE OF MEDICINE DOING ABOUT THE CRITICAL SHORTAGE OF BLACK PHYSICIANS IN THIS COUNTRY?

Plenty!

FOR EXAMPLE:

The Accelerated Medical Education Program (AMEP) will permit college sophomores and

WHAT CAN YOU D

Conside
CAREE
MEDIC

Page 16
THE AFRO-AMERICAN WEEK OF APRIL
CAREER PLANNING EDITION

AT COPPIN STATE COLLEGE

"Reaching Out an Up in '72"

A college with "charisma" — that's Coppin Stat Coppin has "that extraordinary quality of spiritual pow attributed to a person or offic capable of elicitin popular support in the directic of human affairs Everything about Coppin has " smatic communi consciousness," and it embraces the the urban commun as no other college can. It's on 2500 W. North Avenu no other college is as close to the urban populace . . It offers a day and evening curriculum that meets the needs of the community . . . It gives the college to the community in a variety of services and academic program that keeps Coppin's theme of "Reaching Out and Up i '72" a reality — not a slogan.

FINANCIAL AID AVAILABLE

UNDERGRADUATE

For further information,
CALL 383-5990

ARTS & SCIENCES
Biology
Chemistry
English
General Science
History
Social Science with concentrations in
Political Science, Psychology, Sociology

GRADUATE
Earn a M.ED. Degree
Mental Retardation
Emotional Disturbances
Correctional Educational
Also courses for certification in
guidance and counseling, adult
education and elementary edu-
cation.

TEACHER EDUCATION
Adult Education
Early Childhood Education
Elementary Education
Industrial Arts Education
Secondary Education
Special Education

Coppin State College
is accredited
by . . .
Middle States Association of Colleges and Secondary Schools
National Council for the Accreditation of Teacher Education
Maryland State Department of Education

COPPIN STATE COLLEGE
2500 West NORTH AVENUE
BALTIMORE, MARYLAND 21216

Universities, colleges and special professional schools within these institutions are seeking to arouse the interest of Blacks to attend. The top large advertisement of Howard University College of Medicine and the lower one of Coppin State College appeared in the *Afro-American* educational supplement, distributed in a number of cities by this Baltimore-based semi-weekly.

NEWSPAPER ADVERTISING RATES

Newspaper advertising is sold, as indicated, on the agate-line basis. An agate line is a space measurement $\frac{1}{14}$ of an inch high and one column wide. Thus a one-inch advertisement, (14 lines) single column, at 5 cents a line, would come to 70 cents (5¢ x 14 lines). A two-inch advertisement, single column, at 5 cents a line would total $1.40 ($14 \times 2 = 28$ lines $\times 5$¢) regardless of the number of lines appearing. A two-inch, double column ($14 \times 2 \times 2 = 56$ lines) advertisement would be 56 lines x 5¢ or $2.80.

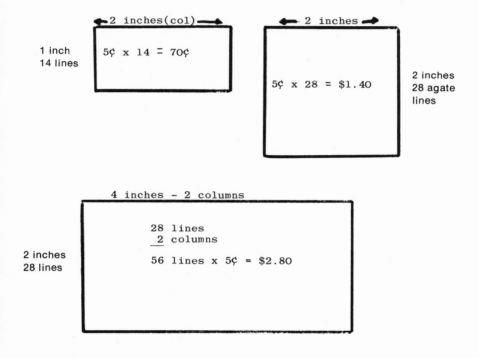

Line rates vary according to circulation, a small paper charging maybe a 20¢ charge per line, a large paper as much as $3 a line. The small circulation newspapers often use the inch rather than the agate line as a space measurement.

Columns average two inches in width. A standard-size newspaper is approximately 20 inches high by 8 columns wide; the tabloids, 16 inches by 5 columns wide. Dimensions refer to the type size, not overall size which includes the white margin. Advertisements are generally referred to with respect to size as 28 lines by one column or 56 lines by two columns.

Rates vary not only according to the circulation and the prestige of the paper, but also according to the amount of space contracted for. Thus, there may be an open rate for a small amount of display advertising, and lower rates when 1,000 or 5,000 or 10,000 lines are used in a single year. Educational advertisers contracting for large space are billed at the prevailing rate for that amount of space. If they do not use all of the space in one year, they are short-rated at the end of the year for the difference between the rate contracted for and the prevailing rate for the amount of space actually used. There are also special added rates for preferred positions.

Common Yardstick

To compare the cost of space in different papers, whose circulation may vary greatly, a common yardstick is the milline, which means agate line rate for reaching a million readers. This is obtained by multiplying the agate rate per line by 1,000,000 and dividing by the given circulation of a certain newspaper. Thus, one with an agate rate of $1.70 and a circulation of a million would have a milline rate of $1.70. A newspaper with an agate line rate of $1.70 and a circulation of 500,000 would have a milline rate of $3.40.

To obtain the insertion of an advertisement in a newspaper two steps are necessary: (1) signing a space contract; and (2) preparing and submitting the advertisement. Each paper has a "deadline" or closing for receiving advertising after which none is accepted.

Magazine Rates

Space is contracted for on the basis of (a) so many issues a year or (b) so many pages a year. The first may include a contract of 13, 26 or 52 issues in a weekly, 3, 6 or 12 in a monthly magazine.

A "Rate and Data" card is usually printed by each newspaper or magazine and representatives of the publications will offer the card, if asked.

SCHEDULE FOR ADVERTISEMENTS

NEWSPAPER	DATE OF PUBLICATION, SIZE IN AGATE LINES
Daily News	January $\frac{2}{200}$ | $\frac{7}{203}$ | $\frac{9}{209}$ | 13 | 14
	February $\frac{3}{100}$ | $\frac{7}{56}$ | $\frac{9}{200}$ | | $\frac{14}{100}$
Tribune	January $\frac{7}{100}$ | | $\frac{13}{100}$ | | $\frac{20}{100}$

Part Four

VISUAL AND BROADCAST MEDIA

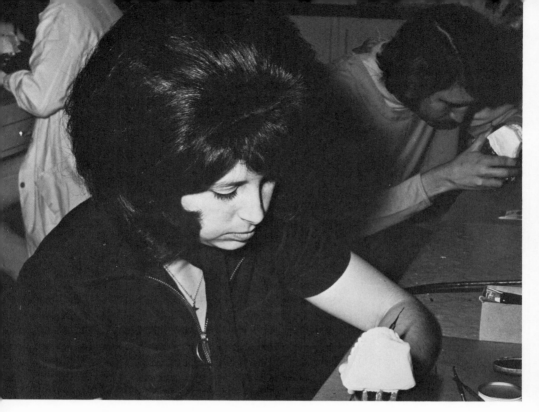

This attractive student was posed in a dental laboratory in a community college as she worked on a denture. The close-up shot dramatizes the subject and omits all unnecessary background or detail.

Students make good subjects for the public relations photographer for most of them cooperate readily. This one was caught in an off-guard moment while sitting on the back of a chair, sketching.

9

Photographs

PHOTOGRAPHS PROVIDE another dimension for communicating the college story to the institution's publics. Pictures can create a strong interest and give important information about the university visually. Snap a picture of a professor writing on a blackboard, take a shot of a student working in a laboratory among test tubes, or selecting a book from the college library shelf—and the action will be recognized readily by parents, high school students, members of the county council. Thus, college pictures provide instant communication.

The photo of a college department may create attention where a written piece of copy may not. Public relations men for universities realize that quality, action photos about their institutions may leave a more lasting impression and be remembered longer than words describing the same action or event. Photos of classes in business administration or music or art, make the viewers feel they are there, because the viewers identify themselves with persons in the picture. When the striking photo is combined with the written news story or feature article, a double impact is achieved. The viewer reads about the event—and he also sees it.

Photos of classroom activities and of current campus events also furnish permanent records of the college happenings, capturing an instant of time in the history of the institution. Such photos will be found useful over the years ahead, when historical pictures are needed, long after the event is over and the people have vanished. When the public relations staff produces a tabloid newspaper or a brochure about the 20th anniversary of the college, the public relations representatives will search for photos picturing graphically the past decades. The photofile will be the most important resource for the pictures.

Public relations men use university photos in a variety of ways. Pictures of college events are submitted along with news and feature articles to daily or weekly newspapers, press associations and general magazines. Often the college representative will deliver to the editor just a photo with deep caption-lines. On the campus, the representative publishes the photos in brochures, or in such college publications as the catalogues and the annual report of the president. The department will need photos for the alumni magazine and the newsletter sent to key officials in government and business. When the representative begins to prepare a college exhibit, he turns to his picture file for illustrations, and he uses photos, both black-and-white and color, for the college's slide shows.

The university public relations department makes full use of photos, because the public wants and responds to the picture appeal. Daily and weekly editors are willing to accept, and are even eager to obtain, good quality campus photos with human interest appeal and action.

USEFUL PHOTO TYPES

The public relations department builds up a photofile for future use and provides acceptable photographs for current college events. The department also develops a classification system to cover the various types of illustrations which will be usually required and files the photos so that they can be retrieved readily.

External Photos

Photos of campus buildings will be used over and over again. To show the extent of the campus, the photographer snaps the entire complex of buildings, shooting from the roof of the tallest building, or he takes an aerial shot of the campus scene. Searching for the most strategic spot, the photographer makes a ground shot of a number of the university buildings. Then he turns to front, back and side shots of the administration buildings and the classroom buildings, selecting striking and unusual angles. Separate pictures of the outside of the science building, and the art or business wings will be found useful throughout the year. Because people in the pictures add interest, the photographer makes sure that, for the ground shots, he includes students walking across the campus, going into or leaving the buildings. The resourceful photographer searches out special spots on the campus, such as the attractive ones around the flowerbed, flagpole, gate or tower which may be landmarks.

For live, current photos and for the photofile for future use, the cameraman takes pictures of the campus and the buildings in the day and evening, and during the autumn, winter, spring and summer sessions. Pictures of the campus in the evening, with students entering the lighted buildings, for instance, will be used to illustrate the articles about the employed

Photos of adult students who work in plants and mills during the day and attend college in the evening, or who go to classes in the daytime and then head for work, make striking illustrations for features that newspapers will use. The college photographer had to go down into the plant to snap Bill Smith's picture working at his big machine. *Below:* The same Bill Smith was photographed in the college television studio as he "worked" the camera in a program.

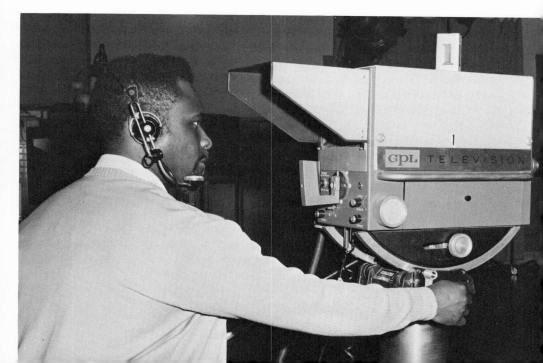

adults who attend classes after work, or the photos will find a place in the catalogues and brochures of the Division of Continuing Education, sponsoring the evening courses.

Internal Photographs

Going into the buildings, the cameraman builds up a group of shots for each department or division, taking classroom and laboratory scenes. Before shooting, he studies the instructional methods used in the departments. He inquires about equipment, maps and audio-visual aids, as these will find a place in the photos. Some of the pictures may be regular overall views of professors and students in classroom situations; other photos may portray instructors at their desks, writing on the blackboard or demonstrating a piece of equipment. When appropriate, the cameraman takes pictures of the instructors using slide or motion picture projectors. Photos may show students at work in the physics or chemistry laboratories, or may picture students testing machines in the mechanical engineering department. To obtain the shot with the most impact, the photographer may decide that he should group several of the students and the instructor in front of a piece of equipment. If the cameraman is projecting the activities in the art department, he may zoom in on one student at his painting easel.

Moving over to the library, the photographer will want a set of photos of its various features. He shoots pictures of students at the card catalogue, or he clicks his shutter as they select magazines from the rack or books from the shelves. He then snaps some photos of students doing their home assignments in the carrels. Maybe the library is building up its microfilm department, hence a student may be pictured reading a 1960 issue of the *New York Times*.

Administration and Faculty

Because they are used many times during the year, photographs of each administrative officer are taken. The photographs consist of the regular full-body or face-and-shoulder shots. The cameraman also creates different pictures of these administrators. The president may be snapped in his office, standing beside the aerial photo of the campus; the vice president may be shown walking in the front door of the administration building; the dean of the faculty may be presented at a rostrum, when he addressed the faculty at a meeting.

Photos of new administrative officers are taken as soon as they arrive on the campus, for in this way, a complete file can be obtained. Because of the changes in clothes, in hairstyles and in general appearance, photos are retaken at stated intervals, such as every two or three years, to keep the files up-to-date.

Both standard head-and-shoulders photos as well as candid and action photos of each member of the faculty will be needed to complete the pho-

Photographs of the president of a university or college are used by the public relations department frequently; however, the pictures have a tendency to become routine. Standard face-and-shoulder shots are needed; but in the top photo, President Harry Bard of the Community College of Baltimore was given a background, a poster about the Allied Health Program in which he was deeply interested. *Below:* An action shot pictures President Bard discussing a proposed program with a dean and his assistant.

tofile. Here again the creativity and imagination of the public relations photographer can be demonstrated. The faculty member will be shown in his office, at his desk, at a file, or telephoning, talking to a student, gazing out the window, or reading. The cameraman shoots him in the classroom, lecturing, using the blackboard, or demonstrating a point with a map, operating a slide projector, or working with a piece of machinery. The physical education instructor may be portrayed shooting a basket on the court. Photos of new faculty members are added to the file early in the year when they arrive on campus.

The personnel and operations of other auxiliary departments of the university are covered by the staff photographer. He makes appointments to take photos of admissions officers, of counselors, of the health aides. He also moves into the audio-visual department, then the cafeteria and maintenance departments for lively shots of their essential activities.

Student Activities

The public relations photographer keeps a file of student activities. Consequently, he shoots scenes of the Student Government Association in action. He portrays the students working on Christmas projects, and he captures students building theatrical sets for the next play. When students are rehearsing for a play, or for the concert a month away, the public relations photographer gets some live shots of these student activities. On the basketball court, he captures a few action shots of players throwing the ball into the basket or passing the ball to team-mates.

CURRENT EVENTS AND SPECIAL EVENTS

The director of the public relations department, keeping abreast of the news, decides which college events should be covered: (1) by written news and feature articles; (2) by photographs; and (3) by both. Public relations men, conscious of the picture-trend and aware of the possibilities of placing live news photos, cover pictorially almost every major and minor event at the university.

Some PR men have discovered that a safe photograph distribution-rule is to send out a photo, or several of them, with each important news story or feature article. The few cents needed for the extra photos will be more than justified with the publication of one or two of the pictures. Effective photos in the hands of editors have a strong chance of catching their eyes and getting acceptance—the daily or weekly editors can't react to photos the public relations man has failed to send in.

Many alert editors are on the lookout for sharp photos which have a genuine human interest appeal, or show the educational side of the com-

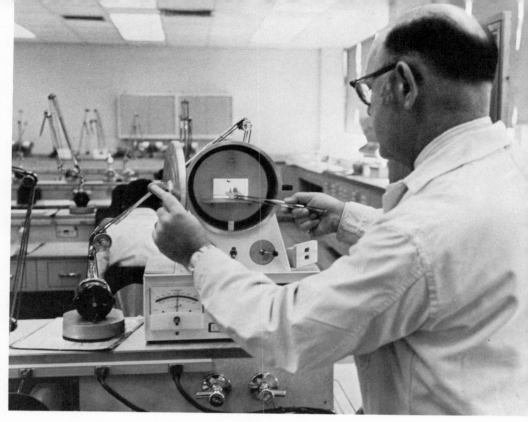

Illustrating his work in a college laboratory, this close-up shot of an instructor was used widely by the public relations department.

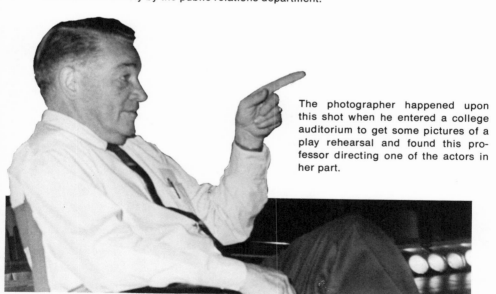

The photographer happened upon this shot when he entered a college auditorium to get some pictures of a play rehearsal and found this professor directing one of the actors in her part.

The photographer went behind the scenes of a play to get this photo of actors, working on their make-up. He found them looking into the mirror and snapped the shot quickly, producing an interesting double-effect.

This posed photo was taken to get the leading characters of a play, dressed in their own costumes, into a single picture with interesting composition qualities. The background prop gives an added touch.

Public relations photographers, covering cultural events at universities and colleges, are challenged to come up with pictures which have fresh and different angles. This is a standard photo of visitors coming to an exhibit at the college. The situation seems realistic, as nobody looks into the camera lens, the visitors' eyes are on the guide and on the artwork, as he explains the picture.

munity pictorially. As in the coverage of campus news by a reporter, the editor faces the same problem with his photostaff: he never has enough personnel to do the complete job. Even if the university photo, for one reason or another, is unacceptable, the editor may be stirred to assign his own staff photographer to get a picture more in accordance with the editor's preferences and needs. But the college PR man has given the editor the starting idea for the pictorial coverage in such instances.

The range of reportable events happening on a campus is wide and has been outlined in the previous chapters on news and features. Photographs of current events on the campus are judged in much the same way as are news stories. The pictures must have currency above all, then general interest. If the photo has human interest elements, chances of the picture's acceptance will be increased. The best newsphotos show action. The newswriter has 1,000 or 2,000 words in which to tell the story of the dedication of the new building being constructed on the campus, or 500 words with which to relate the graduation events. The photographer, however, may have only one or two photos to capture the essence, or the highlights of these events. He has to freeze all the action in a single moment of time. He is compelled, therefore, to get the peak, or a few peaks, of the event for the picture to have the dramatic impact editors are looking for.

What lends particular interest to the current events shots are the people in the pictures. Most live campus newsphotos feature people—students, professors, visitors. It is the job of the campus public relations photographer to get persons into the picture and to show them doing something—not just staring ghost-like into the camera lens.

The public relations photographer has to be just as ingenious as the newswriter when special events are scheduled. The photos have to be conceived and taken long before the day of the event. Preparations for Homecoming, graduation, the rehearsals for concerts and plays, the arrangements for the panel discussion—all these events require photos to be taken. Published by editors, the pictures will arouse interest in the events. As these events are in progress, the photographer also shoots pictures of them.

Some photographs do not portray current happenings on campus, but depend on their general human interest appeal. They may have the desirable ingredient of currency, but the distinctive attractiveness is their human quality. The photo which accompanies the article on the three sets of twins at the college has a human interest ingredient. After the newswriter on the public relations staff discovers three mothers and three grandmothers attending classes, he develops a lively feature article, the appeal of which would be improved with several photos showing these older students in classrooms and science laboratories.

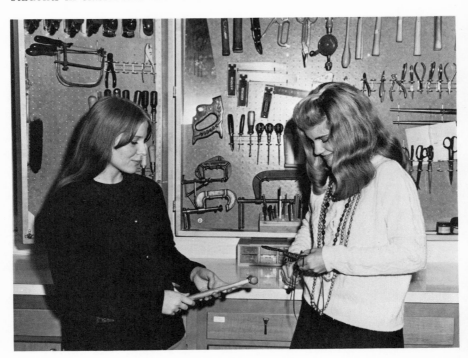

Students in occupational therapy learn to use tools for making and adjusting appliances. Background shows tools on cork board in a classroom-laboratory.

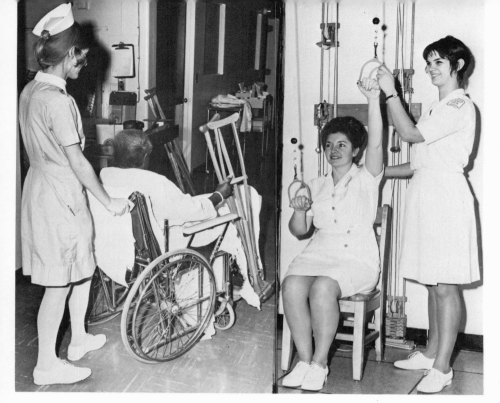

A sequence of photos about the Allied Health Program shows the variety which a public relations photographer can achieve, each picture having a different angle. The editor may choose to publish all the photos, or may select just one or two. (left) Nursing student rolls patient in wheelchair in hospital. (right) Occupational therapy student assistant practices weight lifting methods on another student.

PHOTOGRAPHIC STORIES

With the expansion of photo departments and the increased space given to pictures in newspapers and magazines, editors have become interested now in a group of related photos telling one complete story about an event or a person. One campus picture can catch a highlight of an event, or portray a single action of a student, instructor or department; a series of correlated photos, however, can give a fuller, more dramatic and more interesting treatment of these subjects. Such photos about the college are used not only in daily newspapers, but others with Sunday editions and tabloid supplements, edited with originality.

The college cameraman may produce also a series of related photos of the crowning of the college queen, showing the crowning itself, the entertainment, the dancers, the decorations. Events related to homecoming may include committee preparations, the floats of fraternities being judged, the outdoor barbecue, the meetings of the alumni held at the college, the banquet and the football game.

A sequence of photos of a woman student makes an appeal to editors and to their readers. She is shown at the local Gas & Electric Company, where she works as a credit checker. In the second photo, she is depicted in her class, intently listening to the professor of state government in the evening session.

A sequence of photos on the nursing career department creates interest, with pictures of the girls in classrooms, in laboratories, and at the clinics and hospitals. The editor of a Sunday supplement may find attractive the story and picture layout of the oldest male student on campus who is now registered in the physical therapy assistant program. The photographer shows the gray-haired student: (1) at home, studying, (2) riding his bike to his classes; (3) sitting in classes with younger students; (4) working in the lab with the equipment used in the course. A photo sequence may be shot on the construction of a model house by students in the building construction department, with the cameraman's portraying the steps the students take, from working out a blueprint to constructing the building. The series would prove acceptable to the editor of a building construction magazine as well as to the Sunday feature editor of a daily newspaper.

Although he has planned ahead for most of his shots, the campus photographer is on the lookout for the unexpected, which may produce superior pictures to those he planned carefully. The cameraman finds such candid off-beat pictures in the hallways, in the cafeteria, in the student lounge. He may happen upon unusually appealing shots on the steps of the library or on the campus lawn. Such photos give an informal, human feeling which isn't captured in planned pictures.

METHODS OF OBTAINING PHOTOS

The public relations director has several practical alternatives, or a combination of them, to obtain acceptable photos of his university's activities. The practitioner can hire a professional photographer on a full-time basis, or he can employ a commercial photographer on a part-time basis to do special jobs. Some PR men in small colleges do all of their own picture-taking and developing, or they supplement the work of the part-time photographer. Whatever the situation, the representative needs to develop a picture-awareness. He sizes up a current event for its picture possibilities, and creates a photograph to cover the happening.

Employ a Professional

When the practitioner hires a competent, qualified cameraman, the college usually is assured of professional results. The experienced photographer, particularly if he has been on a newspaper staff, has the picture- or news-sense to select the right action or the best angle to dramatize the institution. The photojournalist knows how to create a newsy photo, and he has the ability to get into the 8 x 10 glossy the appeal for the specific public the PR department wishes to reach. The professional, too, understands what kinds of action prints publication editors want. Besides, the competent, experienced cameraman has the technical knowledge of the camera, lighting and the developing process to produce an acceptable-quality print which can be reproduced easily by newspapers or magazines.

The full-time photographer is on the spot at all times at the college, thinking and planning attractive, appealing pictures, suggesting picture-ideas, consulting with the public relations director. Above all, he is available when the news happens on the campus.

For many colleges, the significant drawback to hiring a full-time professional, however, is the salary cost. Many institutions, particularly community or junior colleges, cannot afford the expense of adding a qualified cameraman to the regular staff. The large university has less of a financial problem, once the officials become convinced that the employment of a pictureman would be desirable.

Hundreds of colleges rely on part-time photographers, in the community or elsewhere, who come to the campus to carry out special photo assignments. These cameramen may be hired for special jobs to snap specific pictures, charging for each shot, or they may be hired on an hourly- or daily-basis. Some public relations men believe that the day-basis is better, for the photographer—with more time—will take more pictures from which the best may be chosen.

Frequently, the cameraman who is employed on a full or part-time basis has not had extensive journalistic experience. Perhaps he has special-

ized in portrait work, or baby or wedding pictures. He may have just graduated from college where he majored in photography. He has the technical
ability necessary to do acceptable, even creative, work but he requires additional training and experience in the photojournalistic work of the
college public relations department—the development of a newsphoto
sense and a grasp of the importance of deadlines for the downtown dailies
and weeklies.

The PR director or his assistant helps the photographer get his photos.
The staff transmits background information to the photographer and often
makes the arrangements for the shooting session in the classroom or after
class. The staffer may have to determine what kinds of photos should be
taken and what poses would be suitable. When a tour of the university
buildings is taken by a high school group, the public relations director may
indicate the nature of the scenes to be snapped, and may suggest beforehand to the instructors the need for cooperating with the photographer. If
the PR director knows that the community weekly newspapers would be
interested in certain students on the tour, he may assign the photographer
to take different shots to fit the needs of these editors.

Take Your Own

Many public relations men adjust their viewfinders, press the buttons
on their cameras and shoot their own publicity pictures. These practitioners may once have been professional photographers who became interested
in public relations, more recently turning to this work full-time. Or they
see the necessity of having photos, but limited budgets prevent the employment of professionals. The staff member may have achieved advanced amateur status in photography previously, but now needs to shoot seriously if
he is to obtain needed photos of the college activities. He has his 35mm or
his twin-reflex camera ready. With practice, he learns to take high contrast,
glossy prints which can be used by outside media, and by himself for the
various public relations publications. His awareness of human interest and
significant picture-possibilities sharpens with time, and he is finally able to
think, plan and snap attractive, appealing pictures. Continuous study of
commercial publications which carry many pictures and reading photography trade magazines enable him to improve the subject matter, composition and angles of his own campus shots. Even if he employs a part-time
photographer, the public relations staff member often needs to fill in when
the photographer may not be available to cover an assignment.

Check With Editor

On big events, the public relations man calls the editor of the daily,
Sunday edition or weekly newspaper describing the picture-possibilities

of the college event. The representative might suggest some types of newsy photos which can be taken. Or he might indicate the prominent person from outside the state who is to be present, or tell about the attractive co-eds who will participate in the event. The editor may decide to send out his own photographers to cover the event; or he may rely on the public relations department to get the pictures to him promptly. As the editor gets to know and to trust the PR representative, the newsman will rely increasingly on the practitioner's news-picture sense and his ability to deliver a publishable photo.

CHECKLIST ON PHOTO-IDEAS

In shooting his own pictures, the public relations man thinks through the photo-idea possibilities of a scene or action. If he uses a photographer, the picture will be the result of their combined thinking. In either situation, the practitioner raises these questions:

1. What basic idea am I trying to interpret pictorially?
   What information do I wish to convey? Or what impression am I trying to create?
2. How can I bring out this idea pictorially?
   What will be the content of the photo?
   Who should appear in the picture?
   What background is needed?
   What props are required?
3. What types of people are the pictures supposed to appeal to? High school students? Parents? Scientists?
4. How many photos will I need?
5. In what media are the photos to appear and what are the editors' preferences?
   What are the editors mechanical requirements for reproduction?
   What are the publications' deadlines?

WHAT MAKES A GOOD PUBLICITY PHOTO?

The ingredients of an acceptable publicity photo are difficult to pin down; however, most photographers agree upon a few essential qualities. Each public relations photographer must read into the following paragraphs their meaning for himself, translating the suggestions into photos for his particular needs and publication requirements.

Stopping Power

The college photographer aims for photos with "stopping power." The first basic step, in communication, as already indicated, is to get attention. The cameraman has to get the reader, who is thumbing through the pages of the daily newspaper or the brochure, to stop and look at the college photo. The photographer seeks, therefore, to achieve impact. The picture must hit the reader in the eye—he may be pleased, startled or moved. The best picture gets some reaction—it is not just another routine shot the viewer has seen a thousand and one times. How is this impact achieved? Basing their opinions on their experience, professional photographers suggest many ways, including the following:

Selection

The photographer selects the subjects carefully to get the greatest impact. For his photo he picks the youngest or oldest student, a pretty co-ed, a blonde and a brunette, or the tallest and shortest student. The cameraman may chose one detail or aspect of an event to obtain interest—instead of photographing hundreds of graduating students at the commencement exercises, he snaps a photo of a small child arranging the graduation cap of her mother.

Arrangement of Elements

The cameraman also gets impact through the arrangement of the elements in the pictorial situation. He shows the student bent over the test tube, peering intently into its bubbling contents. Or the photographer selects two or three students in the typing class at their desks, rather than a single student typing away—on the ground that doubles and triples doing the same job create more interest than a single person would. The mouth-to-mouth resuscitation given by a student nurse to a volunteer student-patient on the floor of a shopping center, where the college exhibit is being conducted, provides a live picture.

The cameraman reduces the picture to the fewest possible elements to convey the message. He cuts the number of people to one or two so he can concentrate the reader's attention. He may get impact by correct timing, by releasing the shutter at just the right moment. When the director of the university orchestra raises his baton for the downbeat to start the concert, the cameraman snaps the photo, producing a picture which will be in demand by editors and which can be used in brochures of the music department.

Action

Impact comes most frequently from picturing action. The photographer times his snapping so that his resulting print conveys a sense of movement. The cameraman has "stopped" the event, he has captured the moment of time. The viewer can imagine easily, or supply unconsciously, what went on before and what will come afterwards.

Human Interest

College pictures with a strong human interest element supply arresting power. Photos may reveal only the outward event, but the print also may portray a face showing emotion—happiness, amazement, fear, dejection. These are the unusual values, recognized everywhere. Some college photos suggest the emotion, but spur the reader to take over and supply his own feelings and experiences. The picture tries to arouse the viewer's previous associations with some universal theme, portrayed in the picture.

Unusual Angles

The cameraman stirs interest by shooting familiar shots from a different or unusual point of view. This explains why the aerial shot of the campus, the long-lens telescopic shot of the student reading in the shade of a tree on the campus, are often exciting. The cameraman shows the reader a viewpoint which is new and often revealing.

The cameraman can change his distance from camera to subject. He can move up close, getting a tight-shot which will give impact. By moving up close to the professor who is lecturing, the photographer eliminates the non-essential, distracting details of the classroom. The cameraman may show just the professor's head, mouth and gesturing hands.

The cameraman also can shoot the picture from a low angle. Instead of standing in the usual fashion, aiming his camera from the waist, the photographer can sit on the floor and shoot upwards. This, too, eliminates a cluttering background and gives a fresh viewpoint. In taking a regular picture of a professor and student conferring over an English theme, the cameraman can mount a chair or stepladder and shoot down on the subjects to achieve variety.

The cameraman uses scale to achieve perspective and relative size of objects. How can the height of a rocket be depicted? Beside the rocket he poses a student looking up the side of the mechanism. Other objects, such as trees or a house, may be used to show relative size, but people generate more interest. On the opposite end of the scale, the photographer may show the smallness of a transistor by placing it in the hands of an attractive girl student who holds the object between her fingers.

Format

Sometimes the college photographer achieves greater interest by altering his picture-format. He may have to picture a number of persons in his frame, say, a board of directors at their meeting. He looks through his viewfinder and thinks, "This will make a better horizontal picture," and he shoots the board members around the table. On other occasions, the cam-

Graduation photos are used widely. Some standard shots may be planned ahead, but others have to be taken by the alert public relations photographer as the photo-situations occur.

eraman turns his 35mm on its side so that he can get a vertical photo. He snaps the shutter, getting a format which emphasizes height, strength; and, although narrow in width, the photo has gained effectiveness, for the cameraman has cut out unneeded details and given a lengthy view.

HANDLING ROUTINE SITUATIONS

The public relations photographer often faces routine picture tasks which give him the least opportunity for originality, and he may thus produce photoclichés. Here are some of the repeated news situations:

The Group. The photographer has to picture the new board of directors, or the student council which has just been elected. A news story about the committee being convened for developing the schedule of cultural events for the year calls for a group shot.

The Plaque. The president, or a dean or a student receives an award for active participation in community affairs; or a faculty member gets a plaque for his contributions to science. These news stories require photos.

(Top) The public relations photographer caught this unposed shot of a father taking a picture of his wife and graduating son—also a father.
(Bottom) A posed photo of a mother, who is graduating, holding a program, with her teen-age children. They look either at the program or their mother, she looks at them.

The Handshake. A visiting celebrity arrives and shakes hands, and the president suggests a newsphoto.

The Check. A state or local philanthropist hands over a large check for the construction of a library wing; downtown editors think that this event would make a usable photo.

Ground-Breaking Ceremony. With a black shovel, the governor breaks ground on the new physical education building, a worthy news event suggesting a photo.

Methods of Treatment

News photo-situations such as those outlined above, no matter how important to the college and its president, produce a sameness of pictorial coverage although the standard shots find acceptance in many newspapers and magazines. Repeated photo-situations put pressure on a photographer's originality and imagination, just as the routine news-situations provoke the reporter into creating a different new lead. How can these routine pictures be improved?

College photographers make a number of suggestions to produce pictures which are different. For some situations, the cameraman can furnish background or props, or he can suggest them to those in charge of the event. Before taking the photo of the check-passing, a large picture of the artist's drawing of the new library wing might be set up behind the persons appearing in the photo. The photographer, as indicated before, can get different effects by switching from a waist-high shot, to a low- or to a stepladder-shot. The cameraman can pose adroitly some of the people in the frame. If five persons are to appear in the group picture, four of them may be posed looking at the fifth one. They may be told to stand and converse in small groups. Persons in the frame should be given something to do with their hands. The photographer also may move the group outside to the campus and pose them informally in front of one of the buildings. By controlling the lighting, better effects might be achieved for some routine shots.

The campus photographer, in handling people, must turn into a stage director. Unless he is shooting candid-camera shots, when he catches the subjects informally, he has to pose the people in his pictures. Before the actual shooting, the photographer has to visualize what he wants to get, what impression he wants his picture to make. Otherwise, his photo may have little value and will fail to get his message across.

Photographers find that most people do not understand picture values, but they will follow the photographer's directions if the cameraman shows them that he knows what he wants. Sometimes, however, he may have to ask the subjects to cooperate quickly so that he can get his job done—other assignments have to be filled.

PRINT QUALITY

University photos may have all the necessary and human interest ingredients, but fail to be accepted by editors. The photos do not have good *print quality*. Print quality consists of a number of elements which will be outlined briefly.

Glossy Prints

Newspaper and magazine editors want glossy prints as the high gloss enables the reproduction camera to produce better printing plates. Usually an editor can blow up, or reduce, an 8 x 10 inch print more easily than a snapshot or smaller size photo. Today the trend is for the public relations photographer or agency to submit pictures which can fit into a 2-column size—4-inches wide; or, if justified, 3-columns—6-inches wide.

Color Photos

The trend definitely is toward the use of color photos in many newspapers and in magazines. Color pictures give a greater sense of reality to the person and the news event, and they generate more attention-getting power. Such photos brighten up a gray printed page, making the publication generally more attractive.

CAPTION-WRITING

Although the university photographer makes every effort to take a picture which will be so graphic it will speak for itself, he obtains few such stories. Some explanation of the photo is needed. This explanation merely may identify the persons in the photo. But more than likely the reader must also be informed as to what the action really represents. Two persons are shaking hands—but who are they and what does the handshake mean? Where did the event occur? When did the incident happen? The reader must be told these newsy facts and learn the identification quickly.

This information is typed neatly on a separate sheet of paper and pasted on the back of the photo. Some brief identification is written lightly in ink on the bottom of the backside of the photo. The editor will re-write your caption line, or he will send yours down to the composing room. The picture, meanwhile, goes to the engraving department. This is one reason for typing the caption on a separate sheet. The second is, if you write on the center of the back of the photo, the writing may ruin the picture for reproduction.

If the public relations man plans on wide distribution of the picture, he has an engraving made. Then he has "mats," or asbestos sheets, produced. These can be sent to the weekly newspapers which do not have engraving departments.

PICTURE DISTRIBUTION

Distribution of the college publicity photos should be studied as carefully as the news publicity distribution. The practitioner realizes that each publication editor has likes and dislikes. Some editors prefer routine shots; others are looking for pictures which are unusual, different. Some editors want face shots, others prefer action. Certain publications prefer pretty girls; others do not seek particularly this type of human interest photo. But all want timely photos.

The practitioner raises certain questions in his own mind: What reproduction facilities do the publications have? Do they make engravings themselves? Do they want glossy prints? What size? 4 x 5 inches? 6 x 8 inches? 8 x 10 inches? 2 x 3 inches for faces? Do they want single shots, or will they take a series for the Sunday edition or magazine section?

What days are best for releasing photos? Monday? Thursday? Sunday? Picture pages may be made up on certain days. Weekend supplements are planned a week or more ahead—sometimes as much as a month.

The practitioner asks himself what newspapers or general magazines would be interested in the subject matter of these photos? Are they suitable for local publications only? What state editors, or photo editors, would like these shots? Any specific editors, or departmental editors, such as financial page, or woman's page, or youth page, or sports page editors? Perhaps a trade or professional magazine would find the cameraman's work acceptable.

The photographer might ask, "Is this wire-service photo material?" Would the *Associated Press,* or the *United Press-International* be interested in this picture for state or national distribution? What about feature syndicates, or special photo services?

Here again a study of possible outlets—what they usually publish, the background and interests of the city editors and the departmental and photo editors—will pay off in placing the campus publicity pictures.

Whatever the publication, speed is the watchword. The practitioner notifies the daily newspaper editor or the magazine editor about the event which is coming up, explaining the picture possibilities. Then the campus representative asks if the editor will send out his own photographer. If the editor can't spare one, he may suggest that the pictures be furnished to him for consideration. In this event, the college director arranges with the editor on the timing. What are the deadlines for pictures? If the pictures are promised for a deadline, the director fulfills his promise.

Newspapers

Newspaper editors are looking for pictures with news value. They are looking also for human interest photos, those which have timeliness, are different and maybe have some humor. Newspapers are not seeking fine quality photos with offbeat composition effects. They are not opposed to routine shots, say, of parades taken from unusual angles.

Regular 8 x 10 inch glossy prints with sharp contrasting blacks and whites are most desired, but, as indicated, many editors wish 4 x 5 inch pictures to fit a 2-column layout.

Magazines

Editors of weekly or monthly periodicals are searching for more quality in the photos. Beautiful, attractive pictures are desirable. If they have currency and are related to a current event so much the better. Editors of Sunday supplements, printed on high quality paper, look for quality photos. These editors may be more interested in a sequence of shots than a single photo.

For trade magazines, feature newsphotos will be of interest. The prose article tells the story, the pictures illustrate the points more clearly, more graphically. This does not rule out the photos of people, nor the fine photograph, brilliantly executed. Photographs of the college's business or engineering departments are wanted by commercial and industrial publications.

EQUIPMENT

What equipment does a public relations photographer need? What essentials does his department require to produce top-quality prints? At one time the press photographer and the PR cameraman were identified by their 4 x 5 Speed Graphic press cameras. The large-size cameras were sturdy and produced large negatives. The 4 x 5 camera became the workhorse of professional photographers for newspapers and magazines. At the present time, most public relations photographers have given up their 4 x 5 cameras, or are supplementing them with the 2¼ x 2¼ twin lens reflex or the 35mm rangefinder and single lens reflex as their standard cameras. Photo journalists give two reasons for this shift. First, the 35mm and the 2¼ x 2¼ aren't nearly as bulky and heavy as the old press cameras. In addition, the smaller cameras can be operated with such rapidity that the photographer, using one of them, can shoot at least four times as fast as snapping with his old 4 x 5. The depth of field—persons and scene in the background—obtainable with the smaller cameras is immensely greater too.

The trend today in most photography is toward available-light shooting by which the natural light of the room, produced by sunlight or the regular electric lights, furnish the only light used in taking indoor photos. A quality light meter, hence, becomes a necessity to the public relations cameraman—with it, he can determine how much light is available and what settings to use on his lens. A sturdy tripod, placed on the floor or a table, enables him to open his lens wide and avoid any shake or blurred photo. Many university public relations photographers avoid the problems involved in natural light shooting and continue to use strobe lights, attached to their cameras, or held aloft by hand.

DATE _____

PICTURE NO. _____

PHOTOGRAPHY IDENTIFICATION FORM

_____ College

NAME _____

LOCAL ADDRESS _____ ZIP _____

TELEPHONE NO. _____

HOME ADDRESS _____, (CITY) _____,(ZIP)_____

MAJOR _____	Freshman _____	Junior _____
	Sophomore _____	Senior _____

FULL TIME   PART TIME

_____   DAY ‗‗

_____   EVENING ‗‗   _____

FUTURE VOCATION

HIGH SCHOOL _____

MARRIED _____ SINGLE _____ CHILDREN _____

IF WORKING:

NAME OF COMPANY _____

TYPE OF JOB _____

****

Section of City where you live

East___Northeast___North___Northwest___South___Southwest___Center___

This is a photograph identification form for use by the newswriter and photographer to identify people in the picture.

10

Motion Pictures

WHEN THOMAS A. EDISON WORKED on the kinescope before the turn of the century, he exclaimed, "Now, you can throw away your textbooks. The motion picture will displace them soon!" He thought that motion pictures would be a great educational tool, but we know that they did not eliminate the class text. Instead, motion pictures became a commercial entertainment medium. Many educational films, however, were produced and documentaries were made. Discovering the value of film, industry invested millions of dollars in moving pictures for public relations purposes.

College PR departments have been alert also to the graphic impact of film as a means of telling the institution's story to a variety of groups. To portray the college's programs and facilities, films are produced and shown before high school students and parents. Motion pictures are projected at freshman orientation at the university to give incoming students an overall view of the campus activities. Public relations departments of universities show their films also to the general public and members of government bodies, such as city or county councils. Similarly, special films about particular departments, such as business or engineering, are presented to meetings of trade and professional associations. To arouse the alumni association to support the university, films are projected on alumni night. Likewise, to get support for bond issues for higher education, films are presented to voters and to influential groups, associations and opinion-leaders.

ADVANTAGES OF FILM

The motion picture has distinct advantages as a communication medium for colleges. The picture compels the audience's attention. You

229

Cameraman gets ready for close-up of student writing a brochure—a sequence in *Client File* (see page 235).

cannot help looking at the moving figures on the screen. The film is usually projected in a dark room, with the doors closed and the window curtains pulled down. The movement and action of the film hold the viewers' attention closely, with no other distractions in the room at the time. Members of the audience identify themselves easily with the persons in the film—students and instructors. People in the audience thus are drawn into the film, emotionally and intellectually. They become involved, participate unconsciously in the campus action. The institutional film combines both sight and sound for its impact. The audience sees students, instructors and administrators in action, and also hears their voices and the sounds on the campus, in the classroom and in the laboratories.

The university public relations department is aware that the scriptwriter and the director must translate ideas and general statements into concrete activities of people on the campus. And this lends interest. If the director of public relations wants to show that the instructors are modern in classroom approach—that they take a personal interest in students—the cameraman will take shots of an instructor using visual aids, motion pictures, slides, tape recordings. Then the cameraman will show the instructor holding conferences with individual students, reviewing their work. The audience can easily understand these actions and is convinced of their reality, because the scenes seem to be actually happening, although many of them may have been staged by the cameraman.

The narrative techniques used in the motion picture enable the public relations department to make college education interesting and college activities exciting. The cameraman can use the newsreel technique to tell about the events on the campus for the past year. Departmental work, for example in science, business, engineering, is made exciting by weaving a "plot" or narrative around their activities and by focusing on individual students during the course of a day, a week or a semester.

Perhaps the outstanding asset of the college film is its permanency. Once the film is produced, it can be used by the public relations staff many times. The picture can be shown to a student group this week, and to a parents' association next month. Closely linked to its permanency is the film's portability. You wind up the 300-feet reel, and you put the film into a small steel can, which can be taken to a meeting of high school groups, or shipped by express to an alumni chapter in another state. The film may also be shown as a special by television stations, widening the audience for the message.

The college film reaches a mass audience at low cost. The cost per exposure is decreased considerably because the film can be shown: (1) to many types and sizes of audiences; (2) in many places; (3) over a period of time, whether months or years. In the industrial world, many public relations films have reached 100,000 persons; some motion pictures made for companies have been viewed by more than 10 million people. The Ford Motor Company's public relations film, *American Cowboy*, and *Green Harvest*, produced by the Weyerhauser Forest Products Company, each have been viewed by more than 12 million people in a decade.

A survey by the Film Steering Committee of the Association of National Advertisers indicated that the total cost ranged from one-third of a cent per person and up. The average was $.046. When the films were used on television, the cost per viewer dropped to $.016.

STAFF ROLE

Whether the public relations department has the college film produced by an outside commercial company or whether the motion picture is shot by the department, the director and staff have important roles to play in its planning, production and distribution. The PR department should be acquainted, therefore, with the potentialities and problems connected with film-making, because the staff will be called upon to suggest certain types of film for the university. With his assistants, the director of the department may write the prospectus of a script, outlining its aims, the types of sequences which ought to be included, the audiences who will view the finished product, and the film's running time. As films frequently cause a heavier drain than usual on the college public relations department's yearly budget, the director has to present the case for the picture to the administrators to obtain the additional funds.

Once the go-signal has been given, the public relations director sits in on the film conferences with administrators, with his own cameraman, with the college's cinematography department, or with the outside professional picture company's representatives. With a knowledge of film possibilities, the college director makes intelligent, practical suggestions for the content of the film and its production. Most important, the director and his staffers are needed to assist the camera crew when they set up scenes, as the staff enlists the support of instructors and students and makes arrangements for the use of classrooms and laboratories.

Later, after the shooting and developing of the film have been completed, the director also participates in reviewing the rough film and joins in the editing session which follows. He may even act as narrator for the college documentary.

It is the responsibility of the public relations department to publicize the premiere of the film and, afterwards, to tell the public when and where the picture may be shown or borrowed from the college. If a number of requests come in, the staffman sets up a schedule for the showings. As already mentioned, the public relations department may undertake the production of a long or short film, with the aid of the college's audio visual department, the cinematography department or the radio-television department.

THE FILM PROSPECTUS

The public relations director starts the action by developing a prospectus for the university motion picture. The prospectus helps to focus on the kind of film which the institution needs and it outlines the possible content of the production. The prospectus will be used in the director's conferences with administrators, with the production team of the film company, or with the public relations film crew. The prospectus serves as a guideline as well as a stimulus to thinking about the film. Here is a general outline for a film prospectus, to which the public relations directors of universities and colleges can add according to their needs:

1. *Title of the film.* A tentative title may be originated at the beginning and improved upon later. The director selects a catchy title which captures the idea and spirit he wishes to convey. Instead of "Franklin University—Past and Present," it might be "Franklin University—Where the Action is Today,"

or "Explore New Worlds at Franklin" or "The Exciting World of Franklin College."

2. *Purpose(s) of the film.* The public relations man thinks through and lists clearly the purpose, or purposes of the film. What will be the specific value to the institution? Give information? Provide entertainment and information? Build understanding and gain prestige? Obtain support? Increase campus enrollment of (a) high school students, (b) working adults, (c) women home-makers?

3. *Publics to whom film will be shown.* A campus film may be shown to the public, to high school students or to parents. Perhaps all of these groups would be interested in the same general film. Specialized science films may be shown to students in high school science classes, or to scientists. Films about the music or art departments may find outlets in particular high school classes, or before music and art groups.

4. *Brief résumé of film content.* The film may be a general picture of the college with scenes of campus and classroom activities. Or the film may deal with the music department, for example, showing the activities of this department, students, faculty and ensembles, bands and orchestras in which they participate.

5. *Length of film—running time.* The length of the film is important, as it will determine the number and length of scenes and sequences. It may be a 20-minute production or a half-hour documentary.

6. *Black-and-white or color.* Many documentaries, shot in black and white, do the necessary job. Color is striking and more costly—but it may be worth the difference. Bright colors of women students' dresses enhance the attractiveness of a film.

7. *Silent or sound.* Will you have narration, dialogue, music or a combination of all of these? If a silent film is decided upon, subtitles would be needed. Should you have magnetic or optical sound? (This will be explained later.)

8. *Size of film.* Good pictures may be shot in 16mm or 8mm or Super 8mm. The decision as to what film to use depends on where the film will be shown and on the projectors available there—for example, at high schools or television stations.

9. *Actors needed.* Both actors and actresses are needed for the college film. Usually they are drawn from the administrative staff, the faculty and the students. Sometimes, however, high school students may have roles in the production if the picture involves them. Other films or sequences might incorporate the work of the board of directors, hence they would be called upon to participate in the film-making.

10. *Props needed.* Some auxiliary props will be needed in certain scenes and sequences. The director of the film may call for laboratory and workshop equipment, typewriters and adding machines.
11. *Locations for shooting film.* The locations for the scenes are determined ahead of time and are correlated with them. A variety of scenes, both outside on the campus and inside the buildings lends interest to the film.
12. *Distribution methods.* The public relations man who thinks through the film-production to the end also considers the methods he will use to tell the publics about the motion picture.
13. *Cost of film production.* The film-cost is difficult to estimate The cost will depend in large part on whether the college hires an outside company to do the production work, or on whether the public relations department does the filming and editing.

THE SCRIPT

To get top quality final projection, the college film needs a planned, detailed script before the production begins. The script serves the film director, the cameraman, the soundman, and the actors, giving them an outline of the objectives and scenes to be shot.

The scriptwriter for the public relations department has to have in mind the general aims of the film. Then he visualizes what specific sequences, scenes and individual shots will produce these results pictorially. As the final film consists of a number of sequences and scenes fitted together into a smooth production, the writer pictures in his mind what purpose each scene serves, how it will be acted and what camera work will be necessary.

The writer uses a *story board* for convenience. The story board is simply a corkboard hung on a wall or put on a desk. Each general sequence of scenes relating to one subject is written on a separate card. These cards are then arranged on the story board in the logical order in which the film is to unfold.

The story line can be followed through by studying the story board, giving the writer the opportunity to polish the script before shooting. Individual parts, for instance, can be dovetailed for a closer fit. Scene lengths can be estimated on cards. The scriptwriter can control the pace by cutting down long scenes, or he can give them variety with close-up or medium shots, and with shots taken from various angles. When sound is to be synchronized later, each scene must be long enough to allow for full explanation.

When the story board work has been completed, the script can be written from the cards. The writer produces multiple copies of the script, to be distributed to cameraman, director and actors.

Here is an outline of the major sequences and scenes of *Client File*, a film dealing with the instructional program of the Department of Public Relations and Advertising, School of Business of Florida State University, Tallahassee. Produced by the students and instructor in the department, the 16mm color film was shot with a Bolex camera. Magnetic sound was added in narrative form later and projected on a Bell & Howell 202 magnetic-optical projector.

The film depicted classroom activities, special trips made to a printing plant and to a state government agency using public relations extensively. Then the picture portrayed students developing their own public relations projects, on which they reported to the class in public relations. Finally, footage was taken on Public Relations-Advertising Day, sponsored by the department and various public relations and advertising organizations.

CLIENT FILE

1. Opening Shot—Location Sequence

   Scene 1: Students entering the gate at Florida State University
   Scene 2: Students entering the School of Business building, where the public relations department is housed

2. Classroom Sequence

   Scene 1: Professor Lecturing,
   Using blackboard,
   Referring to Flip Chart Outline, and
   Employing motion pictures
   Scene 2: Class Participation
   Students discuss topic, argue with professor, become involved in an animated scene

3. Special Trips Outside the Classroom

   A. Class Trip to Large Local Printing Plant

   Scene 1: Students enter building of printing company
   Scene 2: Owner and manager discuss plant operations
   Scene 3: Students visit composing department
   Scene 4: Students visit lay-out artist at work
   Scene 5: Students visit photo-offset department where plates are made
   Scene 6: Students visit printing department, watch machines operate

B. Class Trip to Florida Development Commission (advertising and public relations arm of the state)

Scene 1: Students enter the commission's building
Scene 2: Then confer with the director of the commission
Scene 3: They visit News Department
Scene 4: Photographers section
Scene 5: Printing department
Scene 6: Motion picture film department
Scene 7: Radio department
Scene 8: Students visit research department and library where they talk to director

4.   Student Project Sequence

A. Student Who Selects Recreation Division of Florida Development Commission for special report

Scene 1: Student confers with instructor on report after class
Scene 2: Student leaves campus
Scene 3: Student enters Florida Development Commission Building downtown
Scene 4: Student confers with Director of Recreational Projects in his office
Scene 5: Student, back on campus, sits at typewriter and taps out report
Scene 6: Confers with instructor in his office on progress of report
Scene 7 Student at desk produces brochure—makes layout
Scene 8: Student checks with instructor, re-writes some of the material
          Places brochure on class instruction board

B. Student Who Selects Mental Health Clinic For Report

Scene 1: Student goes to Mental Clinic in downtown Tallahassee
Scene 2: Student confers with director in his office on purpose and operation of clinic
Scene 3: Student talks to social worker in his office to learn about his work
Scene 4: Student makes display for clinic, the exhibit to be shown at the County Fair

C. These and other students report on their work at classroom sessions

Scene 1: Students walk up to rostrum, deliver reports, answer questions from audience

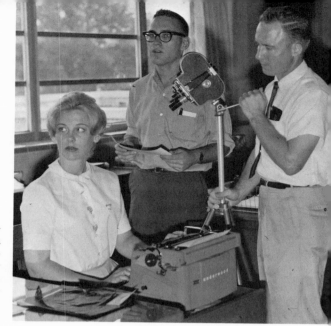

A scene in *Client File*, a public relations film about the activities of a public relations class during one semester. The film was produced by students and instructor in public relations at Florida State University with a 16mm camera.

5. Public Relations-Advertising Day at the University

Scene 1: First Session in auditorium:
The formal speeches by (1) prominent advertisers, (2) public relations men, (3) graduates of the college's public relations department

Scene 2: The special dinner—Speakers Shown—Audience Pictured

Scene 3: The displays of the department

This 20-minute film was edited by instructor and students in the public relations department. The picture was shown to faculty members at the Florida State University School of Business at a special meeting and to students in the School of Business as well as those in other departments of the university who might be interested in the public relations program or special courses of value in their own future professions. The film was also projected at the Florida Public Relations Association at a semi-annual meeting, when officials, after viewing the program of the university, gave $500 to support and to expand the public relations departmental budget.

SCRIPT-WRITING FORM

The script follows a special form, as it is written in parallel columns with "Sound" on right side, "Scene-Action" on the left. Note the time in seconds. All sound is in capitals for easy reading. Here is a sample of one sequence in the film outlined before.

SCENE-ACTION (VIDEO)   SOUND

```
            *************************
            Scene 1 - CLASSROOM SCENE
            *************************
```

5 sec.   (LS) Carol comes in the   NOW HERE COMES A STUDENT
              door of the class-
              room.   WHO HAS PICKED THE RECREA-

                                         TION DIVISION OF THE FLORIDA

                                         DEVELOPMENT COMMISSION FOR

                                         HER CLIENT FOR THE NEXT

         (MS) She checks with   FEW MONTHS...SHE CHECKS
              instructor at his
              desk.   WITH INSTRUCTOR ON THE

                                         SCOPE AND PLAN OF ATTACK...

         (MS) Carol leaves him.   HE APPROVES...AND OFF SHE

         (LS) She goes out of the   GOES ON HER ASSIGNMENT.
              school building.

2 sec.   (MS) Carol walks down the   LET'S FOLLOW HER AS
              footpath in front of
              the building.   SHE GOES THROUGH THE

                                             CAMPUS DOWNTOWN.

```
            ***********************************
            Scene 2 - CARLTON BUILDING OUTSIDE
            ***********************************
```

2 sec.   (LS)(CU) Carol enters the   CAROL NOW REACHES
              Carlton Building.
                                             THE CARLTON BUILDING

                                             WHERE THE RECREATION

                                             COMMISSION HAS ITS

                                             HEADQUARTERS.

```
            *********************************
            Scene 3 - CARLTON BUILDING INSIDE
            *********************************
```

3 sec.   (MS) Carol enters door   AT THE RECREATION
              and talks to Mrs. Jones,
              departmental secretary.   COMMISSION SHE TALKS

                                         TO THE SECRETARY OF

                                         THE AGENCY ABOUT HER

                                         PROJECT.

SUCCESSFUL FILM TECHNIQUES

The scriptwriter and cameraman are aware that a variety of shots provide interest. Several types of shots have been developed by cameramen since the Mack Sennett Days. The long shot (LS) is used for placing the person in the scene. This is usually a wide-angle shot, and shows, for example, the entire campus or a building taken from a distance. In other sequences, the cameraman desires to picture an entire class in action, hence he uses a long shot. The medium shot (MS) is employed to give some variety, with the cameraman coming in and focusing on one student. To get a dramatic effect, and give the scene impact, the cameraman then uses the close-up (CU) showing the face of the student, or her hands on the electric adding machine at close range. With the turret camera, or the zoom lenses, these shots are achieved easily.

The scriptwriter also indicates the angle of the shot, although this is usually left to the discretion of the cameraman and director. A high angle gives perspective, showing the scene from up above: the top of a staircase, the roof of a building. A low shot shows the actor from the viewpoint of the cameraman who is sitting on the ground and shooting up to the top of the building.

Public relations men who produce college films know that their effectiveness depends on the lighting. The lighting can make the difference between a dark, unacceptable scene and a bright professional picture. The cameraman, therefore, makes a special effort to produce well-illuminated scenes. The human eye is deceptive: what appears to be an adequately-lighted scene may be black to the camera eye. The viewer is unaware of the light in the final film, but he is affected by the lack of light. Cameramen take great pains, therefore, to create effective lighting situations. Creative lighting requires imagination and skill.

Many sequences of the university film are shot outside where, usually, natural sunlight is sufficient; but often even outside scenes require some artificial light. Students standing under the administration building's roof which juts out, for example, will appear with dark faces unless floodlights are used.

In a few campus buildings, there is enough light coming in through the windows during the day to do some indoor filming without lights. Large windows give the cameramen sufficient daylight to film students on the far side of a classroom being shot.

CREATIVE EDITING

Many college film production men believe that the moving picture film is *really made* in the editing room. The public relations director, or assistant in charge of film production, takes part in the editing step, because here the film is polished and brought up to a professional level. It may take 10 hours to shoot a film and 20 or more hours to edit it properly. Film editing is just as absorbing and creative as picture-shooting. The film editor's basic problems involve cutting out the film's weak parts—the sections where the scenes are not lit properly and the action seems stilted—and weaving the remaining segments into a smooth-running motion picture. He notes down any shots which are useless because of (1) poor exposure or (2) unsharpness. The film editor needs to run the picture through several times before the final cut.

The object of the editing is to make the events on the film seem as if they actually were happening. Anything in the film which does not look real, very soon breaks the spell, so that people in the audience no longer believe in what they see.

Cutting scenes enables the director to change the viewpoint of the audience, thus adding variety to the film. In the early days, whole scenes were shot from one camera position, and the films suffered as a consequence. Any shots which do not contribute to the story must be hacked out ruthlessly. The editor prunes the finished film of all superfluous scenes, however pretty the photography; for he knows the poor scenes will only weaken the effect of the main story. The pace of the film depends on matching the length of each shot with the events it depicts.

TITLES COMPLETE THE FILM

College public relations men know that a film never really looks complete without titles. They give a polished appearance to the whole work, making the film an individual entity, crediting you for the work you have done, and in a silent film the titles help to tell the story. Subtitles are especially useful for explaining any gaps in the action. The use of subtitles provides a change of pace and sound from the voice of the narrator. An end-title helps round off the film so that it does not just die out when the audience is expecting to see more.

You can buy main titles already prepared on short lengths of film which you splice on to the beginning and end of your own. It is not difficult, however, for the college movie production team to produce its own titles.

Here are some of the titles from a film made by the public relations department of the Community College of Baltimore.

Main title:

COLORFUL EXHIBITS OF
THE COMMUNITY COLLEGE OF BALTIMORE

Secondary title:

Taking the Community College to
the Neighborhoods

Credit Titles:

Produced by Public Relations Department
Dr. Sidney Kobre, Director

Cast of Characters
Students
Administrators, Faculty
Residents of the Communities

Cameramen
Adrian G. Lasker
Sidney Kobre

Lettering Made Easy

Films should have professional-looking lettered titles, available in various forms. Movable letters made from cork, plastic or felt can be purchased. Plastic letters are simple to handle and can be used repeatedly. With adhesive backs or small prongs to fix them to the title board, they come in several colors. Cork letters, which are cheaper, can be used many times if handled with care, and are available in a wider range of sizes with capitals and lower case. Felt letters cling to velvet or similar backgrounds and can be easily removed.

By far the widest range of title letters is available in the dry transfer Letraset and similar series. The director can get almost any size letter. Although they can be used only once, the letters are available with many alphabets and extra letters on each sheet. They are applied by pressure and can be linked up on a transparent transfer sheet. Titles may also be printed on sheets of paper and shot.

Cameramen usually shoot titles by putting on the floor the board with the title and setting the camera up on a tripod over the board. The title also may be placed on a wall and shot. A number of companies manufacture good horizontal titling equipment with lights. These titlers consist of sliding camera supports with a holder to grip the title card at one end. Lights are fixed on either side of the card and at equal distances from it. The director angles the lamps to avoid reflections. Outdoors, titles can be mounted on a transparent plastic sheet and shot with natural sunlight.

SOUND ADDS INTEREST

Sound adds another dimension and interest to the college public relations film, and the public relations director should have an understanding of the types of sound film which can be made, and the pros and cons of each kind. Silent films may be used, with titles being added to explain the scene and the action. But with the application of sound to commercial films and the widespread interest in television, sound becomes essential for most college films. The technical improvements made in adding sound to motion pictures produced both by professionals and by non-professionals enable sound film to be made at a lower cost and with greater ease than ever before. Background narration, live dialogue and music make the campus picture more exciting.

Optical Sound

Optical sound film is produced usually by commercial photography laboratories. The company records the sound at the college, or in the company's own studios, and then, with special equipment, adds a sound track to the film. When projected, the film actuates an electronic lamp in the projector, setting up the sound waves which are fed into the speaker. The optical film can be shown and played on any 16mm sound projector, and there is no danger of an accidental erasure of the sound track. Optical prints can be made from the original film. Most high schools and other organizations before which the college films will be presented have optical sound projectors which can show the films. This is a decided advantage, as the college film can be transported to these locations and projected before large audiences.

Magnetic Sound

A relatively new form of sound motion pictures, magnetic sound film is produced by coating or laminating a magnetic tape on one edge of the film. When sound is recorded on it, the sound can be played back by the projector while the film is shown. The projector, therefore, serves as a moving picture projector and also as a tape-recorder.

Adding sound to the film is easy. Usually, after the script has been filmed and processed in the regular fashion, a magnetic stripe, as indicated, is fixed to one edge of the entire film by a film striping company, or by the public relations department. Then the film is projected. The narrator plugs in the wire of the microphone into the projector and begins the narration, describing the scenes and adding explanation. He may also record music as a background or fill-in to increase the interest. At the proper point, he can incorporate or dub in dialogue recorded on a tape recorder when the original film was shot. The voices and the music are now recorded on the stripe on the film.

After the sound has been added, corrections may be made by the erasure of errors. The film is now ready to be shown and the sound heard. Both 16mm and standard 8mm and Super 8mm film and projectors are available for the use of the public relations department. Bell & Howell, Kodak and Eumig as well as other companies manufacture a variety of dependable magnetic sound projectors which are easy to operate.

Although magnetic sound-on-film is relatively new, in the few short years since the first magnetic projector made its appearance, rapid progress has been made in its manufacture. The full potential of magnetic sound-on-film has yet to be realized. With some experience and proper recording facilities, sound tracks of a professional quality can be made even by small college public relations departments. Magnetic sound reduces the cost of sound-film production to the point where it is within the means of any college which is able to afford 16mm or 8mm silent pictures. Couple this with the inherent ease of magnetic recording, and colleges have the beginning of a new era in the production and use of sound motion pictures.

The increasing use of magnetic sound-on-film will not replace the optical photographic sound-on-film picture, nor will it compete with the commercial film producer. Optical photographic sound is still more economical than magnetic sound if a large number of prints are desired; but in optical film there is no danger of accidentally erasing the sound track. Such film can be shown on television. Magnetic sound, however, opens up new avenues for college public relations departments, as more films, particularly short ones for special needs and for showing departmental operations, will be made.

ADDING NARRATION

The public relations department may write the narrative part of the script, or it can be a joint effort of the public relations director and the commercial film producer. The director remembers that the motion picture is essentially a visual medium, and the addition of a sound track should only enhance, not alter, this basic premise. The film, thus, is planned with the visual presentation as the dominant element. A commentary that is well-written and recorded can make a dull picture tolerable, but it will never take the place of a sparkling, vividly-presented picture on the screen. When picture and sound work well together, the result can be very compelling.

The scriptwriter plans narration as a supplement to the picture, not as a mere representation of what is happening on the screen. We can see that the student is playing on the violin—you don't have to tell us. The director lets the sound track point up aspects of the screen action not evident in the picture. The writer avoids letting the commentary tip off what is going to happen in the next scene. He keeps the comments appropriate to, and timed with, what is happening visually.

The writer keeps the narration brief and to the point, for wordiness tends only to dull the interest of the audience. An apt word or phrase introduced at the proper moment can point up a scene so that, as the audience watches the film, the viewers will fill in and create narration of their own. All details of the college activities cannot be presented. A well-placed word or phrase can conjure up related scenes that never appear on the screen.

Write Narration First

There are two basic approaches in preparing narration for a college film: to write the narration first and then shoot the scenes to fit the narration; or to write commentary for films already completed insofar as the photography is concerned.

In films where the narration is written first, there is a chance for much better flow of the track portion of the film. If the narrative is recorded on tape, the various scenes can be timed and the length of each scene determined prior to shooting the picture. Recording the narration in advance also gives the narrator a much better chance to do a high quality job on this portion of the picture. He can concentrate on what he is saying, without being hurried to keep pace with the projected pictures.

The chief danger in this method is that it tends to put too much emphasis on the sound portion of the picture. If the message being told can be fully communicated with words alone, a motion picture is unnecessary and only a tape recorder is needed.

Shoot Film First

The second approach to preparing narration for a film is the one most often used, with the voice and music being added after the film has been shot. Many university films do not lend themselves to careful planning. They are often shots of incidents as they occur, and the actual film development is not known in advance. It is only when the film record is complete that attention can be given to the necessary verbal description and amplification that would give complete meaning to the picture.

If the public relations director is the narrator, or is helping to write the script, he proceeds to add sound in a series of steps. He first views the film after it has been roughly edited for scenes which are too dark, or under- or over-exposed, or ruined in some other way. He may run the film through the editor or viewer, or he may have the picture projected on a large screen. As each scene appears, he takes notes on the scene content, approximates scene content and points which need verbal emphasis. These notes then form the basis for the commentary.

He now projects the picture for the second time, and using his notes, he talks into a tape recorder conversationally about the scenes being shown. Afterwards, his secretary listens to the tape and copies the script. This rough draft can be corrected and polished.

Using the new script, the director now screens the film again and makes a second tape recording. If a scene is overlong, he may reedit and cut the film, and he may shorten the script. He can leave space for the dialogue which has been recorded when the film was originally shot.

The director is now about ready to record the polished narration. He can record on a tape recorder, with the sound later being channeled into the projector. This step enables him to pick up any errors or repeat any flubs. Or he can narrate directly into the projector. He may narrate himself or secure an instructor or student in the radio-television or speech department for this job; or he may employ a professional newscaster. More than one voice adds interest to the picture.

MUSIC AND SOUND EFFECTS

The director gives careful consideration to the planning of additional music and sound effects. He chooses background music which can greatly enhance the vocal portion of the film. Music, properly used, can create a mood more quickly than other means of communication. Music can be employed in a film in several ways: (1) music can serve alone; (2) it can be used as background in general; or (3) it can be woven into the film alternately with a voice. The music can be recorded on sections of the film, such as for titles or as bridges under scene transitions. The director fits music in where the action is simple and self-evident and needs no words of the narrator. When used as a background for the narration or for dialogue, the music is more or less continuous and is recorded at a much lower volume level than the voice.

Some background sounds can be recorded on campus and used with good effect in the picture. The shot of a busy engineering department may be accompanied with the whirring and clacking of the machines. The sounds can be picked up by the tape recorder and later rerecorded onto the sound track.

THE PRODUCTION TEAM

The public relations director is faced with this important problem: Who should produce the university motion picture? The answer to this puzzler depends on a number of factors: (1) the size of the university or college; (2) the number and kinds of films to be made; (3) the amount of money to be spent on films; (4) the purposes for which the film will be used; (5) the existence of a motion picture department in the institution.

Some large universities, such as Ohio State University, have departments of photography and cinematography; hence, the public relations
film production is turned over to this department. Although other universities have photography departments, the public relations departments give
the actual production of a lengthy film to an outside company. If the department decides to produce its own films, the director may obtain assistance from the audio-visual department, the radio-television department
and other divisions of the institution.

Insiders' Advantages

The public relations department has certain advantages in producing
its own films. Because they live with the university daily, the members of
the department know the inside operations of the institution and know the
audiences who will view the films. The public relations staff is on the campus throughout the year and can film events as they happen. The visit of a
high school student group to the college campus, homecoming week, college convocation, the coming of outside speakers to the campus—all can
be filmed and spliced together in newsreel style. Such a film has a liveli-
ness and spontaneity which a professional job may lack. A film about the
business administration, the engineering, the art or the science departments may be shot for special public relations purposes and for particular
audiences. The cost is low, because the cost of materials is the least expenditure in motion picture-making, and film and striping make up the chief
costs if the film is made by the PR department. The audience is more interested in the message and information than in the technical proficiency.
The development of automatic cameras, magnetic sound striping and
sound projectors makes the job of producing satisfactory sound film easier
than ever before.

Professionals' Assets

The professional commercial film company, on the other hand, comes
into the college and does a complete job. The commercial company's staff
writes the script, or takes over the preliminary one the public relations
staff has prepared. After further study and consultation, shooting begins.
The commercial film organization has the experience and necessary equipment for top-quality film production. The cost is necessarily higher; it is
likely the public relations department will undertake few motion pictures,
however, under these circumstances.

EQUIPMENT

If the public relations department decides to develop its own motion
picture production team for short or long subjects, it will need certain
equipment. The director can follow one of two paths in buying equipment.

He can get the college to buy Super 8mm or 16mm equipment and film.

Generally, the Super 8mm camera, projector and film have certain distinct advantages. This equipment costs less to purchase. Also less costly, Super 8mm film can be shot, processed and shown on a low-cost operating budget. The tendency, therefore, is for the department to take a great deal of film on every occasion and to select what the department needs later. One disadvantage of the Super 8mm film mentioned before, is that the staff member can't show it to large audiences in a large auditorium on a large screen. But this difficulty is being overcome by some 8mm manufacturers who are adding high-powered zoom lenses. Some cameramen claim that the Super 8mm film is not as clear, sharp and brilliant as the larger filmsize. Many outstanding exceptions to this statement are cited by other filmmakers. A significant drawback, however, is that the Super 8mm film cannot be shown directly on television to secure wide audience for the university. Experiments are now being carried on to enable this to be done.

Other film producers claim that the 16mm equipment and film produce clearer pictures and better focused shots. The film can be projected on a large auditorium screen before large audiences. The larger film size can be used, as indicated, on television. Schools and various organizations which would show the university films usually have 16mm projectors. A disadvantage of 16mm film production is that the cost of equipment is greater and the cost of film and film processing is more.

Whatever the merits of the 16mm and the 8mm—and the argument will continue for years—the public relations department needs for its motion picture production and screening a number of essential pieces of equipment.

For Shooting Film:
    Super 8mm or 16mm camera, with variety of lenses or zoom operation
    Lights—floodlights, lightbar and light-on-the-camera
    Exposure meter
    Tripod

For Editing Film:
    Editor-viewer
    Reel
    Splicer
    Titler

Projecting:
    Projector
    Screen

The type of equipment you purchase depends upon the institution's budget for public relations and the frequency and extent to which the equipment will be used. It has been found true by many departments that more motion pictures will be produced when the equipment is owned by, and readily available to, the public relations department. Equipment in good working order will last for years, hence the initial cost may be amortized over such period.

Motion picture equipment is being improved upon constantly by inventors and manufacturers, hence it is desirable to get current information just before purchasing. In considering the purchasing of equipment, public relations directors seek expert advice from manufacturers, professional photo companies and from local dealers.

REVIEWS OF SOME COLLEGE FILMS

In the following pages, we shall present reviews of some university and college films which have been successful in interesting large audiences. In some instances, the films have been produced by the institutions' public relations staffs; in others, by the universities' cinema departments; and in still others, by outside film production companies. These films usually may be borrowed by university public relations departments for detailed study.

Duke University Film

The Duke University's excellent film, *Response to Our Challenge*, is aimed at alumni and other friends of the institution. In color and sound, the 20-minute picture portrays something of the past of the university, its growth, aims and future needs. The clever opening shows an alumnus returning in his auto to the university and depicts what he sees. An aerial shot covers the complex of buildings in Durham, North Carolina, and then the camera returns to the homecoming alumnus who is taken on a quick but satisfactory tour of the buildings constructed during the previous years, perhaps since he was graduated. Long and medium shots are used for variety. The cameraman shows current construction being undertaken, giving long shots of derricks and a close-up of a stonemason's hands working on his materials—all of which give the film considerable flavor.

Ohio State Centennial Film

Another type of film with similar characteristics, but with a different emphasis, was produced by Ohio State University's own Department of Photography and Cinematography, headed by Robert W. Wagner. The picture, *Ohio State University Centennial, 1870–1970*, had as its objective to relate the 100-year history of the college in an interesting pictorial fashion. This was a tough assignment, but with the use of old still photos and motion picture film which, fortunately, had been taken of early campus events, a highly interesting production was achieved. Creativity and imagination went into every sequence and scene, the picture being of absorbing interest to a variety of audiences in Ohio as well as those outside of the state.

The Citadel

Discovering that the previous Citadel motion picture was out-of-date, officials of the Citadel, in Charleston, S.C., decided to produce a new film for public relations and recruitment purposes. The Citadel is a state-supported military school, with strong science and engineering programs.

The production schedule of *The Citadel: Education Plus* lasted over a nine-month school year, as all aspects of the institution's activities were to be portrayed. After an extensive investigation of comparative costs and quality factors, a film-making company was finally awarded the contract.

This effective motion picture opens with a campus scene showing the first week for freshmen, who are assisted by the upper-classmen in becoming oriented. Then the scene shifts to the engineering, science and other classes where the cadets study. Alternating with the educational side are scenes of the students in the physical education program, playing ping pong, and scuba diving "given under expert supervision," rowing, and engaging in rifle practice. The cameraman now turns again to the academic activities at Citadel, depicting the attractive dormitory rooms, the library with its 100,000 volumes, microfilm and foreign language teaching-equipment. The narrator points out that the scholastic averages of the students are high.

One of the best and most persuasive sequences deals with the graduates of the Citadel, as a surgeon is shown at a hospital, a business executive at work in a plant, an editor at a newspaper, a military commander in Vietnam, a senator in Washington, an engineer on a construction job, and a clergyman in his church.

Cleveland State Community College

Using his own ingenuity and resources, Bob Robinson, Director of Public Relations for the Cleveland State Community College, in Tennessee, produced a color film with sound, describing the role of the institution in the community. The 18-minute film, *The Cleveland State Story—Footsteps to Further Education,* was produced for $600 with equipment purchased by the director for this film and for later use. The documentary was shown to 35 different groups since its premiere and was also scheduled on a Nashville, Tennessee, commercial television station as well as on the state educational television network.

11

Radio

PUBLIC RELATIONS DIRECTORS are aware that, to keep up-to-date, their institutions should add radio and television to the other media used to inform the public about campus developments. For most people, the electronic media reinforce or supplement the information and news obtained through print; for many others, the electronic media provide the major, and often the only channel of news communication.

In utilizing the great advantages of the new media, educational PR directors became aware that radio and television bore similarities to the newspaper and magazine, but had important differences. The directors found also that radio and television, both changing rapidly, also differed from each other in scope and methods. Today the university and college public relations directors seek to understand the special values and the techniques of *both* electronic media, for each has something special to offer.

In a small college, the PR director undertakes to write the radio news himself, and produces film clips for television. For the more extended radio and television programs, he makes arrangements with local stations and even participates in the programs when they are presented on the air. He may have the help of other departments at the college for developing such broadcasts. In large educational institutions, desiring to process radio news systematically and to produce a number of radio and television programs throughout the year, he may have on his staff a radio-television specialist who carries out this phase of the department's public relations and publicity work. Some institutions of higher learning have their own radio stations as well as departments of radio and television.

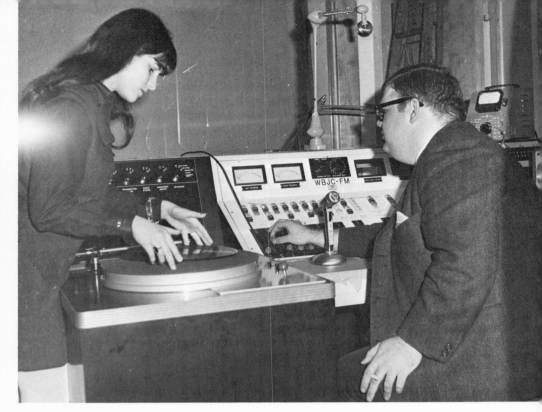

Many colleges and universities have their own radio stations which broadcast college news, features, interviews and music.

PROGRAMS IN THE PUBLIC INTEREST

Both the radio and television station managers know that university and college news is of general interest to the stations' audiences. Most citizens believe in education, and many are now realizing the advantages of higher education for their children and for themselves. Anything which affects their children, therefore, is of interest if it can be presented over the air in an attractive, appealing fashion. The opportunities adults have for learning beyond the high school level are of public concern, and would provide a basis for attractive radio and TV programs. If the institution is a public-supported municipal or county community college, a state college or university, the listening and viewing publics are interested particularly in what is being taught and the quality of instruction that tax dollars are buying. Many radio and television officials, therefore, welcome ideas and suggestions for good, quality programs of general appeal and interest. They believe they have an obligation to give the latest developments in their areas and to inform the viewing public of what is happening of importance in local educational institutions.

Station managers are aware also of the need to present on the air public service programs, or programs in the public interest as they are called officially. By the Federal Communications Commission policies, a percentage of broadcast hours should be educational or cultural. The assumption is that the airways belong to the people. A broadcaster thus may use the airways only under license after showing his qualification for serving the public interest. The FCC awards a license partly on the basis of a proposed program schedule submitted by the applicant. And although a license may be renewed at the end of its three-year term, the license may also be suspended or revoked if the FCC decides that the broadcaster has failed to serve the public interest—or if he has failed to live up to the promises in his original proposal. Rarely, however, have these licenses been revoked, but the broadcasters are aware of the need to provide public service programs and thereby enhance the good reputations of their stations.

Educational programs, involving the university or college, are considered "public service"; hence, such programs help to meet the FCC requirement. News about the institutions, programs that interpret and explain the historical significance of news, or explain scientific and technical developments on campus are in this category.

In this chapter, we will deal with radio programs for colleges and universities; then, in the next chapter, we will turn to the opportunities and problems in producing television shows.

WIDE RADIO AUDIENCES

Radio was once the dominant electronic medium of communication, holding a monopoly over the air, during the 1920's through the 40's—communicating news, plays, special programs, music, and advertising messages. With the rise of television in the 1950's, radio began to lose its dominance, and many persons believed radio would be eliminated from the scene. Although radio broadcasting went into a temporary eclipse, radio made a comeback, finding special audiences and new types of programs. Today radio, going strong, cannot be overlooked as a medium for informing various segments of the public about university and college activities and programs.

Surveys have shown that more than 336 million radio sets are in use. About 200 million are found in homes, while 85 million are operating in autos, with the remainder in public places. Radio broadcasting stations greatly outnumber television stations—more than 4,300 AM stations and 2,700 FM compared to some 650 TV stations.

It is important for the public relations director to understand *who* listens to radio and under what circumstances. Millions of radio sets are turned on in the morning at home by husbands and housewives and are kept on during the day. A daytime college radio program, therefore, can be aimed at the listening women to tell them about happenings at the college, about programs of value to their growing children, about courses the mothers may wish to enroll in, and about cultural events women may desire to attend.

Meanwhile, the car radios are turned on by millions of men and women as they drive to their offices. During the day, salesmen in their autos calling on customers, and many other drivers listen to the broadcasts hour after hour. Thus these men and women drivers may be reached by university radio programs.

During the day and evening, particularly on week-ends, teen-agers flip the radio dials to listen to their favorite programs. The young people may be at home, in the auto, walking along the street, sitting on the beach. The campus public relations representative takes advantage of this listening situation to reach many youngsters who may be interested in college-oriented news, sports, discussion and music programs.

In many restaurants, barber shops and other public places, radio news and music pour in throughout the day and even into the evening, furnishing additional opportunities for the campus representative to appeal to many persons.

CBS Radio To Expand Scope

New York (P)—The CBS Radio Network will add 10 new programs after the first of the year to meet what it says is a growing demand for more service programming.

Some of the new shows will be aimed at specific audiences, such as women, consumers, or businessmen. All of the shows will be informational.

Maurie Webster, a CBS radio vice president, said radio listening has increased and a trend is developing in which FM radio is being used more for music and AM radio more for news and information.

While the advantages of radio as a channel for educational public relations are many, the university director is aware also of radio's limitations. One of the chief shortcomings is that the radio broadcasts lack permanency; you have to be present when the program is being presented on the air. Unless you have the set turned on at the proper time during the day or evening, you miss the college message. This is in contrast to the print media, for you can read in your leisure time about the campus event or the new program in law-enforcement. Likewise, the radio broadcast is presented once, and then usually goes off the air. The news or magazine feature, however, can be read and reread afterwards for details which were missed or not understood the first time.

Commercial Stations

The public relations director and his staff study carefully the radio broadcasting stations in the community, in the county and the state to determine what kinds of programs they use and the types of university-oriented material that station directors might accept. The radio stations may differ in the kinds of programs they broadcast. The director of public relations of an institution located in a small community may find only one or two radio stations available; in a large metropolitan area, he may have as many as 20, both AM and FM stations, to work with, each specializing in a particular kind of program, or offering a combination of appeals.

The educational representative is particularly interested in the newscasts, so that he can fit the campus news into the stations' news patterns. Most of the radio stations have newscasts of various lengths, with some being given on the hour, on the half-hour or every 15 minutes, or all day long.

The college public relations director also studies the musical programs offered. They usually cover a wide range: free-form rock, rhythm and blues; country and western or underground rock. Some may focus on gospel and jazz. At the middle of the musical spectrum, the public relations director might find standard pop; at the other end of the scale, semi-classical and classical music.

The university staff is interested, too, in the longer programs relating to current issues and events, for the staff members may find outlets there for college material.

College-Operated Stations

Some colleges and universities are fortunate in having their own radio stations. The public relations directors of these institutions will find a ready outlet for a variety of programs which the directors can propose to the station's managers. The public relations officer, however, is careful to see that the programs he proposes and the copy he submits to the college station have the same high quality as those he presents to the commercial stations. He assists the college radio news-gatherers and newscasters just as he does the students working on the college newspaper, furnishing news releases and tips on campus news.

DEVELOPING SUCCESSFUL PROGRAMS

The public relations staff members have to have a clear rationale for each college program which they expect to put on the air. There are a number of key questions: What purposes will be served with this program and whom is it intended to reach? In what way will the college benefit from the newscast? How will the concert of the college choir and sym-

Junior College Radio Network Celebrates Third Year

On March 13, 1969, the first broadcast of the National Junior College Radio Network was aired and the system that would link together all two-year colleges with amateur band broadcast equipment was born.

Since that date, WB4GYT of Miami-Dade Junior College in Florida (network headquarters) has broadcast each Thursday from September through June; its mailing list has grown to over 150 schools, including many four-year institutions; and administrators, faculty, and students from colleges in 34 states have had the opportunity to compare curriculums, programs, and campuses.

College presidents have been enabled to compare budgeting, governance, physical plants, and curriculums. Faculty members and course designers have been able to discuss teaching methods and course design. And students have had the opportunity to compare education and discuss current issues.

Perhaps the most important benefit is the responsibility assumed by the student operators of the network as they learn and promote the hobby of amateur radio.

Junior College Journal

phony help the institution? Is the university program on the air to provide information? entertainment? both? Is the program intended to keep the name of the college before the listening public and create a favorable impression of the institution, or is the aim to provide specific information about college activities? Will the program help to increase enrollment of teen-agers? of employed adults? homemakers? Is the aim of the program to entice audiences to come to the college concerts?

By raising and answering such relevant questions, the staff is more apt to find and to design radio programs which will carry out the purposes and gain the objectives.

For news and other programs the public relations staff searches for ideas and information throughout the institution. Unlike the problems of writing for the print media, the staff has to be on the lookout for campus talent to take part in the radio programs. Administrators, faculty and students must be discovered, those who have the necessary ability, the desire and the time to participate in the news, special talk-programs and musical presentations.

Newscasts

The university radio writer makes up a budget of radio news for the day or week, including the outstanding happenings and major developments on the campus, covering less important but interesting events also. Meetings of the Board of Trustees or Academic Council which produce sig-

nificant changes in policy are covered by the college radio staff. Because of
public interest, appointments to top positions are given by the radio reporter. News of important faculty research as well as of student activities
of general interest likewise are reported. The radio staffer may use the
same releases which are distributed to the print media, but he may have
time to develop other news also.

Certain kinds of news may get more prominent spots on commercial
radio than in the newspaper columns. The three-paragraph article on the
theatrical production at the college may be buried in the daily's amusement page, but may receive prominent attention every half-hour throughout the day and evening on the radio broadcasts.

The public relations staff writer follows the radio style in preparing
news for the commercial or college broadcaster. He writes enough for 30-
second or 60-second announcements and, when the event justifies it, produces a longer piece. Many colleges take another route. The staff worker
assigned to radio makes tape-recordings of the news, using his own voice,
or that of an instructor or student. The staffer also gets live interviews with
administrators, faculty and students when they have roles in the events.
The information and interviews are taped and distributed to selected radio
stations.

Special Spot Events

When important events happen on the campus, the public relations
staff contacts the radio station in advance, suggesting live coverage by the
station's own reporters. Special spot events such as dedication of a new
building, an anniversary, lectures of important speakers who come on the
campus. College Opportunity Week and other events outlined in previous
chapters on news, may arouse the interest of the station director or public
affairs director, or news program director.

The university public relations staff assists in making the broadcast successful by providing full written information about the event and the background of speakers, arranging for special interviews. The public relations
staff also arranges for the placing of equipment and getting necessary
hook-ups.

When the stations cannot cover the event on the campus, the university staffer makes arrangements for the coverage by finding out whether
written résumés are desired, whether interviews are needed, whether tapes
would be preferred and what deadlines should be observed.

Interviews

The college staffer is fortunate when he finds stations which have "talk
programs," or "open mike" shows. During these programs radio reporters
interview selected people in the news. They may be government officials,

authors of new books, housewives who have made the news by having unusual hobbies. The subjects discussed may involve current news on front pages, or social and economic problems faced by the state or national government. By studying the programs carefully, the university staffer can find instructors with specialties who may make good interview prospects for the radio reporter. The instructor may be developing or completing some significant research, say, in biology or psychology and would be willing to talk about it. The history department may have a specialist on Africa on its staff who recently visited that continent. The historian may be placed on the talk show when Africa is tops in the news. When new programs of particular interest are introduced at the college, the chairman of the department may be interviewed about the aims of the program and challenges and rewards the courses offer.

If the Board of Trustees or the Administrative Council or the president decides on a new policy or announces a construction program, these actions become news; hence an administrator may be interviewed on the significance and meaning behind the actions.

Panel Discussions, Roundtables

The radio public relations staffer can propose to the station's public affairs director several types of informative panel discussions or roundtable programs which would involve faculty members; or faculty and students; or students. Panel discussions dealing with front-page international and national events affecting everyone, including university people, create interest especially if political scientists, historians and sociologists on the university staff participate. Controversial questions relating to Soviet-American relations, the conflicts in the Far East and the Middle East, the rise of China as a world power, the Common Market in Europe, the problems in East and West Germany and Latin-American issues—all call for discussion via radio.

Other panel discussions relating directly to campus issues and affecting students particularly have been aired successfully over the radio. Student discussions of the drug problem, coeducational dormitories, reform of admissions policies, improvement of curricula and teaching methods are worthy of being broadcast. Equally important as subjects for roundtables are causes for student dissent on the campus as well as the student effort to achieve greater participation in university policy-making. Such panel discussions can be sparked by special events on the campus, such as College Opportunity Week.

Audience Participation

A rapidly growing type of program is radio-audience participation shows, in which listeners are invited to telephone to the station. They participate in the discussion or ask questions of the guests. Originally a small-town radio station program, this format spread rapidly to larger cities. The university's public relations representative can propose an interview with a college official, faculty member or student, or he can suggest a panel discussion, to be followed by questions from the telephone audience.

Dramatic Shows

The radio staff writer can be on the lookout for opportunities to present over the air excerpts or acts from the theatrical and musical productions at the institution. Airing of such programs would serve to bring attention to the institution and appeal to high schoolers interested in theatrical work. If the production were to be open to the public later, the radio program also would stir other listeners to attend the performances.

Musical Programs

The wide range of radio stations devoted to music enables the public relations representative of the college to get all types of campus musicians on the air—ranging from underground rock to pop to classical. The public is always interested in hearing qualified individual singers or instrumentalists. Some radio audiences would like to hear wind or string ensembles or combos. Most universities and colleges have large choirs and symphony orchestras which are worth listening to, and can get hearings on the air if promoted by an alert public relations representative.

With the cooperation of the music department and by contacting students, the representative may find a "hot guitarist" who is tops, or a folksinger, or a gospel choir who give superb performances, hence arrangements can be made to get air time for these musicians. University representatives can build a series of programs around central themes, such as "Masterpieces of Music," "American Folksongs" or "The Modern Sounds." Musical programs over the air demonstrate the kind of quality instruction being given at the college and show the musical talent on the campus.

Sports Programs

Many colleges and universities have their own sports publicity department, working under the direction of the general public relations director, or constituting an independent organization. Local radio stations may be willing to broadcast a running account of the sports events on the campus, or take a tape of the games played at home or in other cities. News and sportscasters welcome material on participants in the baseball, football, basketball, track events; the newscasters look for stories on the forthcoming contents and final scores. Because of their general interest, special events honoring campus lettermen are covered by the radio newsmen.

WORKING WITH COMMERCIAL STATIONS

In working with commercial stations, the university staffer assigned to the job makes contact with the program managers and public affairs directors, just as the newspaper PR writer does for his medium. By conferring with the radiomen, the university representative learns what are each station's preferences in news and special programs. The staffer finds out the proper lengths for news stories, and the deadlines for copy; he learns about the arrangements that can be made for tapes.

The representative may go to the station to explore campus program possibilities. Or he can prepare a definite plan for college programs, perhaps furnishing brief résumés of the content, and listing the campus participants if any would be involved. The written suggestions would provide a basis for the station director or program manager "to shoot at." He can accept a suggestion as is, or modify it. The college representative should be aware that the program manager can give worthwhile tips for increasing the interest and maybe widening the public for the program. The radio manager may reject the program idea—a decision which the university representative takes in stride, without rancor, because he knows that he may be able to walk around to the next radio station and get an enthusiastic acceptance for the program.

The university public relations department does not make the mistake of assuming that the program which has been accepted by the radio station director will get a large and automatic audience. A certain number of people who follow the programs of the station will be tuned in when the campus program is broadcast. But a larger audience can be developed. The university staffer can help to draw attention to the campus program by promoting it in a systematic fashion.

The public relations department can write and distribute a general news release for daily and community newspapers. Some editors feel that radio is a competitor and, therefore, consign such news immediately to the wastebasket. In other instances, the city editor or radio-television editor will accept and use such news, as it involves an educational institution. The news of the radio program may run in the radio news column, or as news in the radio-television page. The program may find space in the regular city section.

The radio station can be given advance spot newscasts telling about the upcoming panel discussion by faculty members or the concert by the campus symphony orchestra.

Attractive announcements about the broadcast can be mailed to leading citizens, high school officials and counselors, organizations, selected alumni, and other friends of the college. Posters can be printed and placed in strategic locations off-campus as well as on-campus. The public relations department may prepare a special release about the program for the student newspaper, furnishing photos of the participants.

WRITING STYLE

When radio news emerged in the 1920's and 1930's, it was written by men trained in the newspaper tradition. Radio news first was fed to the stations through the newspaper wire services, and later through radio wire services which were but stylistic copies of newspaper writing. Gradually, however, it became apparent that radio news *was not just spoken newspaper copy*.

The most distinctive feature of newspaper writing, for example, was the "inverted pyramid," in which the most important facts were told first, followed by the lesser facts in descending order of importance. The first sentence included the five "W's": Who, What, Where, When, Why and sometimes How. The important information was stacked into the opening sentence, and then expanded block by block. The story could be cut from the bottom, without the reader's losing important facts, or the gist of the news.

Radio news had to grab the reader's interest immediately, but he could not absorb, through his ear, all the 5 "W's." Radiomen discovered that, after a concise opening, a narrative treatment of the event would be more natural, for that is the way one person tells about an experience to another individual.

Further, some words or word-parts which look perfectly good in print felt awkward on the tongue—"youths," for example. A newscaster ploughing through a long sentence must catch his breath in the middle, a psychological fact which a newspaper writer need not consider.

The radio listener, moreover, cannot absorb long, complicated sentences with many modifiers and qualifiers. Lengthy phrases or clauses between subject and verb, or between transitive verb and direct object, cause listeners to have difficulty in comprehending the meaning of the sentence coming over the air. For instance, this sentence would make a hard one to listen to:

> President John Brown, of State University, who visited Mills College after a talk with Congressman Jones, cancelled all other appointments.

Over the years, radio newswriters altered newspaper style to suit their own medium. Whatever worked practically was used, whether the style broke with old tradition or not. In the following pages, we will point out some of the main characteristics of the style of radio news writing with which the university staff should be familiar; these characteristics and techniques are applicable also to writing for television.

Main Characteristics

Immediacy. Radio's chief contribution to news communication was, and is, immediacy. Radio can bring the news to the audience more quickly than can newspapers, which are governed by a time element determining that editions be printed at stated intervals during the day. Some dailies have as many as nine editions. Radio news can be broadcast, however, more frequently—say, every half-hour. The announcer also can go on the air even more quickly and often to bring the latest developments. The newscaster thus tells the news while it is happening or relates it immediately afterwards.

Aware of this, the university radio newswriter gives the fast-breaking campus events quickly to the radio news editor, or he aids the station's own reporter in gathering and transmitting the institution's news event while it is happening, or shortly after it has been completed. The event may be the ground-breaking ceremonies for a new building, or the convocation speech made by a distinguished guest. Radio may cover the university president's important report to the faculty and students, or the meeting of the board of trustees when weighty far-reaching decisions are made. Radio covers quickly also the significant crime conference or scientific session on the campus. The station's news editor wants the announcement of the new medical discovery at the School of Medicine as quickly as he can obtain the news.

On the Scene. University radio news is written so that the listener feels he is on the scene. The news is highly personal, as the listener hears the voice of the newscaster or the taped interview with the college president, for the sound comes right into the living room, auto or wherever.

Simple, Clear Style. Radio news is written simply and clearly, for it must be understood instantaneously. The campus newswriter avoids all flowery style and he sticks to a working-vocabulary of one- and two-syllable words. While radio news does not have a particularly literary flavor, the campus staffer can use color to create a scene or portray how a faculty member or student looks. The writer uses strong active verbs to depict the live action going on. While written quickly, radio news does not have to be sloppy or ungrammatical.

Use Present Tense. In radio news, the campus staffer uses the present tense whenever possible. The best radio news is that which covers the news while it is happening. The university radio writer, therefore, employs various technical devices to bring out this feeling of timeliness and immediacy.

On a morning broadcast, he uses, "The Board of Trustees is meeting today . . ." or, "In just a few minutes the Board of Trustees will meet to decide . . ." On an early afternoon newscast, when the meeting has been going on for a few hours, the announcer says, "Right now the Board of Trustees of ―― College is meeting to determine policies affecting hundreds of new students. . . ." Or, "At this moment, the Board of Trustees is . . ." If the meeting has just concluded, the announcer on the 6 P.M. show may state, "The Board of Trustees' meeting is now over. President Raymond J. Smithfield banged the gavel down a few minutes ago. Important decisions came out of the meeting. . . ."

As radio news developed, experienced writers recognized that consistent use of present tense was illogical, and a swing away from present tense became apparent. Today, some stations insist on the present tense being used. Other news editors have returned to the past tense for verbs. Still others have adopted the practice of dealing with individual news situations as they arise, using the most logical tense—present, past, past perfect, or future.

In striving for immediacy, the campus writer doesn't use the present tense for the past tense in an illogical or awkward fashion. In some university news, accuracy and clarity demand past tense.

Accuracy. The radio writer is governed by the same high standards controlling the newspaper reporter. The campus writer for the air seeks to be accurate in all his facts and in all his figures relating to the institution. He avoids any exaggeration just to impress the listener. The represenative does not state the enrollment figures as a "record-breaking 4,000" or "whopping 4,000" when the enrollment has reached 3,500, representing more of a "steady increase" than a "spectacular jump" over the previous year's figures.

Brevity. Because of the conditions under which radio news is broadcast and listened to, most radio announcements and news bulletins are short. Hence, the college radio writer compresses his information into a brief, concise statement. All excess verbiage, all excess and detailed facts are omitted, particularly in the short news.

The campus writer knows it is a mistake to assume that writing news for radio is a much easier task than writing for other media. Radio newswriting demands greater compression, which calls for greater skill. The radio writer must develop the knack for being clear at all times. This does not mean always keeping sentences brief. Generally speaking, however, a short sentence is more likely to be clear; therefore, short sentences are preferable. But it is possible to be brief and still unclear. Some fairly long sentences are easily understood. *The final test is not how long but how clear.*

Announcements and Newscasts

Straight radio newscasts have evolved into the following time periods: 30-seconds; 60-seconds; 1-minute; 5-minutes.

You can't get many details in the brief broadcasts, but the popular 5-minute newscast allows for a longer university program. Some of the newscasts confine themselves to international and national news on one broadcast and, on the second broadcast, focus on local happenings. On many other stations, a combination of out-of-town and local news events is presented over the air. The university representative studies the local programs to learn where his newscast might fit best.

Pad or Filler Items

The news editor of a daily or weekly newspaper needs additional news to fill out pages in an emergency, for he can't tell in advance how many columns of type he will be allowed for the edition. The radio newscaster figures out as closely as he can the number of items he needs for a broadcast, but he may talk too fast or run short of news. He needs, therefore, filler or pad items. If the university news has been sent in, and is on the radioman's desk, the institution's news may be used.

MEASURING COPY

The campus writer has to determine as accurately as he can: (1) the number of words, and (2) the number of seconds or minutes his radio copy will require. There seems to be no agreement on the number of words a "typical" newscaster should read in one minute. One large station says its studies show 175 words-a-minute is ideal. Other stations prefer a count as low as 150; but some newscasters average even more than 175. Hence, the campus writer has to check with the radio, or TV, news editor to find out the policy of the station as to the number of words a minute, so that the writer will have some guidelines for his copy.

Here is a practical way of fitting copy to time:

Set the typewriter margins at 10 and 75. That setting should give you an average line of 10 words. The newscasters will read an average of 15, 16 or 19 of these lines a minute. Therefore, you can tailor your copy to station policy by counting the number of typed lines.

Let us assume that station policy will be 16 lines per minute. You will need:

For a 10-minute broadcast, 160 lines . . . 1,600 words approximately
      5-minute   "   80 " . . . 800 "   "
      1-minute   "   16 " . . . 160 "   "
     30-second   "   8 " . . .   80 "   "
     20-second   "   6 " . . .   60 "   "
     10-second   "   3 " . . .   30 "   "

NEWS RELEASE

OFFICE OF THE PRESIDENT   RELEASED BY :
                                              Public Information Office

Public Service Announcement
(Subject)
 Release No_____
(Date)

_____

Spot Announcement   DO NOT USE AFTER_____
_____ Seconds

ANNCR:

SAMPLE OF 30-SECOND NEWS FORM

SPOTS -- NEW COURSES   NEWS BUREAU
EVENING DIVISION

30-SECONDS

THE AMBITIOUS MAN OR WOMAN WHO WANTS TO GET AHEAD IN BUSINESS,
INDUSTRY OR THE PROFESSIONS WILL HAVE THE OPPORTUNITY AT THE
EVENING DIVISION OF THE COMMUNITY COLLEGE.   ENROL-
LMENT BEGINS AT THE LIBERTY HEIGHTS CAMPUS ON MONDAY, JANUARY 27
AND CONTINUES THROUGH THE WEEK. CLASSES BEGIN ON FEBRUARY 3.
THE COURSES SHOULD INTEREST PERSONS CURRENTLY EMPLOYED WHO WANT
TO LEARN MORE ABOUT THEIR VOCATIONS SO THAT THEY CAN SUCCEED.
THOSE LOOKING FOR NEW CAREERS MAY ENROLL AND EXPLORE NEW TYPES
OF POSITIONS. COURSES ARE OFFERED IN SUCH SUBJECTS AS COMPUTER
PROGRAMMING, DRAFTING AND ENGINEERING, ELECTRONICS AND FOOD
TECHNOLOGY. BACKGROUND COURSES FOR GENERAL KNOWLEDGE MAY BE
STUDIED. THESE INCLUDE PSYCHOLOGY, SOCIOLOGY, ENGLISH, AMERICAN
LITERATURE. DON'T WASTE YOUR EVENINGS! ENROLL AT THE COMMUNITY
COLLEGE.

12

Television

Television provides an exceptionally effective channel for communicating the university story to large and varied audiences. Television combines sight and sound and color to project campus activities and events to many people—enabling them to see and to hear happenings in the classroom, laboratories, music studios and so on. Watching the broadcast, audiences get a sense of identification, a feeling that they are there on the spot watching the action. The entire campus appears to be brought into their living rooms.

Of particular value to the public relations representative is that, as studies have shown, information obtained through visual broadcasts *is understood better and is retained longer* than through any other medium. By the use of television, the college representative can therefore reach wider audiences. Television watching (as much as five or six hours daily) has become a habit with millions of families, and the statistics show the rapid growth of this medium.

The PR representative needs to familiarize himself with the TV stations and their personnel with whom he will deal in getting his news and special programs on the air. Moreover, a general understanding of the techniques of preparing audio and visual materials that will enhance the value of the campus program is essential for successful public relations via television.

Time is the commodity television stations have to offer and to sell, just as space is the "product" of newspapers and magazines. The PR representative therefore seeks to get the best available time for his institution's news and special programs, keeping in mind that even if some of the "best"

266

viewing hours (so-called "prime time") may be unobtainable, he will still be able to attract large audiences in other periods of the day or evening. For example, possibilities of reaching, in the morning, women audiences for colleges exist but have not been fully explored by the directors of institutional programs. There are also the late night and early morning hours. It is of interest and importance to note that viewing habits of television audiences are changing rapidly, with more viewers waiting up for late shows than ever before. Often television time is open to campus programs on Saturdays and Sundays; university relations people may find large audiences listening and watching during these periods too. Campus representatives remember that a broadcast even on these and other periods will reach larger audiences than the usual academic meetings, held at the college or elsewhere.

EDUCATIONAL TELEVISION STATIONS

More than 200 educational television stations, affiliated with National Educational Television Network (NET), broadcast over UHF channels and provide media for exciting and informative university programs of various kinds. These publicly supported stations were established to provide educational and cultural programs not usually available on commercial stations. A station assigned to one of the reserved channels must function on a non-profit basis and make its facilities available to public schools, colleges, universities, and other educational agencies in the broadcast area. Almost all of the nation's major metropolitan areas have at least one ETV outlet.

From early morning until late afternoon these stations generally carry instructional programs for school use. In the late afternoon and evening, they offer programs of various kinds for home viewing by adults and children. This non-school programming for home audiences presents certain well-defined opportunities for the public relations programs of universities and colleges. Many ETV stations, seeking to give a balanced presentation, are providing considerable air time to minority groups, and have built wide followings among them.

The campus representative submits ideas for programs to the managers of the educational television stations, just as he does to commercial station officials. ETV stations may provide facilities for the production of the university program, although station funds for elaborate documentaries are frequently very limited. A finished film may be submitted by the university, however.

Because of the cost of college documentaries, another avenue for support of the college programs should not be overlooked by the campus representative. The educational television station manager and the representative, working cooperatively, may be able to find a foundation, a community-minded company or individual to underwrite the university program. Such programs afford foundations and enterprises—such as utilities, banks, savings and loan associations, insurance companies—an unusually good opportunity to build their own public relations to back up their community-minded and educational support.

Time on educational television is not for sale, and products cannot be advertised, but the underwriter is identified on and off the air with the program or series—screen credits consist of opening or closing visual or audio identification, or a combination of these, consistent with the policies of the Federal Communications Commission. Such identification with the program or series continues through its life on the air—ETV stations frequently repeat a program and often replay it several times in succeeding years. Furthermore, the underwriter's name stays on the print when it is circulated to civic, professional, governmental and school groups for non-broadcast use.

The public relations representative of the campus can point out, too, that the underwriter's name will appear on publicity and promotional material, and on newspaper tune-in advertisements for the program. The sponsor's name also appears on booklets, folders, book lists and reading guides which can be published.

Some universities have radio and television stations holding either educational television or commercial licenses and are able to present a variety of campus programs on the air.

PLANNING THE PROGRAM

Intelligent use of television requires that the university public relations personnel plan carefully the institution's air programs. Before soliciting a station for time, the staffer must resolve certain questions through conferences with other staff members, and with administrators and faculty members if they are on the public relations advisory committee, or would be participants in the program. At the initial conference all angles of the TV program are discussed and on the basis of this, the staff members write a preliminary proposal or presentation. This can be used in later meetings with the faculty people and with television station officials.

Aims of the Program

A clear statement of the objectives of the university program should be made first, focusing on its value to the institution and to the community. In presenting the program later to the station officials, it is essential to stress the general and specific interest the program can generate, and particularly the community needs the program would fulfill.

The program's intent may be to keep the public informed about what is going on currently at the institution. The proposal may stress the fact that the program will keep the public posted about the educational opportunities open to them, leading prospective students to enroll. A program may show the progressiveness of the institution by portraying innovative techniques used in classroom and laboratory. Another program may depict the university's contributions to the economic and cultural life of the community. The broadcast may portray the valuable research being conducted in the campus laboratories, research which may later prove highly beneficial to all citizens. In a roundtable discussion, participated in by faculty, the telecast may provide background for public understanding of current international or national events and social problems being tackled in the local community or the state.

Audience Selection

The public relations officer should determine at what audiences the programs are being aimed. The term "general public" is broad, and it would be preferable to break this up into a series of smaller segments—such as teenagers, high schoolers or college dropouts, adult employees, home-makers, concert-goers.

Content of Programs

Here the campus representative pours in the best thinking of the staff and advisors. He specifies whether the program will consist of news, a special, a documentary film, a roundtable discussion or panel. He may focus on one department, or upon the research activities of a number of the departments. The program may deal with the audio-visual methods used by certain instructors. It may be concerned with the 25th anniversary of the college and show the origins of the institution, its growth and its future plans. An outline of some of the scenes inside and outside the buildings could be presented in the proposal.

Manpower Needs

Unlike the newspaper or magazine article proposal, the television plan has to include the manpower requirements for the program. The staffer thus would include the administrators, faculty members and students who might be involved in the telecast.

Visuals and Other Equipment

The representative knows that the college television program would be made more attractive if visuals were used; hence, he tells about the maps, charts, slides, photographs which can be used and mentions where they can be obtained. He may or may not raise the question of preparation of the slides for television use, preferring to leave this to a later time.

If the program calls for pieces of equipment from the science laboratory, electronics workshop, machines from the business department, or selections from the art gallery, this information would be covered in the presentation.

Promotion Plans

With the aid of the news writers and brochure producers the staff outlines some definite promotion plans for the program to supplement those of the station. Well thought-out plans, to help build large audiences, would arouse the interest of station managers. News articles for dailies, weeklies and magazines may be written by the station or the university's news bureau, and news photos of the participants may be taken by the cameraman. The program may be tied in with other organizations. Letters, brochures and posters may be sent to local and area high schools, calling attention to the television program as of interest to principals, teachers and students. Business, professional, civic and religious groups may be contacted with mailings. Posters and exhibits may be placed in libraries and shopping centers. Internally, the story of the broadcast may be told to faculty and students through campus publications, such as the faculty newsletter and student newspaper. The alumni magazine may carry an article and pictures on the telecast.

Financial Commitment

The program may require no funds, but usually money is needed for producing photographs and visuals. Other expenses may be needed for film and film processing. Professionals may have to be hired for camera work and even narration on documentaries produced by the institution. Although no final figures would be available in the early planning stage of the program, nevertheless some thought might be given to the financial requirements.

PLANNING A COOPERATIVE PROGRAM

Sometimes television managers do not wish to give time for a special program to one institution of higher education. The manager may suggest that the program you propose for your college be broadened to include other similar institutions in the area. Broader representation in a special film or on a panel or roundtable program, for instance, will attract a larger audience, he points out.

You can anticipate this suggestion in some instances by widening your original proposal. The staffer then can contact the public relations personnel of other institutions, outline the program and find out if they are willing to cooperate on the venture. More work will be required to round up the cooperating members and to hold joint meetings, but the effort may be worth it, because of the greater chance of the program's being accepted by the station and, indeed, the wider audience which can be built.

The Community College of Baltimore designed a joint program to include representatives of area community colleges. The program, developed for Community College Opportunity Month, was initiated by this author and carried out by Counselor Lewis P. Mulligan in cooperation with Public Affairs Director David Stickle, of station WMAR, Channel 2, the CBS affiliate in Baltimore.

On the final program were faculty and students from Anne Arundel Community College, Essex Community College and the Community College of Baltimore. With Mr. Mulligan as moderator, the panel discussed questions raised by students about the various college-transfer and career-programs at the institutions, fees charged, extra-curricular activities. Many in the television audience said afterwards that a sound, thorough over-all view of the community college opportunities in the Baltimore area was given, and the program was made interesting because it had a variety of people, involving students and faculty who answered typical questions for which students wanted specific answers.

The 14 community/junior colleges in the state of Maryland joined together to produce *Where The Action Is*, a 30-minute film in color. Each college provided its share of the funds to make the film, which showed the academic and extra-curricular activities at the institutions. It was a professional film that traced briefly the beginnings and growth of each college, then portrayed in graphic style live campus scenes. The film was shown on the Baltimore station WMAR-TV, a CBS affiliate, several times and later on TV stations throughout the state. Prints of the film were made and shown to high school and other groups by all the colleges in recruitment drives in their own communities.

THE COLLEGE WORKING STAFF

The public relations director, as indicated previously, may initiate the television programs for the campus, and may carry out the full assignment or part of the assignment himself. If he has a small staff, he may confine himself to writing the regular news releases for television stations and notifying the public affairs directors or news directors of upcoming events worthy of consideration for broadcasting. If a station agrees to coverage, the PR director may assist the television news reporters and cameramen with their heavy equipment when they arrive. If the director has a special feature program of particular interest to television audiences, he may write the proposal for consideration by the station and attend conferences with the officials.

In large institutions, the public relations director may assign a staff member to the television jobs and place the responsibility on him. In still larger institutions, which recognize the value of television as a medium and wish to have extensive TV coverage, the PR director may obtain funds to employ a director in charge of planning and executing television (and

radio) programs for the university. Where the university has a cinema department for instruction, cooperation of the chairman may be secured for
the production of campus television programs. The motion picture and
photography services of the university may assist, and the active participation of the institution's television station may be sought.

The resourceful staffer responsible for television broadcasts scours the
campus for practical program ideas. He can be as creative in his approach
as his ability, experience and training allow. Going about the job systematically, he checks all campus calendars and all news releases aimed at the
print media, to size up the possibilities for telecast news and special programs. Some news releases written for the dailies may not be suitable for
television; other news will fit into the stations' patterns. The staffer studies
carefully the composition of the college, its faculty and student activities.
Knowing the potential of television and having an understanding of what
stations want, as well as what they can and cannot do with their facilities
and equipment, he selects the university programs which he believes will
be acceptable to station managers.

WORKING WITH STATION PERSONNEL

The college representative should know something of the organization
and facilities of typical television stations, for he has to contact and work
with key personnel. The representative should become acquainted with the
station manager of a local TV station, for he is comparable to the managing editor of a newspaper, and he has control over the entire commercial
and programming operations of the station. It cannot be expected, however, that the manager will go over details of the college program; usually
he prefers that it be discussed with the operating department. But the station manager may have an overall influence on programming; and if he is
acquainted with, and has a favorable impression of, the representative and
of the university, the manager may pass the word down the line to support
the educational institution all the way.

Programming Department

Key man in the station is the program manager. He is the person with
whom the representative deals, and he is responsible for the scheduling
and supervision of the staff.

The public relations officer will work also with the production director, who is in charge of all directors and responsible for all creative departments, such as the art department, which may make slides for the educational project. The production director may be called the production manager, supervisor or coordinator in various stations. Another key executive
is the producer, who is directly in charge of specific programs, such as the
university's. Directly responsible for getting the format of a show into final

form is the director. He will be in charge of rehearsals of the college show, directing it from the control room. Staff announcers present the information before the opening and closing of the show.

Public Service Department

In many stations, the public service department will handle the educational program. The director of this department, which is sometimes called the public affairs department, clears all programs of public interest and has slides for the university prepared if they have not been furnished. In smaller stations, the program director or staff director doubles in brass and serves as the public service coordinator.

News Department

News reporters frequently combine a number of functions. They have announcing backgrounds, hence serve as staff announcers. Some reporters, however, shoot pictures in addition to covering the news with a pencil. In the news department the public relations director may have contact with the news director, the news editor, or the newsmen who do the broadcasting.

Developing Good Relations

Campus representatives seek to develop good working relations with the station's personnel. Representatives try to establish reputations for reliability and honesty in their dealings. Through their actions, the college representatives show they are cooperative, and they demonstrate that they are prompt in keeping appointments and in rounding up "talent" on the campus for the telecasts. College representatives make it a point to deliver on all promises and commitments.

The representatives give evidence that they have a sound knowledge of their institutions' operations, programs and personnel and are current on what is going on. The campus representatives also show enthusiasm and a belief in the aims and value of their educational institutions. Station managers say that lack of technical television knowledge is not an important drawback. If you have a worthwhile program, the stations usually will give you every assistance in producing the program on the air.

The college representative should not feel that television people are too busy. They *are* busy, hence appointments must be scheduled ahead of time. They will find time to talk to a representative of an educational institution who makes an appointment in advance.

The college representative should never make the mistake of assuming that Federal Communications Commission requires the television station to carry all the public service material submitted, for it can select what it wants to broadcast. Most stations exceed the FCC requirements and prefer to feel that they are doing a genuine service to the community with their public service programming. A station manager would resent any implication that he had to be forced to have a public conscience.

CONFERENCE WITH THE PROGRAM DIRECTOR

For the college representative seeking to make contact with a television station for the first time, certain steps are taken to insure a favorable reception and response. Having developed the general idea for a program and having worked out the specifics as far as he can go, the PR staffer writes a letter to the program manager, briefly describing the program, how it will meet community needs, the general intent the program would have, and he gives a few details about the target audience. The representative asks for an appointment. Even when the campus representative is acquainted with the station personnel, a brief letter outlining the general proposal would be desirable, as it gives TV officials something definite to consider.

At the conference with the station executive, the campus representative gives him the written presentation of the program for examination and also asks for help and suggestions. The station director usually is stimulated by the challenge and offers some excellent points. He may outline what additional details the program should contain and a particular slant or angle it might take. He sizes up the proposed program from the standpoint of the station's facilities, and probable manpower needs and cost.

By the end of the meeting, the campus representative should have learned whether the station would be interested in producing the program and, if so, what people and materials the college should provide. If spot announcements about the program will be involved, does the station desire to write them, or will the college public relations staff furnish them? The public relations representative makes sure that he has a clear understanding of what the station expects of the college. Frequently, the program director states that he will have to confer with other officials before determining whether the station will cooperate on the project.

After the meeting, it is wise to write a letter summarizing your agreement and restating what you will supply and when. This insures against misunderstanding and subsequent mistakes. If the go-ahead signal has come through at the first conference, or arrives by mail or a telephone call, further meetings can be planned. If the program is rejected by the station, the campus staffer may ask for another conference, or he may transmit the proposal to another station. On some occasions, the station official may turn down the original proposal but offer to produce at a later date another program with a different slant or emphasis. Come the later date, the campus staffman asks for a conference to develop the new program.

PREPARING NEWS PROGRAMS

In his contacts with the television news directors or news editors, the campus representative learns something about the form the stations prefer in releases, their deadlines and how they like to receive material. The representative listens to each station to check on the kinds of news programs each uses so he can decide what kinds of campus news should be sent to the various stations.

News Standards

The commercial TV news director considers a number of elements in deciding whether or not to use a story. Certain constant factors make an item worth using, factors which are similar to those employed by the city editor or news editor of the daily or weekly press. The television news editor looks for: (1) timeliness; (2) general interest; (3) unusual quality in the news event. Sometimes the campus news may bear on other national educational news the editor has received over the television wire. He evaluates the campus news against other stories he has, and estimates the number of people who may be interested in the campus story. The television news show of one station may use only hard news with no features; but other stations may broadcast a combination of hard news and light features.

The television representative has to work with the TV editor as the news writer does the city editor of a newspaper. The television representative gets the story to the station as quickly as he can, then lets the editor use his own judgment. The campus representative doesn't attempt to pressure the editor to broadcast the story, and never argues with him about his choice. If the campus stories are consistently rejected, the representative may talk to the news editor, asking honestly what the representative can do to select and prepare better stories.

In some areas, photographs or slides of the people or the events described in the television release are welcomed by station news editors. In other cities, such visuals are not used ordinarily.

Some universities also prepare short film clips of happenings on the campus and submit them to area television stations.

In writing television news releases, the university staffer assigned to the job is aware of the special needs of TV station editors. He uses the television form with columns for video and audio shown on the next page.

The appointment of new university board members, their educational philosophy and their plans for the institution may be the subject of a broadcast. A meeting of the board of trustees, where critical university issues affecting the admissions policy involving thousands of high school students, particularly from the low-economic areas, will be discussed and a final vote taken, may be considered newsworthy by the television stations desiring to keep the public informed about educational matters.

SAMPLE OF TELEVISION FORM

COPY
FROM
COMMUNITY
COLLEGE OF
BALTIMORE

CLIENT _____

PROGRAM _____

COPY INSTRUCTIONS _____

PROMO _____

TALENT _____ LENGTH OF COPY

VIDEO	AUDIO

When the station cannot cover the event live with its own personnel and equipment, the campus representative undertakes the coverage. He inquires what the news editor needs and the deadline. The station may wish just a phone call, or may request a written news release with or without photos or other visuals. If the university has its own cameraman or film department, clips can be produced and furnished the station.

INTERVIEWS AND NEWS EVENTS

The public relations representative has the opportunity to get television time on interview shows conducted by a number of stations. The appointment of a distinguished faculty member, or one with an interesting and unusual background, or experiences in other parts of the world, may suggest an interview over the air. The faculty has experts on world history and politics, hence they may be interviewed by the station's key personality on some of the background of significant world events as they occur.

Progressive TV program directors and news editors respond to important events which occur on the campus. When the president of the university delivers his "State of the University" speech, summarizing progress made and announcing significant plans and changes for the institution, he produces news that broadcast editors want. When a nationally known speaker or panel of speakers is brought to the campus to participate in a series of discussions about current international or national affairs, the station wants coverage. Social science conferences dealing with urban affairs, particularly housing, crime and drug problems, produce newsworthy events for TV news editors.

The program director may desire to telecast ground-breaking for a new building or an art or science wing, and later an anniversary of the college may call for extensive coverage. The key event of the year, the convocation at which a distinguished speaker may talk on a significant academic issue, or on some problem in which he is considered an authority, may be newsworthy for special news coverage over the air.

To give the public background information on the bond issue for the construction of a new branch of the college in the downtown section of the city, the station desires a live interview with the college president, giving the reasons for the new off-campus center and presenting some maps indicating exactly where the branch will be located and the areas of the city it will serve. And don't forget the kinds of background and special career courses the branch would offer, the station manager reminds the campus representative.

On the national scene, the campus can furnish experts on history and economics, who can follow up current headlines about governmental wage and price freezes by discussing the previous attempts in this country to control prices and wages and the effects of these earlier efforts. Scientists on the faculty may be interviewed about their research into cancer, or their investigations of urban problems, or may be questioned on their reactions to new discoveries by other scientists. New and significant books on political, economic, scientific and cultural subjects written by professors can provide the basis for exciting interviews. Instructors with unusual hobbies related, or unrelated, to the subjects they teach have general appeal to broadcast audiences.

SPECIAL PROGRAMS

The television staffer searches the campus for specials which portray in sound and pictures exciting aspects of campus life. He talks to each department chairman and division head for program ideas. These specials involve more than interviews on campus or at the television station. Such specials require more extensive film coverage with various location shots on and, sometimes, off campus. Both basic and applied research going on in the physical science laboratories and social science centers produce programs with wide broadcast appeal. The television audience would be interested in imaginative, challenging techniques of teaching used by forward-looking college instructors seeking to improve teaching methods and add something vital to the traditional lecture system. TV specials may also be built around students from foreign countries, adults enrolled at the college, homemakers returning to college.

In a community college, the television coordinator finds many ideas for informative special TV broadcasts. He may develop a program based on the career programs in allied health, or in the business administration, law-enforcement or fire-fighting departments. The efforts of the two-year college to bridge the gap between high school and college for many students, weak in reading, math, writing and science, will produce telecasts with audience appeal. The institution's attempts to reduce the number of college dropouts can be depicted, the efforts to use original and daring methods for arousing interest and recruiting potential students by house-to-house canvassing, conducting shopping center exhibits, opening store-front offices in neighborhood business sections—all such programs furnish the material for appealing broadcasts.

The television coordinator does not overlook any division of the college. The active Evening Division, or Division of Continuing Education as it is called in a number of institutions, may be searched for program-ideas. The public relations TV coordinator and the dean of the division may come up with programs dealing with the types of adult students attending classes after work, their problems in getting home and eating before rushing to their college courses. The dean may suggest as an interesting program the off-campus centers being conducted in libraries, high schools or government buildings in various neighborhoods.

Universities and colleges also produce longer television specials covering more aspects of their activities, or treating them in greater detail. These films may be suggested by special events, such as an anniversary, the opening of a new branch or the inauguration of a new president. The programs may be triggered also by radical departures in curriculum, or the merger of the college with other institutions, the expansion of the college facilities or the institution's moving to a new location.

The campus representative, after consultation with the head of the music department and the student musical organization(s), will be able to develop acceptable musical programs for television stations. The programs may have a wide range, featuring rock to popular to traditional and classical. Singers and instrumentalists, ensembles, choirs and symphonies may be focused upon. During the Christmas and Easter seasons, stations look for quality musical programs. The station may wish to do a live show, film the

In a television studio of the Community College, a press conference is held, announcing the winning of a national award by the college.

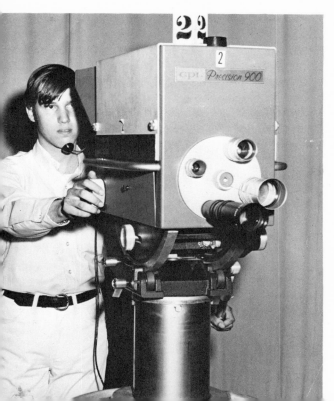

Getting ready to roll, student focuses the television camera at the Community College of Baltimore.

rehearsals and the problems encountered by the directors and players in producing a smooth performance. This footage would be followed by a filming of excerpts from the final performance. On other occasions, the manager may wish to skip the rehearsal and give all the air-time to the concert. Other stations may prefer a special program and performance of the university musicians before a studio audience.

WRITING STYLE

Television news grew out of radio news, just as the latter evolved from newspaper journalism. Television writing style has developed to suit the newer medium. Although there are many similarities, the style of television news-writing differs in certain essentials from that of radio.

When the film is shown, words must relate to pictures. Audio and video elements work in concert to tell the story. Silence is sometimes part of the television script. A good radio story is often trimmed or rejected for television because the story is essentially verbal. A good television film story is often rejected by a radio news editor because it is "weak" verbally.

Give Camera Directions

The TV script writer has the opportunity to tell his story with the camera. He therefore works camera directions into his script. He is in a position to call for any view of any object, person or activity. Furthermore, because more than one camera is always employed in the studio, and all of them are capable of changing their distance and angle, the writer can tell a story through a series of shots that may assume the burden of exposition. The uses of the camera are diverse, and the scriptwriter should learn those terms which enable him to take advantage of these powers.

The basic shots, such as the long or establishing shot, the medium shot and the close-up shot, were described in the chapter on motion picture film.

Camera Position

The scriptwriter can also lend variety to the filming by calling for a change in the position of the camera. He may ask for a FRONT SHOT, which is a head-on view of the situation. Then he can call for a SIDE SHOT, in which the camera is set at an angle to the subject. Or he may ask for an ANGLE SHOT, relating to the subject in terms of height. A LOW ANGLE means the camera should view the subject from below, and a HIGH ANGLE means we are looking down from above at the subject.

Adding Music

The scriptwriter uses music to increase the appeal of his program. Musical sounds create human emotional responses of infinite variety, and these are capable of translation into visual terms. When we hear music, we can identify the mood or impression it creates. We know of "light music," "heavy music," "somber," "witty," "impressive" types of music.

In TV, as in radio, music can be used for various purposes. It can establish a scene. Music can be used also as an emotional bridge by which the audience may be transported from one scene to the next. Music can be employed to punctuate, as in the famous trombone laugh.

To make production people understand what music is required, the scriptwriter will use the same terms which were developed in radio.

MUSIC IN.	Bring the music up so that the primary sound is heard.
MUSIC UP FULL.	Make music louder and let it dominate, as in a sense of finality or crescendo.
FADE MUSIC TO.	Take the music into background so another sound can dominate, but don't permit it to fade out entirely.
FADE OUT.	Take music out completely.
FADE UNDER.	Either take music to background or give dominance to another sound.
UP AND HOLD.	Increase volume of the music and leave it there.
STING.	Sharp punctuation.

Other Sounds

Sound effects can become a re-enforcement of the image-provoking qualities spelled out clearly by the picture. Certain actions call for specific sounds on TV. A door slams—we see and hear it. A gun fires—we see and hear it. We would sense that something is wrong if we witness a picture of an action taking place and not hear the corresponding sounds. Sounds of typewriters or the heavy machinery in the engineering lab, students talking and laughing on the campus, in the cafeteria—these are all sounds which give reality to the university film.

MECHANICS OF SCRIPTING

Splitting the script into its logical divisions of video and audio and running them in parallel columns simplify the task of writing, reading and interpreting for production. Split scripting serves a valuable purpose with all writers in that they are able to see what corresponds to what, in terms of sound and pictures.

Video | Audio

Under VIDEO the writer enters all his instructions about what action is taking place, the setting and locale, description of props and other visuals. All descriptions of talent and characters involved and their actions, movement and business will go also under VIDEO. Finally, all instructions relating to the camera should be entered on the same side.

On the AUDIO side of the page, include all music by writing MUSIC and carrying the underline across your description of it. The same will apply to SOUND and the instruction for its use. Finally, enter the names of all talent and characters in CAPITALS above their speeches, and then write in what they will say.

In writing the script, put slides or other visuals and film scene descriptions or identifications on the left hand side of the page, and all copy to be read by the announcer on the right. Identify at the top of the page the dates, show and times the material is scheduled to run (see the sample script on following pages).

You must also enter all instructions about sound sources in the AUDIO column. The station will select the music recordings unless you provide your own.

Copy must be mailed at least three days before air time. At least three copies should be provided—one for the Control Room, one for the Announce Booth and one for Projection.

ANNOUNCEMENTS AND NEWS RELEASES

Straight Announcer Presentation

There are a number of approaches in writing announcements. One approach, highly acceptable for university announcements, is the "straight announcer presentation" which simply brings together performer and camera with no other visuals.

Announcer Presentation with Visuals

The announcer may use one or two slides or flip cards to help the audience visualize the points, or he may employ a number of visuals such as photographs. In some programs, the announcer is seen and, while he talks, he points to a model of a proposed building or a scale drawing of a new campus addition. In other programs, the audience does not see the announcer, but only hears his voice as the viewers watch the camera move to each visual (called "voice-over").

Combination of Approach

Nothing said above should suggest that these approaches are mutually exclusive. They are merely ways in which messages can be presented to the public. All of these methods must be carefully blended into a clear approach.

Ten-Second Announcements

Short announcements are acceptable to many TV stations. The first basic principle in writing the short ID (Identification) is to remember: You have such a short time that you cannot use a complex or a hard-to-understand visual treatment. The best you can do is to identify your college in quick generalities. Words are an important part of the ID, and one of the most difficult creative efforts in TV writing is bringing together words and picture in sharp impact. This is the scriptwriter's chance to invent clever slogans or catch-phrases. Visually, you can invent identifying symbols, cartoons or "trade mark" characters. Your slogan or theme may focus on quality education, a wide variety of instruction programs, dedicated teachers, or low cost education.

Longer Announcements

Pre-planning and preparation are much more important for the longer forms—the 20-second and one-minute announcements. Longer messages need more than the immediate impact of novelty or humor. The story must be started with something that will immediately attract, preferably a verbal and visual combination that makes a direct appeal to motivations. After the interest is established, the story begins to unfold. In 20 seconds you have time for one major point; in one minute, at least two.

EXAMPLE: NEWS RELEASE PLUS FILM CLIP

```
FROM OFFICE OF PUBLIC INFORMATION          ADVANCE FOR
University of Illinois at Urbana-Champaign  THURSDAY, OCT. 15, 1970
                                            Mailed 10/12/70

COLOR TELEVISION NEWSFILM      :87
"Institute of Aviation, U. of I., 25th Anniversary"
```

TIME	VIDEO	AUDIO
:00	LS - Institute of Aviation sign	The Institute of Aviation at the University of Illinois, Urbana-Champaign, is celebrating its 25th anniversary this Saturday (Oct. 17). In those 25 years the institute has served in the areas of education, research, and public service.

(MORE--"Aviation")

"Aviation"----2

TIME	VIDEO	AUDIO

:13 MS - Student entering "link" flight trainer

Since the Institute of Aviation was founded 25 years ago, about 3,500 students have earned their private pilot licenses, and many of those have gone on for higher flight ratings.

:23 MS - Class with airplane engine running on blocks

A 2-year technical course at the U. of I. Institute of Aviation exposes students to all facets of flying mechanics and airplane maintenance.

:32 LS - Students working on broken down plane

These technical classes break down and completely reassemble and rebuild aircraft for course credit. When the planes are reassembled, they are used by the institute for training and instruction. And they become a part of

:41 CU - rebuilt plane with pan to fleet of rebuilt planes

the fleet of 43 flying aircraft housed at the University of Illinois Airport.

:50 MS - Inside research trainer

Constant research is conducted at the Institute of Aviation with cooperation from many private and government institutions. (Pause)

:56 MS - Exterior of research trainer and computer

And the use of the computer is evident in flying. (Pause)

:62 MS - research plane (exterior)

This twin engine Beechcraft has been completely outfitted with highly technical and extremely sophisticated electronic equipment. This equipment

:70 MS - research plane (interior)

along with the use of the computer will possibly help solve an aviation problem, and will collect valuable data for scientists.

```
:79  MS - Silver anniversary      Alumni and friends of the
     sign                         University of Illinois Institute of

                                  Aviation have been invited back this

                                  weekend (Saturday, Oct. 17) to join in

                                  on the 25th anniversary celebration.

:87

                                  END
```

SCRIPTS FOR TALKS AND INTERVIEWS

When the scriptwriter for the university plans a talk to be given by an administrator, faculty member or student on a television program, the writer considers also attention-getting visuals. For they contribute immensely to a telecast. The scriptwriter can suggest the use of charts, maps, still pictures or models in the talk program as well as in the interview or discussion broadcast.

Talks

It is vital that the speech be so planned and written that it creates a direct link between speaker and audience. In television, a professor discussing a problem in economics has two choices. He may bring in complex charts and figures, and devote his time to an analysis of these facts; or he can bring simple visuals which demonstrate what the *facts mean to the audience*. He must assume that he is speaking to an average citizen with little or no direct interest in the topic unless the interest is created for him.

The most prosaic elements must be given that touch of "show biz" that will take hold of the audience. This means a dramatic opening, step-by-step treatment and demonstration of conclusions in unmistakable terms.

Interviews

In the interview the continuity assigned to the interviewer is of vital importance. He should speak often and ask significant questions. It is too easy to fall into conventional patterns when interviewing. Routine questions are necessary, of course, but they must be phrased differently each time. Good writing will avoid the usual "I see," followed by another question. In many cases, only the questions will be completely written out, but answers should be rehearsed for running time.

Spontaneity in questioning is a vital part of the good TV interview. Though it has been rehearsed, it must not appear so. Pretending the material is absolutely new to him will help the interviewer create a more believable mood. At its best, the interview should actually include materials that have not been rehearsed, but not enough of them to get away from the basic purpose of the interview, or sacrifice more important materials.

Openings

A program opening serves several functions and must answer several demands. The opening must identify the program by title and set the general tone or mood of the program, in its words, music and visuals. The opening always must identify the sponsoring college and have interest values in itself—be catchy or attention-getting.

The scriptwriter keeps the opening short. If possible, he moves the viewer into the situation almost immediately—giving him some clear and definite idea of what to expect. No long and windy introductions, no pomposity or sententiousness. The scriptwriter introduces quickly the central personality, either host, master of ceremonies, speaker or principal figure. The opening should have the maximum visual appeal which the budget will allow. High-action visuals are best. If you have not chosen specific music, describe what you think fits best.

Closing

The closing also serves several specific functions, but is not obligated to catch attention. The closing re-identifies the sponsoring organization, keeps the mood with the same kind of music and sound effects, and includes debts and thanks and acknowledgements. The scriptwriter can include some final visuals or signature materials.

PREPARING VISUALS

Interest-catching visuals will enhance the campus telecast. Without good visual materials, the real impact of the medium is lost. Graphics are used constantly in television announcements, newscasts and programs, hence the college PR representative should understand visuals, be fully aware of what they can contribute to make programs interesting, meaningful, informative and should be familiar with their preparation.

The campus staffer, therefore, studies each proposed program to determine if slides or other graphics are needed. For example, he may develop a broadcast in which the science laboratories are involved. Slides, photos or motion picture film portraying scientific equipment would help the viewer visualize vividly what goes on in the laboratories. Or a faculty panel discussion of social problems may suggest maps of cities and urban areas where the incidence of crime is high, and such visuals may be used to enable the audience better to spot the crime areas.

There are two general types of television visuals—graphics and demonstration materials. Graphics may take the form of charts, maps, slides and Balopticon (Balop) cards, screened by an opaque projector. Demonstration visuals include all items which are non-graphic in nature, and which are intended for use in the live studio—models, pieces of equipment and objects shown or demonstrated by the performer.

Graphics

Flip Cards. A professor, who might be on a panel discussion dealing with U. S. regulatory commissions and agencies, such as the Federal Communications Commission, wants to describe on his program the structure of government and how the commissions fit in. He needs a visual to explain the situation to his audience, and uses a flip card for this purpose.

These cards are usually prepared on medium gray cardboard stock (normally 11" x 14" of 14-ply weight) and arranged on a special stand at lens height in front of the camera in such a way that outer cards may be pulled away or "flipped" over to reveal the cards beneath.

Photo-mounted Cards. Still photographs are frequently mounted on the flip cards. Hence, if the television program is concerned with the new library building, a photo of the facility can be used to advantage. The pictures are generally horizontals, 8 x 10 inches in size. When prepared outside the studio, the photos may be stapled or glued to the cards, but it is better to use a "dry-mount" process in which a hot iron is used to weld picture and card together. A waxy paper serves as the sticking agent. All TV stations are equipped with dry-mounting equipment, and it would be best to take photos to the station for this kind of mounting unless the college's photography department has the equipment. Dry-mounting is the best way to insure the absolutely flat, unbuckled photo which is needed on television.

Artwork. Drawings and paintings of all kinds also may be executed directly upon medium gray flip cards of the 11 x 14 inch, 14-ply variety. If the visual is to be used only once or twice, such direct transfer of artwork to camera is the quickest and easiest way. If the artwork is to be used over and over again, it is best first to make a photographic negative from the flip card. A print can be made then on a matte-finished photographic printing stock of the 11 x 14 inch type. This creates a working flip card for studio use, and a negative which can be filed and used again when the original card begins to get worn and dogeared.

Lettered Flip Cards. On a live TV program an urban affairs professor wants to point up significant factors that may lead to the making of a slum. He has ten points to present. These points can be outlined briefly on two flip cards to increase the audience's understanding of the discussion, and to enable the viewers at home to follow the talk more intelligently.

The basic studio flip card is used for such printed or lettered messages. A combination of artwork and lettering is in steady use in all TV stations. It is possible for cards to be hand-lettered by a non-professional, using either brush or pen on flip card stock.

Depending upon the amount of work to be submitted, it may be wise to invest in one of a number of quick-letter devices that will do the job. Some of the familiar commercial names for such lettering devices include: Art-Type, Paratype and Film-o-Type. Many stations use Film-o-Type, a patent photographic process for creating letters of various types on a photographic strip. The completed printing looks like a photographic picture of the printed words. The strips are then mounted on a standard flip card. For lettering flip cards, the campus staffer can use also stencil sets, cut-out letters, stick-on letters, water-transfer letters and others, sold in art supply stores.

Wall Charts. In a broadcast on population shifts in the United States, a history instructor describes the movement of farmers and their families to the city since 1900. A wall chart showing the flow of people toward the urban areas will help to make this campus television program more understandable and exciting. The wall chart may be a map, graph, chart, a whole series of smaller photographs or drawings, even a list of words. These illustrations are too large to be placed on a single flip card.

Posters. Striking posters can be drawn for the television broadcast, or posters already made for other purposes can be used to enliven the campus TV program. These posters can be seen easily by the audience, and the posters will cause the "talent" to move to them as he discusses his points.

Non-Live Graphics

The processes and procedures which govern use of non-live graphics, such as slides, are much the same as those involved in presentation of studio graphics.

Slides and Balops. The most obvious advantage in using college slides as graphics is economy of manpower. No studio personnel is required. Studio cameras do not have to be "heated up." Lights do not have to be set. An extra crew member is not needed during busy studio hours when he can be used for other responsibilities. Only the projectionist is needed.

A second important advantage in the use of projection graphics is the permanency of the visual. To make a slide requires a photographic process and a negative, which can be duplicated and is always available. Slides require less storage space and are less likely to be dirtied or bent by heavy handling.

Neither a slide nor Balop, however, can permit the focusing of camera-attention upon a given point. The slide is a simple photographic reproduction of the original artwork and cannot be scanned slowly, as when a camera pans over a chart or poster picking out important elements in sequence.

Relative Cost. The cost of the artwork will be the major expense in preparation of all graphics. The well-prepared flip card is easily reduced to slide or Balop form anyway, and the additional cost of photographing and mounting a slide is not prohibitive.

Identification Slide. To open up the university program, an identification slide is desirable. This may consist only of lettering giving the name of the show and the sponsor, but it also may have artwork or a photo to make it more attractive.

Making Slides and Mounts. There are several types of slide mounts which are acceptable for use in the TV projector. It would be advisable for the campus representative to check with the stations on the specific type they like to use. Metal mounts will be accepted normally by any station, although some prefer glass-mounted slides with tape-bound edges. Paper-mounted slides are discouraged unless they are to be used for one showing and then discarded. Some stations may prefer the transparency unmounted, and will handle mounting themselves. Slides must correspond to copy submitted. Give each slide a readily identifiable "slug" word or number. Check with the station's practice on this.

Slide Size Specifications. Over-all slide size should be 2 x 2 inches. The normal film camera which shoots the slide will scan an area of 27.32 of an inch by 1 and $\frac{1}{18}$ inches. Make certain that matting around the slide corresponds to these dimensions.

Film Strips. Some universities have found it more desirable to produce a series of photos on a film strip. The film strip has the advantage of having the photos in correct order, according to a logical presentation. The PR staff provides written copy, or a recorded disc to accompany the strip. This visual is far less expensive than a 16mm motion picture.

Demonstration Materials. In many instances, objects and devices if shown on the air would contribute to the interest in the program. For example, a science telecast may call for the use of microscopes, test tubes and other laboratory equipment.

AUDIO MATERIALS

In planning and preparation of university announcements, the public relations department may be called upon to provide recorded sound materials.

Recorded announcements, on a tape or disc, are used when a certain performer is essential to the presentation, but cannot be present at the station to do it "live." The recorded message would be employed, too, in conjunction with all-visual or filmed "spots" for the sake of convenience, or if a station announcer could not do the job.

Preparing recorded spots presents special problems. Most television stations can provide some tape playback facility, but the majority would prefer disc. These are prepared by a number of commercial companies. Tapes done on a personal recorder may be acceptable if the quality is high.

TV FILM PRODUCTION

A film shown on a TV series can also be used in the lecture hall or at group meetings, as we pointed out in the chapter on motion picture films. The film may be stored and, if it retains its timeliness, used again in the next year's campaign for students or to arouse interest of alumni. The film may be sent to many outlets at once, to be run at different times for different TV audiences. The number of people who finally get the public service message may be considerably larger than the group which sees a one-time-only live telecast.

Film enables the public relations department to control the professional quality of the message. The use of "re-takes" will remove those minor production errors and blemishes which seem to occur on live TV. A nervous speaker can be given new opportunities to re-do bad points in his speech. Lighting can be more carefully controlled. Outdoor scenes and settings can be added, and more "location" material used. The scope of the film is much wider in terms of shifts in time and place.

These advantages of film must be taken into account when the public relations department first considers preparation of material for TV audiences. Expenses will be greater, but such advantages may offset higher cost. The value must be determined by the public relations department.

There are really three fundamental ways in which film is used: (1) as a full program in itself; (2) as supplemental visual material within all types of live programs; (3) in the form of "spot" announcements. There are several basic film production methods:

Silent Film

The cheapest and easiest production method uses 16mm black-and-white or color silent film stock. This is really an easy film to work with. Most TV stations are equipped to process cut film with little or no delay. Film shot at a campus meeting in the morning can be used on an afternoon or evening news show. Such film can be aired as a negative, which saves additional time in processing.

16mm silent film can be used with news stories, with narrational background on regular live shows, or with "voice-over" copy as an announcement. The station can lend a professional quality to such materials. This film may also be used extensively in local documentaries.

Sound Film

This method of production requires more careful preparation and is much broader in scope. It must be used when dramatic action is required. A station performer's voice cannot very well be "dubbed" over a film interview or speech. Sound film is more expensive to produce, but may well be worth the cost and effort.

There are two methods of recording sound to accompany the film—double system and single system. In single system sound production, which is most easily used at local station levels, both sound and picture are recorded on the same film at the same time. In double system recording, the sound is recorded separately on tape or specially treated film, thus assuring higher sound quality. The film and sound tracks are then synchronized and reproduced on a single print. The process of recording quality double-system sound is almost exclusively the concern of professional film-makers.

CHECKLIST FOR PROGRAMS AND SPOTS

The television station will want to get the following information when the college submits film:
1. What is the final date this film should run?
2. What is the film's release date? When should it first be shown?
3. What should the station do with the film after airing? Return it? Throw it away?
4. What is the exact running length of programs and spots?
5. What is the length of the audio message on spots?
6. What is the condition of the print? New? Old?
7. When can you assure shipment, and how will it be shipped to the station?

SOURCES OF FILM

University-Produced
Film may be shot by the university staff or a professional photographer hired by the institution. Spot announcemnts, specials and longer documentaries can be produced by the university team. Film, shot and edited to required length, can be submitted to the television station for use in news programs or as "filler" material in a variety of station programs. Such film may be silent, and sent together with prepared script which is to be read at the station. It may be shot "sound-on," or discs and tapes may be sent with a silent film.

Station-Produced Film
Stations may originate live programs and filmed documentaries dealing with the university or college. In most instances, the station will shoot its own film, although the college may be asked to produce any available filmed records of their activities. Combination of station-originated and campus-originated film may be used within a single format. Public relations staff can cooperate in a number of ways when the station agrees to produce a film.

Casting

Filmed performance is far more critical than live performance in some ways, and deserves professional quality. The public relations department should seek to get the best talent on the campus, whether they be administrators, faculty or students. The staff must ask: who can best represent the campus? The PR department doesn't let anyone provide narration for a film if a professional is available. Non-professionals may be called upon to make statements before the camera, but the heavy burden of narration should be left to the best talent available.

All points should be covered in the first and later planning sessions.

Production Commitments

Once a station sets its film production processing in motion, it must be able to count upon the institution to provide facilities, talent and all other material which the college has agreed to provide. Make sure that the schedule is followed, so that the station crew can be at a certain place at a certain time, as agreed upon, and that all production elements will be on hand for the crew to work with. If you have agreed to have a certain demonstration or activity in operation, make sure it is set up and going at the proper time. Loss of a few hours here and there can play havoc with a tight shooting-schedule. If you have agreed to send talent to a certain place, make double-sure they are there, and have with them necessary props and other elements to be shown or used.

Supplying Supplemental Film

Frequently, the public relations photographer or other staff member may shoot film of certain campus events. Such film may be welcomed by TV stations. If you have supplementary film which can be used, the station would like to know certain facts about the picture. Is it silent or sound? If silent, does a script and shot breakdown accompany the film? The station would like to know what live audio is planned for the silent film. What canned audio? Is the film relevant to the program? Does it meet all station technical standards?

Time Specifications for Films

Most commercial half-hour filmed programs are timed to run approximately 29:30 minutes (29 minutes, 30 seconds) including commercials, but many are so designed that the local station may buy them and insert messages of local sponsors at intervals.

The proper running time for a 30-minute public service film should be anywhere between 28:30 and 29:00 minutes. The extra time will permit the local station to offer a brief open or close. Public relations films may also be timed to 26 minutes, allowing time for separate campus announcements.

You will find greater acceptance for films ranging between 13:30 and 14:30 for the quarter-time slot; anywhere from 26 to 29 minutes for the half-hour slots; and 58 or 59 minutes for the full-hour time periods.

Spot announcements are shot frequently with film. Television announcements are normally 10 seconds, 20 seconds, or 60 seconds in length. The 30-second spot, popular in radio, is virtually non-existent in video programming. In the 20-second spot, the audio message should be just over 18 seconds long. In the 60-second spot, audio should time out to 58 seconds.

Kinescope Recording

There is still another general way in which film has entered the TV medium—a direct off-the-air recording of a live program, called a kinescope. A 16mm film camera is permanently mounted facing a sensitive receiver tube. The camera rolls as the program starts, thus recording on film every part of the program exactly as it is seen on the home receiver. Once it is processed, the recording can be sent to other stations or played at a later time on the same station. It can be retained also by the organization for showing at meetings or public gatherings.

The "kine" seldom has a high technical quality and will not compare favorably with even single-system sound film. There is always some loss of clarity and resolution. It is still the cheapest way to get a filmed record of important materials which can be re-shown to smaller audiences.

VIDEOTAPE

A revolution in television communication was under way as Videotape opened unexplored areas in television in 1957. Within three years Americans witnessed programs of world-shaking events, videotaped, flown to this country and shown within hours of their occurrence. Videotape offered a cheap and instantaneous method of preserving the great events of our time. Engineers agreed that there was little or no difference in quality between a live broadcast and a Videotape recording of it.

For all intents and purposes, VTR is simply a recording of a live TV program. It is limited by the basic limitations of the medium itself. It cannot fully replace film. Videotape should be regarded as a new medium in itself. Since it can be replayed immediately, errors in production can be corrected.

Videotape may prove an effective way to get important meetings into a TV studio. College boards of trustees might be reluctant to hold their entire meetings in a crowded studio, but they may find less objection to a quiet taping session. Unimportant parts of such meetings can be edited out of the tape, and the important elements carried at a later time to the viewing audience.

Tape can also be ideal for announcements. Taping can also be an easy way to get informal interviews. Discussions, debates and talks are no longer subject to "who can be available when, and for how long."

EXAMPLES OF UNIVERSITY AND COLLEGE TV PROGRAMS

In the chapter on motion pictures some university public relations films were reviewed. These films were shown also over television stations. In the following pages, the reader will find a number of specific university and college programs produced for television.

Tulane University

The information office of Tulane University Medical School produced a series of 16mm film strips, each one a minute in length. The strips were produced on an experimental basis to learn if the information office could do a quality job acceptable to television station managers.

Eighteen films were scheduled to be produced the first year, one every other week, but because of lack of time, 11 were made and distributed to three stations in New Orleans. The clips were produced without sound, but an announcer read the script. The information office purchased a 16mm Bolex camera, a projector, splicing set and lighting facilities, which could be also used in the future.

Cornell University

A 28-minute film strip was produced by Cornell University using its own resources. Arthur W. Brodeur, director of Radio-TV Section of the Office of Public Information, desired to update old film of the university's admissions office. The up-dating provided the information office staff with the opportunity to pull together its available facilities and produce an audio-visual device at low cost, yet of high quality.

Entitled *The Cornell Experience,* the film project intended to explain Cornell University to prospective students, and was coordinated with the recruitment drive of the admissions office in cooperation with the alumni's secondary school committee.

Ohio State University

An unusual film designed to build general understanding and support for higher education, *Crisis and the University* was produced by the Ohio State University. A special production of the Office of University Relations, headed by Frederick Stecker, executive director, the film did not follow the traditional patterns of university films. It was an idea rather than an informational picture. It focused on the idea that higher education is one of man's best hopes for a solution of the great problems of this age. This contention was documented by example and especially by referral to activities on the campus of Ohio State University.

The film, running 28:30 minutes, was shown on Columbus, Ohio, television stations five times. Eventually the film was projected over 17 television stations in the state and elsewhere. The value of single broadcast time for the film was estimated at $4,000 to $5,000. Between November, 1964, and April, 1965, *Crisis and the University* reached 1,000,000 potential viewers. Reactions from audiences indicated that the film realized its general objectives as well as its specific goals. The cost ran into thousands of dollars, but the value of the exposure time on the air and the large audiences reached offset the production expenses.

University of Illinois

An extensive, coordinated plan for using both radio and television as public relations media was developed by the University of Illinois for its own stations, and for commercial and educational television stations in Illinois. The university, in adjusting to the television medium, gave special attention to the technical requirements of stations.

Associate director Evans said that one of the most effective services was the use of motion picture news clips of events on campus. These clips ran generally between one and two minutes and were accompanied by a script. News clips were sent regularly to 17 television stations.

The production of public affairs programs on a regular basis was another aspect of the university's use of television. The Office of Public Information worked with the School of Music and the university television station to produce a total of eight 27-minute shows.

The university's Office of Public Information also produced a number of films. They ran approximately 30 minutes and were used on television and were screened at schools, alumni meetings and various conferences. The films were *Beyond Teaching*, portraying research at the University of Illinois; *Serving the Whole State*, showing various types of extension services of the university; *Voices of a Great University*, focusing on outstanding teachers in the university; *The Dedicated*, being based on the medical center campus in Chicago.

University of California in San Diego

Officials at the University of California Campus in San Diego were confronted with a loss of confidence by many persons in the local community. A series of confrontations and disturbances had swept through the campus. They were reported by five television stations, two of which had national network affiliations. Two other UHF stations also broadcast in the area.

The university public relations staff turned to television to present the normal activities on the campus and make them newsworthy. This was done to counterbalance the poor image which had been created by the disturbances. The department employed Mrs. Ardys Heise as a full-time television coordinator, a person who was knowledgeable about the special needs of the electronic media. The department hoped to produce its own TV shows, but had no TV, photography or film department, and no budget. The TV coordinator had to make the material on the campus important enough so that the local TV stations would do the productions.

The news programs, which had prime time audiences, provided the opportunity. The public relations department took the responsibility of working with the TV reporters and helping them to provide accurate reporting. The university representatives helped the cameramen and reporters locate the principals in the hard-news stories, seeking to get a balanced point-of-view by obtaining student leaders and administrators to be interviewed.

The college representatives then turned their attention beyond the hard news to special segments within the news. The staff found professors who were tied in some way to the stories about the national news, giving them a local twist. When the moon flights were in the news, the university staff suggested to TV crews that they interview professors who were working on NASA projects and other faculty members with an understanding of lunar rocks. In the same way, the economics department was called on to have a specialist in international finance help the public understand the English monetary crisis.

The university TV coordinator found that by working with TV reporters responsible for developing specific aspects of the news—such as special reports, sports, people in the news and youth features—they could get opportunities for additional campus exposure.

The coordinator looked for interesting visual activities on the campus which could be used for features on a slow news day. Sometimes when a TV crew came for hard news, the university representatives were able to suggest a feature. The TV crew often returned to its station with two stories instead of one.

The coordinator looked into nooks and corners of laboratories, searching for special projects and activities with great visual impact. The glassblower who made special equipment for the scientists proved a delightful feature. The public relations representative found that a machine designed to slice and photograph the brain was very visual—this pointed up the unique and exciting work done in science. On the Fourth of July, the community had a special treat of hearing the university computer play John Phillip Sousa's "Stars and Stripes Forever."

In one year, 78 special features were used on hard-news programs, in addition to the regular hard news.

The coordinator knew that the university must look beyond the news to other opportunities, checking all locally produced programs, analyzing their audiences and their format. One locally produced morning show was directed toward the 18- to 36-year-old housewives, the children who watched before school, and the senior citizens. The broadcaster announced special events and interviewed important people on the campus, both professors and students as well as the chancellor and the provost. In an afternoon show, aimed at the young housewife, the format was more entertaining, featuring music, interviews with authors, performers and artists. The show manager felt at first that the campus could not furnish such talent. He was proved wrong when the university coordinator provided student musical groups, a potter, a fencing team and a karate demonstrator. Dr. Harold Urey, famous scientist, was invited to talk on "Water On The Moon."

The coordinator prepared 11 30-minute shows for educational television, including discussions, documentaries and two shows on the new sounds of music. The university found another opportunity on radio.

The university officials felt the TV and radio projects were justified. On the limited budget, the public relations department provided more than 300 segments of TV programming. The local air-time alone, if purchased, would have amounted to more than $200,000. The department concluded that the university was able to make the normal activities on the campus worthy of TV coverage. The administrators were brought to the public in more meaningful ways—a positive rather than defensive posture. An increase in moral and financial support of the university resulted. Enrollment applications increased. The results on the state educational bond elections showed positive support from the San Diego area.

Part Five

SPECIAL EVENTS AND ACTIVITIES

HOMECOMING

1970

WELCOME ALUMNI

That fellow with the guitar and the super hat was one of the Sonesta Hotel's strolling mariachi band which livened up the picnic lunch Homecoming Day. Outside the tent where he played, Charlie Parrott LAW '64 (above) came back for seconds at the food table. At Nickerson Field, the pennant vendor found the wind brisker than business, for few wanted to leave their hands exposed. But the day's weather adversities were soon forgotten after the game during a rousing party for alumni (right) which packed The Castle.

OCTOBER 17, 1970, will be remembered superficially as the Homecoming it snowed—first at 12:05, then in intermittent flurries through the rest of the day. But if the chill (40 degrees), the wind (35-mile gusts) and nature's own beautiful air pollution cooled the enthusiasm of returning grads at all, that didn't last; in fact, it seemed to increase the camaraderie among those who revisited the Charles River campus.

Special events for alumni began Friday with class auditing and, that evening, the annual Bell Lecture sponsored by the Alumni Association and featuring William D. Blair, Jr., U.S. Assistant Secretary of State for Public Affairs. He joined alumni at a reception in The Castle after his address.

Saturday over 100 attended the National Alumni Council breakfast at the Top of the Hub. On campus, alumni were invited to three special morning seminars—on drugs, the economics of the poor, and the social responsibility of the university—and to an all-day student show at the SFAA Gallery.

At noon, lunch was served from a wind-blown tent on the lawn behind Marsh Chapel, where a genuine strolling Mexican mariachi band produced hot, happy sounds. Then it was off to Nickerson Field for football with Holy Cross, where the Terriers surged to a big lead early and the Crusaders came back only in the last quarter, uncorking a couple of long scoring plays against second-stringers.

After the game, more than 200 trekked to The Castle for a "Castlefest," where cocktails, hors d'oeuvres, and animated conversation soon removed all recollection of climatic adversities earlier in the day. And if the ranks of returning alumni were thinner than on other (nicer) days in the past, the BU spirit seemed livelier than ever.

Three Saturday-morning seminars for alumni included a discussion of drugs led by Dr. Alan Katz (top) of BU's Student Health Service. The football game with Holy Cross was a 33–23 Terrier romp led by quarterback Sam Hollo, here being hauled down after a rollout gainer. Friday's Bell Lecture was followed by a reception where the speaker, William D. Blair, Jr., chatted with Edward Bernays (left) and Mrs. Calvin Lee.

15

Homecoming is one of the big special events of the year on many campuses and public relations departments, particularly the alumni division, help to organize and carry out the various activities, and then publicize them. These are scenes from the Homecoming at Boston University, with photos from *Bostonia,* the alumni magazine.

13

Special Events

SPECIAL EVENTS, effectively organized and directed by the public relations department, will give the college an opportunity to present dramatic, graphic and concrete demonstrations about the people, the programs and activities at the institution. Such events draw attention in a unique way, enabling the PR representative to interpret the work of the college in a broad, meaningful fashion which no single news or feature article can do. Special events tell the human side of the college operations and take the public behind the scenes.

According to the occasion, these events reach a variety of publics, including potential students and their parents. The general public may become interested, and special professional and business groups or organizations may be appealed to. Often the events reach people not ordinarily contacted and give them an understanding of the college.

If properly executed, these events are newsworthy—the long-range goal is to build up the reputation and prestige of the college. Much of this will overflow and provide the context and setting for news releases to the daily or weekly newspapers, magazines and broadcast media.

The public relations representative is alert for occasions which lend themselves to the full treatment of a special event. They may be:

Opening of the college.

Completion of the construction of a new building or wing or branch campus.

Dedication of a building honoring a president or faculty member.

Anniversaries of the college founding—such as the 10th, 20th, 25th or the 50th anniversary.

302

The inauguration of a new president.

Establishment of a new school, division or department within the university.

Observing "College Week."

Any college can add to this list, basing the selection on local events which will arise and on the needs of the college and the interests of the community. The special event is the most elaborate communications tool of the public relations department, as the event blends together print as well as broadcast media, and uses all the other communication tools: photographs, motion picture film, brochures and the speakers' bureau.

CHECKLIST FOR PLANNING SPECIAL EVENT

	CHECK-OFF AS COMPLETED
Plan carefully, a necessity	————
Determine purpose of event	————
Get a key theme, slogan and picture symbol	————
Appoint sufficient working committees	————
Determine date, time, place of event	————
Budget estimates of cost	————
Develop a timetable	————
Hold a series of progress meetings	————
Write a prospectus of the event	————
Work out a schedule of the event	————
Time all events carefully	————
Prepare necessary publicity	————
Arrange for broad photo coverage	————
Don't forget follow-ups after the event	————
Analyze results objectively	————

The staging of a planned event requires more than news-writing ability, but it brings out this and other skills the representative possesses. He must think through the problem carefully and intelligently, otherwise the event may prove to be a disastrous dud. Each step, each event and each part of the event, as well as each hour must be visualized. By doing this, the representative eliminates many headaches later. He cannot anticipate everything that will happen, but he can reduce the uncertainties to a minimum. The representative must have organizing ability, or develop it quickly. The event he plans may be a complex one, and he needs to pull together the many threads to make it work. The representative, too, must improve on his follow-through ability—once the event begins, he assumes the responsibility for carrying through the details, or of supervising someone else closely and regularly.

PRE-PLANNING

Careful, intelligent planning *beforehand*, when you can think of every possible step and emergency, will produce a more effective special event, later. Success depends in large part on your ability to visualize the event, to appoint the right people to your committees, and to get adequate publicity. All of these essential steps require systematic planning.

You should explore the entire project with officials of your college, or the head of the department sponsoring the special event. This might be called "the scouring-of-the-brains-session." Preparation of some typewritten material beforehand, outlining the suggested project and its purposes and methods you have worked out tentatively, will speed the discussion, helping to focus on the problem. You need the full backing of the institution's officials before you take any concrete steps.

Purpose and Theme

You have now selected the type of special event. At this point it is essential to determine its exact purpose, or purposes. If you define and write down the objectives for the event, you and your committees will be in a better position to design and program it. Is the purpose of the open-house at the college to create a friendly spirit? Then, to accomplish this result, every effort should be taken to convey this feeling, including the instruction of guides and other personnel. Is the aim of the exhibit to inform prospective students about the courses and programs at the college and to show career opportunities? If so, explanatory printed materials and demonstrations will be needed. Similar questions should be raised when other events are planned.

As early as you can, you want to develop a key theme for the event. The key theme will give coherence to the project, furnishing a central idea for conducting it. Events, displays, newspaper publicity, photos, posters may then be linked to the event more closely. Much thought should be given to the recurring theme. The perfect idea may not come to the surface immediately; indeed, you may require several attempts, the exact theme emerging when you least expect its appearance.

The public relations director recalls that the commercial world has successfully built events around such slogans as "Progress on Wheels" and "Better Things Through Chemistry." So, too, a YMCA luncheon designed to raise money to curb delinquency was called "The Fight To Lick Juvenile Delinquency." Similarly, you don't contribute funds to the cancer society, "You Combat a Killing Disease." Thus, we may call the college's week-long event "College Opportunity Week" or "College Career Week," instead of just "College Week." For events which involve the community, we may come up with: "Community and the College: A Partnership," or "Community Progress Through College Education," or "Preparing for Community Participation (or Life) Through Education."

Selecting Committees

Unless you expect to do the entire job yourself, you need the cooperation of several key committees. The chairmen of these committees—and sometimes all the members—may serve as the coordinating or steering committee for the special event. The number and size of the committees will depend on the scope of the event, with responsibilities including such areas as: program; contacts; budget; advertising and publicity.

Although you are the sparkplug of the special event, its success also depends on the personnel of your committees. If you are developing a college event, it is desirable to include representatives of administration, faculty and students for the purpose of getting the cooperation and support of every segment of the institution. A greater variety of useful ideas will emerge, too. If you are planning an event involving the community, the representatives of government and of civic organizations should be asked to serve.

After considering all the relative factors, the coordinating committees should determine the specific date, time and place of the event. Obviously, it should be planned to avoid competing with other events. If you intend to put on a panel discussion and expect to draw 500 people, an adequately sized auditorium must be obtained. If you expect only 100 in the audience, a small place would be filled, hence would be less embarrassing to the out-of-town speaker.

The job of the contacts committee is to interview and explain the special event to persons who would take part or whose organizations would be involved. The committee might have to enlist the cooperation of the governor, or the mayor, who might be asked to cut a ribbon, to speak or to serve as master of ceremonies. The group might have to get the help of the police and fire departments for a parade. The contacts committee may have to discuss the occasion with instructors or students, and with representatives of the college plant maintenance and security department.

Budgeting

Before any steps are taken, the budget committee needs to draw up a tentative budget, which will serve to give direction to the event and obtain better control. Many opportunities to spend will come up. The budget will keep the event going in the direction originally planned, with the aims always in the forefront. Costs usually are underestimated, so a hardheaded person with financial background should head up this committee. Both necessary items as well as desirable ones should be included in the budget of expenses. All items of expense need to be considered and written down. Sources of revenue must be stated, and amounts you can reasonably and realistically expect from each source should be written out.

SOME EXPENSE ITEMS

Personnel	(typists hired, or transferred from other work)	$ _____
Speakers	(honorariums and expenses)	$ _____
Materials	(float for parade)	$ _____

Cups, Plaques, Certificates	$ _____
Advertising	$ _____

Newspaper space	$ _____
Radio time	$ _____
Television time	$ _____
Brochures	$ _____
Posters	$ _____
Sound trucks	$ _____

Food, Dinners, Luncheons, Picnics	$ _____
Rent for Booths	$ _____
Entertainment	$ _____
Talent	$ _____

Orchestra	$ _____
Performers	$ _____

TIMETABLE OF PROGRAM

The members of the program committee have the task of visualizing each step in the program. If a tour of the college is planned by the coordinating committee, the program group must determine where the visitors will assemble. Where will they go first? Who will accompany them? Who will explain the overall operations of the college before the visit begins? Where will the visitors be taken next? What departments have to be side-stepped? What kinds of printed matter can be furnished? When should brochures be provided—beginning or end of tour? How long will the tour require? How many persons should be taken on each trip? When should the next trip be scheduled?

A timetable of the special event is desirable. This would provide a useful working guide and would enable you to start the event on time and end it when it should be concluded. Thus you might have:

COMMUNITY AND THE COLLEGE
Guided Tours Through
Metropolitan College

Wednesday, 9 A.M. to 6 P.M.

Group of 10 Visitors Each Hour on
the Hour—Trip lasts 2 hours

9–11 o'clock Tour

9 A.M.	First group meets in staff conference meeting room
9:10 A.M.	President Sam Longstreet gives overall presentation of college aims
	Vice President Harvey Little tells about programs and courses
9:30	Group taken to admissions office, Admissions Director LeRoy James shows new methods being used in his department
9:40	Group moves to Science Laboratory. Shown latest equipment. Talk by Prof. Fred Balser, head of Science Department
10:10	Group moves to Humanities. Prof. Jerome Cohen describes programs, courses
10:20	Group moves to Music Department
10:30	Group visits Library
10:50	Group moves to Field House
11:00	Group completes tour in Cafeteria. Shown equipment, given refreshments

End of Tour

At regular intervals progress meetings of the coordinating committee are held. Reports of each committee chairman are given, so that an overall picture of the event emerges and total information is supplied the staff. Chairmen report on obstacles still to be faced and receive suggestions on solutions to puzzling problems. The committee, too, learns the state of the finances.

PROSPECTUS AND PUBLICITY

When a tentative outline of each committee's operations has been developed, the chairman of the coordinating committee writes out all the facts in a prospectus. This serves as a guideline for the chairman and for each member of the committee. The prospectus may be furnished also to the college administrators and to newspapers. The prospectus includes these and other items:

1. Title of the event
2. Kind of event
3. Theme of event

4. Date and time
5. Place of the event
6. Objectives of the event
7. Committees—chairmen and members appointed
8. Program of the event with timetable
9. Budget of the event—expected sources of revenue and expected expenses
10. Publicity plans

In addition to serving as the coordinating chairman, the college public relations man usually acts as the chairman of the publicity and advertising committee, or he may appoint one of his staffmen to do the job.

It is necessary to plan the publicity for the special event as carefully and to time it as adroitly as the total program. The public relations representative should seek to get as broad and as thorough coverage as possible for the event. Both spot news and feature articles may be written about the occasion, for all media should be interested in the event if it is newsworthy. Articles may be written for the morning and afternoon dailies, weeklies, state and national newspapers. Magazines, national publications of general circulation and trade periodicals should be considered as outlets. If the event has some wide significance, the news wire services—the Associated Press and the United Press-International—may be contacted.

The public relations man releases the news about the special event according to a planned time-schedule. Articles are sent out as the event develops. The first announcement covers the essential points relating to the type of special event, the underlying theme or slogan, and the purpose, date, time and place. If the committees have been appointed, the names are included. If these appointments will be a much later step, then the names are given in a second story along with other details. As the program develops, and as officials are selected and talent chosen to take part in the event, the public relations representative puts these facts into another article.

It is not desirable to flood the editors and the reporters assigned to the story, but to offer news only when sufficient progress has been made to give definiteness to the event. Special feature articles may be written on particular phases—such as the background of the speaker, some unusual classes to be seen by the public who visit the college on "Community College Day."

Schedule of Releases

To keep track of the features he plans to send out, the public relations man works out a schedule of releases. The schedule enables him to plan more intelligently, to estimate overall impact and to include all media. The schedule contains the type of news in the release, its content and the date of the release.

A special event news and feature schedule such as the following would be of help in planning the coverage effectively:

NEWS RELEASE DATE SCHEDULE FOR
. . . . **Special Event**

Subject	Contents	Date	Publication
Special Event Announced	Kind of event; slogan, date, place, purposes	March 1	Morning papers, Radio
Committees Appointed	Chairman, names; recap on special event facts	March 10	Afternoon papers; weeklies
Tentative Program Announced	Speakers plus background; Exhibit details; Mayor to be master of ceremonies	March 17	Morning papers, Television program
Feature on Particular Exhibit	Unusual exhibit to be displayed; recap some of highlights of event	March 21	Sunday Supplement
Final Program	Complete details of program and event	March 30	All media

Press Conference

The press conference to introduce big promotions and projects to newspaper reporters and, through them, to newspaper readers is still prevalent and a potent device.

City desks have their calendars literally littered with notations for press conferences, some on a large scale with elaborate luncheons or dinners as sidelines (or mainlines). Other conferences are only brief and breezy announcement sessions, with a few reporters asking pertinent and often penetrating questions. Usually, hefty press kits with fact sheets, suggested stories and photos are distributed; but occasionally reporters must make their own notes and take time away from canapés and cocktails to listen to speeches and exhortations.

Civic groups and commercial and industrial concerns have perfected the press conference; colleges may study their operations profitably, adapting the best methods.

Photo Coverage

Advanced photo coverage before the event is carried out by the public relations representative. Photos need to be taken of individuals who will take part, creating ahead of the event some action to give the event reality. Some of these pictures are head-pictures ("mug shots") of the key individuals; but photographs showing people in action would be preferable. Release dates on these photos are coordinated with the news and feature schedules outlined before.

Some editors may be more interested in the photos than in your news or feature story, and will print a picture with deep cutlines in preference to a long news article. This is the editor's choice—but the public relations representative should be prepared for any choices the editors make.

Assistance to Newsmen

The preceding suggestions were written on the basis that the publications and broadcasting stations were not sending out newsmen to cover the advance stories of the college event at the time it occurred. The media may not have the personnel, other events of greater importance may be breaking, or the editors may not think your university event newsworthy enough for a reporter to be taken off some other beat or spot story. But if the editor thinks the special event deserves space or time, because of its interest/importance, he will use the news if you cover it adequately and send in a worthwhile story and/or pictures. College public relations men check with the editors at every stage to learn their plans for the event.

If the editor believes the event justifies his sending a newsman to cover it, the college public relations man assists him in every way. It is desirable to write out the news in regular news form, and to supply also a fact sheet, listing the facts about every detail of the event.

Many public relations men produce, as indicated, a press kit. This folder, in a large envelop, contains each story which has been released; the background of the speakers; copies of the speeches; details of the parade route; names of invited guests for the dinner; the history of the award, if one is given, its purposes and previous winners. The kit is kept up-to-date and given to each reporter whenever he appears, particularly at the time of the special event.

On the day of the event, a quick check with the editor enables the public relations representative to learn if the publication or the broadcasting station will send a representative, or if the editors desire the public relations man to report the event for the media. If the latter, the public relations man asks, what are the deadlines. Should the news be sent by special messenger or telephoned in? How long should the story be?

Advertising

Money should be provided for publicizing the special event. Funds, we have seen, may be necessary for the awards, for the dinner, for the

Guided Tours

Hopkins To Have Open House

The Johns Hopkins University will hold its first University Open House on the Homewood campus, Charles and 34th streets, from 10 A.M. to 2 P.M. Saturday.

The public is invited, and there is no charge.

Visitors may take guided tours of the campus, witness laboratory demonstrations and see exhibits depicting student activities and other aspects of life at Johns Hopkins

A visitors' center will be set up for the day in Shriver Hall, from which point the tours will originate at regular intervals. Among various pieces of scientific apparatus to be demonstrated will be a wave tank used in oceanographic research, and an amino acid protein analyzer in the Department of Biology.

The Lacrosse Hall of Fame at the Newton H. White Athletic Center will be open to visitors until noon. The Baltimore Zoo's "safari train" has been borrowed for the day to transport guests between Shriver Hall and the Athletic Center.

Other events scheduled include the performance of two one-act plays by the Johns Hopkins Barnstormers starting at 11 A.M.; continuous showings of a film entitled "The Noisy Underwater World"; and a concert by the Johns Hopkins Band from noon to 1 P.M.

Special activities have been arranged for young children. Visitors are encouraged to bring picnic lunches, although food will be available on the campus.

The Open House is being sponsored by the university's Office of Community Affairs. The director, Mrs. Dea A. Kline, said the Open House is part of a community impact study and demonstration program.

"Its chief purpose," she said, "is to give Baltimoreans, particularly those who live in the Homewood neighborhood, a chance to gain a broader insight into the university and the many diverse facets of its day-to-day life."

Guides and hosts for the day's activities will be drawn from a number of Johns Hopkins organizations, including the Alumni Association, Alpha Phi Omega, Blue Key, the Student Council, the Student Association, Black Students Union, Graduate Student Organization, Graduate Wives Association, the Urban Affairs Council and the campus radio station, WJHU.

UM Community Day Scheduled Dec. 12 At Westminster High

Carroll County Bureau

Westminster—Faculty and students of the University of Maryland, College Park campus will present a Community-University Day, for Carroll County, December 12 at the new Westminster Senior High School in an effort to broaden the community's knowledge of the school.

The event, being coordinated by Carroll county community leaders, the College Park office of Summer School and the university relations office for special events, is only the third one of its kind to be held in the state.

Previous community-university days were held in the Frederick and Cumberland areas.

The program, open and free to the public will have discussions by faculty experts on topics of interest to all ages, exhibitions, entertainment and programs for children.

News of special events in universities and colleges frequently get strong display and coverage, as these stories indicate. Sometimes the news involves the community residents.

African art

Discussions on the humanities, including Maryland history, folklore, international communications and African art, will be the main feature of the presentation.

The scheduled events, which will start at 1.30 P.M. and continue until 5 P.M. follows:

Discussions in humanities and other topics; 1.45 P.M., two types of contemporary philosophy, history comes to Maryland, ancient myths in the modern world, African art, the spirits of Christmas, the challenge of leisure, basic photography, how to watch a basketball game, language teaching at the university level—the what, when and why?, Maryland medieval mercenary militia crossing the U.S. by camper, and disposition of estates under Maryland law.

At 2.45, folk dance in comparative cultures, sermon in stones: Athenian inscriptions, international communications and propaganda, Apollo 11 experiment, requirements for getting started in farming, the stellar evolution, engineering for the housewife, effective learning techniques, creative dramatics for children, college life on the campus, 1971.

At 3.45, magic: its occurrence in myth and religion, important moments in Maryland history, how we got to modern architecture, creative dramatics for children, synthetic foods of the future, four trips to Russia reading efficiency, home vegetable gardens, small engine maintenance, making Christmas wreaths, new technology in the arts, and the meat we eat.

Demonstrations

Exhibitions and demonstrations will include the impact on agriculture on the consumer, institute of applied agriculture, beekeeping, copper enameling, fire service extension, co-operative engineering exhibit, resume the job help, traffic safety, wealth out of waste, and Maryland medieval mercenary militia.

Also, the many faces of the university, College Park campus organizational exhibit, conversation with a computer gravitational wave exhibit, admissions office information booth, photojournalism exhibit, continuum, and landing on the moon.

Entertainment features include, a dance concert by the University Dance Company at the school auditorium, at 3 P.M., a children's film festival in Room A104-105, continuous from 1.30 to 5 P.M., a reading theater with readings from Charles Dickens' Christmas Carols at Room A-103, continuous from 1.45 to 3.45 P.M., and an organ concert by Debbie Bauerlien in the auditorium at 4 P.M.

Complete programs and additional information can be obtained between 8.30 A.M. and 4.30 P.M. daily at the Carroll County Cooperative Extension Service in the County Office Building, Court street in Westminster, or by telephoning 848-611.

floats, for the exhibition. Part of these funds should be set aside for advertising the event. Advertising should be considered a necessary part of the expense budget.

In addition to newsmen's efforts and cooperation in publicizing the event, advertising space should be bought to tell about your college's special event, reinforcing what has been said in the news columns. For various reasons, including the breaking of big news during the same day, your news article of the special event may be trimmed mercilessly, or find itself on an inside page, buried. Your spot news radio announcement may be crowded off the air. Your advertisement, however, will give proper attention to your event.

The public relations man suggests to the advertising representative of the publication that an effort be made to obtain advertisements from local companies, during "College Opportunity Month" for example, for a special page, section or supplement in the daily or weekly newspaper. Because companies employ graduates and present students of the college, they realize the value of telling about the opportunities in their organizations for trained personnel. The president of the company and his advertising and public relations man may understand the value of having a college in the community to attract other industrial concerns.

Sometimes, for the dedication of a new college building, the commercial companies directly involved will place advertisements in a special newspaper section, showing their part in the campus construction. Or the companies may salute the college on its progress. If it is an event making a contribution to the community, many retail advertisers and manufacturers will want to tie-in with the public affair sponsored by the college and the community.

Many business associations or institutes can, and will, furnish sufficient advertising support to justify an entire section in a weekly, daily or Sunday edition of one or more newspapers. Outstanding tabloid magazine sections have been produced for individual companies and for organizations to tell about their special events. Similar sections could be published to signalize a college or university event.

The public relations man should consider the necessary brochures and booklets which may be distributed at the event. They provide background information, furnish facts about the institution. The brochures may remain lasting souvenirs of the occasion. The public relations man must decide whether the souvenir commemorating the event should be two or four pages, in black and white or in color. What pictures should be used?

FOLLOW-UP AND ANALYSIS

Certain steps should be taken after the event is over. If taken, these steps will contribute to the success of your next event.

Letters of appreciation should be sent: (1) to all invited guests; (2) to all persons participating; (3) to all newspapers, radio or TV stations and magazines covering the activity. These letters will show the courtesy of your organization and will create goodwill for future events.

All experiences you have had contribute to your understanding and knowledge of special events, but your immediate experiences must be analyzed for the best future results. A scrapbook and notebook with various steps and actions taken—containing clippings, photos, invitations and timetables—should be kept. If you make an analysis of what you did, you will discover what the positive strengths of your event were—what contributions the special event made to your organization's prestige, or the image build-up. These contributions might be developed into a report for the president of the college or other administrative officers. The report may be used as the basis for an article for trade or professional magazines, and for inclusion in the public relations department's annual report to the president.

Weaknesses? You do no doubt have some. What were the errors, frankly? Why were they made—lack of planning? Lack of previous experience? Committee shortcomings? Unforeseen, uncontrollable events? The public relations representative makes a conscientious list of these mistakes and failures, and he makes a conscientious determination to discover ways the mistakes can be reduced or eliminated next time.

COLLEGE WEEK

Although there are "Apple Pie Week" and "Gardening Week" and a host of other events of a similar kind, "College Week" can prove a worthwhile project for any four-year or community college. The event can be conducted on a high level, with dignified style. "College Week" will prove a meaningful educational experience for the public and a beneficial special event for the institution.

This author has applied the multimedia approach to this event, concentrating the public relations efforts over a short period of time. The News Bureau of the Community College of Baltimore sought to achieve in its "Community College Week" maximum impact, reaching many people and groups. It was believed that one communication channel would tend to reinforce another. If a person did not see the story of the college in one media, or could not be reached by that channel, he would be exposed to the message in another channel.

While the first "Community College Week" was held solely by this college the first year, the next year the event was made a cooperative effort, with four community colleges, public and private, mostly in the Baltimore metropolitan area, joining in. The advantages of the united effort were apparent. Attention was focused on the community college as a significant institution in the community, rather than directing attention to the advantages and courses in only one college. The belief was held that the colleges were not in competition with each other in obtaining students and in getting the attention and respect of the public. The common problem of the colleges was that of arousing the interest of the thousands of high school graduates who did not continue their education, and in stirring the interest of thousands of adults who worked by day but could enroll in the evening courses at the colleges. Also the aim was to reach homemakers—mothers and housewives—who had not continued with their education beyond high school and might be interested in enrolling in background courses as well as those preparing women for careers in business or the professions.

The joint goal of the colleges, too, was the generating of understanding and support of the general public—including the taxpayers who footed the college bills. Because it was a joint effort, news editors of daily and community newspapers and broadcast media were more apt to judge the event as of general educational interest and value, for "the week" did not give special advantage or publicity to one college. Cooperative advertising also would reduce rates for each college.

Official Proclamation

"Community College Week" is proclaimed usually by the governor of the state during October. The date is a questionable one, and must be given some thought by the public relations men and women. While some high school students in October are thinking ahead and expecting to enroll in a college in the following September, a November date would be preferable for proper planning of the event. If a fall date is found impractical or undesirable, a spring event may be set several months ahead. A proclamation by the local mayor or executive of the county commissioners would give the college week an official send-off. Standing by itself, as it usually does, the proclamation becomes an empty, paper gesture, unless the document is implemented with specific events.

The event may be broken down into a number of steps and actions which need to be taken.

Purpose and Theme

"Community College Week" or "College Week" may be presented as a special event year after year. It has a continuing general purpose, but if the public relations department, in conference with college officials, generates a special theme, the event will produce a unity of pattern and be given freshness.

The general purpose may be stated in these or other ways. "College Week":

Centers attention on the college in a concentrated fashion over a
    short period of time.

> Provides information about the programs and courses and other activities of the college in a coordinated manner and on a broad scale.
>
> Interprets the college's work to varied groups, building understanding and goodwill for the institution.
>
> Shows the value of the college to the community, demonstrating that the community needs the college

The values of a college may be spelled out:

> College provides educational opportunity to high school graduates and adults, enabling them to broaden their intellectual horizons, to acquire courses and credits which may be transferred to four-year colleges and universities, and to train for many careers.
>
> College raises level of citizenship for community living and participation through courses in social sciences.
>
> College develops cultural interests of citizens for general understanding of arts and literature, and furnishes basis for constructive leisure-time pursuits and interests.
>
> College provides trained personnel and manpower for business, industry, professions, government service.
>
> College builds future citizens to fill jobs with greater income possibilities, giving them greater taxpaying abilities.
>
> Community is making a good investment in the future when it supports the college.

These themes are expressed in talks before community groups, included in the news publicity about the event, and repeated in the exhibits and posters on display.

Targets

The publics which the "Community College Week" aims at are varied. Included are high school students who will become better informed about the specific educational opportunities at the college and will take advantage of them later. The parents of high school students will learn about the programs at the college by visiting one of the exhibits, listening to a talk, or reading about the college in the daily or community newspaper. Many adults who have thought only casually about enrolling in college will be stimulated as a result of the concentrated effort to tell the college story, to consider seriously enrolling for occupation advancement or acquiring a better background.

The public relations man seeks to enlist the interest of the general public—those who provide the climate in which the college operates and who furnish the finances through taxes. Also in the public are those who would attend the cultural events at the college if these were brought to their attention during "Community College Week."

Overall Plan

"Community College Week" is concentrated, as indicated, in a one- or two-week period. The public relations director uses these media:

1. Daily Newspapers—regular and Sunday editions; tabloid youth supplements.
2. Community Newspapers—all areas represented.
3. Special Publications—trade and professional magazines.
4. Radio stations—spot news; interviews.
5. Television stations—spot news; features; interviews.
6. Speakers Bureau—speakers for high schools; speakers for civic, merchants' and women's associations.
7. Exhibits and Displays—in shopping centers; in libraries; in merchants' windows.
8. Supplements in High School Newspapers—two- or four-page supplements; news and features about the colleges in high school papers.

News of "Community College Week" in the Baltimore metropolitan area was sent to the daily newspapers as well as to the community newspapers. Arrangements were made with principals and counselors in high schools for special programs featuring the speakers from the colleges. Advance news articles were sent to high school editors, who gave the news strong display in their publications.

Other college speakers had engagements, arranged by the public relations representatives, to speak at various civic and merchants' organizations in various parts of the city. This news was carried in local community weeklies.

A four-page tabloid newspaper was produced jointly by public relations personnel of four community colleges. The tabloid was inserted in high school newspapers, public, private and parochial. The special edition tied in the stories with "Community College Opportunity Week," as it was finally called, and covered both college-transfer and career programs at the institutions. Features told about extra-curricular activities, such as sports, special-interest clubs, theatricals. One article dealt with social activities. The tone of some articles was factual and serious; other features had a lighter touch, aimed directly at the high-schoolers. Photos were used on each page to illustrate the articles and to give eye-appeal. Pages one and four of the tabloid were written by each college representative, who slanted the copy toward his own college and stressed the points he desired. The printer replated these two pages for each college involved. Pages two and three, which remained constant throughout all editions, covered opportunities at all community colleges.

The Community College of Baltimore had 35,000 copies of the tabloid printed and distributed in Baltimore City high schools. In Baltimore County, Essex Community College and Catonsville Community College distributed 40,000 copies, while in Hagerstown, Maryland, the junior college there distributed 12,000 copies. The tabloid was a vehicle aimed directly at the high school market-target. Coupons were printed on page four. They listed courses and programs at the colleges, and the students could check them off and send the coupons in for brochures and catalogues. The response was very favorable.

Sam and Mary, Frank and Susan Learn About Jobs The Hard Way

Sam Jones, typical high school graduate, thinks he has had enough of formal education.

He got his diploma — that's enough. Or Sam—because of economic reasons has to find a job after he graduates.

Sam goes downtown to get a job in a business concern, or an industrial company, or even a professional office. The personnel manager says, "You've got a high school diploma. That's great! But we need employes with some specialized training and knowledge beyond the high school level."

Now here's Frank Applegate. Frank has been working for the U.S. Stone Company for three years. He can't seem to move up to the better jobs. One day he goes into the employment manager's office and states his beef.

He gets the standard reply, "You need some more education, Frank. To get ahead in this company, you have to acquire some more knowledge at a school and improve yourself. Have you ever considered studying business organization, accounting, engineering, data-processing?

The same stories can be told about Mary Johns, Susan Folks. They are ambitious. They want the better-paying jobs with more prestige—but they require further training.

Smart high school seniors know today that you can't get a well-paying job, or move up in business or industry without some special training. They realize they have to have additional background beyond the high school level and specific knowledge and practical skills to make any headway in the commercial world.

The community college nowadays is the gateway to successful careers. The community college graduates do well in business, or industry...

This feature in the high school college tabloid was written in a lighter style.

The most extensive production by the public relations department of the Community College of Baltimore consisted of outdoor exhibits and displays, placed in shopping centers in the city. It was thought that shoppers coming for their groceries, clothes, furniture, auto supplies, would see the college exhibits if they were made convenient and attractive. Community weeklies featured the news of the exhibits when they opened in their areas, some editors printing the news on page one.

The displays, put up in cooperation with the merchants' associations at the shopping centers, drew several thousand people. The exhibits were shown from one to three days at Mondawmin, Reisterstown Road, Parkville shopping centers and at Federal Hill Park. At Federal Hill, the college joined in with other groups in putting on the South Baltimore Spring Festival. Residents came to see the exhibits of elementary, junior and senior high schools, of the Boy Scouts, the YMCA, and various churches. A high school rock-and-roll quartet played. It was a gala occasion that drew more than 5,000 persons. Because of the strategic location of the Community College exhibit at the entrance of the park, the exhibit was seen by most visitors.

Interested in acting and the theatre, two visitors examined the posters of the Baltimore Community College's Drama, Radio and Television Department, displayed at shopping centers in connection with Community College Opportunity Week. On the opposite panel the visitors could learn about the college radio station.

At all of the outdoor exhibits, brochures about the college programs were distributed by administrators, departmental representatives and students, who told about the courses and answered visitors' questions. Both teen-agers as well as adults visited the displays. They provided a direct contact with the public in various communities, drawing attention to the day and the evening classes, as well as the informal courses offered by the college.

The author developed a questionnaire about the displays for visitors to fill out, patterned on the surveys that had been conducted successfully by the Bell Telephone System at its exhibits throughout the country. The Community College survey showed that: (1) the visitors were impressed by the college's variety of programs and activities, and (2) that they became better informed about the institution after seeing the exhibits. This survey, combined with the fact that thousands of residents took the time to go through the 100 displays and the fact that the visitors asked for hundreds of brochures, would lead to the conservative conclusion that the exhibits served a useful public relations purpose.

An adult looks over the table displaying trophies won by the various teams of the college. The poster for the Recreation Aide program was put up for the Department of Physical Education.

COMMUNITY-UNIVERSITY OF MARYLAND DAY

Each year the University of Maryland has conducted a highly successful Community-University Day at its campus in College Park, Md. Designed for every member of the family, the program featured faculty experts who discussed drug education, vacation photography, how to watch football, and getting the most out of your dollar. Plans also called for an extensive recreation program, including swimming, softball, tennis, bowling, archery and pitching horse shoes. Entertainment highlights of Community-University Day featured a live drama production, musical presentations and a continuous cartoon show. The event was held on Sunday, between 11 A.M. and 4:30 P.M.

Displays of art, glassblowing, art welding and weaving were scheduled also through the day. The National Aeronautic and Space Administration and Goddard Space Flight Center, located near the University, presented a space science lecture and exhibitions. Visitors also toured the University's Cyclotron Laboratory, the largest of its type in the world, the Astronomy Laboratory and the Center of Adult Education.

Food service, at a very nominal cost, was offered in the university's Student Union Cafeteria. The program, a project of the University of Maryland's Summer School, was developed with the assistance of the mayor and other active civic leaders in the district in which the university is located. Publicity was sent to state and area dailies and weeklies weeks before the event.

Here is the full program for the event, as published in the *Baltimore, Md., Sun.*

Community-University Event August 2

Exhibtions and Demonstrations

Glassblowing.
Computer Science.
Art Exhibit.
Weaving.
Jewelery.
Art Welding.
Dairy.
Laser Exhibit.
Spacemobile.
NASA's Space Demonstration Unit.
Astronomy Laboratory Tour.
Goldard Space Flight Center Exhibitions.
Cyclotron Tours.
Center of Adult Education Tour.
Horse Show.

Recreation

Gymnastic Participation.
Swimming.
Softball.
Volleyball.
Badminton.
Horseshoes.
Tennis.
Bowling.
Archery.

Food Service

Student Union Cafeteria—11 A.M. to 2 P.M.

Seminars

Crossing the United States by Camper.
Arfican Art.
Introducing to Reading Efficiency.
Educational Technology.
Leisure Time.
Terrace Gardening for Apartment Gardeners.
What Goes on Behind the TV Show.
Drug Education.
H. L. Mencken.
Drama Wing One Act Play.
Campus Unrest.
Human Relations.
Obesity and Weight Reduction.
Engineering for Housewives.
Vacation Photography for the Beginner.
Getting the Most Out of the Family Food Dollar.
Wills.
Pollution.
Urban Transportation Problems in the District of Columbia area.
Use of Accessories in Decoratign.
How to Watch a Football Game.
How to Watch a Basketball Game.

Entertainment

Musical Presentations.
Live Drama Production.
Continuous Carton Show for Children.

14

Exhibits and Displays

COLLEGE EXHIBITS with a dramatic, visual impact become useful tools of the public relations department in its efforts to tell the college story to a variety of publics in a meaningful, forceful fashion.

Exhibits pictorialize and make realistic the institution's message. The displays project the college buildings and programs beyond the walls or grounds of the institution. The exhibits lift up the college, so to speak, and take it outside—downtown, into schools, meetings, community and shopping centers—where the outside public is. There the college's facilities and programs can be viewed without the visitors' coming out to the campus. In a sense, the displays make the brochures and news and feature articles come to life, for the exhibits present the same or similar information in different ways through a different medium. When they are manned by college representatives, the exhibits provide the opportunity to get direct, personal contact with various publics the college wants to reach.

To achieve his purposes, the public relations officer uses pictures and copy. To enliven, humanize and personalize his exhibits, he adds live personalities and student demonstrations of work done in classrooms and laboratories. He puts on a slide show to strengthen the appeal of the exhibit and has brochures ready to be distributed to persons whose interest has been aroused by the displays.

The officer seeks to make his show an attention-getter. The displays may tell the college story to already deeply concerned people as well as partially interested persons. The exhibits often, however, attract many persons who overlook the newspaper or magazine article that the representative has had published about the college; other persons who don't listen to

321

Single panel displays compress much catalogue information into small space. This display had prose and two photos to tell about the Northern Off-Campus Center of the Community College of Baltimore. The display gave the (1) name of the college (2) the off-campus center (3) main courses being offered (4) time and place of registration (5) and a final line on the Liberty Campus registration.

radio or view television see the displays in the store windows. Still others who would not read the college brochure may be attracted to the exhibit and become informed about the institution. In many instances, the exhibit reinforces whatever communication message the viewer has already received in the press, or the exhibit adds more to his stock of information.

Instead of hundreds of persons, thousands may stop to view the college exhibit at a shopping center or city fair. At the exhibit, crowd enthusiasm helps generate interest. The visitor thinks, "Other people are watching. Why shouldn't I? Maybe there is something interesting over there at the college show. I'll drop over and see . . ."

Displays of the college are presented on a number of occasions and in a variety of places, both outside the college as well as inside.

OFF-CAMPUS EXHIBITS

Here is a suggested list of places and occasions for the showing of university exhibits outside the campus:

Commercial Establishments

Stores and store windows—during the year, on special occasions such as "College Week," or before the beginning of the semester.

Bank lobbies.

Airports, train and bus stations.

Shopping centers.

Educational, Cultural Institutions

Schools in the city, county, state—when "college-days" or "career-days" are held. During the year, the exhibits may be displayed in the schools' exhibit cases.

Libraries—main and branch library windows and inside the building on special occasions and during "College Education Week."

Fairs

City, county, state fairs.

Off-Campus Meetings

Parent-Teachers Associations Meetings.

Teachers', Counselors', Science Associations.

Conventions of professional, education, or trade groups related to college programs.

ON-CAMPUS EXHIBITS

Places and occasions for on-campus exhibits at various traffic spots include:

Regular Exhibits

College library.

Student Activities Center.

Lobbies of Administration Buildings.

Special Occasions for Exhibits

Open House for Various Groups

Parents; civic leaders; government officials; visiting school groups; alumni; board of trustees.

Other Special Events on Campus
College Week; dedication of new building or center; Freshman Orientation Week; arts and science meetings held on campus; panel discussions, workshops sponsored by college; outside speaker events.

Displays may be mounted and moved by truck from neighborhood to neighborhood, from city to city. Once the extensive exhibit or the small displays have been developed, and their effectiveness and value recognized, the public relations department will get calls from the president, the deans and the department heads as well as from the counselors and directors of student activities, for the showing of exhibits for special purposes.

In a small public relations department, where the director wears many professional hats, he develops the exhibit himself. Perhaps he is aided by an assistant, or the artist on his staff who does the brochure-designing. In larger institutions, the departments have "special events representatives" or "coordinators of special events." Working under the general direction of the public relations department head, the coordinator, aided by an artist, organizes and produces the displays. He studies the requests for the exhibits and sets up a schedule for the month or year. He also arranges the transportation for the displays and gets them manned.

The problem in presenting displays is the same as that of all public relations efforts: get the right message to the right people at the right time . . . and in the right way.

Exhibits are made to be seen instantly by the viewers and not read or studied carefully over a long period of time. People move quickly in front of the displays. Before the public relations representative starts to plan his exhibit, he asks these significant questions:
1. What is the message, or messages, I wish to present?
2. What techniques can I use for attracting attention? Arousing interest? Giving information about the university interestingly and quickly?
3. What materials can I use?
4. What personnel do I need to man the exhibit most effectively?

The public relations man first investigates the following factors bearing on the presentation of his exhibit. These factors determine the extent and character of the displays. He wants to know: (1) the physical location of the exhibit; (2) the time of year; (3) the audience.

Physical Location

The public relations representative first sizes up the place of the exhibit. How big will be the display area—what are its exact dimensions? Will there be enough room for a small exhibit or for a large display? Has a booth been. assigned to the college? If so, what are its dimensions?

The representative asks also in what building will the exhibit be held.

First floor? Second floor? What electrical outlets are available there? The special events director wants to learn what will be placed next to the college display. With what exhibits will his display be in direct competition? Will the noise of the musical group or the record-playing in the adjacent booth at the county fair be apt to drown out the college slide show which also has sound? If so, can another exhibit location for the college display be found at the fair?

Time of Year

Sometimes the time of year will determine whether the exhibit will be given at all, or what the content and character might be. If an exhibit is suggested for December or even in March at an outdoor shopping center, the chances for success are dim. Shoppers will not spend time in the cold air, or wait in the rain, to visit the exhibit. Moving the exhibit to an inside mall for December, and shifting the displays to the outside shopping center in April, might solve the problem.

Audience: Most Important Factor

The public relations man responsible for the exhibit will seek to discover as many facts about his potential audience as he can. He can select the photos and objects and materials and personnel which will suit best the audience. Will the audience be composed of the general public? Even men, women and children who have some interest in education already have to be attracted to the college exhibit by some attention-compelling means. Perhaps special demonstrations will be advisable; maybe a three-piece combo from the college music department will be needed to attract attention at the county fair.

Will special interest groups be present at the event where the college exhibit will be displayed? A Parent-Teachers Association convention will draw mothers and fathers with a specific interest in children and education. These parents are concerned about the educational programs, buildings and costs of tuition. A meeting of high school music teachers off or on campus suggests special displays relating to the college's music department, showing students playing or singing, and instructors teaching. Other displays can pictorialize music studios, orchestras and bands rehearsing, as well as previous concerts which have been performed.

In preparing for a meeting of the state engineering society attended by college faculty members, the university public relations man would focus on the institution's engineering program and the machinery used by students. When counselors from a community college visit a technical-vocational high school during "College Career Week" to talk to students, displays of the college's construction, mechanical and electronic engineering departments would strengthen the counselors' presentation.

PLANNING THE EXHIBIT

Once he determines the facts about the location and the type of audience, the public relations man is ready to plan his next step. He must work out a display plan. He selects, out of the many possibilities which bubble up in his mind, the plan with the maximum potential. Not every idea can be carried out, nor every object used.

In producing the exhibit, the representative may call on the college's art department, college art students, and the maintenance department for assistance in actually carrying out the ideas. If this is not practical, he may engage the services of a commercial display company which will produce the design and the exhibit, or furnish the panelboards or stands needed. A professional signpainter may supply the posters, artwork and lettering required. The public relations representative participates in the preliminary as well as progress conferences so that the exhibit, when finished, will express and present the message he desires. He may furnish the necessary photos from his file, or have the pictures taken.

The content of the displays has to be determined early in the planning stage. Some exhibits are general and give a wide-scope view of the institution. The department may decide on only one permanent exhibit which will last a year or two, and will be useful for all occasions. The department, however, may determine that a group of smaller displays provide flexibility, and individual posters or panels be built so they may be changed to fit special occasions and particular purposes. The ideal pattern is a combination of a permanent exhibit and interchangeable, flexible displays.

One exhibit or part of an exhibit is frequently devoted to the history and progress of the institution. The public relations man desires to show the advancement made in student enrollment, in courses and programs, or in the departments, and he wants to indicate the growth in the building facilities from the small institution it was years ago, until today. The public relations director may wish to show in another panel the present overall campus with an aerial shot, or individual buildings in the complex photographed from the ground level. Or he may desire to focus on the new construction going on.

In other displays, the representative may desire to concentrate on a number of the departments or divisions at the college. He wishes to build up displays for each department, as the displays can be changed and used on a variety of occasions. He asks himself what would the viewers want to know about the departments, then he jots down some of the significant points. Now he consults with the department heads, explains the purpose of the exhibit and requests suggestions for content, pointing out that the departmental display would be a brief, striking *pictorial presentation* of the value and work of the department. As the department head, or the instructor assigned to the conference may not be accustomed to preparing exhibits, the public relations man submits a preliminary sketch with the content to the departmental representatives, as a basis for further discussion.

In presenting a view of the department, the public relations representative focuses on a number of points: (1) value of the subject for general background or for career-preparation; (2) the variety of courses offered by the department; (3) the qualified faculty. He may wish to show (4) the classrooms and laboratories and other facilities used by instructors and students. Or he may desire to demonstrate (5) the new teaching methods and audiovisual aids used by the instructors to make the classes interesting and to get the students involved in the learning process. Photos of field trips taken by the business administration department to industrial plants, or illustrations of the geology students' trip to the mountains to dig for fossils, would bring out other phases of the college activities.

At the community/junior college, the special events coordinator usually wishes to stress (1) the transfer-to-college programs and (2) the career programs offered at the institution. In addition to the regular information about the programs, he may wish, therefore, to devote posters and panels to the career opportunities open to graduates of (1) the entire college; (2) business administration department; (3) allied health section; (4) engineering department; (5) art courses; (6) radio and television department, (7) other curriculums.

In designing the content for the panel on the radio and television department, for example, the representative may wish to focus on the excitement and personal satisfactions of radio and television newscasters, scriptwriters, floormen, cameramen and others. A panel to show what some graduates of the department are doing in broadcasting stations enlivens the exhibit.

In seeking to develop a special exhibit which would appeal to high school students, the public relations representative may go further. In addition to presenting his own college's advantages, he may desire to stress the value of a college education to high school graduates. The display may feature: (1) college education stimulates better citizenship; (2) college education provides for leisuretime pursuits; (3) college courses enable students to explore further interesting subjects begun in high school; (4) college furnishes the opportunity to open up new and interesting worlds not explored in high schools; (5) college gives the necessary preparation for study in professional schools of law, medicine, social work; (6) college preparation is needed for entering graduate work in the physical and social sciences; (7) college graduates earn more during their lifetime usually than high school graduates.

Special exhibits may be developed for adults who are employed dur-

The poster display for "Upward Bound" consisted of (1) a poster, stressing the purpose of the college program for high schoolers who received intensive preparation for college entrance, and (2) five pictures showing the activities students engage in when they enroll in the "Upward Bound" program.

ing the day, but wish to continue their education in the evening. Such displays may be placed in factories, business and governmental offices. The exhibits may find a place in local libraries and in shopping centers. The displays focus on the particular advantages of continuing education for employed persons.

Similar exhibits can be designed for homemakers, housewives, mothers and grandmothers, who can be aroused to attend courses in the morning, afternoon or evening at the main campus of the college, or at off-campus centers in libraries, high schools and other places in the neighborhoods.

Different kinds of exhibits are developed by the coordinator for different events. If a library or building is dedicated and named for a prominent person, living or dead, a special event may be held at the college, when an exhibit would add much interest to the occasion. Some of the posters might be devoted to the life of, say, the president of the college who is being honored. Photos of his early life, school and college days may be obtained from his family. Part of the exhibit could be focused on the president's various roles and activities at the college, with some reference being made to his contributions to the institution. The expansion of the college during his administration could be portrayed, with a display of the magazine articles and books he has written.

If the official has been active in community life, a section of the display could be devoted to his role as government consultant, and to his membership on the board of city library trustees. To give the exhibit a lively and newsy flavor, front pages of newspapers during the previous decade would be of interest, as they would show the world, national and state events which occurred and perhaps influenced the president during his administration. These blow-ups of front pages could be supplied by local editors as their contribution to the event.

If state, county or city officials are invited to an open house at the college, the public relations man prepares a fresh exhibit or readapts some of his other displays for the occasion. He focuses on the contributions made by the institution to the state, county or city. His exhibit would show the value of the college education to residents. In the display would be photos of some graduates who entered the business world; pictures of other graduates who became doctors; and shots of still other graduates who became lawyers and now plead the causes of citizens in courts. Panels would show graduates participating in community life, joining civic organizations and neighborhood groups, serving on the boards of directors of libraries and schools.

DESIGN AND CONSTRUCTION

Photos

Photos tell the university story graphically in displays, enabling the public relations department to project the college's programs, faculty, students and building facilities beyond the campus. As far as possible, ideas about the institution must be translated into visuals. The space given to the photo display should be three or four times that given to copy.

The special events coordinator begins by drawing on the photo file of the public relations department. He selects the photos most appropriate for the particular display, and from the negatives makes positive prints. In many instances, he will need to have new photos shot to bring out the messages he wants to convey.

The 8 x 10 inch glossy photos used for newspaper and magazine purposes usually do not suffice for displays. Although 8 x 10's have their value for certain spots in the exhibit, such photos cannot be seen readily from any distance. Photos of 11 x 16 inch, and even larger, give more dramatic effect, catch the eye and may be seen from a distance. The photos can be mounted on cardboards of various sizes and colors.

Lettering

All photos in exhibits need some explanation, for they do not tell the college story or give the message by themselves. Lettering is also needed for the headlines and the other explanatory copy. Various sizes and styles or families of letters make the exhibits attractive.

The public relations man in a small department may have a full- or part-time artist on his staff, or he may have the inclination or the ability to do his own lettering. Bookstores and art supply shops have a variety of useful pens, brushes, posterpaints and cardboard to help the display-maker. He can buy lettering stencils or press-on letters which give a professional appearance. He remembers that visitors usually will be looking at the exhibits from a distance; consequently, letters 2½ inches high are needed even for window displays.

If the public relations man doesn't have the time, inclination or ability for such lettering work, he may enlist the interest of the college art department's instructors or students. Many PR men employ the services of a professional sign-painter or poster-maker, who will prepare layouts from copy and photos supplied, and will produce finished work.

Construction Design

Exhibits range from a simple group of posters attached to panel boards to elaborate designs in various shapes, sizes and materials.

Easy to construct are the one-, two- and three-panel displays on large cardboards of various colors. Standard cardboards are 11 x 16 inches. They may be cut in different shapes: (1) rectangle, (2) square, (3) triangle, or (4) circle. They are stapled on bulletin boards or display panels which stand on their own feet and are joined together with hinges in pairs or triplets. These display panels may be built, or purchased from school supply houses.

The practitioner who wants a more substantial display for his posters may place the photos and lettering on wooden boards such as plywood, a material which is light and may be transported easily. Beaverboard and Celotex, purchased in a variety of lengths and widths, may be obtained. Some companies specialize in easily mounted displays, consisting of Celotex blocks with fitted hinges. These cubes can be hooked together in various designs and dismounted easily for other exhibits.

Exhibits made by professionals are designed especially to suit the needs of the university. The displays may involve several panels or sections, with attractive photos, striking lettering and effective artwork. Two-dimensional lettering heightens the exhibit's appeal.

Lighting

The college representative finds that the lighting of his exhibit is an important factor in its success. He desires to heighten the effect by having his own spotlights, hence he purchases them for present and future use. Before setting up a display anywhere, the public relations man asks what lights are available there. Are they ordinary fixtures? Are spotlights furnished? When he makes the arrangements for the college exhibit at a local high school, he finds out if electrical outlets are nearby, and exactly where they are located.

Transportable Exhibits

Some public relations men design their exhibits to be shown one time, then dismount the entire project. In other institutions, the representatives plan the exhibit so that they can be used over again. With a few changes, the displays can be adapted to different audiences and different physical locations. The aim, then, is to produce an exhibit which can be folded up easily and can be transported. Cardboard sheets, instead of wooden boards, prove useful for backgrounds. Lightweight materials can be carried in a case or large box. On several hours' notice the public relations man can set up the displays for almost any occasion.

MANNING THE EXHIBIT

Now the photos and the copy, no matter how unique, are lifeless. A live person—instructor, counselor, student or public relations representative—at the exhibit attracts attention and adds value. The college personnel can answer questions about the displays, point up features of the exhibit, and tell about the institution. When the exhibit is held at the city auditorium or the county fair, the visitors have the opportunity to talk directly to a college representative, particularly about enrollment.

Live Demonstrations

Student or departmental demonstrations, or projects, add immensely to the exhibit. The opportunities are many, but cooperation is needed. The electronics engineering students may develop a computer which hums a song. The dental laboratory students in a community college may bring some of their equipment and show how they make dental appliances. The food service and hotel management department may bake cookies at the college, and ice them at the exhibit for free distribution. If the area for the display is large enough, the art students may paint at their easels.

As an adjunct to the exhibit, color-slide shows may be projected. Screens with hoods or special daylight screens have been found useful for this purpose. The effectiveness of the physical education department's exhibit on recreational leadership may be increased with the presence of some team members in uniform and with a table displaying the trophies won by the basketball or football team. Community College of Baltimore's public relations department aroused the interest of the history department in an exhibit; as a result, Prof. Beverly Chico developed a display of "Hats Through the Ages," reflecting the economic, political, cultural and military life of various nations.

Brochures

Visitors may want to take home printed material about the college from the exhibit after they have seen it. The public relations department head may furnish a catalogue, a schedule or a list of courses for the next semester; he may have available general brochures about the college or specific brochures about departments in which the visitors are interested. A one-, two-, or four-page tabloid newspaper covering the history of the college, the programs, costs and other information, will be found useful for distribution at many exhibits.

Newspaper articles telling about the exhibits may be released before the displays are shown as well as during the period when they are presented.

CHECK LIST FOR DISPLAYS

1. Title or top heading for the exhibit (general theme or themes).
2. Purpose of the exhibit.
3. Place(s) where it will be shown.
4. Audience(s) to whom it will be shown.
5. Dimensions of the exhibit space selected (for table: 6 x 4 feet; large space 10 x 10 feet; larger area 15 x 15 feet).
6. Dimensions of 1-, 2-, or 3-Panel Display.
   left panel _____ middle panel _____
   right panel _____ floor area _____
7. Materials to be used:
   Pictures—type, sizes, content
   Objects—
   Models (houses, printing presses)—
   Motion pictures—
   Other
8. Attendants and demonstrators.
9. Literature to be distributed.
10. Draw on a large sheet of paper (or double 8½ x 11) the design for the display.

15

The Speakers' Bureau

MANY UNIVERSITIES AND COLLEGES have established speakers' bureaus because they have demonstrated their value as public relations channels. The well-organized and capably staffed speakers' bureau gives the university an opportunity to reach a variety of publics directly. The speakers generate a personal feeling about the institution, replacing the impersonal impression many people get from "cold print" about the college. On many occasions the speakers are requested to talk about the college—its programs and personnel, its physical facilities, and the institution's contributions to the community.

On other occasions, the bureau establishes a strong, durable relationship with community organizations by supplying knowledgeable speakers who talk on general and specific cultural, scientific and business topics as well as on current issues. The topics are selected by these groups, hence the subjects are of special interest to the audiences. Organizations may desire a panel of speakers to discuss important subjects, with the panel including instructors as well as students.

Frequently, the speeches lead to audience-questions about the courses taught by the professors who are on the platforms. Members of the audiences may desire to learn more about the issues just discussed. Others in the audience want to know more about the college courses relating to the topic presented by the lecturer.

To make the speeches more graphic, speakers are supplied with audio-visual aids, such as color slides, motion pictures or tape recordings. Posters or exhibits relating to the college or specific programs may be furnished the speaker, or delivered to the place where he gives his talk. Many

Enthusiastic and knowledgeable instructors, assistant and
associate and full professors,
as well as deans and chairmen
of departments, enlist in the
speakers' bureaus. The speakers perform a service to community organizations and act
as goodwill agents of the public relations departments of
universities.

instructors have their own visual aids prepared, as they know the value of such materials in making their subjects come alive.

SPEAKERS' TOPICS

Several general categories of topics are offered by the speakers' bureaus. One group deals with higher education, with the speakers discussing universities and colleges in the state or area; lectures may present also an overall view of the state's system of higher education. People want to know what are the requirements to enter the various universities and colleges, what programs and courses are offered, what are the costs, and whether personal counseling is available. This type of speech would be of direct value to the college which the speaker represents. The second general category relates to current social, political and economic issues. A third type of lecture is concerned with background topics; and a fourth type, personal problems of individuals.

The public relations department assists the professors in formulating appealing and catchy titles. The professors may be highly knowledgeable and concerned primarily with the content of their talks, but to attract a wide audience, the titles of their discussions should be framed as interestingly and as provocatively as possible.

In the spring or fall semester, the director distributes through the campus mail a speakers' bureau form to each administrator and faculty member. The form is accompanied by a brief note which tells the importance of the speakers' bureau, and outlines the satisfactions the administrators and faculty members can derive from speaking to a wider audience, usually adults who are interested in special topics. The forms are filled out by the staff and returned to the public relations department. The director proceeds to have a brochure designed and printed.

Most faculty members volunteer their services to the speakers' bureau, desiring to reach the general public outside the classroom, telling about what is going on in their subjects, discussing current government or social problems before a wide audience. The instructors are told about the publicity releases which will be sent out in connection with the talks. Department heads and college officials will be sent copies of the releases also. In some instances, a faculty member with elaborate, well-prepared lectures, slides or motion pictures, is offered a regular honorarium for outside lecturing on his specialty. The amount may be stated in the brochure and during the pre-lecture arrangements when they are made.

UM Speakers' Bureau Guidebook Is Available

College Park—Publication of the new University of Maryland Speakers' Bureau Guide for 1970-1971 has been announced by Jean Greenwald, bureau director.

Mrs. Greenwald, said the guide lists 276 faculty and staff members who are prepared to discuss more than 700 subjects before Maryland civic, educational, religious and service groups.

Presentations by faculty and staff members are normally determined by their area of expertise, although speakers often draw on personal experience in discussing such topics as "European Travel Today" or "Student Dissent at the University of Maryland."

Student Speakers

In addition to providing its normal service of arranging for faculty and staff speakers, the bureau will have additional capabilities this year, Mrs. Greenwald said. "We are now able to honor requests for student speakers," she noted. "In addition, we are in the process of arranging panels of students, administrators and faculty members to discuss the campus scene with members of community groups."

Copies of the Speakers' Bureau Guide may be obtained by phoning 454-3324 or by writing to; the Speakers' Bureau, Public Information Office, Graduate School and Administrative Services Building, University of Maryland, College Park, Maryland 20742.

A news release about the speakers' bureau sent out by the University of Maryland

SPEAKERS' BUREAU
FORM   FOR SPEAKERS

(filled out by administrators, faculty members, others)

Name _____

Department _____

Room Number _____ Telephone Number _____

Topic(s) I Can Speak On:
    1.
    2.
    3.

General Content of Lecture (100 words) (May be by topics)
                    (use other side)

Significance of Subject:

Possible Groups Subjects Might Appeal To:
    1.
    2.
    3.
    4.

Length of Speech (may be more than one length, according to audience
  needs)

30 minutes _____   1 hour _____   2 hours _____

(Series of lectures)

Audio-Visual Aids Used:
    Slide projector ___   Motion Pictures ___   Tape Recordings ___
    Still photographs ___   Charts ___   Graphs ___   Demonstrations ___
    Performances (music) ___

When Available:
    Day _____   Evening _____   During Week _____   Week-ends _____

Educational Topics

The speakers' bureau may offer a speaker who will combine general information about higher education with specific facts about the university or college where he teaches. Thus, he may speak on "New Developments in College Teaching Today," or "New Techniques for Reaching the College Student," which would cover developments throughout the United States and also touch upon "The Innovative Methods Used At_____ University." A more direct missile might be "What_____College Has

SPEAKERS' BUREAU FORM

BACKGROUND INFORMATION ON SPEAKER

Name _____

Department _____

Telephone _____

Colleges attended   Dates   Degree

_____   _____   _____

_____   _____   _____

_____   _____   _____

Appointed this Institution _____

General Interests _____

Research Activities _____

Publications:
      (Title)   (Date)

To Offer Your Son, Your Daughter, or You." Some audiences may prefer the lecture to cover just the single college, as they may want direct personal information.

When disturbing headlines about students on college campuses appear in the newspaper, the public is concerned about these activities, hence speakers focusing on student problems get a ready ear. College bureaus list such topics as "The Meaning of Student Dissent Today," "Roots of the Student Revolt," "Some Results of Student Protests." Where campuses have increased their student participation in college decision-making, speakers discuss "Increasing Student Participation in Governance at _____ College," or "The Significant Role of Students in Planning at _____ University."

Current Issues

As the instructors have expertise in the subjects they teach, the speakers' bureau may offer their services to discuss current issues of importance to the community. These instructors may be looked upon by the community as persons who will present more objectively the background and causes, the pros and cons of the issues. This does not imply that instructors have no opinions on such problems, but they have greater detachment than many other persons and possess the ability to articulate the background causes and the various sides of the issues.

One of the key issues today and during the decade ahead is the racial problem. From the sociology or psychology department may come instructors who have done research, and have acquired background and opinions, on problems of the minority groups. These instructors may seek especially a larger audience than the young people sitting in the classroom, and wish to talk on such subjects as "The Black Attitude Today"; "Neglected Americans Today—Puerto Ricans, Mexican-Americans and Indians"; "Civil Rights Progress We Have Made—and Lost." Other instructors may select a broader topic such as "The Struggle of Minority Groups For Rights— Economic and Political"; "How You Can Break Down the Barriers of Prejudice"; "Practical Solutions to the White and Black Problem."

Because of the steadily-rising rate of crime and the glaring headlines about muggings, robberies and murders in the city streets, crime, its causes and means of prevention, provides topics in which many organizations are interested. From the sociology department, the urban affairs department, or the law-enforcement and psychology departments come lecturers on the crime issue. The instructor may give the background in such topics as "Roots of Criminal Behavior"; "The Deeper Causes of Crime"; "Why the Rising Crime Rate?" He may have some solutions in his speeches "The New Juvenile Delinquents," or "Preventing Crime Before It Gets Started." The law enforcement department chairman may wish to talk on "Police: Friend or Foe?" or "Protecting Yourself in Your Own Home." The instructor, dealing with correctional institutions in his classes, may select "Prisons, Schools of Crime"; "Do Correctional Institutions Correct?" or "Prisons: A Revolving Door For Offenders."

The widespread use and abuse of drugs and the genuine alarm expressed by many parents have led to frequent requests for discussions of the drug topic. The conflicts parents have with their teen-age and college-age sons and daughters have pushed this to the No. 1 topic in many communities. These residents want to know how widespread is the taking of drugs, why do young people engage in this activity, how harmful is it, and what they, as parents, can tell their children. Instructors from the physiology department, the psychology or the sociology departments can be encouraged to list their names as outside speakers with the bureau. "Are Drugs Really Harmful?" "What Do Young People Seek to Gain Through

Getting a Fix?" are some topics used. "The Social and Commercial Factors Behind Drug Pushing" or "What To Tell Your Son and Daughter About Drugs," are subjects which have wide appeal.

As the political scene changes, the topics which can be presented by members of the political science or government departments also alter, reflecting the current interest, such as "The Disenchantment with the Electoral College Today" or "Electoral College: Outmoded or Living, Viable Institution." The political scientist and historian may also deal with broad international topics relating to U. S. foreign policy and involvement in the Middle-East or Far-East. Such topics may be titled: "The Changing Image of Uncle Sam" or "Enough Involvement in . . . ." Instructors in the government department may seek the opportunity to give their views on "What's Right, What's Wrong at the UN"; "The Mistakes We Made at the United Nations"; "Can the UN Survive?"

Professors in the business administration or economics departments lecture to their classes on the advancements in technology, the wonders of the computer, the stock market trends, the influx of Japanese cameras and German mini-autos, plus other topics of current interest which would appeal also to community groups looking for useful information and enlightenment about our economic world.

Background Topics

Some community groups are less interested in current issues than in acquiring cultural background. Organizations may ask for a speaker to deal with art, hence the public relations department would offer the art instructor whose topics might be "Art Trends: 1910–1970's"; "The Meaning Behind the Picture"; "What Contemporary Artists Are Trying to Say and Convey." To broaden the appreciation of his audience, another art instructor might select: "How To Get More Out of Art" or "Adding Another Dimension to Your Life." With reproductions and color slides, the instructor illustrates his talks. From the music department may come an instructor whose views on traditional and rock music would be covered in "Is Rock Music Really Bad?" or "Is Traditional Music Really Dead?" An instructor with a strong community feeling, might discuss "Music in the Community" or "Some Contemporary and Avant Garde Musicians." Instrumentalists from the music faculty or students who play at the lecture-demonstrations would add to the interest or, if these musicians are unavailable, recordings would help.

The department of English or the department of literature can supply speakers who deal interestingly with American literary trends and personalities. A number of universities and colleges have courses in world literature, dealing with the works of Europeans, Africans and Orientals. The lectures in these courses may be briefed and highlighted for a lively and different program offered by the speakers' bureau. Many literary or book review groups welcome university speakers who are knowledgeable about current novels, biographies or other non-fiction of significance.

At one time, scientists were considered the gods who, with the inventors, gave us our great affluent society, and the scientists still are held in great esteem. In the departments of physical or biological science in every college or university, there are a number of scientists who can "make science come alive" and they have something significant to say about their subjects. They may talk on "New Horizons in Chemistry"; "What Genetics Have to Tell Us About Human Beings"; "Social Consequences of Artificial Insemination In the Decades Ahead."

Self-Improvement Topics

College speakers' bureaus get calls from organizations which want experts to help them with personal problems. The psychology department may supply a speaker who will deal with the problem of reducing the communication gap with the younger generation. The business administration department may be asked by the Chamber of Commerce or a trade association for a panel of speakers on successful operation of small businesses. A woman's organization may want a lecture on attractive home decorating. The art or home economics departments may have just the person for this assignment. Another group requires a series of lectures which will enable the members to understand modern art better, and the art instructor who has put his name down on the speakers' list is selected.

ORGANIZATIONS LOOK FOR SPEAKERS

A variety of groups with general and special interests are on the lookout for effective, informative speakers. Other organizations would invite such lecturers if the idea were suggested to them and the advantages were pointed out. The chairmen of program committees for local women's groups which meet regularly search for worthwhile speakers who provide the main lure for audiences, or are used to round out a program of business. But whatever the reason for requesting a list from the speakers' bureau, the college public relations representative has the opportunity to reach an influential public. Among the members of women's groups are parents of potential students and adults who also might enroll in day or evening or summer classes. Book review and literary groups, composed largely of women, provide an outlet for the speakers on literary topics.

Church, synagogue and temple organizations which believe they should link their programs to current issues confronting members, ask for speakers from the college. During the week or on Sunday mornings, the college speakers have the opportunity to present informative talks and, at the same time, build goodwill and understanding for the institution.

Parent-Teachers organizations desire lecturers on current educational topics. They may wish to understand what the local community colleges offer in the way of transfer-to-college and career programs for high school graduates. Or the members may wish to learn about the student revolt on the campuses. Some groups of this kind want to get more facts about parent-child relationships, hence welcome the professor of psychology who specializes in this subject, and who has something new and different to say.

At high schools, student clubs frequently seek outside speakers on topics of current issues, on science or literature. These speakers can be supplied by the college speakers' bureau. The instructor may take along college exhibits as well as brochures regarding science courses or literature courses.

Local civic improvement and neighborhood improvement associations are on the lookout for speakers to complete their weekly or monthly programs. The Exchange Club and the Kiwanis Club desire to liven up their weekly or monthly meetings and, after the chicken dinner with apple dumplings and ice cream has been consumed, the members will listen to a representative of the college on an issue of general interest. Desiring to fit in with "Community College Week," the chairmen of the program committees will respond to the suggestion of the college representative that the speakers' bureau provide a dynamic speaker and 20-minute motion picture that day.

PROMOTING THE SPEAKERS' BUREAU

The college public relations department makes a careful study of the city directories for lists of community organizations and clubs which might be interested in the speakers' bureau. The college list covers also church organizations, community or local neighborhood improvement associations, and those obtained from the Chamber of Commerce, or a state agency which has compiled such groups. Sometimes such lists are found in the local or the state library.

To these groups the director then circulates an attractively printed brochure about the bureau, with information in easy-to-read, parallel columns, about: each topic which lecturers are prepared to discuss; general content of each topic; length of the lectures; and audio-visual aids to be used; speakers and their available dates. In the mail he encloses a letter to the president or chairman, and makes sure to include also a return-card and envelope.

Upon receiving a request from an organization the public relations news writer or director of the speakers' bureau, writes a news release, telling about the speaker, his topic and the time and date of the meeting. A sentence about the program chairman would be desirable. A glossy photo

MONTGOMERY COLLEGE SPEAKERS PROGRAM 1970-71

mc

Brochures for speakers' bureaus have attractive covers. The insides give the lecturers, subjects and other information of value to organization presidents. In various ways, the covers convey the idea of the speaker in communication with the listener. Montgomery College shows a section of an entire audience.

of the speaker is included in the packet. The news release and photo may be sent directly to the news editors of the media, or may be forwarded to the program chairman of the organization. Usually the procedure is left to the college representative. However, if the news is sent to the print or broadcast media, a copy is distributed to the program chairman anyway, because it may be used in the next edition of the association's newsletter —all of which adds to the interest in the speaker.

If the university public relations department is alert, it will make an effort to get a résumé of the topic from the instructor before the speech is delivered. A news article on the contents of the talk may be released following the meeting. Sometimes a telephone check about this news event with the city editor, or educational departmental editor, may prove productive.

Mail to:
Public Information Office

REQUEST FOR SPEAKER

COLLEGE SPEAKERS' PROGRAM

1. Name of Organization

2. Contact Representative

   Address

   Telephone: Business _____
   Home _____

3. Location of Meeting

4. Date Speaker Desired _____ Time _____

5. Subject Desired in Order of Preference (Number and Title)

   1.
   2.
   3.

6. Type Affair (Check as applicable)

   Luncheon   Dinner   Business Mtg.

7. Time to be allowed for Presentation

8. Audience (Check as applicable)

   Male   Female   Male and Female

9. Audience size _____

10. Remarks:

Date   Signature

Sample of Request Form For Speakers Used
By Montgomery College (Rockville, Md.)

To create a speakers' bureau which will be successful, the public relations representative has to get the support and enthusiasm of the administrative officials as well as of the chairmen of the various departments and of the instructors. The bureau cannot be just another extracurricular activity for instructors, an activity dreamed up by the public relations men. The value of the bureau has to be perceived by the administrators who, at informal meetings and at luncheons, express the administrators' interest in the work of the bureau and show their understanding of its public relations value to the institution. Chairmen of departments, if aware of the importance of the bureau, are needed to speak to the outside groups as well as to give the speakers' bureau their backing within their college departments.

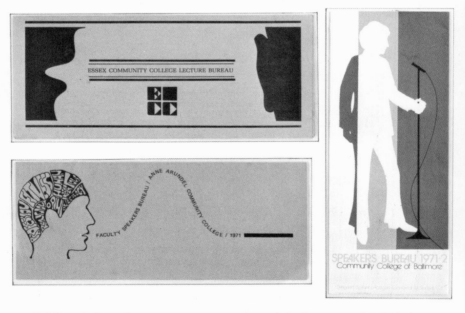

Public relations departments use a variety of designs to make their brochures for the speakers' bureaus attractive.

16

Alumni Relations

COLLEGES AND UNIVERSITIES TODAY face a new and changing world, and they need all the good friends and supporters they can get outside the campus. Alumni and former students are the best ambassadors of goodwill for institutions of higher learning. If well-informed and interested, each alumnus can multiply many fold the work produced and effort exerted by the college's public relations department. For each alumnus can generate far-reaching understanding and goodwill in his area. Former students may be located in many states of the nation, thousands of miles away from the campus.

Universities now and in the decades ahead face the sharp competition for top-flight, qualified students. The graduates of these institutions can spread favorable reports about them and, directly or indirectly, assist in acquainting such students with the universities' advantages. Because of violence and other actions of some students on campus, public reaction toward the universities has been, in many instances, unfavorable. Responding to the headlined news events, many alumni turned against their own alma maters, believing that the administration was too permissive, or the student body wrong and uncontrolled in their illegal actions to accomplish change. Readers of the alumni magazines and news-letters have become informed about the real situation, however, and are in a position to help counteract misunderstandings of what is going on.

The day of single large benefactors of educational institutions is mostly gone too. Many foundations are somewhat hesitant about making contributions or have other outlets in poverty-areas for their excess funds. Government support is uncertain and subject to cutbacks. Yet, rising college costs have not equalled the income obtained from student fees and other sources. A critical situation exists, particularly in many private educational institutions. Large amounts of money are needed to attract and hold capable faculty members, and to meet the urgent needs of college libraries for books or science laboratories for equipment.

A large number of the 1,200 private colleges and universities, educat-

SFAA

alumni news

BOSTON UNIVERSITY SCHOOL OF FINE AND APPLIED ARTS   OCTOBER 1970

Former theatre arts student Dennis Allen was a familiar face in student productions such as Beggar on Horseback (above). Now he has become a regular cast member of Rowan and Martin's Laugh-In (see page 2).

High school musicians who participated in BU's Young Artists' Program at Tanglewood this past summer performed under the baton of several internationally known conductors, including Michael Tilson Thomas, associate conductor of the Boston Symphony Orchestra. Leonard Bernstein and Seiji Ozawa also conducted in rehearsal. Regular Young Artist Symphony conductor is James Yannatos.

Music Launches Experimental Plan

An experimental plan for assigning music students to performing organizations has been inaugurated by the Division of Music.

In an attempt to increase the variety and scope of musical experience in both performance and repertoire, each instrumentalist in the division will participate in several different ensembles under different coaches or conductors during the next academic year.

Each student will be assigned to a particular group, such as string ensemble, woodwind choir, brass choir, percussion ensemble, or chamber orchestra, for a time block of four or five weeks. At the conclusion of each time block, the instrumentalist will be reassigned to a new group and new instructor.

In addition, students will be brought together from time to time to perform in the more traditional performing organizations such as the symphony and wind orchestras.

According to Dr. Wilbur Fullbright, chairman of the music division, the program — believed to be the first of its kind for professional music schools — will make it possible for students to cover music literature that was impossible to perform when students were assigned solely to so-called large ensembles.

"Baroque literature, for example, was something a music student rarely performed if he or she was assigned to large symphony orchestra or concert band for the whole year," Dr. Fullbright explains. "Under the new plan, each conductor will be able to cover a more diverse repertoire, work more closely with individual students in rehearsing the literature, and at the end of the time block begin on something entirely different with the next group."

(continued on page 2)

Boston University's individual schools have their own news-letters, each carrying the same masthead *"Alumni News,"* with code or initial changes. The above publication is printed for the School of Fine and Applied Arts, carrying the initials SFAA.

Number One

Harvard University may enjoy the reputation of being the top school in the nation, but university officials aren't smug about it.

In an intensified recruiting campaign, the Harvard admissions office for the first time has enlisted students as talent scouts.

Early in November, Harvard fresh-

men received letters asking them to help recruit high school seniors from their home towns for next year's freshman class.

Explains director of admissions John P. Reardon, "There just aren't that many outstanding students in the country. Moreover, there are about 2000 colleges competing for the best."

To gain an edge in the competition, Reardon hopes that present freshmen will identify promising future candidates and help persuade them to apply to Harvard.

"There isn't a stronger student body anywhere," Reardon claims. But if you were Hertz and you just sat back, Avis would overtake you."

Parade

Even Harvard University is engaged in a recruitment campaign for top students.

ing about one-third of the seven million students enrolled in higher education, are in the red, according to Joseph T. Hughes, administrative trustee of the Richard King Mellon Foundation in Pittsburgh, in an article several years ago on the financial problem in the *Bostonia,* the alumni magazine of Boston University. He pointed out that a *Fortune* magazine study on 20 selected colleges in the late 1960's, estimated that by 1978 their total combined annual deficit will have risen to $110-million. Because of the rising costs and relatively static income, private colleges will have to curtail their services and reduce the quality of their education, or raise tuition fees. Some may have to go out of business altogether, or merge with other private or state institutions.

The consequences of a major decline in the number and quality of independent colleges would be undesirable, in the view of many responsible persons. Students would lose a freedom of choice in selecting the college with the curricula they desire, or be unable to select a small college with small classes. The existing competition and cooperation between private and state colleges are desirable and should be maintained. Each type of institution is stimulated by the advances in knowledge and the innovation in teaching methods developed by the other. Many private colleges are small, emphasizing close student relations in small classes, permitting face-to-face contacts with teachers of experience rather than teaching assistants.

Strong financial support from the alumni is needed, therefore, to assist the hard-hit colleges to keep in the black and to make progress. The colleges, too, need help in fund-raising activities for long-range projects and new buildings. Such assistance can be supplied by interested, active former students.

Universities also need friends in the community and in the political life of the local area or state, friends who understand the value of these institutions and the contributions they make to the community's economic and cultural welfare. Alumni who are government officials or members of educational commissions and agencies are influential when legislation affecting institutions of higher learning is considered and when budgets are decided.

HOPKINS GETS
$100,000 GIFT

The Commercial Credit Company has made a gift of $100,000 to The Johns Hopkins University, it was announced by Robert D. H. Harvey, chairman of the University's Board of Trustees.

The grant was made in honor of Dr. Milton S. Eisenhower, president of Johns Hopkins University, and a senior member of the Board of Directors of Commercial Credit.

In making the gift, the company said it would be used to expand an endowment of the school, the Dunning Memorial Fund, the income of which is for the unrestricted use by the school.

The H. A. B. Dunning Foundation was founded by Dr. Dunning, former president of Hynson, Wescott and Dunning, a local pharmaceutical firm.

Baltimore (Md.) *Sun*

MAINTAINING GOOD RELATIONS

A key factor in arousing and keeping the interest of former students is systematic communication. The alumnus and the alumna need to be kept informed about the institution—what activities are being carried on, what progress is being made, what changes are under way, and what the institutional needs are. Alumni lacking in information are less likely to work for the college and give it essential support.

Too, a feeling that the graduate is still a part of the *college family* has to be conveyed. The alumnus should be given tangible reasons to believe that the college is still interested in him—that he should continue to be concerned about the institution which prepared him for adult living and laid the groundwork for his profession or business.

Although he may have graduated some years ago, his friendly ties with the institution should be maintained and strengthened. He should be encouraged to continue his interest in the university, to return to it when he can, and to enjoy the meetings and fellowship with other alumni. It should be reemphasized that he is still a member of the "family." The university, through seminars, can provide him with the opportunity to bring his professional or business knowledge up-to-date, furnishing him with a kind of useful continuing education beyond graduation.

It is fatal for the alumnus to feel he is wanted only for his financial support—that he is forgotten throughout the year, and "hit" only when the time comes for annual gift-giving or when faculty and building funds need alumni dollars. Strong psychological relations have to be maintained before money is contributed.

For the public relations department to develop understanding with alumni, and through this, their support, certain requisites are essential. The president is a key figure in all alumni relations and any effort to build goodwill needs his full, actve cooperation. He must have an understanding of the important role played by the former students in the total university-relations program. He sets the whole tone of this effort, as he is looked up to and respected by the graduates. He figures prominently in all the alumni activities, offering his services as speaker at reunions of individual classes, or as the keynoter at Homecoming and other events involving the alumni. He contributes a special column to the magazine mailed to alumni, and his special presidential report also is sent to them.

The second requisite is a strong alumni association. Although the offices are held by the graduates (and they do much work), the main thrust is accomplished through the alumni office, a part of the public relations department. A special staffer, often called alumni relations director, is assigned to carry on the duties and works under the overall direction of the public relations director. On the alumni staff may be several assistants in charge of different projects and special alumni events. In most institutions, the large alumni association has former students organized by classes or schools and regions. The alumni relations director seeks ways to increase the effectiveness of the affiliated associations, and to generate the interest and support of more alumni. Some of the graduates are interested in the university from the time they get their degrees and hence respond readily; others lose interest immediately and have to be re-awakened.

CHANNELS OF COMMUNICATION

Various systematic channels of communication have been developed by public relations departments to keep alumni and former students up-to-date regarding happenings at the college.

Newspapers and Broadcast Media

Alumni, as members of the general public, read university news and features appearing in newspapers, and listen to or watch the institution's news on broadcasts. The alumni relations director takes several additional steps in connection with this publicity in the mass media. He also sends a story about the university to the presidents of the alumni chapters, suggesting that they take the releases to the local newspapers, and point out to the editors the large number of alumni in the area who would be interested in such news, if published. When meetings of area chapters are held, the alumni director prepares releases which may be distributed by the local officers to the newspapers. When a large state newspaper expects to carry an article in the Sunday edition on the college, letters may be sent to alumni in the area calling attention to the upcoming article. Similarly, when radio or television stations broadcast special college programs, alert-cards may be sent ahead to alumni in the area.

The Alumni Magazine

In most universities and colleges the alumni magazine has long been the main channel of communication, although supplemented by other printed media. The magazine furnishes an opportunity to keep former students aware of what is going on at the institution, while generating a feeling of pride in it. By means of news stories, feature articles and lively photographs, information about current happenings at the university and about other alumni can be provided.

To catch and to hold the interest of thousands of former students are formidable tasks of the editor and his staff. In reality, they are competing with many commercial magazines. Surfeited with publications, the college graduate today has to choose from among many, those which he will take time to read. The alumni magazine, therefore, has to be on a high-interest level, with pictorial and typographical quality equal to general publications. The alumnus has to find in his university magazine something of general educational or cultural interest as well as something specific about the institution. The editor must treat readers as serious-minded, intelligent persons with a potential interest in the affairs of the college.

Content

The content of the magazine designed for former students is similar in some ways to other periodicals produced by the public relations department for other segments of the college family. These publications have been described in some detail in another chapter on periodicals. The alumni magazine frequently publishes the news which appears in other campus periodicals, and also prints the same news releases sent to daily and weekly newspapers.

The articles in the alumni magazine, however, are frequently written in feature-style, because of the more extensive space available and because editors believe the readers would be more attracted to a human-interest method of presenting the facts. The alumni magazine also differs from the other public relations periodicals in its news and features about graduates. The first section many former students read is the news of other graduates, and their accomplishments are also of interest. The alumnus wants to know about class meetings and events, hence such news is covered regularly.

The alumnus would be interested in the general progress made by the university, thus articles on the growth of the institution appear in the magazine, the writers telling about the expansion and changes made in departments and the construction of new buildings. Wishing to keep former students up-to-date on developments, editors usually include profiles of new officials, deans and faculty members. Interesting research activities of instructors and students furnish the basis for readable articles. Feature writers develop personality sketches of distinguished professors, and those with unique experiences and unusual hobbies or interests. Other college magazine reporters cover major events, such as Homecoming, important conferences, commencements, news of interest to readers scattered in the 50 states and unable to attend the events on campus.

To keep former students acquainted with current issues on the campus, most of the alumni magazines publish articles dealing with the general problems faced by the university and, often, by all institutions of higher learning. These problems may be discussed by the president in a speech or report and then reprinted, in whole or part, in the magazine. Other articles, written by staff members deal with financial problems experienced by the university, the changing character of the student population, the coming of women students to the campus, or the drug problem. There is a syndicate which produces special broad-gauged educational articles dealing with issues confronting most institutions of higher learning, and these features are sold to alumni magazine editors. This editorial service was started by a former editor of the Johns Hopkins University alumni magazine in Baltimore.

Striking Photos and Layouts

The alumni magazine staff is aware of the need for having a strong pictorial appeal. Action photos of a high quality may be found in many of these magazines, illustrating the news and features. For alumni readers the editors also use photographs with special graphic appeal to capture the spirit and events on campus. Candid shots of professors and students lend special interest. For some articles, a sequence of related photographs is used and spread over several pages.

Experienced editors of the alumni publications make strong efforts to produce lively and varied layouts. Besides attractive covers, the magazines have inside pages carefully laid out to appeal to the eye of the readers. The editors blend pages of print and pictures into a unit, using lively headlines to call attention to the news and feature articles underneath. Many of the magazine designers use considerable white space on each page. Modern layouts are employed by the creative and bold editors.

EXAMPLES OF ALUMNI MAGAZINES

Bostonia, issued quarterly by Boston University, is a typical high quality magazine aimed at alumni. Produced by the Office of Public Affairs in association with the General Alumni Association, the 8½ x 11 inch magazine has a smooth-finished cover, printed in color. The magazine is filled

The alumni magazine or newspaper, one of the principal means of reaching thousands of alumni and former students, is issued in a variety of formats. *Bostonia* is a slick-cover production of Boston University; the *City College Alumnus* is a pocketsize periodical, produced by the City University of New York.

Vol. 3, No. 1, Winter 1970
A PUBLICATION OF THE OFFICE OF UNIVERSITY RELATIONS AND DEVELOPMENT

R. W. FLEMING APPEALS FOR UNDERSTANDING OF YOUTH

R. W. Fleming, who has spent as much or more time than any college president in interpreting tod's oft-maligned youth, states, "T... clder

bombings, they have no capacity to influence other students.

"In somewhat larger numbers, but still insignificant in the total

The *University of Michigan Today,* although crammed with news and features, has a tabloid newspaper format.

with university news, general educational articles and features about the institution. Sections are devoted to letters-to-the-editor and to class notes and the doings of alumni, while the final section covers sports. Many black-and-white photos illustrate the news and features. The editorial staff consists of editor Richard C. Underwood, an associate editor, two assistants and two designers as well as two photographers.

City College Alumnus, published by the City University of New York for its alumni, has a unique pocketsize format. Published in 5½ x 7½ inch size by Executive Editor I. E. Levine, assisted by Lillian Simon, the publication has an attractive photo on the cover and is filled with human features about campus personalities and general educational articles as well as alumni activities.

The provocative quarterly, *Johns Hopkins Magazine,* which pioneered new paths in alumni publications, was revamped in 1971 and published by a new editor, Thomas J. Kleis, assisted by an associate editor, news editor, art director, photography editor and circulation manager. The opening editorial stated, "There will hopefully be the same interesting, informative and provocative stories and the same fanatacism for quality. Oh yes—one other thing isn't new. That's the shortage of funds needed to produce the *Magazine.* With budget cuts and rising costs, it gets harder and harder each year to get out the kind of coverage that interests the *Magazine's* more than fifty thousand readers . . ." The magazine was placed among the top ten alumni publications by the American Alumni Council. The publication also received, for the third consecutive year, the Atlantic Award for excellence of staff writing. Articles cited for award were those on the Applied Physics Laboratory, women's rights in the university, and the use of drugs on the campus. Distinctive-merit citations were given for additional coverage of the institution and the faculty.

Columbia Reports issued by Columbia University is an 8-page monthly in tabloid form. It contains feature articles on significant happenings at the university. Page one of the May-June, 1971 issue published the president's review of his first year under the banner:

Dr. McGill Reviews His First Year in Office

He discussed the problems he faced, the finances and the administrative changes. Inside pages told about the acquisition of the Roosevelt Hospital and St. Luke's Hospital Center, the meetings of the university senate and student aid. A full article was devoted to a review of the highlights of the 1971 commencement, topped by a banner headline. Sports events were recounted under the head:

A Roller Coaster Ride for Spring Sports

The article was written by Bill Steinman, assistant director of sports information. Page six gave the reports from various schools within the university to their alumni. The former students at Columbia University were busy writing books, hence almost a full page was devoted to "Recent Alumni Authors."

SUPPLEMENTARY PRINT MEDIA

Newsletters

Public relations departments have now recognized the value of briefer, to-the-point periodicals that can be read quickly by the alumni. The editors increasingly are using newsletters to reach alumni and former students. Such 4- or 8-page newsletters are easy and inexpensive to produce. They may be printed by mimeograph or offset methods as well as by letterpress. Such newsletters cover the happenings and progress at the institution in rapid journalistic style, so that the reader gets quickly an overall view of what is happening of importance at the college. These periodicals are distributed to the entire alumni, or to a special segment which the editor wishes to reach.

Individual colleges or schools within the university family also produce special newsletters for their alumni. The *Alumni News Letter* of the University of Pittsburgh, Graduate School of Business, is filled with news and information of particular value to the businessmen who are graduates of the institution. Printed on heavy colored stock in an 8½ x 10½ size, the Winter 1970 issue carried on the front page a message from the dean, who summarized the progress being made at the institution.

Special newsletters are published for the graduates of various schools at Boston University. In 8½ x 11 format, the publications are printed on colored paper. Although all are called *Alumni News*, with the masthead printed in deep red, each division is marked with initials: the newsletter of

FROSTBURG STATE TODAY
NEWSLETTER TO ALUMNI

NEW ACADEMIC YEAR BEGINS, PRESIDENT SETS TONE

The 1970-71 academic year is now well underway at Frostburg State with 2331 students enrolled. A total of 2005 undergraduates are registered and 180 persons are taking graduate course work. Additionally, there are 146 individuals studying in the extension division.

Along with the new faces among the student body, 27 new faculty members, three librarians and six administrators have assumed duties.

Students returned to the campus earlier than usual this fall as the college initiated a new academic calendar. The fall semester began August 31 and will be completed December 19. Classes for the second semester will begin January 18 and ends May 19. Commencement is set for May 23.

The new academic year also marks the beginning of the second term in office for President Nelson P. Guild. Speaking to an assembly of students, faculty and staff shortly after classes resumed, Dr. Guild

Dr. Guild also warned that violence,   attention to political or military mistakes.

called for d᷉
higher edu᷉
extremism.

"We as ᷉
identity—w
preserve th᷉
that a coll᷉
collection o᷉
existing in ᷉
said.

"A real
trained, am᷉
a mold. No᷉
can reign s᷉
dor and civ᷉
which self᷉
tongues di᷉
a man or v᷉
self on a c᷉
come a larg᷉
when he ca᷉
of greater ᷉
dissonant ᷉

JC
Hagerstown Junior College Alumni Crier

VOL. IV, NO. II   HAGERSTOWN, MARYLAND 21740   DECEMBER, 1970

April - May Activities To Mark 25th Anniversary

Plans are in full swing for the 25th anniversary of Hagerstown Junior College - oldest of Maryland's 16 public community colleges.

The official observance will open on Sunday, April 18, and will continue with activities, displays, and special commemorations through the college's commencement ceremonies on May 23.

In addition to the 11 members appointed by the Administrative Council, Dr. Atlee C. Kepler - who has been chief administrator of the college for almost two decades - announced that Odell Rosen and Mrs. Marie Byers of the Board of Trustees have consented to serve on the committee.

The committee has also invited as members William Diehl, former assistant superintendent of schools, and Evan Crossley, local attorney, who for many years was an active member of the college's Advisory

FIRST MUG--Dr. Atlee C. Kepler (left), president of Hagerstown Junior College, receives the first mug offered by the HJC Alumni Association to commemorate the college's 25th anniversary. Leon C. Brumback, alumni president, makes the presentation in the President's Office.

Tentative plans call for this evening of fun - open to the students, faculty, and alumni - to be staged on Saturday, May 1.

versary period. A President's Report in booklet form would be compiled and would be widely distributed in the ᷉

Smaller state colleges and junior/community colleges also issue alumni publications to keep the former students informed about happenings at the institutions and to gain their support. The PR Department at Frostburg State College in Frostburg, Md., distributed the news-letter *Frostburg State Today*, while *JC* was issued by the Hagerstown Junior College in Maryland.

the School of Nursing is designated as "SON," The School of Education, "SED" and the School of Fine and Applied Arts, "SAAF."

Reports

When the president gives his annual report at a convention attended by faculty and students, the report may be printed and mailed to alumni. The report is another way to keep alumni up-to-date. Now the report does not have to be printed in solid type; it would attract more interest if the speech were broken into segments and set off with summarizing subheads. The report may be illustrated if such photos would help build interest and break up the solid and sometimes forbidding type.

Bulletins

When important legislative issues or significant internal issues arise, involving faculty or students and administration, the public relations department can produce bulletins covering the situation. The bulletins provide correct, complete information supplementing, in some instances, newspaper and television reports.

PHOTOGRAPHIC MEDIA

Motion Pictures

The alumni director can make full use of the motion pictures and slide series to stir the interest of former students. In the chapter on motion pictures we have mentioned some of the excellent university and college films which have been produced by and for public relations departments. Such films have general interest, but they have particular appeal to former students who recognize some of the buildings and professors on the screen. The alumni viewers enjoy the film, as they would any good motion picture. In addition, upon seeing the film, the alumni feel pride in the institution, its accomplishments and progress. Of particular interest are those films giving the highlights of the year on the campus. The sequences on the previous annual meeting, or class meetings, of the alumni association can be added to the main film. General college films and newsreels-of-the-year may be shown at area meetings of the alumni as well as at the general annual meeting of the association.

Slide Show

Often slide shows serve the purpose of keeping alumni informed in an interesting and appealing pictorial fashion. The color slides may be shot throughout the year and then compiled into an enjoyable and informative sequence about college activities and developments. A lively script can go with the slide show, or a record or tape-recording can be made to give it an aural dimension. The slide show may be easier to produce than a film, and can be shipped to chapters readily. Even if films are produced, some colleges make slide shows as well, for it may be more difficult to get film projectors than slide projectors for area presentations.

REACHING ALUMNI DIRECTLY

Although alumni directors know the advantages of the print and pictorial media, they use other direct and personal channels to reach former students. In public relations there is no real substitute for human contacts.

Speakers' Bureau

The public relations department makes use of its speakers' bureau as a channel to reach in a personal way the general public and the alumni and to build goodwill. Suggestions can be made to area officers by the alumni director for the college speakers to appear at dinners and meetings. The president himself fills some of these speaking engagements, but he can't be expected to fill all of them, and he can't be in two places at once. Other administrative officers and faculty members can well represent the college. They can speak on the happenings and the progress made at the institution, or they may be asked to talk on their own specialties—government, history, social problems, psychology—as they relate to current issues in the world. Likewise, student leaders may be called upon to talk about student activities and needs. The local alumni have an opportunity to learn about the university and to ask questions of concern to them.

Alumni Meetings

The heart of the alumni relations, as indicated, is the alumni association. The alumni director promotes the growth of the large association and helps to organize and develop area groups. The meetings promote fellowship among the graduates and keep them abreast of college developments. The meetings take the form of luncheons, dinners, outings and even home parties. College public relations departments supply speakers, films and slide shows to make the meetings interesting and worthwhile attending. The alumni magazine can publicize the meetings ahead and cover them fully afterward. Likewise, the public relations writer develops news releases for daily and weekly newspapers in the area. The releases may be sent to the editors from the college, or may be mailed to the area alumni officer for local distribution.

College Events

The alumni can be notified beforehand regarding the university's football, basketball games or tennis matches when they are held in regions in which alumni live. Many graduates follow the games and scores of their college teams, hence would be particularly interested in attending such games. Similarly, when university choirs or orchestras play concerts in the area or theatrical groups put on performances, the alumni director can mail out cards and letters to alumni in the vicinity calling attention to these events. Calendars of events, as mentioned, are published in alumni newsletters and magazines.

Homecoming

"Homecoming" provides an unusually good opportunity to welcome graduates back to the campus and renew their interest in the institution. The event also gives the alumni a chance to renew their acquaintance with members of their class and of other classes. The alumni director makes a special effort to have a variety of events of a cultural, social and athletic character. At the president's reception for the alumni, and at luncheons and dinners, the director seeks to provide a feeling of good fellowship.

At Homecoming, some of the institutions have programs devoted to progress made at the college, when speakers are presented, exhibits of departments are shown, and movies and slide shows are screened. Class reunions are held and officers for the year are elected. During Homecoming Week, recognition of alumni may be given formally to outstanding alumni for their work in behalf of the university. Gold medals and certificates are awarded. Usually held in the fall of the year, Homecoming features a football game between the university team and a rival.

Reunions

In some colleges, class reunions have been held over a weekend, following commencement exercises. The college provides housing and meals and the best dormitory rooms. Special guides from the public relations department take the visitors on tours. At the reunions, college speakers bring the alumni up-to-date on what has happened to the college during the past year. The alumni director and association officer arrange social events and concerts.

Special Weekends

Some universities believe it is desirable to bring back the former students for a special week-end. The university president has an opportunity to become acquainted with the guests, and other officials can give on-the-record and off-the-record information about the institution, telling the alumni which way the university is heading and what its needs are. Held during the spring, outdoor facilities of the college can be made available so that the alumni can enjoy golf, tennis, baseball.

Alumni College

A more serious, educational project of the alumni association is the operation of an Alumni College. Refresher courses are offered for businessmen and professionals who want to learn about the new advancements made in their areas. College speakers and others may do the instructing. Small fees are charged for the courses and low rates are put on dormitory rooms. At the same time, the former students are gaining knowledge, they are becoming reacquainted with the college and they appreciate the service performed for their benefit. In some cities, where the university is located and many graduates live, regular seminars are held for them on business and professional subjects. The University of Pittsburgh and Boston University, for example, promote such seminars.

PERSONAL SERVICES

Informal Visits

The alumni director is particularly conscious of the value of welcoming in a cordial fashion alumni who return to the college for informal visits. The alumnus or alumna may have planned to be in the area and hence notified by mail or telephone the director beforehand; or the former students may just happen to be in the city or town and drop in. Whatever the circumstances, the alumni staff gives special attention to these interested alumni. The visit affords the opportunity for personal acquaintance with the alumni, to stimulate interest in the college, and to inform the graduates about campus events.

Although the alumnus may show up during a busy day, the staff makes sure that time is provided for an unhurried chat, that the alumnus gets a tour of the institution, and that he has the opportunity to meet some of the officials.

Correspondence

Many alumni don't have the time or opportunity to visit the campus but desire information by mail. The alumni letter-writers may be scattered all over the country, indeed over the world. Wherever the correspondents may be located, their letters are not given the mimeographed-form-treatment, but are answered personally by the alumni director, who sees the alumnus as a person definitely interested in the institution. If the alumnus addresses his letter to the alumni office, but the correspondence should be answered by the college president, the mail is forwarded for a personal reply by that official. The alumnus's letter is answered promptly, with specific information furnished and questions honestly answered.

CHALLENGE OF FUND-RAISING

Fund-raising, involving both the alumni and the public relations department, is of great importance to the progress and educational health of universities and colleges. More funds mean an opportunity to provide better educational service to students; to improve faculty salaries; and to attract capable instructors. Additional funds enable colleges to aid students by furnishing additional scholarships and grants. With more capital funds, officials also can construct needed campus facilities. Not only do private universities and colleges need funds, but state institutions require money beyond their operating expenses to achieve the best educational results.

Fund-raising campaigns range from low-key alumni fund drives to highly-organized campaigns, conducted by the universities' development staffs, who are aided by hundreds of volunteers and by outside professional fund-raisers. Successful drives depend on continuous, well-designed publicity and vigorous selling effort. The goals range from the construction of a single physical education center to an entire complex of buildings. Financial aims range from a $30,000 fund, to be collected in one year, to a $50 million development fund, extending over a ten-year period.

In addition to increasing the funds of the university or college, fund-raising drives usually produce more donors among the alumni and friends of the institution than before, while the regular annual gift-givers raise their individual amounts as a result of the well-organized campaign. In addition, the drive causes the general public and the alumni to be better informed, to have a deeper understanding of the institution's educational value and its significant contributions to the community. The campaigns also develop stronger feelings of friendship toward the university or college.

While successful fund-raising principles have been developed by the trial-and-error experiences of many institutions of higher learning, each institution must study its own situation. The staff adapts the best methods of other colleges, but works out special techniques and goals to fit its own particular problems.

The weekly, monthly and yearly efforts of the public relations staff furnish the needed spadework for the fund-raising campaign. The publicity helps to lay the foundations and build a receptive climate for the drive.

The university news releases, which have appeared in the daily and weekly press; the broadcasts, over radio and television; and the articles, published in the alumni magazine—have provided an understanding of the university's goals and accomplishments. This publicity has interpreted the college, giving an account of the educational services performed, the research achieved and the potential of the college. Some of the press articles and broadcast programs have already explained the contributions of the college to the community's business, industrial and cultural life.

Generally, the 12-months-a-year publicity has built up among potential benefactors a favorable impression and goodwill toward the university. This is why every news or feature article which appeared in the daily and weekly press, and every 30-second newscast over radio and television stations count. The spadework has been done for the fund-raising harvest.

To be successful and achieve its goals, the fund-raising campaign *still* has to be planned skillfully, organized effectively and carried out systematically. The drive *still* requires continuous publicity.

CAMPAIGN BUILT AROUND
SPECIFIC NEEDS

University and college fund-raising drives are varied, being built around the needs of the institutions. These needs are determined by careful studies and projections of the future, made by the president and other officials of the college, and by department chairmen. The admissions officers and the sociology and economic instructors on the university staff, or outside experts employed for the purpose, are called upon to forecast possible future enrollment growth. Student representatives examine the needs of students enrolled currently and those who will attend in the next decade or two. An architectural firm studies the present and future requirements for acreage and building facilities.

Long and Short-Range Plans
The studies may suggest (1) a long-range development plan over a 25-year period, involving all aspects of the institution, or (2) short-range objectives, or immediate goals.

Unrestricted, Restricted Gifts
Some of the university plans call for unrestricted funds, the university officials' using the money as they deem best, the donors' relying on the executives' good judgment. In other drives, the donors are told that they have a choice to determine what their contributions will be used for, hence they can designate specifically the school or college within the university which will receive their money. The benefactors may have graduated from one of the professional or graduate schools, consequently feel closer to it and its faculty. Combinations of the unrestricted and restricted campaigns are developed by many development officers.

Capital Improvements
Most drives center around capital improvement programs or include, in part, the constructing of some facilities. The capital improvement funds are used for buildings, such as classroom, physical education or science buildings, or art centers. Akron University campaigned for an auditorium, to be used jointly by the institution and the community. Other drives have specified as goals additional library resources or audio-visual equipment. Some institutions have sought additional acreage.

Faculty Assistance

Funds, obtained during an annual drive, are earmarked for strengthening the educational service by raising faculty salaries, putting them on a par with similar institutions. The college wants to hold its effective instructors and to attract new and capable ones. Funds are used also for employing certain distinguished scholars or research professors, and "chairs" are endowed for professors and for special subjects. Additional faculty funds may be employed advantageously in giving instructors more time off for laboratory or library or social research; for field investigations; or for writing books which will make contributions to the professors' areas of interest. In some instances, funds are sought to establish or to strengthen a particular school, such as graduate school of business, or provide research money for the department of chemistry.

Student Assistance

Some colleges need additional funds to assist students to get their education. The funds thus may be used for additional scholarships, grants or loans to students; or to assist, particularly, minority undergraduate students to secure a liberal arts education, or to pursue journalism degrees. Frequently, funds are earmarked to aid campus athletes pay tuition and other fees.

SIGHTING THE RIGHT DONORS

Key to the success of the fund-raising is the accurate sighting of the possible donors or benefactors, who vary in kind and size of contribution as well as where they may be found. In some drives, development officers focus on certain specific groups; in other campaigns, the officials search for donors among all publics. The scope of the campaigns may be narrow or wide, some drives aiming at local donors, others at state and area gift-givers, while still others are directed toward national and even international benefactors.

The most interested and frequently the largest group, the alumni provide the backbone of the drive. Some are wealthy persons who were graduated from the university 30 years ago; or they may be alumni with modest incomes, who received their degrees only a few years ago. The institution seeks to interest the maximum number of alumni and former students. Many officials believe that a large number of small contributions are better than a few large gifts. For the effect of the drive is to awaken the interest of many alumni who become active workers for fund-raising.

Parents of students also form another group which is solicited by volunteers, as mothers and fathers may be appreciative of the educational value of the institution for their sons and daughters. Some institutions, large and small—such as St. Lawrence University, Stephens College, Villa Nova University and Colgate University—have conducted successful parents' campaigns.

JULIAN CLARENCE LEVI

Hail Huge Levi Bequest

Julian Clarence Levi '96C, the architect and painter who was Columbia University's oldest living alumnus until his death last August at 96, bequeathed the University $5 million.

Columbia officials considered the bequest extraordinary not only in size but in terms. It directs that the principal and interest be used for faculty salaries, the establishment of professorships and fellowships, the creation of student loans and scholarships, the support of research and experimentation, and, most unusual, "the support of continuing studies of the University's problems and methods of solving them." This final provision is made "to the end that, through the united efforts of students, faculty, trustees, and administration, the University may most effectively and satisfactorily discharge its duties of research and education and thereby make a maximum contribution to the common good."

President William J. McGill, hailing the bequest as an outstanding example of perceptive and enlightened philanthropy, said that "it should serve as a model for all alumni and corporations seeking wise and thoughtful support of our institutions." He said that "for several years we have been exhorting alumni and corporations for support of the general purposes of the University. Now in one document Julian Levi has laid down near-perfect guidelines for all of us."

Mr. Levi, who was graduated from the College the year before the University abandoned its Madison Ave. and 49th St. campus for Morningside Heights, came to the "new" campus this year on Commencement Day to receive the University's Certificate of Distinction. Even then, Dr. McGill called him a "friend and benefactor of this University," mentioning Mr. Levi's gift to Columbia that had made possible, in 1966, the purchase of the Laura Boulton Collection of Traditional and Liturgical Music.

At college in the '90's, Mr. Levi joined crew and became a coxswain. He later attended Columbia's School of Architecture for two years before leaving to complete his education in Paris, at the Ecole des Beaux Arts.

Mr. Levi's entry in the current *Who's Who in America* runs nearly five column inches—particularly unusual for a person who was well past retirement age. He was a member of the New York architectural firm of Taylor and Levi from 1907 to 1962, when he was 87, and in recent years he painted 30 to 40 watercolors each summer, both here and abroad.

Story and photo of an alumnus who gave $5 million to Columbia University.

Columbia University Report

In some colleges, *faculty members,* knowing the needs and value of the educational programs and student services, make contributions; in one instance, faculty members pledged 2% of their annual salaries. Aware, too, of the lacks of the institution and believing that they are being given a sound education, *students* organize teams and solicit from the student body. At Marquette University, successful annual campaigns have been carried on among 10,500 students. The drive was originally formulated by the development office and sponsored by the Student Senate. It was thought that students would become alumni, with a feeling of continued responsibility toward the university when they were graduated. The objectives were $10,000 in cash gifts from the freshmen, sophomores and juniors, and $25,000 in three-year pledges from seniors.

An important segment of fund-givers in a number of institutions, particularly private ones, is the *trustees.* Often wealthy businessmen, industrialists or professionals, they make large contributions. The trustee in one college provided the Challenge Gift of $750,000, to be matched by other donors.

Going outside the immediate university family, the fundraisers aim their efforts at *special individual donors.* They may provide $10,000, $100,000 or $1 million for the unrestricted use of the institution, even setting a "Challenge Fund," to be matched by other donors. Large local or national *corporations* receive the attention of the campaign managers. In many other drives, *community business* and *professional leaders* have proved to be excellent supporters. The development officer in many institutions widens the campaign to include *community residents* who may not be in the top economic income level. Georgetown University in Washington, D.C., concentrated on a community-wide support program.

National foundations, such as the Ford and Rockefeller, known to be benefactors of institutions of higher education, are put on the list; sometimes, *local foundations,* knowing the university's contributions, prove to be large donors. Universities with plans for buildings approach the *federal government* which either gives an outright grant or one which calls for matching funds by the institution. Some church-founded institutions aim their drives first at church members in the state and then in the nation, but later seek community support, on the grounds that only 60% of the students belong to the church, which founded the college. The remainder come from all denominations.

In every section of the country, universities such as California Institute of Technology, Clark University, Marquette University and University of Houston, have found that campaigns aimed at deferred givers have been highly successful. The development officer works out a drive to arouse the interest of both men and women in placing money for the university in their trust funds, or in their wills. The development director, aided by lawyers and investment counselors, provides valuable information for these alumni and friends of the university, rather than engaging in a hard-sell campaign for funds.

The public relations director working with the development officer has to overcome a number of built-in problems in obtaining funds for the institution. Lack of information about the aims and educational programs of the university, and lack of understanding of the important role the institution plays and its many contributions to community living are primary obstacles. This lack of information is exhibited by many alumni, friends of the university, foundations and others.

The officers also have to face the apathy of both alumni and others; their money is drained off elsewhere. Many are not wealthy, but have modest middle-class incomes. They believe that unless they can give $100, or $1,000 or $10,000, the college is not particularly interested; besides, they are embarrassed by being able to contribute only a limited amount.

Still other former students and community leaders and residents are unfavorable because of the exhibition of student dissent and violence on campuses. In various states and cities, the local college is considered by many persons to be just an extension of the high school and provides low-quality education.

For one of several or all of these reasons, financial support is not forthcoming. The director and the public relations staff, aiding in the fund-campaign, seek to overcome these drawbacks by analyzing the roots of the unfavorable attitudes, the lack of knowledge and the misinformation, and then meeting these difficulties by furnishing adequate communications.

PARTICIPANTS IN FUND-RAISING

Universities and colleges who want to succeed in their fund-raising activities, put much thought and effort into personnel and organization. Most of the mistakes are made in such campaigns by not picking the best professional help, selecting and training the right staff, screening and organizing the working volunteers.

Internal Section

So important is the fund-raising for many universities and colleges, that a special person, director of development, is selected to head up the drive. Employed full-time, he develops long- and short-range plans, organizes the effort and acts as a coordinator in the execution of the campaign. He works with the institution's president and public relations director as well as alumni director.

In other colleges, the head of the drive may be the alumni director, assisted by other staff members. In small institutions, the public relations director, wearing many hats, may conduct the alumni work, hence the fund-raising job would fall in his lap too.

In the campaigns for additional funds, the public relations director helps to analyze the attitudes of the various publics who might become donors, advises on courses of action, and furnishes the communications needed, where no staff writer is on the developmental staff. Key person is the alumni director who is acquainted with alumni leaders, and has lists of alumni and others. Publicity writers may be drawn from the regular development office or the public relations staff; or additional writers can be hired and assigned to the campaign. Full-time secretarial help and part-time secretarial and clerical workers are essential for large-scale mailings.

Administration, Faculty, Students

Because of his prestige, the university president plays an important role in fund-raising. He speaks at meetings, writes special appeals and solicits the large individual donors and corporations and foundations. In some institutions, the presidents realize the importance of the drive to the progress of the college, and hence devote 15 to 25% of their time in this activity. Many presidents object to the fact that they have to spend so much of their time on campaigns, The administrative assistant to the president and the vice president often relieve the president of many fund-raising details. Participating, too, are other administrators and chairmen of departments, because they know specifically the needs of the university and are good speakers. Well-informed students with good voices, attractive appearances and pleasing personalities, serve in many colleges as excellent fund-raisers, speaking at alumni and other meetings. In many institutions, trustees, well-informed and prestigious, are enlisted in the campaigns, giving generously themselves to the funds, but also soliciting for their contributions, professional and business men who are friends and business associates.

External Volunteers: Alumni

The alumni, as indicated, are the backbone of the volunteer section. They have had an interest in the college, or their interest can be awakened. Many become active, willing workers, with a knowledge of the institution. Called "Task Forces," "Clark (University) Regulars" or "Huskies," after the mascot of the university, the alumni group may be broken down by regions or states. Some universities have organizations or representatives in 50 states and 53 foreign countries, because their graduates are scattered in all parts of the globe. Seeking efficiency, the development officer and the alumni director develop these alumni into close-knit organizations with active chairmen and workers. Often honorary chairmen are appointed from among industrialists or bankers.

The most successful drives result when the volunteers are carefully chosen, informed thoroughly and have their enthusiasm aroused. Presidents find some way to recognize and reward their hard work.

Non-Alumni

University fund-raisers do not rely entirely on institution officials and alumni, for they have found that "friends of the university," contribute time and fruitful effort to the campaigns for new buildings. Business leaders, who recognize the educational value of the college to students and its educational, economic and cultural value to the community, often become active workers in the campaigns. They are selected as chairmen of the "Business Task Force," or the "Industrial Task Force," or "Community Task Force." Other community leaders, such as professional men, civic-minded men and women, clergymen, join in the volunteer army. Professionals, such as lawyers and investment counselors, serve as consultants and speakers at seminars for those interested in deferred giving, and help prepare specialized brochures.

Professional Fund-Raising Organizations

For drives of any substantial magnitude, officials of universities and colleges employ professional fund-raising organizations. They are hired on a full- or part-time consulting basis, sometimes giving two days a week in critical periods to the campaign. University officials often say, after the drives are over, that they made a mistake in not employing professional companies, or not using their services more.

Such organizations have previous experience in fund-raising, and know the procedures and methods which have proved successful elsewhere. Before the campaign gets underway the organization's personnel analyzes the attitudes of the community toward the educational institution, sizes up the financial goals most appropriate. Sometimes their analyses and goals are not accepted by the officials. In one campaign, for example, the professional group estimated the goal the college should aim for; the college officials, however, thought it too low, raised the objective and gained it. The professionals may assist with the setting up of lists of potential donors, advice about the organizaton of committee structure, and carry out the planned program.

ESSENTIALS OF SYSTEMATIC PLANNING

For the fund-raising to produce the financial and other results, university officers and the outside professionals spend much time planning every aspect of the campaign. Many drives fail, in whole or in part, because of the lack of a well-designed plan, or the omission of a certain step in the plan. In the middle of the fund-raising drive, officials go back and erect a hasty stop-gap to shore up the situation.

Determine Objectives

In the planning sessions, which may extend a month or a year, officials determine the financial goals. Should the drive be for $30,000? $1 million? $10 million? Should "Challenge Grants" be sought at the beginning, which will give a definite goal and inspire and stimulate others to contribute? If the Ford Foundation gives $2 million, the university drive will have to get $4 million or $6 million, depending on the stipulation of the grant.

What specific capital improvements should be included as objectives of the campaign? What teaching or research equipment is necessary? Should the funds be employed for strengthening the faculty or for providing needed student services and scholarships?

The planning meetings are also concerned with the prospective donors. Will the campaign seek alumni support? high income donors? Will the drive be extended to include the community? industrial leaders? Will an appeal be made for deferred-givers?

Determine Appeals, Themes, Symbols

Fund-raising is a selling job and the methods of business and merchandising are used advantageously. College officials have to work out the effective appeals to alumni and other publics. What appeals can be made to cause these various publics to contribute? Will the appeal to the alumni be on the grounds that the university provided a foundation for their economic advancement? Should the appeal be based on their interest in promoting higher education for all students? In appealing to the community, will the fund-raisers focus on the contributions of the college to the economic and cultural life of the residents? Should the volunteers in their solicitation point out that students of today are earning, responsible citizens next year? Can the same general appeals be made in all solicitations; or do the volunteers have to make special appeals to special audiences? These approaches will be reflected also in the news releases, brochures, letters and broadcasts. The officials try to find a theme or slogan to epitomize the drive, and create a symbol to portray the campaign graphically.

Link to College Events

To give the institution a peg on which to hang the fund-raising and thereby to gain strength, some universities link their drives to anniversaries. The institution may be observing its 25th, 50th or 100th anniversary next year or two years from now, hence it would be strategic to initiate the capital improvement campaign then. The drive would have a spectacular send-off. Fund-raising drives are also connected with the retiring of presidents—a new scholarship fund may be established, a new library may be built in his honor, or a chair of geology may be established, as that was the subject he taught before being appointed president.

Develop Active Organization

In the planning stage, the development officer, aided by others, works out the blueprint of the organization which will do the soliciting. The organization, as indicated, may be local, state, regional or national, and sometimes international in scope. The role and function of the professional staff are defined.

Plans are also made to weld the volunteers—the alumni, friends of the university and others—into an active, efficient organization for the fund-raising. They may be organized into task forces with chairmen; plans have to be made for training the volunteers, for holding regular meetings, and for developing methods to inspire them with the importance of the educational job they are doing.

Publicity Plan

In the planning sessions, a systematic publicity plan is designed. The public relations effort has to fit in with the kind of fund-raising being programmed and the objectives. The publicity design takes into consideration the groups of contributors being aimed at and the basic appeals. Officials work out a plan for needed brochures, news releases, radio and television broadcasts, as well as articles for the alumni magazine and special reports which may be issued. Slide shows and motion pictures may be included in the publicity plans.

Schedule of Events, Meetings

Anticipating as accurately as possible what will happen and what should happen during the next 12 months, or the next three years, is no easy task. But the success of fund-raising campaigns depends on such forecasting. Development officers schedule each step and each meeting, timing the entire campaign. While the schedules follow generally a time-sequence, officials are wise enough to make the schedules flexible so reshuffling of events may be accomplished if necessary. Emergencies arise—the downward swoop of the stock market; the bad weather which interferes with important meetings; the student confrontations, producing an unfavorable impression; the shift from a private university to a state institution. These situations have to be met and solutions found by the developmental officer and the public relations director. Two of the biggest headaches are the overlapping of meetings and the overlapping of fund-raising campaigns; the new capital improvements drive, for example, will be conducted at the same time as the yearly parents' gift-giving.

In the schedules, time must be provided for the kick-off dinners, the local luncheons, national meetings. Most universities provide time for progress meetings and for final wind-ups of the campaign.

Sample Schedules and Cost Estimates

Cornell University sought to build its Cornell Fund, with a goal of $3 million—20% higher than the previous year's record-breaking total. The existing plans for the 1969-70 campaign were scrapped when in April, 1969 a news photo of rifle-carrying black students polarized alumni opinion, abruptly adding an entirely new dimension to the Cornell Fund. The campaign had to assure virtually all alumni and friends that the university had successfully met a severe challenge and was moving forward.

A key factor in the revised campaign was the history-making Million Dollar Challenge Grant, announced after solicitations had begun. A donor who insisted on complete anonymity offered to match every increase of $10 or more over an individual's largest gift in previous five years, and to equal every gift of $10 or more from a new giver. If the Cornell Fund reached its $3 million goal before the challenge grant money was credited, the entire $1 million would be added to the fund.

Here is the general schedule of the Cornell Drive:

Mar.–Apr., 1969	Preliminary Planning: leadership recruitment, scheduling, preparation of pledge cards, writing of other supporting material.
June–Aug., 1969	Emergency re-planning, determination of new theme, writing new supporting material.
July–Aug., 1969	Production of new supporting material, search for challenge donor begins.
Sept., 1969	Staff orientation, visits with alumni leadership.
Oct., 1969	Direct mail campaign begins.
Oct.–Dec., 1969	Regional personal solicitation begins.
Nov., 1969	Challenge donor found, terms of challenge grant announced by mail.
Jan., 1970	Regional campaign, direct-mail follow-ups.
Feb., 1970	Class personal solicitation campaigns.
Mar.–June, 1970	Class campaign, direct mail follow-ups. Leadership gifts follow-up program.

While it is difficult to estimate accurately the costs of fund-raising at the beginning of the campaign, some general fixed expenses can be anticipated. Salaries of the development officer and of the public relations director may or may not be included in the total. Funds are derived from development office funds, general budget, or alumni funds. Here is the usual breakdown of expenses:

General Help	Motion Picture Production	Advertising
Part-time workers	Office expense	Postage
Entertainment	Art Work	Telephone
Travel	Printing	Miscellaneous

Clark University sought to obtain $150,000 annually in its low-key alumni-staffed annual fund drive. Its organization was staff-oriented and used volunteers on a limited basis only. Here is the budget, broken down: Note that the largest items are for salaries and printing expenses.

Secretarial and professional staff time	$10,000	
Part-time student and clerical help	757	
Entertainment and Travel	1,045	
Office Supplies and Printing	5,318	
Postage	2,304	
Telephone	1,261	
Miscellaneous	125	$20,810

The University of Akron sought to raise money for the Performing Arts Hall, which would meet a long-standing community need and serve as a facility suitable for academic programs. The cost was estimated at $6 million, which became the principal objective of the $10 million campaign. Here is the budget for Akron University's drive:

Part-time personnel	$12,440	
Office Supplies, Postage	14,596	
Equipment	963	
Printing and Duplicating	41,008	
Travel and Promotion	9,058	(excluding salaries
Miscellaneous	456	$78,521 of officials)

After 18 months of campaigning, the Akron board of trustees approved the construction of the auditorium. Over-all attainment was $8.1 million at this point.

California Institute of Technology instituted a deferred giving program at a cost of $5,473 in 1967, with this as the budget:

Art work and engraving on advertisements	$ 991.	
Layout and design of booklets	1,021.	
Printing personal information booklet (10,000 copies)	2,000.	
Printing bequest booklet (10,000 copies)	954.	
Envelope, reply card and postage	516.	$5,482

In a period of less than a year, Caltech mailed 4,768 booklets and received 87 responses. The institute realized $287,064 in income trusts, and the value of known wills in favor of the institute was $1,535,000.

Development officers in many colleges figure on an even lower percentage of returns, believing that if the institution gets 10–15% above costs, the effort is justified.

EXECUTING THE PLAN

In carrying out the plans for the fund drives, specific steps are taken, and some of these have been indicated already.

Producing Publicity

The preparation of publicity materials is usually the responsibility of the public relations director and his writing staff. Facts about the university and goals of the campaign and what they will achieve for the institution are researched and weighed. This information becomes the basis for the publicity efforts, and is used by the volunteers in their solicitations.

The information finds its way into news and feature articles in the alumni magazine and special fund-raising reports. The staff writers use the facts in brochures produced for the campaign, and add photos and drawings to enhance the appeal. In many universities, special brochures are designed and written for alumni, and other publications are aimed at parents. Still other brochures are designed for the community. Some publications are also prepared for men and women who need information about including educational institutions in their trust funds and wills.

The public relations department also prepares news releases about the fund-raising campaign for general distribution; news stories are also localized for area and local meetings of the task forces. The public relations department also produces radio and television programs which will acquaint the public with the fund-raising drive. These programs focus on the college's contributions to the community, on graduates of the institution, and on donors who explain why they are contributing. The public relations departments frequently produce slide shows and motion pictures which can be used in the campaign as well as shown afterwards for general public relations purposes. Some of these films have been described in previous chapters on motion pictures and television programs.

Meetings with Workers

The planned meetings are now carried out at the breakfasts, luncheons and dinners held locally and in various states. The speakers outline the purposes and the goals of the campaign to provide information and background for the workers. Brochures and other literature are passed out, slide shows or motion pictures are shown. Gifts are obtained at these meetings. Names of prospects are suggested, and lists of prospects are assigned to volunteer workers. To get best results, drives have follow-up meetings and progress meetings. Campaign officials keep in continuous communication with volunteers, listening to their reports, assisting them to overcome obstacles and to answer questions of prospective donors.

Mailings

Officials at headquarters compile lists of prospects from various sources: alumni names from the alumni director and parents' names from the admissions officer. Business leaders may supply names of top prospects. City directories may furnish others. The mailings can be anywhere from 500 to 8,000, or more.

For large mailings with personalized letters to parents, St. Lawrence University used a computer. An IBM 360-30 computer was used in the 1969 appeal. The letters were individually addressed, with personal salutations and students' name being included. The university's addressograph list was key punched on IBM cards. Copy for the appeal letter was fed into the computer along with key punched parent and student cards. The IBM machine with two companion machines typed the letters, with one original and one carbon. The letters referred to individual sons and daughters by their first names. The letter program increased participation by 70%, and the total gifts by 17% over the previous year. Parents of graduates nearly doubled their participation.

Personal Solicitation

While the mailing of letters and brochures produces a certain number of responses, development officers know that most of the funds will be raised through personal solicitation: the president of the university, development officer, alumni volunteers and other friends calling on possible donors at their homes, or visiting them at their business offices, where the university representatives have the opportunity to talk, explain, answer questions, while adapting the appeals to the particular prospects.

Phone Calls

When personal visits cannot be made—because of the great number of prospects to be seen, or because they live in other towns and cities—the next best type of solicitation is by phone calls. Chairman of class chapters find their former classmates scattered everywhere. The phone call technique has proved successful in many university drives. Volunteers get the names, addresses, and if possible telephone numbers, and put in the calls to the prospects 100, 500, or 1,000 miles away.

Brown University Annual Fund

WHAT IS A PHONOTHON?

Alumni and Alumnae are joining forces in the Washington area (and in 15 other cities) to record pledges for the Brown University Annual Fund.* We'll be calling all alumni, alumnae, parents, and friends of Brown in the local area in about 2 weeks time.

WHO IS DOING THE CALLING?

Class Agents form the backbone of the team, but we've also signed up other alumni and alumnae, graduate school alumni, and even some parents of present students (you might like to hear their views on contemporary campus events). In fact, if you'd like to help, we'll find a place for you if you'll call me at 202-963-5454.

WHY ON THE TELEPHONE?

The University ran 5 PHONOTHONS last year on a trial basis. People liked them! They were fun for the workers and convenient for the donors (pledges and billing instructions confirmed in one telephone conversation - no more solicitations after that). And best of all, they raised money for Brown in 3 out of every 4 calls that were made.

THE NEED FOR ANNUAL SUPPORT

Brown needs generous support every year to keep a first-ranked faculty, and to keep the tuition somewhere near the grasp of intelligent and deserving students. BROWN IS RUNNING A DEFICIT despite a no-hiring policy and overall belt-tightening. We have nowhere else to turn but to our own to make up the difference. That is why we are especially turning to you.

WILL YOU PLEDGE WHEN WE CALL?

We'd love to share some stimulating conversation about Brown when we call, but our main purpose is to record pledges. And our specific goal is to raise larger pledges from everyone than each gave last year. Why? because, if we want to keep Brown the kind of institution we all respect, we simply have to increase our support.

We look forward to talking with you soon.

Truly yours,

Nancy L. Buc

Nancy L. Buc
Area Chairman

The **Brown University Annual Fund is the newly-formed organization through which all alumni and alumnae support the University with annual gifts. It was created by combining the Brown University Fund and the Pembroke College Fund. The National Co-Chairmen are Edythe Wiedeman Smith '53 and Richard J. Ramsden '59.*

The Phonothon has been used to good advantage by a number of institutions of higher learning. Arrangements are made with the telephone company to have the long-distance calls put through at a certain time. The mass solicitation is conducted by a number of volunteers at the same hour. Brown University conducted five Phonothons a year on a trial basis and got responses in three out of four phone calls made. Colgate University's three-day Phonothon was participated in by 93 parents who contributed 186 hours of phoning time. They attempted 3,278 calls, completing 67 per cent of them. At the close of the year, Colgate recorded a total of 790 confirmed pledges worth $27,030.

Donor Recognition

Various methods are used by officials to recognize the hard work and the effort which volunteers put into the fund-raising campaigns. The alumni, and friends of the college are given recognition in the alumni magazine, with special articles and names listed. Volunteers are put on the "President's List," and are given certificates, with the top workers being presented plaques. The president also sends follow-up letters, expressing his appreciation to each volunteer after the campaign is over.

Results

Those university and college officers who have reported on their campaigns list a number of direct and indirect benefits resulting from the drives. Some of these benefits were anticipated; others came as a surprise. The university officials noted these favorable results:

An increased number of donors
An increase over amounts of money regular donors had previously given
More funds for educational purposes; for faculty and students; for buildings and equipment.
Increased publicity in the press and broadcast media.
Favorable editorials in media.

The officials said they observed a heightened general public awareness of the existence and value of the institution, and they recorded more "friends of the university" than ever before. One college declared that the fund-raising campaign caused a breakthrough to church members who never knew about and didn't support the college before. Besides developing useful mailing lists of prospects for future giving, the universities built permanent organizations for future fundraising. Administrators also noted an increased "warm and friendly correspondence" after the campaigns and observed more attendance by the public at university events.

Part Six

FEEDBACK AND MEASURING RESULTS

Cougars Fall For First Time To FSU

The Florida State basketball team pulled its second biggest upset of the season Saturday night in Tully Gymnasium when it defeated the highly-touted Houston Cougars, 76-69, before 4,200 fans.

Just as when FSU played the Miami Hurricanes, the Seminoles were "sup-posed" to lose, but instead Coach Bud Kennedy's crew tripped up the favored Houston, which had never lost to the Seminoles in any sport.

The game pushed the Seminoles into the winning brackets. The Seminoles have now won 10 contests and lost in nine games.

Again, just as in the Miami game, the two big shots of the Seminoles were forward Charlie Long and center Dale Reeves. Long played the entire contest and scored 20 points, while Reeves came in late and tallied 21 markers.

Reeves, a 6-7 Kentuckian, also pulled down nine rebounds, while Long, a fellow Blue Grasser, grabbed seven missed shots.

However, the high-scorer for the game was a Houston cager--Lyle Harger, a potential All-American who measures in at 6-7.

Harger sliced the nets for 22 points, and proved that he was dangerous at the free throw line by scoring eight charity tosses. The tall man also got eight rebounds.

When the contest opened, it seemed that Coach Guy Lewis' Texans could do no wrong, for the towering Texans dropped the ball through the nets with alarming alacrity.

But the Seminoles met the power push by gradually pulling within scoring distance of the Texans, and a field goal by center Jerry Shirley tied the game, 13-13.

The Cougars slipped on their next scoring effort, and FSU's Long tallied a field goal and a free throw to give the Tribesmen their first lead at 16-15.

Moments later, the Cougars erased this margin, but then Long sank a 20-footer for a 20-18 score to give Flo-rida tate a permanent lead, which was always in danger of being destroyed.

By the time of the half, the Seminoles had a 10-point lead, 39-29. In the second half, the Houston basketballers came on just as they did at the start of the game: hard and fast. And they managed to slice the margin to three points on one occasion, but the Seminoles, relying primarily on the shooting of Long and Reeves, pulled in front to as much as 11 points before the Houston onslaught began anew.

Three more times during the game, the Cougars came with five points; and, in the final seconds of the game, (continued on page 4)

FLORIDA'S FIRST COLLEGIATE DAILY

THE **FLORIDA FLAMBEAU**

Vol. XLIX, No. 86   Published Daily By The Students Of Florida State University   Monday, January 28, 1963

Flambeau Policy Supported

Poll Reveals Interest In World, National Affairs

An overwhelming majority of FSU students and faculty, polled in a cross-section study, believe that the "Florida Flambeau" should be concerned with news outside the university.

A large majority also think that the publication should have columnists of various political beliefs comment on the news. The survey showed that an even larger majority believe the "Flambeau" should print news of local student political parties.

FSU'S FIRST WIN OVER HOUSTON

... in any sport came Saturday night in the 76-69 basketball victory. FSU's Dale Reeves (15) and Cal Huge (33) successfully fight two tall men from the Lone Star state, Don Scheverak (55) and Lyle Harger (43). (Photo by Art Campbell)

Student and faculty opinion was revealed in a poll taken last week by two classes in public relations under the directions of Dr. Sidney Kobre, professor of communications and public relations, School of Business. The polling was a class project, as the students were studying public opinion and the methods which organizations and companies use to get basic facts through research.

"No member of the 'Flambeau' staff was allowed to participate in the poll, either in interviewing or tabulating," the professor said.

The poll surveyed 411 persons. These included 345 freshmen, sophomore, junior, senior and graduate students. They were enrolled in Arts and Sciences, Business, Education, Music and other schools and departments. The 69 faculty members represented various schools. Students interviewed persons in the History, Conradi, Education, Business, Meteorology buildings, the Student Center and dormitories.

In answer to the question, "Do you think the 'Flambeau' should be concerned editorially with current news events outside the university, students and faculty responded with 286 "yes's" and 122 "no's," with three questionnaires being rejected, there were not clear or no answers were given.

"The ratio, therefore, was about two to one in favor of the editor's being concerned with outside happenings," Dr. Kobre explained. "The faculty had a higher ratio-three to one on this question."

When asked, "Do you think the 'Flambeau' should publish news relating to student organizations interested in national politics?" the response was even stronger than on the previous question. For 318 members of the student body and the faculty believed that such news should be printed, while only 87 were opposed. There were six rejects. Faculty ratio was five to one in favor of publication.

Students and faculty think the FSU daily should publish columns written by students with various political views, as the ratio was 4 to 1. They answered with these results: 326 for printing such articles, 76 opposed. Nine rejects were recorded.

A fair distribution of students and faculty was made, according to political beliefs. Of those polled, 196 considered themselves, "liberal," while 153 thought they should be classified as "middle-of-the-roaders." One socialist gave his opinion, but 46 gave no clear-cut answer, or didn't answer. All of the questionnaires were anonymous.

The question of the type of news and columns the "Flambeau" should publish was raised recently by Dalles W. Matthews, a student who opposed such publication because he had to support the "Flambeau" through payment of student fees, and didn't want such a publication because it printed views opposite to his.

As the poll-takers sought to get some comment on the questions, the interviewers asked "why" the person believed as he did on the three issues. A variety of answers was given.

One freshman, voting "yes" to the question, "Do you think the "Flambeau" should be concerned editorially with current news outside the university?" gave this typical reply, "News of the outside world is of concern to everybody." In answer to the question regarding the publication of news of student poli-

(continued on page 3)

By Van Assenderp

Model U.N. Is Rejected

By KATHY VALLETTA
Flambeau Staff Writer

Ken van Assenderp has rejected invitations to the Model United Nations General Assembly at Florida A and M University and the regional conference at the University of North Carolina, Feb. 21-23.

The basis of the rejection of the invitations was given by President van Assenderp as not having enough time to prepare for the conferences because details were sent late, and the meetings usually bogged down in college rivalry.

FAMU put on its first local conference last year; FSU did not participate in this conference either.

The invitation to the FAMU conference was extended by Willy Adams, president of the Student Government Association. Willy Carl Rogers is acting chairman of the FAMU planning committee.

The purpose of the conferences is to discuss international problems, relations and debate on pertinent issues. The college delegations must research the countries they are representing in the Model UN, and debate on issues with their particular country's interest in mind. Other delegations are allowed to challenge the nation's stand on certain issues, protesting that it is not in line with economic and political demands of that nation. That nations must support its stand and attempt to pass resolution in its favor.

The model UN General Assembly works similarly to that of the official United Nations Assembly. Committees are established to thrash out world problems in debate. They are then put on the agenda for debate in the General Assembly.

Election Filing Begins Tomorrow

By SUSIE RHOADES
Asst. News Editor

Declarations of candidacy for major Student Body offices may be filed tomorrow at 5 p.m. Declarations may be obtained and returned at the Main Deck in the Longmire Bldg.

Any candidate filing for the office of-Student Body President must be of Senior standing and have completed at least 70 hours at the time of his filing.

Qualifications for Chief Justice of Honor Court are that he must be of Senior standing and must have one full trimester of court experience.

Candidates for all other offices must be of Senior of Junior standing (40 hours prior to the time of elections).

Candidates for Clerk of Honor Court and for Chairman of University Court must have over one trimester's experience on some university court system.

Board of Student Publications candidates must be of Junior or Senior standing. They must have worked two trimesters on any student publication at any college or university, one of which has to be at FSU.

All candidates for major offices shall be required to have achieved an overall 2.3 scholastic average. Transfere students who wish to run for office may count their grades for full credit.

Secretary of Elections Ron Jones

(continued on page 3)

Change Of Major

Any Basic Division student wishing to make a change in his intended major or area of interest should make this change in the Counseling Center, 302 Westcott, between Feb. 15 and March 15.

Survey of student interest on world and national affairs is featured in Florida State University *Flambeau* on page one.

17

Research, Surveys and Feedback

DISCOVERING HOW THE EDUCATIONAL INSTITUTION STANDS in the opinion of its publics—faculty, students, graduates, members of the outside community —is important for the continued progress of the university. What is the reaction of each of these groups to the university's policies, programs, practices and plans? Officials want to know what the students' attitude is toward the new trimester system. What do students recommend for the improvement of the system's operation? The administrators also desire to learn how the faculty reacts to the "No-Grade Plan," proposed for next semester. What modifications would they urge? Turning to graduates, would they recommend the institution to others? The college would like to learn if the community residents in a certain area will support an off-campus center. What suggestions do area residents have for courses to be offered?

Such fact-finding obtains the essential "feedback" university officials need to make wise decisions. If careful systematic surveys are conducted by the public relations department, the college officers have more definite facts and alternatives in making changes in policy, or in instituting new plans of action. Research reveals the trouble spots before they become cancerous, and it uncovers methods of eradicating or reducing the cause and effects of problems, enabling officials to initiate remedies in time. Public relations research can discover also the amount of misinformation and the erroneous ideas the publics cling to.

Objective research regarding his own public relations projects also enables the director to increase the effectiveness of his communications. These aspects of surveys and fact-finding to obtain communication feedback will be treated in this and the following chapter.

379

In making studies of the attitudes and opinions of various publics regarding the institution, the scope of the work of the public relations department is widened, and an essential service performed for the institution. The charge is sometimes made that the public relations department is largely a publicity arm of the institution, and that the production and distribution of news or the writing of brochures are the sole functions of the staff. Fact-finding about the information which people have, and their opinions and attitudes, will increase the scope of usefulness of the public relations department. Such research will bring the PR operations into line with the highest standards and goals of the profession: to analyze institutional problems, find solutions, produce communications and obtain feedback to improve overall performance.

SURVEYING UNIVERSITY PUBLICS

The public relations department, in making fact-finding surveys, aims at various publics of the institution and seeks to learn any one or a number of facts, such as:
1. Amount of knowledge these publics have of the educational institution.
2. Their opinions of the institution.
3. Their attitudes on current issues and problems facing the university.
4. The publics' preferences for certain choices on programs and policies and practices.
5. The location, type and extent of significant institutional problems which now or in the future will exist.
6. The publics' suggestions for correcting or improving the current problems or undesirable situations.
7. The kinds of, and the extent of, misinformation and erroneous ideas the publics have about the institution.

Problems and issues are similar in many colleges at any one time, but variations occur too. Likewise, the problems change from year to year in each institution. Here are a few of the types of problems that universities, four-year colleges and junior/community colleges can survey. Each director can use these problems as a base, and add to them, according to his local situation.

Students' Views

The college wants to know what the students "feel" about a variety of policies and activities. Through systematic surveying, the public relations department can discover how students react to the current method of registration, and how they might react to a pre-registration technique employed in some other colleges. If certain new courses were introduced, would students register for them? Which courses would be preferred? What do students think of various methods of instruction? Do freshmen derive benefits from the counseling services? If so, which ones? And how would the students improve the counseling conferences being held?

Faculty Attitudes

It is important that the university officers learn the attitudes and opinions of faculty members on current practices and suggested plans being studied for adoption. How would the faculty rate the institution's cooperativeness in instituting new programs? Its procedure for initiating new courses? The college wants to know also how the faculty would rate its procedures in purchasing new equipment. What do instructors think of the communication network in the college—how could the communication system and media be made more efficient?

Graduates' Opinions

The university may wish to discover the reactions of graduates to their university. The survey might inquire what the graduates think are the strengths of the institution. What do the graduates like most about the university? What recommendations would they offer to improve instruction and the relations between faculty and students? Would the graduates recommend the institution to others? Why? Why not?

Community Attitudes

The university is an integral part of the community in which it is located, hence the attitudes of governmental officials, businessmen, residents, are important. What is their general impression of the institution—favorable or unfavorable, or are they indifferent? How do the residents rate the college—as a benefit or as a liability to the community? Do they think the institution adds prestige to the community? What contributions to the community does the college make—economic? cultural? intellectual? What knowledge do the residents have of the faculty's participation in community organizations and activities?

TECHNIQUES OF SURVEYING

Surveys differ widely in scope and methods employed, each survey possessing unique aspects in the problems faced or the approach used. Hence, each director must set up his own organization for surveying and must develop his own schedule of forms. Still, many of the procedures and forms used in various surveys will require only slight adjustment to fit the special needs of the proposed survey.

Basically the public relations department must take the following steps in conducting a survey:

1. Plan the survey carefully.
2. Draft adequate forms (called schedules or questionnaires).
3. Organize the surveying team.
4. Write clear instructions to the interviewers.
5. Determine the sample to be surveyed.
6. Conduct, if necessary, a pilot study.
7. Carry out the survey.
8. Interpret the results fairly.
9. Write a report of the survey.
10. Reproduce and distribute the completed report.

The public relations director becomes acquainted with the techniques which have been tried and found wanting and those procedures which have been found useful. He is aware of the pitfalls in surveying and avoids them. He needs to understand such problems as securing the proper sample, and developing pertinent, unambiguous questions. The ultimate aim is to produce a survey which has validity, is truthful and can be relied on.

INFORMATION SURVEY

```
        EVENING  STUDENTS          Date_____
        _____ COLLEGE        Location___(Main)
                                   Off-campus
                                   Center_____
```

Please fill out the following questionnaire, as we wish to become better acquainted with you and to learn something of your background and educational goals. Your information will help us plan better courses and programs for you and others.

```
Name (Mr._)(Mrs._)(Miss_)_____
                         First     Middle      Last

Address_____(zip)_____Telephone_____

Major subject _____

Present Courses in which enrolled_____,_____
_____,_____,_____

Some Previous Courses Here_____,_____

_____,_____,_____

Are you working toward a degree?  Yes__No__Which?_____

Are you working toward a certificate?_____subject____

Are you studying (Mainly) to improve your skills for your
job?_____

Are you studying (Mainly) to obtain more knowledge about
your job?_____
```

Are you studying for a combination of both of the above?
_____

Are you studying mainly to get general background?_____

Are you enrolled mainly to acquire certain skills in art, music writing? electronics?_____

Other reasons for enrolling_____

What courses not given now, would you like this college to offer?_____,_____,_____,_____

Place of employment_____Location_____

Your title or type of work you do_____

Single__ Married__ Number of Children__ Grandchildren__

Special interests or hobbies_____

High School you attended _____ Graduation date 19____

Any college? _____ WHICH _____ Degree?_____

READERSHIP SURVEY

Please check this information as we wish to learn what publications you read, and, perhaps, where you received your information about this college. You may check more than one newspaper, or radio station, or television station.

Newspapers - Daily	Read Regularly	Sometimes	Never
Sunpapers			
Evening Sun			
Morning Sun			
Sunday Sun			
News-American			
Daily Edition			
Sunday Edition			

Community Press			
Afro-American			
East Baltimore Guide			
Northwest Star			
South Baltimore Enterprise			
Harford Road Reporter			
Community Times			
Jeffersonian			
Affiliate (AFL-CIO)			
Jewish Times			
Catholic Review			
Other Publications			

Radio Station	Listen to Regularly	Sometimes	Never
WFBR			
WSID			
WITH			

Television Stations	Watch Regularly	Sometimes	Never
WBAL - Channel 11			
WMAR - Channel 2			
WJZ - Channel 13			

Public relations is not an exact science, but it is an applied social science—dealing with human beings, somewhat different from physical molecules. Besides, we cannot put the human beings in a laboratory or a test tube, so we use other methods to discover facts about people. Sometimes qualitative techniques reveal brilliant and illuminating insights. Quantitative methods, on the other hand, give the results more exactness. Thus, public relations uses methods derived from the work of the psychologist, sociologist, political scientist as well as from the research of other behavioral scientists. Public relations uses both informal and formal techniques to learn about public attitudes and opinions.

INFORMAL SURVEY METHODS

Personal Contacts
Public relations men get out and talk to people informally. University PR directors and their staffs seek wide acquaintanceship. They may interview administrators, faculty and students, and also go into the community to talk about college affairs with mayors, city councilmen and residents.

There are definite shortcomings in this informal method: the strong possibility that the public relations representative gets only one set of views, or obtains the opinions of biased, prejudiced individuals. These persons may have had only limited or unique experiences with the college. The individuals being interviewed may be influenced by their attitudes toward particular college officials. We say, in science, that the sample is unrepresentative. But such personal methods do give some information, insight and "tips" frequently not provided for in more formal questionnaires.

Mail and Telephone Check
The university PR man watches for the incoming mail. Such mail increases after a flare-up on the campus. Sometimes the correspondent reveals information about a problem or shows attitudes which are enlightening. Similarly, telephone calls are considered seriously. The steady drift of opinion in one direction as revealed by the mail and the telephone calls may provoke thinking about a policy and lead to further investigation.

Press Clips
Some universities and college departments of public relations subscribe to clipping services to discover the attitudes of general or special publics toward higher education. News and editorials influence the public. In other institutions, the director, or a designated secretary, watches the newspapers for clips of educational interest and is on the lookout for state and local news and editorials relating to the institution.

Public Opinion Polls

Many newspapers publish the results of nationwide surveys taken by George Gallup and other pollsters. Sometimes, on critical educational issues, these polls compare the attitude of the public today with the opinion two or five years ago. The public polls seek to break down the audience by regions, by age, by educational backgrounds. Public relations men clip these polls for present and future use. Other research organizations may be employed to make limited surveys of the attitude of the public toward a university or college.

FORMAL SURVEYING TECHNIQUES

From a variety of valid, proven formal techniques for surveying opinion, the educational public relations director can select one or several to obtain information from the several publics. It is not unusual to find combinations of methods employed in many investigations.

Here are some of the successful techniques which can be used by the public relations surveyor of a university or college:

1. Personal interview (face-to-face contacts).
2. Telephone interview.
3. Mail questionnaire and ballot.
4. Panel techniques.

There are advantages and limitations to each method; hence the director should choose the one most suited to the problem confronting him. Any method, however, can yield misleading or incorrect results in the absence of careful planning and attention to details.

Personal Interview

The PR director may find that the personal interview is most suitable and efficient for his purposes. The interview method involves direct personal investigation. The *form* of the interview depends on the type of information to be ascertained. In the usual procedure, the interviewer uses a *schedule form* containing definite items about which the information is to be secured. He records the responses to questions.

Free-Story Technique

One procedure that is popular among some surveyors is the free-story technique. The interviewer encourages the informant to talk about the subject matter, and from these remarks the interviewer obtains a general impression of the subject's attitude or situation. This method frequently results in chance impressions and includes the interviewer's own biases. The information cannot be treated statistically afterward.

Focused Interview

A modified free-story technique known as the "focused interview" has replaced the completely unguided type. In order that the interviewer may obtain the same type of facts about each issue, he may carry a reminder or a list of questions about which he is to secure the informant's reactions. The focused interview is usually more time-consuming than when a set schedule is used.

Group-Interview

A variation in interview technique is to present the schedule to a group of people assembled in one place. To measure the response to certain questions, the persons are asked to record their reactions on questionnaire forms.

Mail Questionnaire or Ballot

The public relations surveyor for the college may choose the mail questionnaire or ballot for any of his institution's publics. The mail questionnaire consists of a sample of questions sent by mail to persons on a list or in a survey sample. The form is supposed to be filled in by the recipient and mailed back to the sender.

This procedure may vary, depending on the manner in which the form or question is placed in the hands of the potential informant. The questionnaire may be distributed to faculty members by being placed in their mail boxes, or may be brought to the instructors' offices to provide a more personal touch. Students may receive the questionnaire at the time of registration, or later in class. The questionnaire also may be printed in the student newspaper. To survey members of the general public, or certain groups, the public relations department may mail the questionnaires.

The advantages of the mail questionnaire are many. If such questionnaires are used, it is possible to cover a wider geographical area and to reach a much larger population with given funds than could be accomplished by personal interviews with each informant. The lower cost applies primarily if personal follow-ups are not made. Mailing costs are relatively low compared with the transportation and time costs for a field staff.

Telephone Interview

Surveys of the opinions of a large number of students and their parents as well as of community residents can be conducted by telephone interviews. Respondents can be queried on their reaction to college programs and policies. The telephone interview can be used in checking on college press publicity and the radio and television programs of the institution. These techniques will be discussed more fully in the next chapter relating to communications feedback.

Panel Interview Technique

The panel technique, mentioned before in informal approaches, has been used successfully in systematic surveying of attitudes and opinions. This method consists in making more than one contact with the groups being surveyed. The technique may be applied to public relations surveying for institutions of higher learning, with the PR department setting up panels of students and faculty or of people in the community.

CONSTRUCTING THE QUESTIONNAIRE

The public relations director is concerned about planning (1) the physical design of the schedule and (2) the careful selection and phrasing of the questions.

The information included on the schedule may be classified under three headings: (1) identifying information, (2) social background or factual data, (3) questions on the subject of the survey. Some of the information is essential for all surveys; other questions may be omitted; still others may be added if necessary.

Questions on the survey topic may be asked in any of several different ways. The informant may be asked a direct question on the facts as he understands and remembers them. The respondent's answers to such questions as what concerts he attends or what courses he carries, are secured by straight-forward questions. The opinions he holds, however, are not so readily ascertained. There are many pitfalls into which the unwary question-designer is likely to fall. Questions should be selected and worded only after considerable deliberation and testing.

The task of drafting questions which can be relied upon to reveal what the respondent thinks about a given issue or educational service, should be approached slowly and carefully. Surveyors and pollsters have recognized the importance of this phase of their work, therefore they are constantly experimenting with different types of questions and with different phrasings in their search for unbiased questions. No form will ever meet the needs of all who try to gauge opinions. Some surveyors prefer types of questions which will get at the intensity of feeling which the respondent holds toward the question at issue. Other surveyors lean toward questions which enable the informant to talk freely about the survey topic, while others prefer questions which ask the respondent to make a definite choice between two or more alternatives.

The type of question used by the college public relations researcher will depend upon what information is being sought, and the amount of explanatory work needed to reveal the breadth and intensity of the opinion. The questions will grow also out of the extent to which the opinion has been crystallized on the subject. The surveyor will need to consider these points and the limitations of various forms of questions when he selects them. Here are some of the more commonly used types of opinion questions and their advantages and shortcomings.

Open-End Questions

During the exploration phases of the survey, it is usually necessary to employ questions which give the respondent free latitude in his responses. He expresses fully what he thinks, no holds barred.

Such general open-end questions might be:

STUDENT QUESTIONNAIRE

What do you think of the proposed trimester system?
Do you think it will benefit the students? If so, how?
Do you believe that the plan will help you?
In what way?

FACULTY QUESTIONNAIRE

Do you believe the present cut-system should be kept?
If so, why?
Do you think your department is getting the proper amount of funds for research?

Free-Story and Case Method

Instead of asking specific questions, interviewers can ascertain opinions and attitudes from extended conversations with the informant. Sometimes case histories also contain expressions of opinion. The case method most applicable to survey procedures is probably the controlled interview. After an extended interview with the informant, the investigator writes up a summary in which he calls attention to various statements which seem to indicate attitudes. If he follows an outline and can classify each informant's reaction to all questions, the data may be of value in statistical analysis.

Dichotomous (Yes or No) Questions

Usually poll questions present opposite alternatives to elicit a response of yes or no, agree or disagree, true or false, right or wrong, approve or disapprove, good or bad, fair or unfair. The following are typical yes or no questions applied to university issues:

(1) Do you approve of the cafeteria arrangements?
   Approve   Disapprove   No opinion

(2) Do you think that the present cultural events satisfy the needs of the university?
   Yes   No   No opinion

(3) Do you agree that the university newspaper should have a separate, independent publication board?
   Agree   Disagree   No opinion

(4) A community question: Do you know that the Community College grants only the A. A. degree?

Yes   No

The first three of these questions ask for an opinion, the last one is directed toward determining the informant's knowledge. Although these questions are designated as "dichotomous," they usually should and do allow for a third response, such as "don't know" or "no opinion" or "neither." Surveyors have found that if the non-committal third alternative is not openly mentioned by the interrogator, relatively few people will fail to make a choice between the two presented. However, it is preferable to use all three choices for completeness.

Questions by mail may be so framed that the respondent puts a plus (+), a minus (−), or a check (✓) in the appropriate column or box, crosses out one or the other of the terms (xxxx), or circles (◯) or underlines (_____) the word which represents his reaction.

Chief advantage of the dichotomous question is its simplicity, both from the standpoint of interviewing and of statistical handling later. The questionnaire takes relatively little time to ask, and gives a clear-cut answer which can be easily recorded and tabulated. The yes-and-no question is useful when opinion is so crystallized that the university issue can be reduced to a specific proposal.

UNIVERSITY LIBRARY QUESTIONNAIRE

To evaluate and improve our service, we are making a study of the use of the Central Library departments. Will you please complete this questionnaire before you leave this department, and drop it in the box provided near the desk. Your cooperation will be appreciated.

---

1. Please indicate if you had any difficulty using the catalogs in the Central Hall:
   _____ a. knowing which catalog to use
   _____ b. found book catalog difficult
   _____ c. found card catalog difficult
   _____ d. hard to know where to go after finding call number

2. In terms of library service, were you:
   _____ a. completely satisfied
   _____ b. only partially satisfied
   _____ c. not satisfied

3. If you found the department's service satisfactory, please indicate whether it was because:
   _____ a. you know your way around
   _____ b. you found the right book through the catalog
   _____ c. you found the right book on the shelf
   _____ d. the librarian helped you
   _____ e. other reasons (please give)

4. Give the reasons why you were not satisfied:
    _____a. book or books wanted were out
    _____b. book not owned by Library
    _____c. couldn't locate material on the subject
    _____d. material on too elementary a level
    _____e. material on too advanced a level
    _____f. material out of date
    _____g. other reasons (please give)
    _____

5. Please indicate if you had any difficulty in using this department
    today:
    _____a. room too crowded
    _____b. books out of order on shelves
    _____c. arrangement of books on shelves confusing
    _____d. staff too noisy
    _____e. staff not helpful (please indicate how)
    _____
    _____f. staff didn't know subject well enough to help
    _____g. took too long to get materials from stacks
    _____h. signs not clear
    _____i. other (please give)
    _____

6. If librarian gave help, did he:
    _____a. point out area where book might be on shelf
    _____b. go with you to shelves to find book
    _____c. identify book
    _____d. help with using catalog
    _____e. show how to use indexes
    _____f. show how to use pamphlet file
    _____g. find information for you from any source
    _____h. refer you to other sources
    _____i. refer you to other departments
    _____j. suggest alternative titles if book you wanted was not
             available
    _____k. other (please give)
    _____

7. Could the librarian have helped you better by:
    _____a. pointing out the area where the book was located
    _____b. going to the shelves with you to find the book
    _____c. giving help with using the catalog
    _____d. giving help with using indexes
    _____e. giving help with using the pamphlet file
    _____f. finding information for you
    _____g. referring you to other sources
    _____h. referring you to other departments
    _____i. suggesting alternative titles of books
    _____j. other (please give)
    _____

    If you have further comments or suggestions, please make them below.
    _____

STUDENT POLL

SHOULD FLAMBEAU (WEEKLY COLLEGE PAPER) PUBLISH CERTAIN MATERIAL

1. Do you think the Flambeau should be concerned editorially with
    current news events outside the University?   Yes_____ No_____

    Why?

2. Do you think the Flambeau should publish news relating to student organizations interested in national **po**litics?Yes_____ No_____

   Why?

3. Do you think the Flambeau should publish columns written by students with various political views?   Yes_____ No_____

   Why?

BACKGROUND INFORMATION

4. Are you a freshman___ sophomore___ junior___ senior___ graduate student_____ faculty_____

5. Do you classify yourself as "liberal" or "conservative" in politics? Liberal_____ Conservative_____

6. What school are you enrolled in?_____

7. What is your name?_____

Interviewer_____

Check Lists

In a sense, checklists are perhaps the most common of the multiple choice questions, but they deserve separate discussion. They usually consist of a statement of a problem or question followed by a list of from 3 to 15 possible answers from which the respondent is asked to check his choice of a reply. Examples of the checklist type of question follow:

(1) If the communication system fails at the university, whose fault do you think it is?

President__
Dean of Faculty__
Vice President__
Associate Dean of Day Division__
Dean of Day Division__
Evening Division Director__
Departmental chairmen__
Other_____

(2) Here is a list of some things which the college might try to do next year. Which two things on the list would you pick as the most important to make a start on?

Improve cafeteria food__
Institute a three-semester system__
Get more research funds from the government__

Obtain more secretarial help in each department__
Introduce more off-campus centers of learning__

As a rule these lists are made up after some preliminary surveying has been done to determine what types of replies may be expected. Only by *pretests* can the surveyor be sure that most of his answers will not fall in the "other" category which is usually provided with a limited list.

The advantage of the checklist is that it serves as a reminder for respondents who might otherwise fail to give a certain reply only because they had not happened to think of it at the moment. On the other hand, the checklist might suggest answers which the respondent checks for some extraneous reasons, such as that it is first or last on a list, or because he thinks it is the "proper" response to make. It is a well-known fact that the number of responses within a given category is higher with a checklist than when no suggestions are made to the informant.

If the checklist is presented orally it should be short, with preferably fewer than *five items* for the listener to grasp. If the list is long, or if each item is complicated, it is better to print the list on a card which the interviewer can hand to the respondent for him to read. There is still some danger that the informant will not bother to read the list but will pick out an answer at random. But this is a problem which can be handled by instructing the interviewer to explain all the questions carefully to the interviewee.

The checklist type of question is popular in mail questionnaire surveys, where the respondent may be asked to indicate his choice in any one of several ways: He may be asked to place a check mark ($\checkmark$) or cross (x) in an answer box. He may be told to cross out answers which do not apply. The technique is sometimes used also in the measurement of attitudes.

Ranking of Items

The ranking or order-of-merit method is also used in attitude measurement. In this type of device the informant is asked to arrange a list of statements, words, phrases, pictures, or other forms in the order of his preference. The following is an example of this type of question:

How important to *you* are these features of a college?

Place (1) beside the most important, (2) next in importance, and so on.

( ) Its faculty
( ) Its football team
( ) Its general sports record
( ) Its accreditation
( ) Its library facilities
( ) Its annual tuition cost
( ) Its location

One limitation of this technique is the fact that in arriving at an individual attitude score, no assumptions are made with regard to the size of the intervals between the steps. For instance, in the above example the difference between the statement ranked (1) and the statement ranked (2) may be much greater or much less than the difference between the statements ranked (3) and (4). However, even with this drawback, the method provides important information about attitudes.

Multiple Choice Questions

Multiple choice questions are so framed that the informant must choose which of several possible answers represents his opinion or comes closest to it. Such questions are particularly useful when the issue is not clear-cut and cannot be represented accurately by a dichotomous question.

With the multiple choices, all degrees of opinion can be given an opportunity for expression. The difficulty lies in *framing questions* which represent the *whole range* of opinion on the issue. It is important that the list of the alternatives or categories must be complete enough to cover the possible answers or the issue. If the list is incomplete, there is grave danger that the respondent will think that one of the specified alternatives takes care of his response. He will read into it something which belongs to an entirely different category. It is difficult to phrase statements which are mutually exclusive so that the respondent will not be undecided between two equally desirable choices. Long or complicated lists of questions also prove confusing and irritating to informants. Frequently, respondents choose the middle course and thus give too much weight to the intermediate categories in the scale.

Multiple choice questions may take any of several different forms. The most popular are the rating or intensity scales which use three, four, or five points, and the check-lists which also may take various forms.

Rating or Intensity Scales

In these scales the informant is asked to choose among various degrees of opinion on a given question. The number of degrees presented is largely a matter of judgment and depends on such general considerations as the purpose of the survey and the nature of the issue. The degrees may vary from three to the maximum number the tester believes the informant capable of differentiating. Generally speaking, no more than five steps are used by surveys employing the interview method. The rating scale attempts to get a quantitative expression of responses that are supposedly at various steps on an attitude continuum.

The following is a typical example of the presentation of items on a three-point rating scale: "How important do you think it is for each department to be represented on the public relations advisory board? Very Important, Only Fairly Important, or Not Important At All?" Another question might be surveyed among community people: "How do you think

the university compares with similar institutions in the state?—Higher__
the Same__ Lower__"

Other words or phrases commonly used in three-point scales are:

Harder..................About the Same......Not so Hard
Greater ....Equal..............Less
Yes ....Depends............No
Above Average...........Average ....Below Average
Most....................Many ....Few
Exceptionally Good ......Average ....Poor
Definitely Agree ....Middle Position......Definitely
                                            Disagree
More than most people.... Like most People ....Less than
                                            most people

SAMPLING PROCEDURES

In a small college with 500–1,000 students and 50–75 faculty members,
the director's problems of securing information are not too difficult. He can
survey the entire "public." But even in this survey he has to make sure
that he gets sufficient responses or answers from representative students
and faculty to draw valid conclusions, which can be depended on for decision-making. However, to survey a community of 10,000-plus population in
which the college is located requires some sampling procedures. In larger
institutions with 5,000–10,000 or even 25,000 students, and a faculty which
ranges from 150 to 2,000 and more, the task of surveying becomes formidable. This is equally true when large numbers of alumni are questioned or
outside community publics in a metropolitan area are surveyed.

The university public relations director, however, is particularly concerned in using the most efficient sampling procedures to conduct his polls.
It is important that he understand the significance of sampling and the various methods which can be successfully used to produce a reliable picture
of what the publics of the institution believe. He should know, too, the key
advantages of each method and its limitations.

The director appreciates the value of using sampling procedures instead of taking complete enumerations. If small samples are employed, an
estimate of the characteristics of the total can be secured in a much shorter
time than would be possible otherwise. This is especially true where conditions are constantly changing. The saving in time applies not only to securing the data, but tabulating and interpreting it.

The director of the college survey aims at certain standards and
avoids a number of pitfalls in developing his sample.

1. He wants the sample to yield an unbiased picture of the population which it purports to sample. The sample should constitute a true cross-sectional picture of the whole "public."

2. The sampling method chosen should be the most efficient for securing information with the funds available. The type of sampling should be suited to the survey design, hence the sample should be relatively easy to plan, to select, to collect information from, and to test and interpret.

The director of the higher educational survey has a number of sampling techniques to choose from, and he may combine several to get adequate results. He should become acquainted with the basic principles and procedures of each major method and what claims have been made for them as well as what criticisms have been raised.

Random Sampling

Random sampling is the term applied when the method of selecting ensures that each individual or element in the universe has an equal chance of being chosen. That is to say, the selection is regarded as being made by chance. Many surveyors have assumed that they could achieve chance selection through an unpremeditated or unsystematic procedure which follows no law of chance. This is not the case. Unless every precaution is taken to avoid biasing the elements, and a conscious effort is made to ensure the operation of chance factors, *the resulting sample is not likely to be random.*

Before a random sampling technique can be properly designed, knowledge of the university publics and their characteristics is essential. The surveyor must know the characteristics of students, faculty or community to include a representation of all persons involved in the issue. The director, for example, cannot eliminate by accident seniors in a survey of student attitudes. Nor can he omit, say, the working student, or the female student if their opinions would influence the outcome of the survey and, hence, affect decisions which would be made on the basis of the survey.

Certain procedures are commonly used to select random samples: (1) drawing by lot numbered slips of paper from a container, capsules from a goldfish bowl, or balls from an urn; (2) using tables of random sample numbers (1, 10, 20, 30, etc.); (3) using a roulette wheel; (4) selecting units at regular intervals from a list or card file or map; (5) selecting numbers of fixed positions.

Stratified Sampling

Stratified sampling is recommended frequently as the most efficient procedure for ensuring representativeness. It consists, first, of classifying the university into two or more strata and then drawing a sample from each. An example will illustrate the technique. It is desirable to get a 10% sample of both men and women in the college to determine their views on some critical issue. Two lists are prepared, one containing the names of men and the other the names of women. A sample of one in ten from each list is drawn. This is a random sample without separating the men and the women. However, if by chance only a small number of women on the list answered or were available to respond, the director could not be certain that the sexes would be fairly represented in the final tally. If the number of men outweighed the number of women, the final sample would not indicate this. Stratification by sex, however, guarantees proportional representation of the sexes and eliminates the possibility of drawing an inadequate random sample. The final selection of the cases within each stratum is made at random; however, this is done according to a carefully-designed plan, such as selecting every sixth or tenth person on the lists.

There are several types of stratified sampling. The number of cases selected within each stratum may be proportional or disproportional; the number may be the same from stratum to stratum or vary from one to another, depending on the sampling plan. If the stratum is not represented in the sample proportionately as in the university, the findings may be weighted or multiplied in such a way as to give a truer picture.

In proportional sampling, the cases are drawn from each stratum in the same proportion as they actually occur. If the strata have different totals, the representativeness (proportionality) for each stratum is achieved by drawing a constant proportion of cases from each one. For example, if the freshmen class has 1,000 students and the sophomore class contains 500, a list of the freshmen is drawn and from it, a 10% sample (or 100 students) would be taken, and similarly 10% would also be taken from the sophomore class (or 50 student names). The proportional stratified sample should closely resemble the random sample. The only difference is that the sampler can be sure that he is obtaining the right proportions from each stratum. If he drew a purely random sample from the 1,500 students listed alphabetically, the correct proportion of each class would not be maintained; he might get more responses from the sophomore class, although that would be the smaller of the two classes.

Area Sampling

It may be desirable to include in the survey representative opinions from students living in various parts of the state, or in various sections of the county or the city. Hence, it would be necessary for the director of the college survey to determine what proportions of the present students are from each of the areas, and then to design a sample which would take these residental areas into consideration.

18

Measuring PR Results

THE ANNIVERSARY celebration is over. The posters for the shopping exhibit have been taken back to the storage room. The first issue of the alumni magazine is off the press. The year's public relations program has come to an end.

Should the public relations department just file and forget these events? Move on to something else which is pressing for attention? We can file and forget, but we would benefit if we stopped to ask the simple question: "How did we do?" After each event is finished and, at the end of the year after the public relations program has been completed, the practitioner sits down and takes a hard, objective look at:

1. What were our aims?
2. What was accomplished?
3. What were the points of greatest success?
4. Why were the successful points successful?
5. Where did we fail—and why?
6. How can we avoid such mistakes next time?
7. If we had the opportunity to repeat the program, what exactly would we do?

Using these questions as guidelines, the university public relations director periodically audits his individual projects and the total program of his department.

Everyone gets a second chance—even university PR men. The wheel turns, the year spins, another special event will come up. The next issue of the alumni magazine will be published within six months, and what we have learned from the current issue can be applied—in part, at least. Or, looking over the program for the anniversary celebration, we notice that we did not allow enough time for sending out and receiving the invitations, or we failed to budget enough money for the food consumed. Now we write down our shortcomings for use next time.

The director would like to develop yardsticks which will determine the exact value of the public relations program in strengthening the favorable impressions of the institution's various publics, and in getting their support and cooperation. Tracing the origins of goodwill is difficult, admittedly. Pin-pointing the roles played by the PR department in giving the public a better understanding of the college and in making operations function more smoothly is equally difficult. Nor is the task of relating the public relations activities and projects to the effect on enrollment easy.

The director can "sense" the favorable effects of the public relations program and may be satisfied with the general results, but measuring them accurately is hard. The director knows generally that his communication messages are being received: Most of the college's releases are printed— faculty and students remark they have seen in the daily press the news article about the incoming members of the faculty—some persons in the community, whom the director meets, tell him casually about the community weekly's feature on the new University-Community Symphony Orchestra's being formed. But this is not measurement in any systematic or scientific sense.

The difficulties of measuring should not allow us to escape from the problem of trying earnestly and systematically to evaluate—qualitatively and quantitatively, and at periodical intervals—what the public relations department has done in all of its projects throughout the entire year.

The evaluation will prove valuable to college practitioners who are seeking better solutions to their own public relations problems and to those practicing the profession in other institutions. Evaluation and measuring, however inadequately done at this point in the development of public relations, will enable the director to present with some degree of confidence a yearly report to college officials who are concerned about the cost, the value and the results of the public relations activities.

RESEARCH TOOLS AND YARDSTICKS

We have pointed out in the previous chapter some of the research tools used to learn about the opinions of the various publics of the institution regarding its operations. Similar tools are employed to determine the effectiveness of specific public relations projects and the entire program. The director can use the questionnaire in a random or cross-sectional survey, or he can seek to get a quota sample on the response to a public relations activity. He can employ the in-depth interview or can organize an advisory panel.

Readership Survey

He may desire to get the reaction of any one of the university publics to the public relations program, especially its communication messages. He may survey the general outside public to obtain their overall reaction to the college's publicity efforts, asking also what they know about the college's courses or programs or what more would they like to know. Such information would enable the public relations department to include in future news and feature articles, information which is not being given. Facts about the reading habits of certain segments of the public may be obtained. What do the members of this public read? What daily newspapers and what part of the daily newspapers—city news; women's page; feature section; Sunday edition; tabloid section? Do they read community newspapers? Which ones?

On the day following the publication of a university article, a check-up can be made to determine if the group being surveyed saw and read the news in the daily, in the weekly or in both. Is there a possible explanation for the results. Did they read or neglect to read the news because of its treatment in the press—headline, length of article, page on which it appeared, position on the page?

Readability

One of the important problems in communication is its level of readability. The central question is: was the printed matter written over the heads of the readers? Are the sentences too long? too impersonal? Rudolph Flesch, one of the early pioneers of the readability movement, sought to develop a tool for determining reader-ease. His method was based on the difficulty of words—which depended on the number of syllables in each word. Reading-ease also depended on sentence length, he said. Human interest in the writing was determined by the number of personal words per 1,000 words and the number of personal sentences per 1,000 sentences. Other investigators, such as Robert Gunning, following a similar procedure, determining reader-ease by the average length of sentences. Irving E. Fang developed the Easy Listening Formula for radio and television news.

Pre- and Post-Tests

These tools might be used in determining the readability of college brochures and catalogues. A pre-test may be conducted before a brochure finally goes to the printer. The public relations department may run some tests on sample audiences to determine: (1) whether the material is understandable; (2) whether the brochure is interestingly written; (3) whether the photos and layout are appealing.

Comparative tests of material and layout can be conducted. Copy might be written in a straight factual style in Sample A; for Sample B the material can be recast in a personal, human interest style. The reactions of the reader audience to Sample A and Sample B may be compared, with the conclusions serving as guidelines for the final copy. Similarly, two types of layout may be presented for audience reaction, with the editors choosing the layout which received the more favorable response.

Post-publication testing may also be carried out by checking on what sections of the brochure or alumni magazine were read most widely; which sections of the publication were read by only a few readers; and which articles were skipped altogether.

Survey of High School Students

Similar studies of the attitudes, opinions and reading habits of high school students and counselors can be conducted. Certain questions have to be included of particular value to the college surveyor. He can include such questions as: "What do you think generally of the college?" "What are your (students' or counselors') reactions to the college's publicity program?"

Going deeper then, the surveyors may ask what newspapers do the high school students read. What dailies? What parts or sections or pages of the dailies do they read regularly? Again, checks might be made immediately after the publication of university news to learn whether the students read the newspapers, and if so, did they see the college article. In which paper(s) did they read the college news?

Other questions might deal with the students' stock of information about the college. What information did they have? What more would they like to know about the institution?

A similar survey can be taken of the college's newspaper tabloid published for high school students and issued by the department of public relations. The director can pre-test sample news articles or brochures to be read by high school students; and later he can conduct post-publication tests.

INFORMATION, READERSHIP SURVEY
GENERAL PUBLIC

_____ College   Date

BACKGROUND INFORMATION

    Mr.
    Mrs.
Name:Miss_____

Address:_____Zip:_____

High School attended:_____Graduated:_____

College attended:_____Graduated:_____

Children:_____,age___;_____,age___;_____,age
        (name)   (name)   (name)

INFORMATION ABOUT COLLEGE

What degrees do you think (name of) College grants: A.B.__;B.S.__;
M.A.__;Ph.D.__;B.Litt.__;A.A.__

What are some of the major departments_____,_____,
_____

What careers can you prepare for at (name of) College: _____,
_____,_____

What is the yearly tuitition fee, approximately? Free__;$300__;$500__;
$750__;$1,000__;$1,500__;$2,000__

Can students enroll in day___evening___summer sessions__

When should you apply for admission_____

READERSHIP INFORMATION

Do you see in newspapers the publicity of (name of) College?
regularly_____;sometimes_____;never_____

What do you read:

Daily Newspapers	Regularly	Sometimes	Never	Do you see (name of) College News in
Daily A				
Daily B				
Community Press				
Comm. Weekly A				
Comm. Weekly B				
Comm. Weekly C				

Where do you get most of your information about the college:
friends_____;newspapers_____;Which of the following depts._____?

BREAKDOWN BY DEPARTMENTS

In "Daily A" Do You Read:	Regu-larly	Some-times	Never	Do You Read the college News in these department Regularly	Sometimes	Never
Weekday Edition						
City News						
Feature Section						
Sports						
Entertainment Section						
Music Column						
Editorial Page						
Sunday Edition						
City News						
Magazine Tabloid						
Teen-Age World Tabloid						
Educational Section						
Amusement Department						
In "Daily B" Do You Read:						
Weekday Edition						
City News						
Feature Section						
County-Section						
Entertainment						
Sports						
Columnist Jones						
Editorial Page						
Sunday Edition						
City News						
County News						
Feature Magazine						
Young World Tabloid						
Columnist Jones						
Editorial Page						

Where do you get most of your information about (name of) College?

_____

_____

_____

The College Crier
(Weekly Newspaper)

Student Opinion Poll

REMARKS ON ANY QUESTIONS ARE ENCOURAGED
USE BACK OF SHEET OR PAGE THREE IF NECESSARY

I. Background Information
   1. Sex
      Male___
      Female___
   2. Class Standing
      Freshman___
      Sophomore___

   3. Number of credits as of
      June _____
   4. Curriculm _____
   5. Contemplated major _____
   6. Number of semesters at BJC
      (counting present) _____
   7. Age _____

II. General Information
   1. Are you interested in what is going on at the
      College? yes___ no___

   2. Do you take an active part in campus life by par-
      ticipating in clubs, special programs, SGA, etc.?
      yes___ no___
      If YES please list: _____

   3. Do you attend College functions:
      a. GIGIF's regularly___ sometimes___ never___
      b. Major dances regularly___ sometimes___ never___
      c. Sports events regularly___ sometimes___ never___

   4. Do you read the College Crier?
      regularly___ sometimes___ never___
      If you read the paper tell generally why: _____

      If you do not read the paper tell why: _____

III. Questions to be answered by readers of the Crier

   1. Do you read all of it?___ Some of it?___

   2. Do you read the front page?
      regularly___ sometimes___ never___

   3. Do you read the editorial (2) page?
      regularly___ sometimes___ never___

   4. Do you read the sports (3) page?
      regularly___ sometimes___ never___

   5. Do you read the back page?
      regularly___ sometimes___ never___

   6. Do you look at the pictures?
      regularly___ sometimes___ never___

   7. Would you like to see ___ pictures in the Crier?
      more___ same number___ less___

   8. Do you like to read reports of events at the College?
      yes___ no___

(continued)

9. Would you read comments or background articles on
   events happening outside the College: such as
   Ku Klux Klan, Vietnam? yes___ no___

10. Do you read news about club meetings?
    regularly___ sometimes___ never___

11. Do you read news about speakers?
    regularly___ sometimes___ never___

12. Do you read personality sketches about students?
    regularly___ sometimes___ never___

13. Do you read personality sketches about instructors?
    regularly___ sometimes___ never___

14. Do you read book reviews?
    regularly___ sometimes___ never___

15. Do you read editorials on College affairs?
    regularly___ sometimes___ never___

16. Do you read editorials on national affairs?
    regularly___ sometimes___ never___

17. Do you think a college paper should comment on
    national events? yes___ no___

                        SPORTS

18. Do you read articles on boys' sports events?
    regularly___ sometimes___ never___

19. Do you read articles on girls' sports events?
    regularly___ sometimes___ never___

20. Do you think the Crier misses any facet of BJC
    activity in coverage? yes___ no___
    IF YES please specify: _____

21. If you have a criticism of the College or Crier,
    would you write a letter to the editor? yes___ no___
    If NO please state why not: _____

22. Do you think the paper is placed easily within your
    reach at distribution stations around the College?
    yes___ no___
    If NO please state where you think it should be:
    _____

23. Do you think the general format of the paper is
    good___ fair___ poor___

24. How might the format be improved? _____
    _____

25. Do you read ads regularly___ sometimes___ never___

Newspaper Editor-Reporter Survey

The public relations department wants to find out the reaction of editors toward the college news, features and photos supplied by the department. The first check is to determine what news and editorials are being printed by each newspaper. But an in-depth survey might give information which would improve the relationship between editors and reporters on the one hand, and the university and public relations department on the other. The editor may reveal that he can't get through to the president as quickly as he needs to on some occasions. The reporter may say that he could not get background information on a certain college-trend feature he was developing. The college fails to give any information on controversial issues involving students or concerning faculty, a newsman may claim.

The city editor or educational reporter may reveal that he is not kept posted on big events far enough ahead to prepare for coverage. He may indicate that the university news may be written too long for his particular needs. He may reveal that more features about students would be desirable, and indicate that certain types of pictures would be acceptable but aren't submitted.

For those editors who do not use college news or publish only a few pieces occasionally, the survey perhaps would reveal the causes. Editors usually are busy, hence the mail questionnaire, unless kept very short, will find its way quickly to the wastebasket. A personal visit to the editor during some period in the week when he has a little leisure, will get better results.

Radio and Television Check-Up

Radio and television stations have developed a variety of methods for testing their programs. Some of these companies are using mechanical devices placed in the home and attached to the radio or television sets, but other surveys are based on personal interviews with radio listeners and television viewers. The public relations department of a university can check on its radio and television programs by initiating a telephone checking system. Several techniques can be employed.

The first is called the *co-incidental method.* The person answering the telephone is asked whether or not his radio is turned on, and, if so, name the program. If the university has a program on the air, the surveyor can determine quickly whether it is being listened to or watched. In the *recall technique,* the informant is asked to report on the programs he has heard in a certain period preceding the phone call. The length of time covered varies from survey to survey—from a few minutes to four hours or more. In the *aided-recall method,* the informant is told the names of programs that were on the air and he is asked to identify those to which his radio was tuned. In the *unaided-recall technique,* no attempt is made to assist the informant in remembering the data asked for.

Personal interviews can be conducted also to determine whether the university programs on the air have been listened to or viewed. The informant is shown a printed list of programs that were on the air during the period the college was on the air. He is asked to check the programs to which he listened.

Coupon Check

When a college schedules an advertisement for a newspaper, the director can conduct a coupon-check to determine the effectiveness of the advertisement. The coupon, to be returned by the reader, states that he will receive a free catalogue or brochure about a special program or course. The coupon is sent to the director of admissions, a particular division of the college, or to the department of public relations. If sent to various departments, the coupons should be returned eventually to the public relations director for record-keeping purposes. The coupons can be coded to determine in which newspaper the coupon appeared. For example, the code can read (DN-1-6), meaning that the advertisement appeared in the *Daily News* on January 6. Similarly a news or feature article can carry the line, "For further information write Director of Admissions,_____University, or telephone_____"

Hence, the director can measure, to some extent, the results of the advertisement or news. Now it is true that the coupons don't determine the entire results of the printed article. Many persons do not take the trouble to return coupons. They come directly to the college to get information or a brochure, or to apply for admission. The advertisement or news story plants a seed, however, for many readers don't respond immediately. They may not be ready. Later when the psychological and economic conditions are suitable, they remember what they read and then react. This writer has had the experience of getting coupons from college advertisements six months after the advertisements were printed; it is likely the appearance of a new advertisement and the opening of a new semester stimulated the readers to respond by sending in the old coupons. Public relations news and features, when not keyed for an immediate response, lay the groundwork for a later favorable reaction. The coupon gives the public relations director a feeling of confidence that the news or advertisement has been read. For every coupon returned, thousands of readers have seen and absorbed the information without responding.

LEVEL OF RESPONSES TO PUBLIC
RELATIONS COMMUNICATIONS

Various levels of responses are exhibited by the publics to a university news story, feature article, photograph or advertisement published in a newspaper or broadcast. There is also a variety of responses to a brochure, catalogue, motion picture or college speaker. Public relations directors constantly make analyses of the behavior reactions of the publics of the educational institutions. Here is an outline of such an analysis, which each director can refine, add to and make more precise, according to his experiences.

1. IMMEDIATE RESPONSE MADE

After seeing the news, viewing or listening to the broadcast, certain members of the "public" take action: they may enroll in a course now, attend the lecture tomorrow, or visit the opening of the art gallery Sunday.

The psychological, economic or "time" elements are just right; hence the news triggers their immediate response.

2. FAVORABLE ATTITUDE CREATED

From the public relations message, still other members of the public gain information and develop a favorable impression of the institution.

In the network of communications and of interpersonal influences and relations, the individuals so conditioned may affect others to react favorably. Parents influence other parents and their own sons and daughters. Concert-goers who can't attend the university concert tell others about the affair and they attend.

Informed and favorably impressed voters are not called upon to react and vote upon any college construction loan immediately, but a year later, when the vote comes up, they cast their ballots for the construction. Similarly, government officials who determine the amount of the institution's budget, may be favorably impressed by the college news now, but will be called upon to act only next spring when budget-making time comes.

3. DELAYED RESPONSE MADE

After absorbing the information, other members of the public make no immediate response because of psychological, economic, time, and other conditions influencing them.

These persons act late: they enroll in programs next semester, attend concerts in the spring, visit art galleries when personal conditions are favorable.

4. NO RESPONSE DEVELOPED

Many members of the public are not interested in a particular piece of college news, or any college news whatsoever. They do not intend to enroll in any course because of various reasons, psychological, anti-intellectual, economic, age. They do not expect to attend college cultural events.

Telephone Call Check

When telephone calls are to be received in response to a news article or advertisement, the public relations department may receive the calls. Or if it is more convenient, the director of admissions may handle the calls; but it is important to make a record of the person calling, as he may not want a catalogue, but only verbal information over the telephone. Each telephone call represents a response to the PR message.

Special Events Check

If tickets are sold or given free, the director can obtain easily the number of those who attend a special event. But when no tickets are involved, the task of checking on those who attend is made more difficult. The public relations staff, however, can institute an informal check of the number of persons who come to the art gallery, or visit the shopping center for the college exhibit.

Large companies such as the Bell Telephone System, have run extensive checks on visitors who attended their exhibits. The surveys were made on visitors as they stood in line before they saw the exhibits, and then the visitors were interviewed afterwards. The surveys checked on (1) the visitors' increased knowledge of the company, (2) the changed (if any) attitude toward the company, and (3) the response to the exhibits. Similar systematic studies can be conducted by the college PR teams, made up of staff members or students, drawn from public relations classes, from college service clubs or employed for the occasion. The surveys may be undertaken at university events to which the community is invited.

The Community College of Baltimore instituted a survey of those attending the institution's exhibits at shopping and community centers in 1970 and in 1971. The purpose was to find out what knowledge the visitors had of the college's degrees and programs, what they thought of the college and what was their response to the exhibit of 25 departments. A brief questionnaire was used and a short newspaper reading survey was taken. The name and address of each visitor together with his special interests were obtained. The information and lists were supplied, according to the interests of the visitors, to the director of admissions for the Day Division; as well as to director of Continuing Education, sponsoring evening classes; and to the Division of Community Services, offering informal programs. The visitors were furnished later with requested catalogues and brochures.

One student from the radio and television department was assigned the job of interviewing via a tape recorder the impressions and reactions of the visitors in all age groups. The printed information plus the verbal information were analyzed later to determine what people knew about the college and what they would like to know. The surveyors listed the visitors' reasons for liking the college, and also the reasons for not attending. The information was used later in determining the appeals and content of news stories and advertisements as well as broadcasts. Many older persons, for example, said they did not enroll in the special courses because the residents felt they were too old. The theme, "It's Never Too Late to Learn," was used afterwards in promotions which cited certain adults who had attended, profited by and were graduated from the institution.

PARKVILLE SHOPPING CENTER
SURVEY FOR COMMUNITY COLLEGE OF BALTIMORE

Name_____ Address_____ Age range____

EXHIBIT INFORMATION

How did you like the exhibit of CCB? Excellent__ Informative__
                                        Fair _____ Not Too __
                                        Poor _____ Informative__
What did you like best about the exhibit _____
After seeing the exhibit, what was your impression of the
  college? very favorable___; not too favorable___

What else would you like to know about the college? ___

KNOWLEDGE OF CCB

Did you ever hear of the Community College of Baltimore
  before? yes___; no___

Is CCB a four-year college or a two-year college?
  four year___; two year___

Generally, what types of programs does it offer? _____
_____

Does the college give a degree? yes___; no___
  Which degree? _____

Do you know what the cost of tuition is? _____

COLLEGE RATING

How would you rate CCB as a community college? tops___;
fair___; poor___

ENROLLMENT

Have you ever enrolled at CCB? yes___; no___

Have any of your children or other relatives enrolled at
  CCB? _____; none_____

READING

Do you read the Parkville Reporter? yes___; no___

Where did you get your information about this exhibit?
_____

Coupon-Enrollment Check

The public relations director can check the coupons from advertisements and news stories, telephone calls, and surveys made at special events against enrollments. The names of respondents and inquirers can be checked with the admission applications in various divisions of the college.

Index of Exposure Check

The public relations department should keep a monthly check on the university's Public Relations Exposure Index. The Exposure Index developed by this writer is a combination of all units of exposure received by the institution during the month. The public relations department checks on the amount of publicity the college has received, and then compiles a yearly total.

The compilation of the unit of exposure follows the method used by newspapers and magazines to determine cost of advertising. The media advertising manager bases the advertising cost on 14-agate lines-to-the-inch rate which is, in turn, dependent on the circulation of the publication, and on other factors. Some advertising unit has to be worked out for most types of merchandise or services being sold, and for whatever customer places the advertisement. Results from the advertisement do not enter the rate. The only variations in the rate are granted by a publication to organizations when large amounts or bulk advertising is used. The theory or principle behind the advertising rate is that, out of the total circulation of the publication, the manufacturer or retailer with a suitable, wanted product will gain a certain percentage of results. What the publication is selling is "advertising exposure," based on the size of the advertisement, the frequency of insertion, taking into consideration the circulation of the publication and its readability. Radio and television advertising rates follow the same general principle, but the rate unit depends on time, not space.

A similar Public Relations Exposure Index can be developed by the public relations department of any educational institution. The index would be based on the column inches of (1) headline space, (2) inches of news or features, (3) inches of photo space devoted to the institution. This barometer is not too difficult to compute, consideration being given to the fact that a one-column headline measures, for example, one inch, and a two-column headline would total two inches.

A more sophisticated and accurate Index of Exposure would take into account the fact that a two-column headline receives far more attention than a single-column headline, and likewise a three-column headline captures even more attention. While this could be determined with trial tests, an arbitrary figure of $1\frac{1}{2}$ times or 2 times ($1\frac{1}{2}\times$ or $2\times$) might be assigned the two-column headline value.

Similarly, the attention-value of a photograph about the university is worth far more than the same amount of space devoted to printed matter.

Hence a $2\times$ value can be assigned to photos; thus, if a 4 x 5 inch photo is printed, its unit value would not be 20 inches, but 40 inches.

Whatever formula is used, the important point is that the formula be continued year after year for comparison purposes. The public relations director may include the advertising space devoted to the institution to get a total exposure barometer. Similar computations may be made of the radio and television publicity and the advertising over these media. These units would be time-units.

The statistical measurement of space inches and time-units is a controversial issue in commercial and educational public relations. Many writers and practitioners have claimed that such statistical measurements do not indicate *effects* of the publicity nor the *attitudes* toward the company or educational institution. To determine the value of the university's public relations program, you must consider all aspects and the total program for the year, rather than just one measurement: inches of newspaper space or radio time.

On the other hand, the statistical measurement and presentation of exposure are definite and concrete. Such measurement can be understood by college officials, and comparisions can be made with last year's figures. No excessive claims, however, should be made for the index of exposure; it is *only one way* to measure results of public relations efforts, and it measures only one aspect of the year's program: amount of inches and time the institution received on a free and/or paid basis. This does not rule out the director's making a study of the attitude changes of the various publics toward the institution, as outlined in the previous chapter.

For the public relations man, the study of the figures can give him clues as to the response he has received in the newspaper and broadcast media. It may confirm certain of his daily analysis of the acceptance of articles by some newspapers and the rejection by others. The figures may give him a better-balanced picture than his daily on-the-spot observations. If the figures are compiled properly for each daily and department within the daily, and for each community newspaper, the public relations director will observe strengths and weaknesses in his own operations. The photo coverage by the community newspapers, for example, will be shown in the computations; perhaps, the figures will suggest that the public relations department should supply these community editors with more and better pictures. According to the figures, the feature section of Daily A is weak in university coverage, pointing to the fact that the feature editors may accept more articles than the institution has offered.

Here are a series of forms which can be used for determining PR Exposure Index. The forms include: (1) weekly check by events covered, which would be added up to produce (2) monthly check, which would be totaled for (3) the yearly breakdown by individual publications and broadcast stations, producing (4) overall yearly exposure index for all media grouped.

PUBLIC RELATIONS
EXPOSURE INDEX

Date: From _____
      To   _____

All Media-Weekly Check Form
(By Event)
News and Features

NEWSPAPERS	EVENT	HEADLINES COLUMN SIZE	LENGTH OF ARTICLE	PHOTO NUMBER	SIZE	TOTAL	CIRCULATION
Daily A							
Daily B							
COMMUNITY PRESS							
Community Weekly A							
Community Weekly B							
Community Weekly C							
(TOTALS)							

RADIO	NUMBER OF PROGRAMS	SEC.MIN.HOURS
Station A		
Station B		
Station C		
(TOTALS)		

TELEVISION	NUMBER OF PROGRAMS	SEC.MIN.HOURS
Station A		
Station B		
(TOTALS)		

PUBLIC RELATIONS EXPOSURE INDEX

Monthly Check
Publications, Broadcast Stations

NEWSPAPERS	NEWS AND FEATURES		PHOTOS		TOTAL	CIRCULATION
	Number	Inches	Number	Size		
Daily A						
Daily B						
COMMUNITY PRESS						
Community Weekly A						
Community Weekly B						
Community Weekly C						
TOTAL						

RADIO	NUMBER OF PROGRAMS	Sec.	Min.	Hours
Radio Station A				
Radio Station B				
TOTAL				

TELEVISION	NUMBER OF PROGRAMS	Sec.	Min.	Hours
Television Station A				
Television Station B				
TOTAL				

PUBLIC RELATIONS EXPOSURE INDEX FORM

YEARLY BREAKDOWN BY MEDIA AND
INDIVIDUAL PUBLICATIONS, BROADCAST STATIONS

NEWSPAPER SPACE

Publicity--DAILIES	Number of Articles	Inches	Total	Circulation
Daily A				
Daily B				
COMMUNITY PRESS				
Community Weekly A				
Community Weekly B				
Community Weekly C				
TOTALS				

RADIO STATIONS	Number of Programs	Sec.	Min.	Hours
Station A				
Station B				
Station C				
TOTALS				

TELEVISION STATIONS	Number of Programs	Sec.	Min.	Hours
Station A				
Station B				
TOTALS				

PUBLIC RELATIONS INDEX EXPOSURE FORM

(Space and Time Measurement)

197..

OVERALL YEARLY FIGURES

NEWSPAPER SPACE	Number of articles	Inches	Totals
Publicity			
Daily Newspapers			
Community Press			
Paid Advertising			
Daily Newspapers			
Community Press			
T O T A L S			

RADIO TIME	Number of Times	Sec.	Min.	Hours
Spot News Publicity				
Program Publicity				
Paid Programs				
T O T A L S				

TELEVISION TIME	Number of Times	Sec.	Min.	Hours
Spot News				
Programs				
Paid News				
T O T A L S				

GRAND TOTAL _____

Based on simple addition of number of articles and amount of inches; number of broadcasts and minutes. No attempt to assign additional value for larger headlines or photos.

ANNUAL REPORT

The public relations director should make an effective comprehensive annual report of the department's activities to the president. In the report the director may review some of the key purposes and goals of the department and the publics aimed at. The director can call attention to the significant public relations problems of the institution and indicate how they were solved, or partially solved, or not solved. The report can relate the highlights of the year's work in the public relations department, mentioning some of the innovations attempted and the continuation of the successful projects of previous years. The director may include a résumé of what progress he thought was made and review some of the results from qualitative and quantitative standpoints.

Outstanding news stories and feature articles about important educational and cultural events at the university during the year and how they were treated by the media can be pointed out. The Public Relations Exposure Index which the department has compiled can be presented and compared with figures of the previous year or years. The director can cover in his report some of the public relations problems which will be faced by the college during the next year, and suggest how they might be handled. And, finally, he can outline his projected public relations program for the year ahead.

The compiling and analysis of such a report have distinct benefits for the public relations department and for the university. In the process of reviewing the past year's problems and the public relations objectives and projects, the director has the opportunity to look at the overall program in one compressed report, and to evaluate the program in some systematic, organized fashion. He has the opportunity also to discover where the weaknesses in the public relations program lie and to develop fertile ideas and practical techniques for overcoming them. By analyzing the figures, he may discover new areas of publicity which might be followed up. Doing the research and writing the report will spur the director to analyze more deeply and articulate more completely his philosophy of educational public relations. He will develop also new insights by assessing the department's work.

The report will show the university officials a comprehensive picture of the operations and will enable them to evaluate the department's contributions to the progress of the institution. The report may be distributed to faculty members as well as to the board of trustees, giving all an understanding and an appreciation of the important role of the public relations program in the university operations.

CHECKLIST FOR PUBLIC RELATIONS ANNUAL REPORT

What should the annual report of the public relations department cover? Here are a few of the important sections the director of public relations can include in his report to the president.

1. Key purposes and goals of the department during the year
2. The various internal publics aimed at
3. The external publics for which the program was designed
4. Significant public relations problems faced by the institution
5. Highlights of the year's work of the PR department
6. Innovations in communications attempted
7. A qualitative analysis of the progress made in public relations
8. Some quantitative summaries of results
   Daily newspapers
   Community newspapers
   Radio
   Television
   Coupons
   Surveys
   Telephone calls
9. Outstanding news articles of important campus events
   Educational events
   Cultural events
10. Feature articles about the institution which appeared
11. Radio newscasts and special programs
12. Television newscasts and special programs
13. Brochures produced and distributed
    Department A
    　　　　　 B
    　　　　　 C
14. Motion pictures produced and shown,
    slide film shows produced, shown
15. Exhibits shown
16. Periodicals edited
    News-letters
    Magazines
17. Photographs taken and processed
18. Assistance in publicizing fund-raising campaign
19. Problems faced by the college, university during next year
20. Plans and projects of the public relations department
21. Recommendations by the director and staff

Bob Robinson, Director of Public Relations at Cleveland State Community College, in Tennessee, has developed another method of measuring the results of his year's effort. It will be noted that he figures "the typed lines" for each news release, then adds these lines for one yardstick. Included in his annual report, too, are the number of stories he sent out from month to month, and then the number of different media to which he distributed his news. At the end of the year, he adds up his figures for a grand

total. Mr. Robinson gives a "News Release Summary," breaking down his
releases by subjects, and finally lists the photos he distributed.

CLEVELAND STATE COMMUNITY COLLEGE

SUBJECT: Report September 1969 through May 1, 1970

FROM: Bob Robinson, Public Relations Office

The Public Relations Office mailed out 157 different stories about activities
at Cleveland State between the reporting period. This is an average of 20
different stories each month.

A total of 59 pictures were made by me during this same period for distribution to 59-plus news media representatives since many newspapers received
the same picture. This is an average of eight pictures a month which I
have made.

There was an average of 260 typed lines a month produced in this office in
the form of news releases, or 11 typed pages with an average of 24 typed
lines to a page. These releases were mailed to the 32 news media representatives, including radio stations, newspapers and television stations, in a
seven-county area surrounding Bradley County, as well as to the hometown
newspaper, if not in this area, of each of those named in the release.

We have sent news releases to all community colleges in Tennessee on an
exchange basis.

During each period when our student newspaper is being distributed, copies of
it are mailed from this office to every news media represented on our list,
as well as to 28 guidance counselors at high schools in the seven-county area,
in addition to 53 colleges and universities in Tennessee on an exchange basis.

Special news feeds to area radio stations are not included in the above figures
on news releases, but would average at least three a month.

A breakdown by month on the workload is as follows:

MONTH	TYPED LINES	NUMBER OF STORIES	DISTRIBUTED (Different News Media)
September	379	20	531
October	269	18	165
November	583	28	147
December	410	28	192
January	281	11	188
February	441	16	98
March	267	21	179
April	453	15	149
Grand Totals	3,083	157	1,649

19

The Effective PR Team

THE UNIVERSITY OR COLLEGE PUBLIC RELATIONS DEPARTMENT needs to have independence and a high-level status in the institution if the director is to do his job efficiently and successfully. The director requires also a large enough staff and sufficient budget to carry out the various functions of the department.

If the public relations department is to serve the entire educational institution, it should be a separate one and not attached to other departments as an auxiliary. A central department coordinates the public relations work that is done, and plans the publicity, for all university divisions and departments. Through the one department flows the news releases, radio and television broadcasts, the brochures and other publications. The department supervises the operation of the speakers' bureau, and coordinates the special events and the exhibits. Special divisions for each of these activities may be established, with associate or assistant public relations directors. Such a broad-scope department provides a uniform presentation, a consistent institutional image and, above all, avoids duplication.

THE DIRECTOR

However large or small the public relations department, the director requires top-level status and unbegrudged official recognition of the importance of his job and of the contributions his department makes to the institution. The public relations director needs to be on a par with university deans or vice presidents, and should report directly to the president, or to

419

a key vice president in charge of community affairs. To be effective, the director must report directly to the top officials so that in times of crises public relations officers can act with dispatch. He cannot be encumbered by the necessity of communicating with other administrators who, in turn, will check with the president. There is no time for that delayed clearance when working with the media on a fast-breaking news story. The director's value as a liaison representative also is based on the newsmen's recognition that the director deals directly with the president, and is close to presidential deliberations and thinking. To gain the confidence of faculty members, likewise, the director must have high status in the institution, receiving a salary equal to other vice presidents or deans.

The title of the public relations representative reflects the character of his work and its scope. Depending on the institution, he is given any one of a variety of titles:

EMPHASIS ON BROAD PUBLIC RELATIONS PROGRAM

Titles Showing Closeness to President:
Assistant to the President
Assistant to the President for University
Relations
Administrative Assistant, Communications

Titles Showing Broad Public Relations Scope:
Director of Public Relations
Director of Community Relations
Director of College Relations
Director of College Affairs

EMPHASIS ON NEWS AND INFORMATION FUNCTIONS
Director of News Bureau
Director of Information
Director of Informational Services
Coordinator of Information Services

The selection of the title, or the change of title to one of the above, should be considered carefully before this step is taken. If the representative is to be on a high level, covering a variety of programs, it would seem appropriate that "Director of University Relations" or "Director of Public Relations" might indicate his job. If his work is confined to publicity, then "Director of Information" or "Director of Informational Services" would be more suitable.

OFFICE OF UNIVERSITY RELATIONS

Objectives

—provide on a continuing, daily basis creative public relations;
—make current resources continuously available to meet established public relations goals and objectives throughout the University;
—establish a strong information publication to attract important attitudinal and financial support to the University;
—build the faculty-staff publication into a strong voice of University policies;
—establish a viable system of public broadcasting to take advantage of public service potential in commercial broadcasting and the new State educational television network;
—create and maintain an Information and Visitors Center, utilizing staff and volunteers;

University of Maryland
University Relations Organizational Booklet

Daily Work

Because it is necessary for the director to keep informed about immediate actions and long-term university plans, he attends administrative council meetings and those of the board of trustees. There he acts in a consulting capacity, expressing his views when the issues involve both the internal and external public relations. In meetings with groups of government officials or representatives of other educational institutions, the director may be designated by the president to serve as spokesman. As pointed out in the section on news publicity, the director acts as liaison representative with the press corps.

Because of the nature of his job, the public relations director circulates through the entire organization and crisscrosses boundaries of authority. He works with deans and chairmen of other departments daily, and he has to be able to communicate easily with all levels of the faculty and with student leaders. In fact, most university public relations directors find that they have to do a great deal of explaining within the universities. The director must be able to talk, write and promote his work constantly. He needs to keep administrators and faculty aware of what he is doing and thinking, and to respond to their enthusiasms and plans to advance their departments. Some public relations men estimate that 20% to 30% of their time is devoted to explaining various aspects of their objectives and projects, for the directors declare that such internal effort is necessary to make the public relations' operations successful.

As he works with distinguished faculty members and often with ambitious deans and chairmen, eager to have their departments secure public recognition and to acquire additional students, the director must have emotional stability and an even temper which does not boil easily, no matter what the circumstances. He has to possess the ability to withstand the frustrations of not getting university news copy accepted by city editors, or of having the feature article trimmed badly, or of learning that the hard-to-get photo was cast in the wastebasket.

Because of the steady volume of work and the necessity of meeting deadlines of the media, the public relations director has to develop steady work-habits. He must be able to work at a rapid pace over a period of time, and, without blowing up, rise to meet emergencies which inevitably occur. These situations may range from writing news stories when the information from a college department head arrives just on a newspaper deadline, to consulting with the president when a student confrontation is about to take place. The ability to forget quickly the inconsideration and lack of cooperation sometimes shown by officials and faculty ranks high among the assets of the director. In spite of the many roadblocks and temporary setbacks he runs into during the day, the director gets the public relations job done and the projects carried out on time.

Professional Knowledge

Directors grow on the job. They seek constantly to improve their writing and speaking abilities which are basic to the job, for they have to be able to write a news or feature article, develop a brochure, or speak before a Rotary Club. They work to get a better knowledge of all communication media, particularly art and photography. As professionals, they are interested, too, in subjects, such as sociology, psychology and social psychology, which bear on public relations. As a vital part of the educational institution, the directors aim to get a deeper understanding of higher education, its goals and accomplishments, and to learn about new instructional techniques and general educational trends.

To broaden their professional scope, to widen their knowledge and to improve their skills, the public relations directors read *College and University Journal,* a bi-monthly, and *Techniques,* a bi-monthly magazine exploring practical methods in public relations, issued by the American College Public Relations Association. On the broad professional level, they subscribe to the *Public Relations Journal,* published by the Public Relations Society of America. This magazine presents case studies and current discussions. The directors also read the *Public Relations Quarterly,* which offers in-depth articles. Current news is published in *Public Relations News, PR Reporter* and *Jack O'Dwyer's Newsletter.*

Staff members in the community college public relations departments get a rich understanding of trends in this area of higher education in the

Community and Junior College Journal, edited in a modern style by William Harper for the American Association of Community and Junior Colleges. To keep posted about what is going on in journalism, the information officer subscribes to the weekly trade magazine, *Editor and Publisher,* and the newspaper, *Publishers' Auxiliary.* For in-depth researched articles on journalism developments, members of the department read the *Journalism Quarterly.*

Public Relations departments also send representatives to national and regional meetings of the American College Public Relations Association and to the public relations sectional meetings of the American Association of Community and Junior Colleges. As significant questions bearing on communications and journalism are discussed at the annual meetings of the Association for Education in Journalism, the university public relations director makes an effort to attend the conventions, where sectional meetings are devoted to public relations.

THE PUBLIC RELATIONS STAFF

The extent of the staff working under the director depends generally on the size of the institution and its total budget. The number of assistants and specialists and the character of their work in the department grow out of the scope and functions of the public relations activities of the university and the amount of money allowed the department.

In a small college, the entire department may consist of a director and a secretary. The director doubles in brass or changes public relations hats, depending on the tasks confronting him. He writes news articles early in the morning, then produces a radio broadcast and shoots a picture at midday, and in the afternoon works on a college exhibit for a community center. His tasks change daily according to immediate pressures and needs.

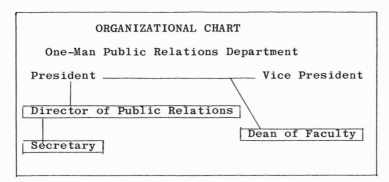

Simple Organizational Chart of One Man-and-Secretary Public Relations Department, Reporting Directly to the President

With a variety of public relations jobs to be done, large university departments employ larger staffs to handle the volume of work. The director coordinates and plans the work, checks for readability and accuracy of copy, producing new ideas and spurring his staff to create new and meaningful forms of communication. The director is responsible for the production of the department and sees that the work gets done. He recommends the hiring of staff members, and he works on and submits the departmental budget to the president or director of finance.

Here are some of the specialists on his staff.

News Bureau Writer. This specialist covers news events and writes feature articles about the institution. He may assist the director in this job, or if the institution is large enough, the news bureau writer may be solely responsible, with the final check being made by the director. The bureau head may write press releases plus radio and television publicity.

Radio-Television Writer. This specialist is knowledgeable regarding the needs and the deadlines of the electronic media, producing copy which fits their requirements. He may originate more extensive radio and television programs involving administration, faculty and students. Skilled in motion pictures, he may direct the production of a college film, or assist a commercial company in such a job.

Artist. This trained individual may be responsible for the artwork, including drawings and photos which go into brochures, catalogues, and periodicals issued by the college. He works in conjunction with the public relations director, carrying out assignments, creating new ideas and making recommendations for visuals.

Photographer. The cameraman shoots pictures for the entire department, getting his assignments from the director as well as other specialists. He develops creative pictorial ideas and recommends them to the director, and, upon getting approval, proceeds to execute the job. More than one photographer may be employed in a large university's public relations department with a huge volume of photo work.

Publications Director (Editor). The brochures and catalogues of the college require an experienced person, and the director may do the job himself or may employ a publications editor. The specialist may also serve as editor of various periodicals.

Alumni Relations Director. In many universities, the job of the cultivation of the thousands of alumni and of keeping them posted about the institution's developments requires the services of a single individual, whose complete time is devoted to the alumni. He produces the alumni magazine or monthly reports and he organizes the meetings of state groups.

Coordinator of Special Events. If the university conducts many functions involving the community or parents, a coordinator of special events will be found desirable. He plans the events with the director of public relations and other officials, and executes the plans. The coordinator may be in charge of the speakers' bureau. To do this work, the coordinator may need the assistance of other staff members, such as the news writer and photographer.

Secretarial Staff. The success of the public relations department frequently rests upon the efficiency of the secretarial staff. The staff keeps the office running efficiently, handling visitors and telephone calls, but also typing letters. The secretarial staff operates the mimeograph or multilith machine, when the public relations department does its own duplicating work. The secretaries also keep the newsclipping book and photo and records files in order.

Here are some organizational charts of the public relations departments showing the relationships of the directors to the president and other staff members.

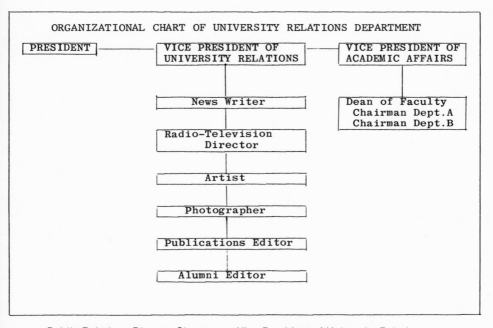

ORGANIZATIONAL CHART OF UNIVERSITY RELATIONS DEPARTMENT

PRESIDENT — VICE PRESIDENT OF UNIVERSITY RELATIONS — VICE PRESIDENT OF ACADEMIC AFFAIRS

News Writer — Dean of Faculty / Chairman Dept.A / Chairman Dept.B

Radio-Television Director

Artist

Photographer

Publications Editor

Alumni Editor

Public Relations Director Shown as a Vice President of University Relations

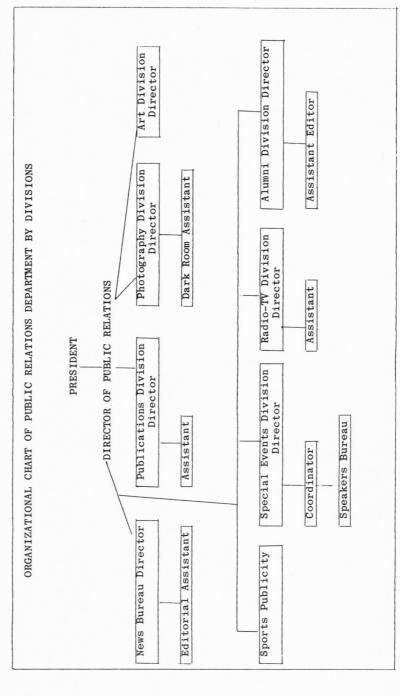

Horizontal Chart Showing Different Divisions Within the Public Relations Department.

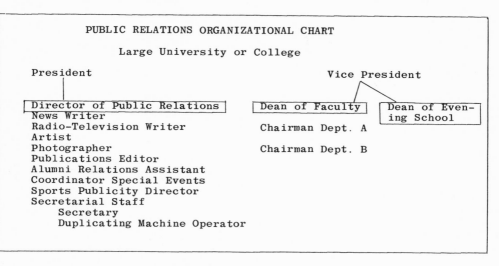

Director Public Relations Reports Directly to President

PROFESSIONAL RELATIONSHIPS

To conduct the public relations program efficiently, the public relations director needs to get cooperation from three different groups— from the administration, from the faculty and from the students. The director, in turn, also must be of assistance to these groups in helping them with their public relations problems and their publicity.

Administration Relationships

The whole college should be given to understand, through presidential example as well as by decree, that the publicizing and the interpretation of the institution's work are functions second only in importance to the educational program itself. When the president provides the PR director with a salary equal to that of vice presidents or deans, the director will more likely be accepted by the administrators if he is on their level. Because of the position's responsibility, the president should pick for the job a well-qualified expert in the area of public relations, selecting someone whom he can respect and trust, as he does the heads of academic departments.

The president has the obligation to inform the public relations director of all that goes on within the institution. The director cannot be expected to inform the public and to interpret the university when he does not have full knowledge of happenings or plans. The president and other officials should invite the public relations director to all high level council meetings

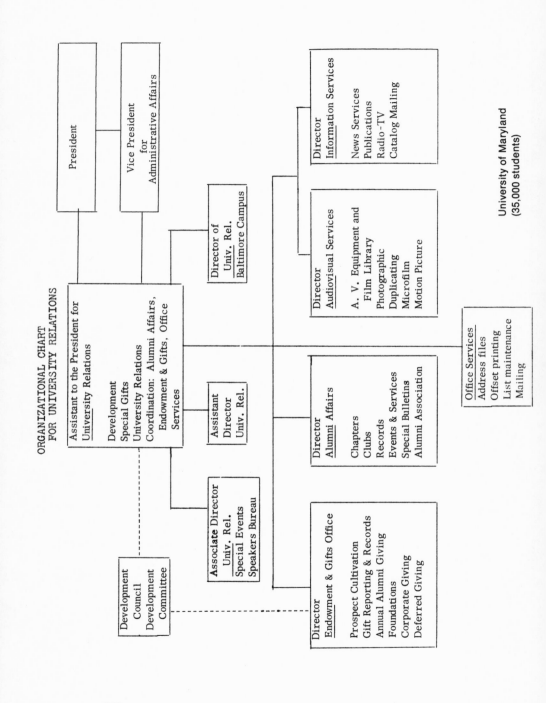

ORGANIZATIONAL CHART
FOR UNIVERSITY RELATIONS

President

Vice President
for
Administrative Affairs

Assistant to the President for
University Relations

Development
Special Gifts
University Relations
Coordination: Alumni Affairs,
Endowment & Gifts, Office
Services

Director of
Univ. Rel.
Baltimore Campus

Director
Information Services

News Services
Publications
Radio-TV
Catalog Mailing

Director
Audiovisual Services

A. V. Equipment and
Film Library
Photographic
Duplicating
Microfilm
Motion Picture

Assistant
Director
Univ. Rel.

Director
Alumni Affairs

Chapters
Clubs
Records
Events & Services
Special Bulletins
Alumni Association

Office Services
Address files
Offset printing
List maintenance
Mailing

Associate Director
Univ. Rel.
Special Events
Speakers Bureau

Development
Council
Development
Committee

Director
Endowment & Gifts Office

Prospect Cultivation
Gift Reporting & Records
Annual Alumni Giving
Foundations
Corporate Giving
Deferred Giving

University of Maryland
(35,000 students)

428

and other meetings of the administrators and faculty. He should be invited to sit in on important conferences with outside individuals and groups, when their meetings have a bearing on university-community relations. The president in daily and weekly conferences with the director outlines the public relations problems the college faces and gets the advice of the director before any important step is taken. All announcements made by the president's office go through the public relations officer, and contacts with the press are funneled through the public relations office also.

Faculty Relationships

The public relations director gains faculty respect as he acquires a knowledge of the whole institution and its individual departments. He seeks to become well-informed and keep up-to-date on activities at the university, and to demonstrate this fund of knowledge in his conversation and writing.

Directors develop a wide acquaintance with faculty members, getting them to talk about their work. As a result of casual conversations, the director can build up a storehouse of "tips" and background for future news and feature articles.

An important way for the director to gain faculty understanding and support is by talking before departmental and other faculty groups. The information representative creates opportunities to discuss the public relations program. Directors realize that the lack of understanding of public relations is widespread, and that most faculty members are critical; hence, the directors prepare their talks carefully. Searching questions will be asked, therefore the directors are ready for these faculty queries. The director may follow-up with meetings in individual faculty offices.

Faculty members should be encouraged, as indicated in an early chapter, to bring their news and public relations problems to the director's office. To keep good relations, the director checks back with the sources before he releases the news. As pointed out previously, the faculty members should be encouraged to furnish the public relations director with a written résumé of the news or the public relations problem to prevent any misinformation and to save time.

Opinions differ as to what to do with newspaper and magazine clippings about the institution. Some directors place all clippings in scrapbooks which are put into filing cabinets. Other colleges keep only enough of a sampling of the clippings to constitute a historical record.

Many university public relations representatives send duplicated clippings to the news source or to the faculty staff member involved in the news article. In this way, the public relations office gives evidence that it is on the job and that it is getting publicity results. The faculty member usually appreciates the thoughtfulness when he receives the clipping of interest to him or the article involving his department. Some directors send duplicates of the original news releases immediately to the college persons involved to show them the publicity being issued for them, whether the newspapers print the releases or not.

Various devices are used for faculty reminders to send in the news to the public relations office. The publicity director of one institution attaches to every telephone on the campus a tag, reminding telephone users that they should call the news bureau regularly with suggestions. Still another director distributes blotters carrying a similar message. A third representative presents cleverly-written and illustrated booklets to all faculty members, telling of the publicity efforts of the office. Many publicity directors send mimeographed news blanks to their faculty members once or twice a month, so that instructors, with a minimum of effort, can give information about their speeches, meetings, research.

One large university obtained good results by asking each of the 70 academic departments to select one of its more news-conscious staff members as departmental reporter to send "tips" and stories to the news bureau of the public relations office. These reporters are called together regularly for detailed instructions.

A spirit of helpfulness on the part of the director can go a long way in building faculty confidence and support. The director may hear that certain faculty members or departments are planning a conference or convention. Before being asked, the director volunteers to help or assigns one of his assistants to the event. At the same time, by participating in the planning from the early stages of the event, the public relations officer has an opportunity to give guidance which will produce more and better publicity for the event.

In other ways, the public relations officer can practice good internal public relations. He can make friends and increase cooperation by taking the time to send brief notes to staff members, expressing congratulations on promotions, achievements, marriages and new arrivals in the family, and also extending sympathy in death and misfortune.

Relationships With Students

Cooperation of students should be sought. The exact nature and extent of work with students varies with the size of the institution, and the director has to determine what is best for his particular situation. In some universities and colleges, the student leaders may look upon the public relations office as part of "the establishment," hence to be avoided. The director must seek to build strong relations in spite of this attitude; a fair policy which considers student interests and needs throughout the year may serve well in crisis situations. The PR director publicizes, as shown in previous chapters, all newsworthy student activities.

The public relations door should be open to all students desiring advice and assistance. The director and his staff may serve thus in the role of consultants. In some colleges, the information officer becomes active in student projects, especially where publicity will result. In a large institution, the student international debate, or the musical festival may be deemed worthy of major news-attention. In a small college, the public relations officer with a student committee may handle entire events.

The student newspaper is an important media for internal communications and for interpreting the institution and its policies. Some directors believe it is the cornerstone in the internal public relations program, because the student publication reaches all or nearly all the students and most of the faculty. Other institutions find that they need to publish internal newsletters for the faculty, as indicated in a previous chapter.

An open door should be maintained for staff members of student newspapers who come seeking the director's advice. He should treat them as he would representatives of off-campus publications. The director supplies the student editor with all publicity releases and tips him off as to what events are coming up. Often the public relations director has first, or early access, to high-level decisions and events, which the student reporter may not have learned about. If the news has been cleared, the director may tip off the student editor. Sometimes news articles or features may be more suitable for the student press than for outside publications. In these instances, the director supplies the facts for the articles to the student reporters.

Problems regarding the distribution of significant news cause trouble. The public relations news bureau may have an important story concerning the appointment of a new dean or other major policy change; then the director has to decide whether the news should be given first to the student newspaper or first to the downtown press and broadcasting services. The student editor does not want to get scooped on an important university story; neither do the downtown news-editors. Some satisfactory method of releasing the news to meet the deadlines of the various publications has to be developed by the director to handle this sticky situation.

Opportunity for students to learn about news and public relations is afforded by public relations directors in some colleges. Students are employed as assistants; these are usually recruited from the journalism department, particularly from reporting or public relations classes. Opinion is divided on this practice. Some officers believe it is undesirable for students to go about the campus representing the public relations department, and interviewing administrators, faculty and students. The copy the students produce may contain embarrassing errors, with the public relations director being blamed for them. If student assistants are employed, the director has the obligation of giving careful instructions about interviewing, urging the students to keep down the arrogant posture or self-important tone the student assistants may assume. The director also has to check the copy carefully before sending out releases produced by students. Careful instructions should be given if students are engaged to handle details in the special events on-campus or off-campus, for the director may decide to hire qualified students as guides on the campus tours or as helpers at the exhibits in the community centers.

MAINTAINING ADEQUATE RECORDS

To operate the department efficiently, the director needs to maintain basic records, files and references, because often accurate and complete information about the institution is needed quickly.

Historical Records

The director should have available for instant use complete background information on the college and its various buildings, organizations and activities. It is essential that he have a history, if one has been written, or historical materials about the institution. In his office storeroom should be kept bound files of the student newspaper, yearbook, magazine and other institutional publications such as the catalogue and alumni magazine.

Morgue

A photofile of still photographs, as already mentioned in the chapter on photographs, should be kept in kraft envelopes in steel cabinets. The photos should include those of administrators, staff members, past and present; campus buildings and scenes. Files of trustees and alumni leaders and student leaders should be maintained, along with shots covering principal special events in the history of the college—anniversaries, dedications and commencements. College publicity offices which serve weeklies and small dailies find it profitable to have on hand newspaper "cuts," or metal engravings, and stereotype mats of leading staff members. Such cuts and mats serve well when editors at the last-minute ask for them.

Biographical Records

Every year hundreds of occasions arise calling for specific and detailed data on faculty, students and others. The news bureau of the public relations department cannot function effectively without having such material within easy reach. Biographical records of faculty members are obtained most readily at the time the appointments are made. When trustees are appointed, such information should be obtained quickly. As student leaders are elected or appointed to office, biographical records are acquired by the public relations office. Also the director should obtain biographical data on the founders of the institution and on men and women who have played prominent roles in its history.

Mailing Lists Maintenance

The publicity director compiles and maintains mailing lists covering the various outlets for his materials. Some offices keep these lists in card files with a card for each newspaper, magazine, radio and telephone contact. Most of the directors, however, keep their lists alphabetically by classifications in 8½ x 11 notebooks. The classification for newspapers might be broken down for morning and evening papers, Sunday papers, as well as for internal departmental editors, such as feature, women's pages, amusement, educational. The radio list or television list will include at least three classifications—newscasters, commentators and program directors.

STUDENT RECORD
For Public Relations Office

Date _____

Name _____ Age _____

Campus Address _____ Telephone ___

Year Entered College _____ Class _____

Major at College _____

Clubs Belonged To:

_____ Officer _____

_____ Committees _____

Secondary Education:

High School attended _____ Yr. Graduated _____

Location _____ Major _____

Outside Work:

Place _____ Type of Work _____

College Employment:

Place _____ Type of Work _____

Special Interests _____

Hobbies _____

Parents _____

Home Address _____

Reference Library

To obtain information quickly, completely and accurately, the public relations office has to have a number of handy references. The staff will find considerable need for a standard dictionary, *Roget's Thesaurus, World Almanac* or *Information Please Almanac*.

Considered essential also are *Editor & Publisher Yearbook, Standard Rate and Data Guide, Broadcasting Yearbook*. Essential also are *Who's Who in America* and *Who's Who in American Education, Accredited Higher Institutions* (a U. S. Office of Education publication). Needed, too, are *Public Relations Directory and Yearbook*, and bound copies of *College Public Relations* and *College Public Relations Annual*. The last-named publication contains an index to hundreds of articles and reports which have appeared in publications of the American College Publicity Association and the American College Public Relations Association since 1924.

SCHEDULING WORK

Before the start of the academic year, the director surveys the months ahead for such major opportunities as local anniversaries and special events. He searches for tie-ins which may produce good news articles. A preview of the year's possibilities by the entire staff will produce suggestions for additional opportunities.

He may desire to set up a public relations and publicity committee for the college. Some colleges use such a committee to develop a broad scope policy. The planning group would include interested administrators and faculty members together with the public relations staff. Special committees may be set up during the course of the year to plan for particular events. The director may make plans to call on administrators and departmental chairmen during the year, and he also may program meetings with editors and reporters of outside publications as well as the student press.

The publicity director operates similarly to the managing editor or city editor of a newspaper. He keeps a calendar or assignment book to assure complete news coverage. Such a "futures book" enables the office to operate smoothly. The staff writer knows what is coming up, when the copy is due, and when it must be delivered to the daily press, to suburban weeklies and to the broadcast media. The publications assistant knows when the information should be gathered for the brochure, when it should be written and when it should be delivered to the printer.

The director wisely plans a week, two weeks, even months ahead. Work schedules are used for every phase of the public relations program. Lack of adequate planning not only makes it necessary for many public relations offices to work under undue tension but also causes the loss of many opportunities for increased effectiveness in the use of media.

THE ANNUAL REPORT

In the previous chapter we have outlined the need for the director to develop a complete annual report of the department and we have indicated the scope of its contents.

PREPARING THE ANNUAL BUDGET

The director, in conjunction with the director of finance, develops the details of the annual budget for the department of public relations. The director includes all necessary salary and expense items for the efficient operation of the department. The typical proposed budget covers the salary items for the staff, then the printing and photography expenses. The cost of advertising would rate a separate line. The director includes also travel expenses for local and out-of-town destinations, meetings of professional educational and public relations organizations. If the public relations department subscribes to a variety of newspapers, both daily and community, as well as professional magazines, this publication expense is included. Capital expense for typewriters and other equipment is incorporated. The experience of one year serves as a basis for the following year.

SAMPLE ANNUAL BUDGET
Public Relations Department

Salaries		Advertising Costs	
Director	$	Daily Newspapers	$
News Bureau Writer	$	Weekly Newspapers	$
Artist	$	Radio	$
Photographer	$	Television	$
Publications Editor	$	**Other Expenses**	
Alumni Relations Assistant	$		
Secretarial Staff	$	Travel:	$
Printing Costs		Local $	
		Out of Town $	
Catalogues	$	Conventions / Meetings	$
Brochures	$	Newspaper Subscriptions	$
Periodicals	$	Capital Equipment	$
Photography Costs		(Typewriter, Duplicating Machines, Filing Cabinets,	
Film	$	etc.)	
Outside Processing	$		
Darkroom Costs	$		

Although a breakdown of printing and advertising costs is often difficult to project, it is necessary to have a basis from which to start the year. Revisions can be made as new projects are proposed and receive approval. Again, the experience of one year serves as the basis for the next year's calculations.

PROPOSED BUDGET OF ADVERTISING
BREAKDOWNS BY ITEM

Date _____ 7_

Advertising Expenses   TOTALS

     Daily Newspapers $_____

         Daily Newspaper A
         (Jan.$_____   June $_____   Sept.$_____)
         Daily Newspaper B
         (Jan.$_____   June $_____   Sept.$_____)

     Weekly Press $_____

         Community Weekly A
         (March $_____   April $_____   Aug.$_____)
         Community Weekly B
         (March $_____   April $_____   Aug.$_____)

     Radio $_____

         Station X
         (March $_____   August $_____)
         Station Y
         (March $_____   September $_____)

     Television $_____

         Station Z
         (March $_____)

PROPOSED BUDGET PRINTING EXPENSES

BROCHURES

Art Department; Multilith, 2,000 copies $_____

Science Department;Letter-Press,5,000 copies $_____

Music Department;Mimeograph,2,000 copies $_____

Physical Education Dept.;Multilith,1,000 copies $_____

_____ $_____

_____ $_____

_____ $_____

_____ $_____

_____ $_____

Bibliography

PART ONE: BACKGROUND FOR PUBLIC RELATIONS

Public Relations in Higher Education

American College Public Relations Association, **Casebook of Institutional Advancement Programs.** Washington, D.C.: American College Public Relations Association, 1970. Excellent detailed cases of many colleges' experiences with special events, news bureaus, fund-raising and other aspects of public relations.

Bertrand R. Canfield, **Public Relations, Principles, Cases and Problems.** Homewood, Ill.: Irwin (4th Ed.) 1968. Detailed chapters on all aspects of public relations. Chapter 12 deals with educational relations.

Scott M. Cutlip, **A Public Relations Bibliography, and Reference and Film Guides.** Madison: University of Wisconsin, (2nd Ed.) 1965. Only complete bibliography on subject; has both books and magazine articles listed and annotated.

Scott M. Cutlip and Allen H. Center, **Effective Public Relations.** Englewood Cliffs, N.J.: Prentice-Hall, 1971. A standard text, well-written and researched, it has informative thoughtful chapters on university public relations.

Richard W. Darrow, Dan J. Forrestal and Aubrey O. Cookman, **Dartnell Public Relations Handbook.** Chicago: Dartnell Corporation, 1967. Useful, explicit volume on basic principles of PR, covering many tools at length.

L. L. Golden, **Only By Public Consent.** New York: Hawthorne Books, 1968. A top consultant and writer on public relations explains the subject and gives fresh insights.

Leslie W. Kindred, **School Public Relations.** Englewood Cliffs, N.J.: Prentice-Hall, 1957. An earlier volume, but well-organized and articulate regarding philosophy of school public relations; deals with school information programs, but philosophy and approaches can be applied to college public relations.

Sidney Kobre, **Dynamic Force of Public Relations Today.** Dubuque, Iowa: Wm. C. Brown Co. Publishers, 1964. Concise statement of public relations key ideas; gives considerable attention to educational public relations, defining publics; outlines practical steps in developing communication tools.

John W. Leslie, **Focus on Understanding and Support: A Study in College Management.** Washington, D.C.: American College Public Relations Association, 1969. A fresh approach to organizational side of university and college public relations, showing scope and functions.

Philip Lesly, **Public Relations Handbook.** Englewood Cliffs, N.J.: Prentice-Hall, (Revised Ed.) 1971. Has excellent chapter on university relations as well as detailed chapters on media.

Edward J. Robinson, **Communications and Public Relations.** Columbus, Ohio: Charles E. Merrill Publishing Co., 1966. A valuable contribution, stressing social science approach to communications and applications to public relations.

Howard Stephenson (Editor), **Handbook of Public Relations.** New York: McGraw-Hill, 1971. Thorough discussions of nearly every phase of public relations makes this more than a handbook.

Student and Campus Issues

Howard S. Becker (Editor), **Campus Power Struggle.** Chicago: Aldine Publishing Co., 1970. Seeks to probe underlying problems of students, faculty and administration.

Cox Commission Report, **Crisis At Columbia.** New York: Vintage, 1968. Fact-finding report on confrontations and student-faculty issues at Columbia University in April and May, 1968.

Seymour Martin Lipset, **The Berkeley Student Revolt.** Garden City: Doubleday, 1965. Penetrating study of causes and events leading to disturbances at the University of California.

William J. Scranton, **The Report of the President's Commission on Campus Unrest.** New York: Avon Books, 1971. Detailed coverage of causes of student confrontations and events on various campuses; has extensive bibliography.

PART TWO: PRINT MEDIA—I

Newspapers

Warren J. Brier and Howard C. Heyn, **Writing for Newspapers and News Services.** New York: Funk & Wagnalls, 1969. Authors focus on readability of copy; based on their extensive experience, the suggestions for improved journalistic communications are practical and useful for public relations work.

Mitchell V. Charnley, **Reporting.** New York: Holt, Rinehart and Winston, (Rev. Ed.) 1966. A comprehensive text, with many specific examples of reporting and writing news.

John Hohenberg, **The Professional Journalist: A Guide to the Practices and Principles of News Media.** New York: Holt, Rinehart and Winston (3rd Ed.) 1973. Uses informal style, but volume is packed with information on writing styles for news, human interest features and interpretatives; treats print and broadcast journalism.

Curtis D. MacDougall, **Interpretative Reporting.** New York: Macmillan, (6th Ed.) 1972. A thorough-going text, covering principles of gathering and writing news; has step-by-step procedures for producing professional copy, making news fresh and readable.

Harry H. McNaughton. **Proofreading and Copyediting: A Practical Guide to Style for the 1970's.** New York: Hastings House, 1973. Includes down-to-earth information on editorial style.

Paul V. Sheehan, **Reportorial Writing.** Philadelphia: Chilton, 1972. Has lively style, clear discussion, good examples of news writing.

Publicity Methods

Babette B. Hall, **Public Relations, Publicity and Promotion.** New York: Washburn, 1970. Useful chapters on publicity which can prove helpful to university PR departments.

Jerry L. Morrow, "Two-Year College in Toledo Area Shows How Weekly Newspapers Will Cooperate in Running Localized News Releases." **College & University Journal,** Vol. 10, No. 4, September, 1971. Has ideas of value to college staff writer.

James W. Schwartz (Editor), **The Publicity Process.** Ames, Iowa: Iowa State University Press, 1966. Important book, with practical principles, good examples.

Feature Articles

George L. Bird, **Modern Article Writing.** Dubuque, Iowa: Wm. C. Brown Company Publishers, 1967. Comprehensive and valuable volume which deals with steps in feature-article writing.

PART THREE: PRINT MEDIA—II

Brochures

Alfred A. Crowell, **Creative Editing.** Dubuque, Iowa: Wm. C. Brown Company Publishers, 1969. Unusually practical, has new approach to layout of pages.

Peter Croy, **Graphic Design and Reproduction Techniques.** New York: Hastings House, (Rev. Ed.) 1972. Highly useful for the PR man or woman called upon to produce professional communications; discusses printing processes, letterpress, silk screen and offset; has detailed instructions on camera-work, and lettering.

John E. Cogoli, **Photo-Offset Fundamentals.** Bloomington, Ill.: McKnight & McKnight, (2nd Ed.) 1967. A comprehensive manual for understanding the step-by-step procedures in offset printing processes, from copy preparation to printing the final product.

H. C. Latimer. **Advertising Production Planning and Copy Preparation for Offset Printing.** New York: Art Direction Book Co., distributed by Hastings House, (2nd Ed.) 1969. A standard "how-to" work with useful illustrations.

Bruce Westley, **News Editing.** Boston: Houghton Mifflin, (2nd Ed.) 1972. A basic, informative text on editing news and feature copy to make it understandable and meaningful, at the same time interesting.

F. W. Wills, **Fundamentals of Layout for Newspapers & Magazine Advertising, for Page Design of Publications & Brochures.** New York: Dover Publishing Co., 1971. Stimulating chapters on layouts and the use of photography and drawings.

Periodicals

Edmund C. Arnold, **Modern Newspaper Design.** New York: Harper & Row, 1969. One of earliest authors to advocate fresh approach to attractive layout of front and inside pages; applicable to college PR publications.

Floyd K. Baskett and Jack C. Sissors, **Art of Editing.** New York: Macmillan, 1971. One of best texts on subject, deals in depth with principles and practices of editing copy; useful for all who issue publications for PR.

Bertrand R. Canfield, **Public Relations, Principles and Problems.** Homewood, Ill.: Irwin, 1968. Has excellent chapter on "Public Relations Periodicals," of value to college PR writers.

William C. Halley, **Employee Publications.** Philadelphia: Chilton, 1959. An earlier but thorough ·and informative study, based on author's experience with DuPont publications. Many examples and illustrations.

See also, Crowell and Westley volumes on editing cited above.

Advertising

Philip Ward Burton, and J. Robert Miller, **Advertising Fundamentals.** Scranton, Penna.: International Textbook Co., 1970. Broad-scoped, gives detailed information about print and broadcast media as well as outdoor and mail advertising; has chapters on copywriting, research and marketing.

Roger Barton (Editor), **Handbook of Advertising Management.** New York: McGraw-Hill, 1970. Would give PR director an overall view of advertising—major principles, media selection, copy strategy.

Charles J. Dirksen and Arthur Kroeger, **Advertising Principles and Problems.** Homewood, Ill.: Irwin (3rd Ed.) 1969. Comprehensive treatment of dynamics of consumer demand and detailed instructions on copy work and layout; covers media in detail; has several chapters on advertising research.

S. W. Dunn, **Advertising: Its Role in Modern Marketing.** New York: Rinehart & Winston, 1969. Detailed exposition of every aspect of advertising; will prove highly useful to PR staffman assigned to advertising jobs.

Darrell Blaine Lucas and Stewart Henderson Britt, **Measuring Advertising Effectiveness.** New York: McGraw-Hill, 1963. Although an older volume, still is highly useful because of its systematic, thorough treatment of measuring results.

Daniel Melcher and Nancy Larrick, **Printing and Promotion Handbook.** New York: McGraw-Hill, 1966. Contains useful technical information for college PR personnel who produce communications.

Patrick J. Robinson, Homer M. Dalbey, Irvin Gross, Yoram Wind, **Advertising Measurement and Decision-Making.** Boston: Allyn & Bacon, Inc., 1968. Concise statements about application of scientific methods in solving practical marketing problems.

C. H. Sandage and Vernon Fryburger, **Advertising Theory and Practice.** Homewood, Ill.: Richard D. Irwin, Inc. (8th Ed.) 1971. Gives step-by-step procedures in producing advertising copy.

Gene F. Seehafer and Jack W. Laemmar, **Successful Television & Radio Advertising.** New York: McGraw-Hill, 1959. A classic of its kind; thorough coverage of every step in producing copy and shows for electronic advertising.

John S. Wright, Daniel S. Warner and Willis L. Winter, Jr., **Advertising.** New York: McGraw-Hill (3rd Ed.) 1971. An up-to-date volume with stimulating chapters on media and on creating advertising; research and advertising budgets are given attention.

Stanley M. Ulanoff. **Advertising Today: The Theory and Practice of Persuasive Business Communication.** New York: Hastings House, 1974. Surveys all phases of the art of advertising and the media employed. Clearly written and illustrated.

PART FOUR: VISUAL AND BROADCAST MEDIA

Photography

Milton Feinberg, **Techniques of Photojournalism.** New York: Wiley, 1970. Has chapters of practical value to university PR cameraman.

Andreas Feininger, **Basic Color Photography.** Englewood Cliffs, N.J.: Prentice-Hall, 1972. A master photographer presents some basic information on steps in taking color photos.

Rodney Fox and Robert Kerns, **Creative News Photography.** Ames, Iowa State University Press, 1961. A stimulating volume with many creative ideas for producing photos with human interest appeal and with impact; has superb illustrations.

Irving Lloyd, **Creative School Photography.** Topeka, Kansas: American Yearbook Company (2nd Ed.) 1964. This book has hundreds of attractive, appealing photos dealing with all aspects of campus life; many unusual angle shots bring routine photo situations to high professional level.

Richard H. Logan III, **Elements of Photo Reporting.** New York: Hastings House,

1971. A comprehensive and practical reference work for people assigned photographic jobs; includes chapters on the picture story, sports and news photography, and photo editing.

Robert B. Rhode and Floyd H. McCall, **Introduction to Photography:** New York: Macmillan (2nd Ed.) 1971. A standard work, up-dated with fresh angles for the cameraman.

Arthur Rothstein, **Photojournalism: Pictures for Magazines and Newspapers.** New York: Amphoto, 1965. An expert who will sharpen your photographic eye for news and feature photos.

Motion Pictures

W. Hugh Baddeley, **Technique of Documentary Film Production.** New York: Hastings House (Rev. 3rd Ed.) 1973. Latest volume on documentary film-making which can be of considerable use to college PR film producers.

John Burder, **Technique of Editing 16mm Films.** New York: Hastings House (Rev. Ed.) 1971. Covers each step in vital process of editing films to make them move.

Henry Provisor, **8mm/16mm Movie-Making.** Philadelphia: Chilton, 1970. Simple explanations of various techniques from shooting to editing film.

Karel Reisz and Gavin Miller, **The Technique of Film Editing.** New York: Hastings House, 1968. Enlarged edition of original great classic in film editing; principles of this important step were first enunciated here.

Mario Raimondo Suoto, **Technique of Motion Picture Camera.** New York: Hastings House, 1967. Simple, but valuable explanations of filming; gives practical suggestions for producing appealing, well-lit pictures.

Radio

Mark W. Hall, **Broadcast Journalism. An Introduction to News Writing.** New York: Hastings House, 1971. A foundation volume for public relations staffman who has to understand broadcast journalism.

Robert L. Hilliard, **Radio Broadcasting. An Introduction to the Sound Medium.** New York: Hastings House (Rev. 2nd Ed.) 1974. Standard textbook on fundamentals and station operation.

——, **Writing for Television and Radio.** New York: Hastings House (2nd Ed.) 1967. Fundamental and specific; includes chapters on special events, news, talk programs; illustrated with script excerpts.

Arthur Wimer and Dale Brix, **Workbook for Radio and TV News Editing and Writing.** Dubuque, Iowa: Wm. C. Brown Company Publishers, 1966. Excellent material, many "do's" and "don'ts" tips given.

Television

A. William Bluem, John F. Cox, Gene McPherson, **Television in the Public Interest.** New York: Hastings House, 1961. Has much useful information for university TV departments.

Irving E. Fang, **Television News.** New York: Hastings House (2nd Ed. Enlarged) 1972. A specific how-it-can-be-done volume.

Mark W. Hall, **Broadcast Journalism, An Introduction to News Writing.** New York: Hastings House, 1971. Cited above.

Robert L. Hilliard, **Writing for Television and Radio.** New York: Hastings House, 1967. Cited above.

Norton S. Parker, **Audio Visual Script Writing.** New Brunswick, N.J.: Rutgers Univ. Press, 1968. Valuable addition to college PR library for its specific recommendations.

Edward B. Roberts, **Television Writing and Selling.** Boston: Writer (3rd Ed.) 1968. Gives current practices in scripting for television programs.

Edgar E. Willis, **Writing Television and Radio Programs.** New York: Holt, Rinehart & Winston, 1967. Gives specifics, covers all phases of program writing.

PART FIVE: SPECIAL EVENTS AND ACTIVITIES

Special Events

Hal Golden and Kitty Hanson, **How to Plan, Produce and Publicize Special Events.** New York: Oceana Publications, 1960. An early book, but the only complete volume on the subject; has wealth of details on practical procedures.

Public Relations Books With chapters or sections on Special Events. Cited above.

Scott M. Cutlip and Allen H. Center, **Effective Public Relations.** Englewood Cliffs, N.J.: Prentice-Hall, Inc. (4th Ed.) 1971.

Sidney Kobre, **Dynamic Force of Public Relations Today.** Wm. C. Brown Co. Publishers, 1964.

Philip Lesly (Ed.), **Public Relations Handbook.** Englewood Cliffs, N.J.: Prentice-Hall (Rev. Ed.) 1971.

Alumni Relations

Casebook for Institutional Advancement Programs. Washington, D.C.: American College Public Relations Association, 1971. Invaluable sections on campaigns of many small and large educational institutions.

D. Ray Hostetter, **The Challenge Grant and Higher Education.** Washington, D.C.: American College Public Relations Association, 1966. An authoritative volume, giving philosophy and specifics of fund-raising.

John W. Leslie, **Focus on Understanding and Support: A Study in College Management.** Washington, D.C.: Cited above.

Advancement of Understanding and Support of Higher Education. Washington, D.C.: American College Public Relations Association, 1958. An early, but still highly useful study; has many good examples of campaigns.

PART SIX: FEEDBACK AND MEASURING RESEARCH

Opinion Research

Robert O. Carlson, "Public Relations Research—Problems and Prospects," **Public Relations Journal,** Vol. 26, May, 1970. Author takes a hard look at research methods and results.

William P. Ehling, "Public Relations Research: A Few Fundamentals," **College and University Journal,** Vol. 1, Fall, 1962.

Charles Y. Glock, (Ed.) **Survey Research in the Social Sciences.** New York: The Russell Sage Foundation, 1967. An overall view of what research is being carried on.

Ralph O. Nafziger and David Manning White, **Introduction to Mass Communications Research.** Baton Rouge: Louisiana State University Press (Rev. Ed.) 1963. A basic work, dealing in an understandable fashion with planning and executing various types of research.

Edward J. Robinson, **Communication and Public Relations.** Columbus, Ohio: Charles E. Merrill Publishing Co., 1966. Has easy-to-understand, but detailed chapters on scientific surveys.

———, **Public Relations and Survey Research.** New York: Appleton, 1969. Excellent as guide to researching public relations problems.

Measuring PR Results

Willard Bailey, "Program Evaluation," **Public Relations Journal,** Vol. 24, September, 1968.

Richard W. Budd, Robert K. Thorp, and Lewis Donohew, **Content Analysis of Communications.** New York: Macmillan, 1967. Has a method to help college PR determine favorable or unfavorable image of institution.

Charles F. Phillips and Delbert J. Duncan, **Marketing: Principles and Methods.** Homewood, Ill.: Irwin, 1968. Has extensive chapters on research methods.

Wilbur Schramm and Donald F. Roberts, **Process and Effects of Mass Communication.** Urbana, University of Illinois (Rev. Ed.) 1971. A pioneering work in research methods and results updated.

Daniel Starch, **Measuring Advertising Readership and Results.** New York: McGraw-Hill, 1966. A pioneer in the research field shows how to check on what you have done.

See volumes by Robinson and Lucas as well as advertising texts cited above in *Advertising.*

The Effective PR Team

John W. Leslie, **Focus on Understanding and Support, A Study in College Management.** Washington, D.C.: American College Public Relations Association, 1969. Cited above.

Ernest E. Rydell, "Public Relations Directors of Colleges With Over 10,000 Students are Long-Time Veterans, Age 45, Earning $18,000–$19,999." **College and University Journal,** Vol. 10, No. 4. September, 1971.

Index